"JoAnn Hackos has provided the definitive roadmap for the challenges that every organization will face over the next decade as they move to capture and reuse their information assets. As we move forward all good content systems will need to meet the goals of

- Efficient capture and reuse
- Publish dynamic tailored content

"She has provided us with an end-to-end view of what it takes to effectively manage this dynamic content delivery system by defining an information model through user requirements and content analysis. JoAnn is one of the few authors to recognize that the information model is at the heart of every content system that meets these goals. Her book breaks down the content management challenge into its core issues and provides us insights to navigate the pitfalls. This is a must read for managers and technologists alike who have the task of providing complex content management systems from the creation processes through final delivery."

Marc Gunning
Manager, IPS e-Business
Hewlett-Packard Company

"Content management has definitely hit the mainstream in terms of both technology development and business need. However, in the rush to buy or build content management systems many organizations build systems that ultimately don't meet their user's needs. The most frequent cause of unsuccessful content management implementations is the lack of a well-thought-out information model. JoAnn's many years of experience helping companies build successful information models and systems, combined with her articulate writing, make this unique book a must-read for anyone hoping to build a successful content management system."

Frank Gilbane
Bluebill Advisors, Inc.

"For anyone wrestling with delivering information on an increasing variety of media while improving information quality and controlling costs, Dr. Hackos has written an invaluable reference. This book will arm you with the knowledge to turn your information into a real competitive advantage."

PG Bartlett
Vice President of Marketing
Arbortext

D1534494

"JoAnn Hackos' book on content management should be the first book that you read on this topic. It is an excellent introduction to the issues and helps guide you along the decisions that you will have to make. When you are betting the future of your business on an infrastructure choice, don't you think you want to be knowledgeable and a bit careful? I will likely take arguments directly from this book to reinforce my message for the need for Corporate ownership and responsibility."

"*Content Management for Dynamic Web Delivery* offers a thorough and clear look at complex concepts in the knowledge and content management field. Dr. Hackos's style offers pleasant reading for professionals, paired with real value and insight into the topic. If you're in this field, *Content Management for Dynamic Web Delivery* should definitely be on your reading list."

"Finally! A book written for technical publication managers who want to move their departments into the 21st century. JoAnn provides a road map starting with why content management deserves careful consideration and ending with making a business case. Along the way, she provides advice on how to process and where a manager might find bumps in the road.

I learned a great deal reading this book because JoAnn makes the concepts easy to understand. A must read for all publications managers even for those who do not think content management is in their future."

Content Management for Dynamic Web Delivery

Content Management for Dynamic Web Delivery

JoAnn T. Hackos

WILEY COMPUTER PUBLISHING

WILEY

John Wiley & Sons, Inc.

Publisher: Robert Ipsen
Editor: Theresa Hudson
Managing Editor: Angela Smith
Text Design & Composition: RDD Consultants, Inc.

This book is printed on acid-free paper. ⊚

Published by John Wiley & Sons, Inc., New York

Published simultaneously in Canada.

Library of Congress Cataloging-in-Publication Data:

Hackos, JoAnn T.
    Content Management for Dynamic Web Delivery/ JoAnn T. Hackos
        p.   cm.
    Includes bibliographical references and index.
    ISBN 0-471-08586-3 (cloth : alk paper)

Printed in the United States of America.

10   9   8   7   6   5   4   3   2   1

To my husband, Bill Hackos, who has survived a fourth major book-writing effort. He helps to clarify my ideas and keeps me moving forward when I get tired and discouraged at a lack of progress.

Contents

Preface

Inside organizations, content has a life cycle. It moves from design through creation at the desks of business planners, information architects, and individual authors. Once created, content must be reviewed and approved before it is ready to be published. Publication takes place through both electronic and traditional media, often in multiple languages, although publication through the Web is fast becoming the most important means of reaching many user communities. In the process of publishing, content may be customized for special user communities, either by line of business, product lines, geographies, or job-related requirements. Finally, content must be archived, either at the end of its valuable life or when it is repurposed to accommodate new needs.

Throughout the content life cycle, content must be managed. In the past, this management has been done by people working hard to ensure that all the right pieces come together at the right time. Despite their efforts, the hands-on nature of the processes has led to delays in making the right content available when users need it.

But time-consuming, expensive, manual processes are only one part of the problem. Perhaps the greater problem is that content has been tied up in proprietary formats, in large compound documents, and focused on presentation rather than message. We have delivered these large documents, only to learn from our users that they are rarely if ever read in their entirety, are frequently out-of-date, and are often difficult to use. They make searching for just the right piece of information to answer a question or solve a problem nearly impossible.

Content management is no longer an option, given the increasing volume of content being produced and the increasing complexity of information access and retrieval.

Content management is a necessity in any organization large enough to have more than one file cabinet. If you find yourself asking: Where is the right information? How was it categorized and filed? Is it in the right form for reuse in a different context? How do we get it from a proprietary authoring system into other media? then, you need content management.

Where does content management fit in?

Content management provides a process for answering your questions by encouraging you to categorize and organize information for future retrieval and development. Grounded on a vision of the user experience, content management focuses not only on keeping track of information assets and making them accessible to users, it also focuses on finding new ways to deliver information to customers, employees, and business partners who need it. Content, well structured and organized for future uses, is available for dynamic Web delivery. That means content is ready to be delivered in multiple channels, targeted to the needs of particular users, placed in new contexts, restructured into compound documents, and made available for end users to manipulate and reconfigure on their own.

For most organizations, content management has two important goals:

- make information more accessible and usable by diverse user communities
- reduce the costs of guiding information through the content life cycle

Throughout this book, I have emphasized the importance of both goals. Too often, I find organizations quick to look for cost savings without taking advantage of the potential benefits for the users. Organizations will elect, for example, to translate whole documents into SGML or XML without rethinking the structure of the documents or reconstructing them into reusable modules. As a result, they reduce costs in deploying content to multiple media (print, CD-ROM, and Web) but forego the benefits that come with a new information architecture.

Consequently, I emphasize from the outset the prime importance of a sound Information Model. The Information Model provides the foundation for all future use. It provides a categorization scheme, a set of well-structured information types, and a plan for assembling and linking content both statically by authors and architects and dynamically by filtering and user preferences.

The Information Model is supported, in my view, by XML standards. XML means using a non-proprietary language to label information modules; it means separating content from presentation; it ensures that modules are consistently structured. Most important, it provides a tool for the future, allowing businesses to present information in new ways, through new channels—many not yet developed.

Turning content into information assets requires work to implement new processes and a new information architecture. It requires discipline to ensure that modules of content are reusable in many contexts. It requires using standard structures and labeling information by its meaning so that it can be searched, changed, and reconfigured automatically. It requires an investment in infrastructure, much like investments in relational databases that helped organize and repurpose other well-structured data. It means having the foresight to know that the content life cycle can no longer be managed haphazardly.

Is content management in your future? I believe it is. I hope this book will show you that content management is the right path to take.

Who should read this book?

If you are contemplating a content-management solution for your organization, then you must be a business executive, a chief technology officer, a Web content manager, an information architect, or a manager of technical publications, training, customer support, human resources. In every case, you are someone who sees a problem with information creation and dissemination in your organization, and you know that the problem has to be solved. You've discovered that you can no longer manage documents as a whole, that you need to look inside the collections of content to find the information assets of genuine value to the corporation. You have learned that those information assets play a vital role in ensuring that staff, customers, and partners find the information they need quickly and easily. You have learned that simply putting documents online, whether on the Internet, an intranet, or an extranet does not make content reusable and useful. You have come to recognize that for content to be a corporate asset, it has to be developed and stored in small enough units that it can be leveraged among many different deliverables. You know you have to be able to create a single source of content that can be used in many ways to meet the needs of many different people.

If you find your thoughts echoed here, then this is the right book for you. I hope that it provides you with an agenda for action. I have outlined the thinking and planning processes you need to embark on to make your journey into content management successful. I have tried to warn you about the pitfalls of premature technology decisions or attempts at quick fixes by moving all your legacy content into XML.

How is the book organized?

Following the introduction to content management strategies in Chapter 1, you will find a five-phase program outlined in detail. That program is my blueprint for success as you move into content management. The details about setting goals, establishing a vision, designing an Information Model, and implementing that model are the focus of the rest of the book. In Chapters 2 and 3, you will find an outline of content-management technologies and a guide to making decisions about which content you need to move into a technology solution.

The heart of the book is in Chapters 4, 5, and 6, which outline how to form a sound and comprehensive Information Model, from user community, through the dimensions of use, into information types and content units. Chapters 7 and 8 lead you through the process of turning content into multiple delivery channels. My focus, certainly, is on electronic delivery through the Web, but I don't neglect other channels, including paper, context-sensitive help, CD-ROM, and new media in cell phones and handheld devices. Chapters 9, 10, and 11 outline the challenges of introducing content management into your working environment, including developing a reuse strategy and staffing a content-management initiative. Finally, in Chapter 12, I return to the beginning by discussing how to formulate a sound business plan to fund a content-management effort in your organization.

Acknowledgments

Many people have contributed to the success of this book over several years. Although I have used many of the strategies described here for more than 20 years, the specific outline began to take shape about five years ago. At that time, I conducted, with my colleagues at Comtech Services, Inc., a benchmark study of content-management strategies in the high-tech industry. That original study was sponsored by companies such as IBM, Cisco Systems, Dell Computer, and others that were interested in learning about the state of the art of content management and in pursuing a single-source strategy for their enormous libraries of technical information.

As the ideas about enterprise content management began to gel, I worked with Dr. William Hackos and Tina Hedlund at Comtech and Henry Korman at Wordplay to form an initial public workshop focused on planning a content-management strategy. Added to the mix were many conversations with Judy Glick-Smith at Integrated Documentation, Inc., Ginny Redish at Redish and Associates, Ann Rockley at The Rockley Group, and others in technical communication who were also beginning to see the need for a new way to manage documents among their clients. When it finally came to collecting all the ideas and designing this book, I have been ably assisted from the outset by Henry Korman, who helped me gain precision in the design of the Information Model.

As the book was forming, I was influenced by the many individuals in client companies who were working on solutions to the problem of content management. These included Chuck Barrett and Wayne Weiseler at Cisco Systems, Julia Cronin and Ron Manns at Nortel Networks, Glenn D'Amore at ADP, Beverly Dunson and Kathryn McKibbon at NCS Pearson, Steve Elliott and Jimm Meloy at Autodesk, Susan Harkus at Ion Global Australia, Theo Heintjes and Mike Poepping at Lucent Learning, Ben Martin and his team at J D Edwards, Vesa Purho at Nokia Networks, Rosaline Tsai at Lawson, Matthias Vering and the team at SAP, and Daphne Walmer and her team at Medtronics. All of these individuals and the organizations that support them expanded my understanding of the problems to be solved and some of the possible solutions.

I have also found my thoughts challenged by the contributions of very clever technology specialists from some of the best software developers in the content-management field. These included PG Bartlett at Arbortext, Kevin Brown at Lightspeed, Daniel Chang and colleagues at Hynet, David Davidoff at Enigma, John Devlin at XyEnterprise, John Eger and Steve Newcomb at Epremis, Eric Freese and Kent Taylor at Isogen, Mark Peters at Chrystal Software, Robert Reich at Ecosystems, Keith Thomas at i4i, and Paul Trotter at AuthorIT.

At the same time, I was assisted by others who read and commented upon manuscript drafts of earlier stages of the book. These included David Davidoff, Tina Hedlund, Henry Korman, and Ginny Redish, as well as George Bradley at J D Edwards, Diane Davis at Synopsys, Marc Gunning at Hewlett-Packard, and Michael Priestley and David Schell at IBM.

A number of people contributed their stories for the vignettes that appear in the book, including Barbara Douma at Compuware Europe, Trudy Evans at AuthorIT, Penny Fairbanks at SBC, Bill Gearhart at BMC, Mark Homnack and Adam Jones at Simultrans, Nancy Howard and George Tamas at Governet, Tom Kelly at Cisco Systems, Kathryn McKibbon at NCS Pearson, Eddie Moore at CSW, Susan Orge and Scott Youngblum at Arbortext, Rich Pasework at XyEnterprise, Palmer Pearson and Amy Witherow at Cadence Design Systems, Lou Petrella at Hewlett-Packard, Ri-Shea Schlitter at Agilent, Judson Slusser at Prosoft Training, Doug Takach at Tweddle Lithography, and Daphne Walmer, as well as staff members at National Geographic and Little, Brown.

Last, but not least, have been the outstanding contributions made by my staff and colleagues in completing the manuscript. Tina Hedlund has made invaluable contributions to the technical content, including working out all the XML examples and writing several of the detailed technical sections of the text. She's done an excellent job of keeping everything accurate. Christina Meyer at Comtech has contributed many hours reviewing for details, checking copyright permissions, calling people about contributions, and generally watching out for all the little problems that occur in every effort of this sort. Lori Maberry worked on all the proofreading and copyediting. Jill Nicholson proofread everything early in the process. Rodney Sauer is again the stalwart book designer I have relied on for many previous books. He puts all the final pieces together, assisted by cartoonist, Jeff Maclachlan. The chapter introductory cartoons were planned by Beth Barrow, who claims she had great fun doing them. Finally, all of this would not have taken place at all without the support of Terri Hudson, editor at John Wiley & Sons, and her staff.

Thank you all.

1

Is Content Management in Your Future?

"All of this money is being spent on information and yet customers can't install their own equipment!"

I s content management in your future? If you think it isn't, think again. Organizations are flooded with content, but that content doesn't become information and information doesn't turn into knowledge unless someone knows it's there, can get to it with minimal pain, and can repurpose it by creating new information from existing content. Content that is inaccessible is not yet a corporate asset. Content that is hidden away in long documents and impenetrable manuals lacks the flexibility we need to act upon it as a corporate asset.

Joe S. is drowning in content from his suppliers—catalogs, white papers, product literature, technical manuals, bulletins—all of them delivered either in paper form or over the Internet. He would be much happier if his suppliers managed the content more effectively for him and if his suppliers made more of an effort to understand his needs. He rarely gets updated information when he needs it. Most of the information is duplicated or is almost the same in five or six different sources. When he reports errors in the information, they are never corrected. Even in new versions of technical manuals, the same errors are repeated year after year.

Isabel H. is an account manager in a service company. She feels overwhelmed with information coming from her colleagues and from outside her organization. She gets volumes of official and unofficial documents and memos sent through email. When she looks for information she needs, she finds it is stored on multiple servers, some of which she doesn't have access to. She has access to an intranet, an extranet, and the Internet, but none of them seems to make the resources she needs any easier to find. Add to the electronic media all the content she has stored in paper form. It's pretty obvious to Isabel that she needs a way to manage content. She just wishes it were as obvious to her technology professionals and management.

Content management is an enormous challenge for every organization that offers information to customers, employees, vendors, and partners. To be useful and to meet the expectations of a host of different users, content must be

- easy to find
- accurate, up-to-date, and continuously refreshed
- complete enough for users' needs
- well organized for quick search and retrieval
- readable in the right languages
- linked to other relevant content
- targeted to each person's needs and levels of experience and knowledge

In most organizations, information resources are hidden away on personal hard drives, in accessible servers controlled by other departments, in office file cabinets in several offices or even on several continents, in personal file drawers, in piles of paper on somebody's desk, or stuck in the company library. Looking for a needle in the proverbial haystack is a lot easier than finding the right piece of information for the task at hand.

To make content most accessible, organizations are beginning to recognize that they have to move their most current, up-to-date information to a Web site. They need to make information resources accessible through corporate intranets and extranets or even through the Internet. To be usable, information resources must be accessible electronically. Although many users of information tell us they prefer to read from paper rather than from a screen, they also recognize that paper is likely to be easily misplaced and soon out-of-date. As information architects, we know that paper is not easily repurposed to meet previously unrecognized needs.

Dynamic, ever-changing publication of information resources at all levels by using internal and external electronically supported systems is a solution that many organizations are vigorously and actively planning, developing, and implementing today. If they are not, they will soon find that they must or be mired in information wasteland.

To be manageable and effective, retrievable and useful, all this publishing and disseminating of information must be structured within the framework of a comprehensive Information Model and under the control of a content-management system.

Nonetheless—be warned! Content management is not about tools or technology although both play an important role. Content management is not exclusively about SGML, XML, databases, or Web publishing.

Organizations frequently make the mistake of assuming that technology will magically solve the content-management problems they face. A colleague once asked me in frustration if it weren't possible just to buy a tool and do what it said. I laughed and said, "No, unfortunately, the tools don't say anything." As I will emphasize and reiterate throughout this book, content management is not just about tools and technology.

Content management is about organizing, categorizing, and structuring information resources so that they can be stored, retrieved, published, and reused in multiple ways. As an information architect, information developer, quality manager, communication specialist, or Web administrator, content management has as its foundation your thorough understanding of the goals and needs of multiple user communities when they want to find and retrieve information. Successful content management is founded on your ability to create and implement a sound vision of your users' needs.

Content management necessarily starts with an Information Model. The Information Model is the framework for organizing content in response to users' needs and establishing the structure in which the content is stored.* Building upon your Information Model, you provide methods for efficiently authoring, categorizing, storing, retrieving, and using content. If you build a sound Information Model and manage it with the appropriate content-management technology in a well-structured repository, you will be able to deliver information to your users in a multitude of innovative and dynamic ways.

In Figure 1-1, note that the foundation of your Information Model and your content-management solution is your user community. The better you understand their needs, the stronger your Information Model will be. From your Information Model, you will develop processes to author and categorize content, house it in a repository, repurpose it, and deliver it effectively in multiple media, using personalization and customization techniques.

The promise of content management

Content-management solutions hold an attractive promise—that all relevant content can be quickly and easily available to those who need it to do their jobs, make decisions, acquire new knowledge, and satisfy their curiosity. Achieving that promise takes the hard work of developing a comprehensive Information Model.

Only by creating the appropriate content to deliver to users, storing it for active retrieval by people or by technology, can we keep the promise. By creating content that is available for reuse (written once, used everywhere), we can build custom-

---

* The Information Model is discussed in detail in Chapters 4, 5 and 6. In these chapters, learn how to create an Information Model for your enterprise.

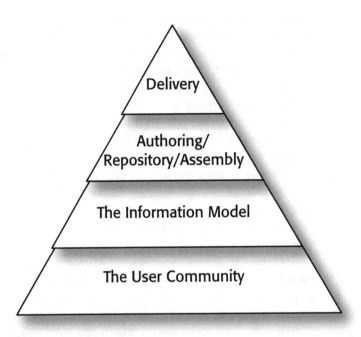

Figure 1-1 This conceptual model of a content-management solution shows that the foundation of the model is the user community or multiple user communities. Built upon the user community is the Information Model(s), which support the development of processes and technology for authoring, categorizing, storing, assembling, delivering, and using information.

ized (fit for special customer needs) and even personalized (fit for special individual needs) deliverables that are always up-to-date and correct, and deliver a consistent, well-branded message.

Opportunities to deliver targeted content anywhere at any time are supported by technology solutions today and will be better supported as technologists better understand our needs. But technology only *assists* in fulfilling the promise of better information everywhere. At the core of the content-management promise is sound and careful planning based on a vision of the user's experience. That vision is supported by flexible, standards-based tools that allow for an evolution of processes without requiring massive recoding of the organization's information assets.

In this chapter, I explain the opportunities and challenges of a content-management strategy for three primary activities of the enterprise:

- content to serve the needs of the supply chain
- content to serve the needs of the support chain
- content to serve entertainment and new content delivery

Before we talk about the solutions, it may be useful to examine some of the current problems in more depth. Let's look at typical scenarios that show the impact of the absence of a well-structured content-management solution.

Scenario 1—Wanting to buy, but no place to go

As head planning engineer at the southwest area phone company, Ed wanted to evaluate the latest optical fiber systems so he could advise his management about the need to improve performance and speed. He'd been talking with the area sales representatives from two of the top companies. They'd dropped off technical white papers and sent him the URLs for their corporate technical Web sites. Using the product catalogs, Ed reviewed a lot of the information. Now he needed more detailed specifications about several of the devices.

Ed, the planning engineer, is increasingly frustrated at being unable to find the right information.

He tried searching the sites for device specifications and came up with too many hits. Nevertheless, he dove into the first several that seemed promising and came up with not one but three sets of specifications for one of the devices he was interested in. Problem was—the specifications were all slightly different. Which one was correct?

A call to tech support didn't help much. When he mentioned the differences in the specifications, the support specialist Ed was talking with only got more confused himself.

"I'll have to get back to you. I don't know why the numbers aren't the same. The purchasing database is usually pretty reliable, but the second set is from the engineering department and they're the experts," Ed was informed. That meant another delay in his evaluation project. Somebody in management was going to be quite unhappy. Maybe he better go with the other company—even if he didn't like their products as much. Customer service was key.

Scenario 2—Where, oh where did the customer go?

Claire is responsible for taking calls from customers who have had problems with their new product shipments. Typically, something is missing from the box or something arrives damaged. When a customer calls, Claire uses one system to find the customer's order information. To get to the shipping summary, she has to log into another system. If she wants a copy of the invoice, she has to call accounts receivable and have them fax it to her. Then, to send a problem report and get the shipping department to send the correct products, she creates an email message. Because she has to keep a copy of her message, she prints it out and puts it into a customer-problem report file that she keeps in the file cabinet by her desk.

Claire, the customer-service representative, is plagued with handling information stored in multiple computer systems and paper-centric file cabinets.

Scenario 3—Customer service gone awry

Jason tries the search button for the third time on his company's intranet site. He is looking for the phone number of the IT contact at the remote location in Jacksonville, Florida. The phone number should have been in the company phone directory, but the listing for Jacksonville gave him a fax machine. Somewhere, someone should have updated the information. He received a call to the service hotline from a secretary in the St. Augustine office who needed help connecting to the company network. Ordinarily, he could dispatch an IT person within an hour, if he knew who to call.

"I'm really tired of plowing through all of this old junk on the intranet. Nobody ever takes anything off. And they usually forget to post new information as soon as it's available." In desperation, Jason starts walking from cubicle to cubicle in his work area. He finally finds the Jacksonville phone number he needed—on a sticky note tacked to the wall by one of the other service reps. A problem that should have taken minutes sends Jason on an hour-long wild goose chase.

Jason is having a difficult time trying to use the company's intranet to find information he needs to do his job.

Scenario 4—No instructions are better than the wrong ones

"I don't understand. I just downloaded this technical manual from the manufacturer's Web site, but the drawings in the installation instructions don't look anything like the model I just bought," complained Audrey to her husband.

Audrey had already spent two hours trying to install the new skis on her snowmobile following the printed instruction that had come in the box. When she finally realized that the instructions had to be for a different model machine, she went right to the company's Web site. Sure enough, instructions for her model were easy to download—that is until she realized that the information in the 45 pages she'd just printed was also out-of-date.

Audrey is an increasingly annoyed customer faced with a broken snowmobile, new skis to install, loose pages of instructions, and a Web site that causes more problems than it solves.

Scenario 5—If it happened last year, it doesn't do me much good today

Blake likes to look at several Web sites each day because they provide information about unusual, out-of-the way travel locations. Most of the sites have links to specific locations, such as local chambers of commerce, museums, resort hotels, small bed and breakfast inns that Blake prefers. About half the time, the links go nowhere at all—all he gets is one of those Web error messages "page not found."

The other half of the time, he's likely to find the site so completely out-of-date that it is useless. Doesn't anyone ever update events lists? He found one site where everything was over a year old.

Blake is tired of finding information that is almost always out-of-date. He'd like at least some of his Web information sources to make an effort to keep information current.

Essential content management

Is there anyone who hasn't experienced frustrations identical to or similar to these? How often do you find yourself dropping out or looking for a competitor's Web page when you're using the Internet? How long does it take before you give up looking for internal information and start writing from scratch?

My purpose in writing this book is to show you how to implement a successful content-management solution. Will it take planning and time? Yes, more than you'd like if you're into instant gratification. Will it take process changes and commitment across the organization? Yes, because every significant improvement requires changes and commitment. Is it easy? Not necessarily. Is it worth doing? Definitely, or at least almost always.

Content management will make you money—because it turns disorganized content into corporate assets. In doing so, you enable content to become information, by making it accessible to the people who need it, as soon as they need it. You can significantly reduce the amount of time people spend searching, often unsuccessfully. You can reduce the amount of information that people rewrite because they can't find it. You can ensure that information is written only once, checked for correctness and completeness, and published everywhere. You can simplify the updating process and reduce the number of people involved. You can improve the quality of the information you deliver by giving your customers the advantage of customized and personalized content without a lot of labor-intensive tweaking. And you can publish to all the promising new electronic devices that carry information directly to the users' hands, and you can be prepared to publish in ways not yet invented.

The content-management challenge for the enterprise

Some years ago, I led a study for Federal Express Corporation to determine how employees who worked in ground operations used their information resources (30 manuals updated quarterly, loads of bulletins and emails, video broadcasts from the corporate office, and training programs galore)*. In more than half the cases, I found a pattern that is typical in every corporation worldwide I've studied and even in most households: when people need critical information, they first turn to other people, even if that means making a phone call to someone on the other side of the world.

- Where is the contact information for that new client?
- What happened to the last revision of the proposal we sent?
- What is our company policy on this matter?
- What procedure are we supposed to follow in this case?
- Where is that email notice that came from the CEO last month?

When the written information isn't easily accessible, everyone relies on other people.

Employees need access to information—consumers need access to information—technical experts need access to information. Information exchanged between businesses and consumers (B2C), information exchanged between your business and other businesses (B2B), and information exchanged within your business among your employees (B2E) provide the core of knowledge, experience, and expertise that support both your company's supply chain and your customer support chain. Without information, the wheels grind to a halt.

It has long been the assumption among executives and information technology (IT) professionals, especially those responsible for keeping the computers running, that the information to drive business comes primarily in the form of

---

* Hackos, JoAnn T., PhD. and Julian S. Winstead with Sadie Gill and Mary Hartmann, 1995. "Finding Out What Users Need and Giving It to Them: A Case-study at Federal Express," *Technical Communication*, second quarter (May), pp. 322–327.

numeric data. Numbers drive financial reporting by letting you know if you're making money or losing it. Numeric data is certainly essential to support the supply chain from sales through fulfillment, from payables to receivables, and from revenues and expenses to profits. Nonetheless, qualitative data is often just as valuable or even more valuable to the success of the enterprise.

Numeric data without context is often pretty meaningless. People place value on numeric assets and honor the role of such data in financial reporting, but they have given short shrift to finding, preserving, updating, and communicating qualitative information. People have talked about doing knowledge management but often lack the motivation to collect and maintain a body of knowledge.

Although knowledge management often sounds esoteric and unachieveable, content management sounds more approachable. You know what content is about—it's all those documents piled up on your desks or cluttering up your email system. It's the documents in the file cabinets, storerooms, and thick binders. It's the documents preserved on your personal hard drives. You know what you need is in there—somewhere—you just can't find it. Nor can anyone else.

The problem, however, is that no matter how cooperative you want to be, most people have limited memory capacity and a terrible time with details. No matter how much technology has to offer, human hard wiring hasn't changed much over the millennia.

For someone who wants the right information, it's easy to get a mass of wrong or incomplete information from people who are trying to be helpful. If we could just find the definitive source, we'd be certain that we've gotten the best information available. As we all know, we have to write it down to remember it.

Turning content into knowledge

On the other hand, people have knowledge about how things work that never gets written down anywhere. We all know the complaint—the official procedures are all well and good, but that's not how the work really gets accomplished. Tacit knowledge, the information hidden away in the heads of the experts, has to be accessible because experts retire, forget, leave for other jobs, and their hard drives crash. Their knowledge usually goes with them.

Historically, to collect the information out there and make it accessible has required that we create documents. We have defined them to include text alone, text and graphics, images, and rich media, including video, audio, and animation. The collected information could be in the form of official company documents, training materials, interoffice memos and notes, forms, reports and proposals, email, and slide presentations.

But just collecting the information is only the beginning. Once collected, the documents have to be easily accessible, or they will not be used. They have to be readily understandable, linked to other related information resources, and capable of being repurposed in part or in whole. The very documents themselves may make their content inaccessible. We have to find ways of breaking apart long documents and storing smaller, more self-contained modules of information that can be reused and repurposed.

The information resources themselves can't be neglected. They must be kept current or archived when they are no longer relevant. Many of them must be placed into a review and approval cycle so that they remain correct and complete. They must be protected against unauthorized retrieval, reuse, or change.

Content itself has a life cycle. A product manager writes a product plan. Engineering replies with an engineering specifications document. This document is used by sales and marketing to create data sheets and sales brochure. One set of content, especially if it is designed and structured in modular chunks, becomes available to fulfill multiple purposes. The content life cycle demonstrates that content is a corporate asset that itself must be managed.

If the content itself is developed in a modular and structured form, we can ensure that smaller chunks of content are updated without having to recreate the entire collection. Chunking, structure, and labeling turn content into a valuable commodity.

Like any numeric data that our organizations spend time and effort to maintain, our qualitative business content must be part of a process designed to ensure their integrity. Given the volume of information being created, disseminated, and stored in our organizations, we need the support of technology to keep the system alive and well. The technology that best supports information creation, storage, and dissemination is content management.

Placing content at the core of the information value proposition

When we explain that information provides value, we must look at the information that is held by the experts in our organization. Consider these three scenarios:

Scenario 1—Sam, the marketing guy

Sam, the vice president of product marketing, has come up through the ranks, becoming knowledgeable about a wide variety of the company's products over the past ten years. He knows what it takes to bring a new product to market. Over the years, he has developed supplier contacts—his relationships with key people are part of his store of knowledge. In addition to knowing all the steps of the process, he knows which ones you should start worrying about and managing early, which ones will take care of themselves, and which ones come toward the end of the process.

The knowledge that Sam brings to the organization keeps things running smoothly. In fact, the CEO lives in fear that Sam will leave and take his wealth of experience with him. Capturing Sam's knowledge about process and people will take time and effort but might make the difference between a rocky or a smooth transition in the future. The process captured and written down will also allow some of the up-and-coming product managers avoid the problems that continue to plague them.

Capturing Sam's knowledge means developing content and collecting it in documents. The documents are most likely to be written procedures, statements of policy, timelines, pricing options, lists of trusted suppliers—they might even include a videotape of Sam describing a particularly harrowing experience and what he would do to avoid the pitfalls in the future. Right now, Sam's knowledge is in his head and in notes, memos, and email, none of which can be understood out of the context of Sam's experience. Sam's knowledge must be institutionalized and made available to everyone who needs it. As the company expands globally, this information might even have to be translated into multiple languages to accommodate the needs of a far-flung staff.

Scenario 2—Jamie, the product manager

Jamie, a new product manager, is part of the company's supply chain. In fact, he's right at the start of the supply chain process when it comes to bringing out a new product. His experience involves interacting with myriad suppliers and establishing a workable schedule of activities.

Jamie provides value to the company by efficiently and effectively getting the product to the customers. He works closely with the product developers to ensure that everyone understands the customers' needs. He reviews the product designs and prototypes to ensure that the customers' desires have been realized. He has information about customers coming in from the human-factors experts who conduct highly detailed site visits with customers and put the early design ideas and later implementations through rigorous usability tests. All the information about the customer is communicated regularly to the development team and Jamie's marketing professionals. It's also available to trainers, authors, customer services representatives, and the sales team so that they're ready with supporting information when the product is ready to go live.

The information produced by the supply chain initiators in Jamie's organization becomes part of the support chain once the product is out.

Scenario 3—Julie, the support manager

Julie leads the organization's support chain. Once Jamie's product is in the hands of the customer, Julie's organization assumes responsibility for supporting customers. The information-development manager reports to Julie. Her job is to ensure that the user manuals, help systems, technical services manuals, service bulletins, and bug reports are all up-to-date. Some information goes directly to customers through paper manuals packed with the product. Some information is available over the Internet and through CD-ROM. Other information goes directly to the field staff and the customer support staff, who also work for Julie. The internal training organization develops laboratory experiences that help the field service and support techs come up to speed. Some of the training is also done through the intranet and on the extranet that the company shares with its sales partners. All this information has to be updated as customer and field staff gain experience with the product, learning its peculiarities and uncovering problems that have to be fixed quickly.

Post-sales support in Julie's group includes consulting services, upgrades, and product accessories. These sales have an extremely high profit margin, but they depend heavily on the ability of the sales support team to know what they're talking about. They usually don't have a lot of time to come up to speed on the new products before the phones start ringing and inquiries start coming in through the Web site. Once again, having the right information at the right time is a key to success.

If information is available on time, up-to-date, accessible, accurate, and complete, everyone's job is made easier.

Content management in the supply chain

The supply chain, as illustrated in Figure 1-2, represents the processes that ensure that products are developed, marketed effectively, and sold and delivered to the customer. The supply chain process moves from ideas to decision making through development to sales, accounting, and order fulfillment, including all the business processes that track costs and revenues.

Figure 1-2 All the business activities associated with the supply chain require rapid access to critical information resources.

The supply chain uses significant amounts of pure numeric data, much of it coming from the company's ERP (Enterprise Resource Planning) system. But the supply chain also produces a significant amount of content that must be tracked through the design and development workflow and content that must be used to manage all activities relating to the sales cycle and order fulfillment processes. Much of the information produced during these activities is eventually moved into the support chain to assist customers in the successful implementation and use of the product and to facilitate follow-on sales.

Content management in the product-development life cycle might involve tracking the design and development documents. Analysis reports, customer studies, requirements definitions, engineering drawings, software code, documentation, and so on—all these documents provide a record of what is happening, when it is happening, who is responsible, and what can go wrong.

Content management in the supply chain extends into the realm of Customer Relationship Management (CRM), although CRM is primarily an activity of the support chain described in the next section. Information about customers improves sales opportunities by recording each interaction and transaction involving a customer. Analysis tools lead to additional opportunities to know which customers to target with information specifically focused on their needs. That targeted information might come from people, product literature, advertising in print and other media, new business proposals, as well as through the Internet in the form of catalogs, technical literature, product comparisons, and more.

All these channels for providing information are best developed, controlled, and published under the umbrella of content management. Content management is a valuable tool to support the product-development process, from the early planning stages for new and updated products through marketing and sales. Many of the documents produced throughout the process might be sources of text and graphics for customer service and support after the product is launched, as well as being available for reference and reuse during myriad supply chain activities.

Content management is not a single, simple tool. As you learn more about its potential, you will recognize that it is a way of doing business that includes creating new policies, procedures, tools, and processes. The implementation of a content-management solution requires the same planning and perspective that you may already have experienced with enterprise resource planning and product development in your organizations.

Content management for product development

Information developed during the product-development life cycle is an important candidate for content management. Key life-cycle documents such as feasibility studies, requirements definitions, test plans, source code, code specifications, and engineering drawings should be placed under workflow and version control. Workflow control implies that the review process will occur automatically; that is, everyone in the review chain will either be emailed draft copies or alerted to their readiness for review in the repository. Not only do the drafts travel among team member and managers, but their progress can be tracked. It's often easy to see who is delaying a document's progress.

In addition, the life-cycle documents are placed under version control. Most version control systems keep track of all changes to a document, the date of the change, and who was responsible for the change. Version control facilitates audit monitoring required in ISO (International Standards Organization) and other process certification programs.

Content produced in the product-development life cycle also becomes available for reuse in other documents, including technical manuals, training materials, technical catalogs, and product bulletins.

Content management for product marketing

Product-marketing content management includes both information created during the product-development life cycle and information that supports the marketing of the product. Some of the technical information produced by the engineers or programmers might become part of product literature and advertising and catalog copy. Information about target markets, buyer characteristics, product placement, and so on, can effectively be reused by sales, training, and technical information development as part of their source.

Consider graphics that are created first in engineering and become part of product catalogs, technical manuals, and training materials, produced in paper and made available through the Internet. If they are placed under content management, the same drawings can be reused in many contexts without having to be recreated. Content management enables you to avoid making multiple copies of text and graphics simply because different departments need access to them.

Content management for sales support

A shared repository of product information can enable marketing, engineering, and sales to avoid reinventing the wheel. Text and graphics can be reused in new business proposals, correspondence with potential customers, product bulletins and alerts, and so on. In addition, the sales organization might want to use the content-management system to single source proposals. If proposal content is developed in modular form—for example, modules that describe prior experience with similar customers—the modules can be easily assembled into new proposals. The core information in the proposal will come directly from the database with unique information added for a particular proposal. Because each module of information exists only once in the database, when it is updated, the update will be immediately available to everyone.

We have also found that many proposals include specifications and other standardized information that comes from engineering, testing, quality control, and other parts of the organization. If this information is available in the content-management system, it can more easily be located and repurposed into new collections of modules.

Content management can also assist sales people and account managers in keeping track of documents produced during the sales cycle. Contact information, relationship notes, emails and memos, meeting notes, decisions and recommendations, all of these documents must be accessible to a variety of team members, often in widely dispersed geographic locations.

Sales support includes documents produced by such diverse organizations as contracts, pricing controls, risk management, proposal development, implementation, and account management.

Content management for order fulfillment

Consider all the content generated by the order-fulfillment functions in an organization. Order fulfillment includes documents that account for relationships with suppliers, detail standard processes and their exceptions; provide schedules for activities, and track results. All this content should be considered for content-management control. As I detail in Chapter 2, *Implementing a Content-Management Solution,* one of the first steps in planning for a content-management solution is the analysis of your information resources. The analysis of what you have, what you really need, and how it will be managed becomes a core part of your planning process. For more information about the planning and implementation process, see the phases detailed at the end of this chapter.

Transition of content from the supply chain to the support chain

Content is being created throughout the supply chain to support internal processes and knowledge transfer. At some point following the sale of a product or service, much of the content produced for internal use must be transitioned to the customers and those who support the customers. Unfortunately, without a well defined Information Model, the development of modular content, and a focus on reuse in new contexts, much of the information produced in the supply chain will not be usable after the point of sale. If you begin to focus on content management and sound Information Modeling at the earliest stages of product and service development, you will find that the costs of the transition to customer support will be significantly reduced and the quality of the information you deliver will be substantially increased.

Content management in the support chain

The support chain, illustrated in Figure 1-3, is the set of activities that occur after a sale has been completed, the product has been delivered and installed, and the user is about to begin operations. The activities that occur within the support chain include responding to customer questions about using the product, providing

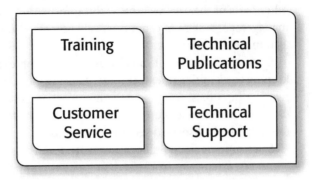

Figure 1-3 All the business- and customer-centric activities in the support chain require the creation, management, and dissemination of content.

training on the product, selling spare parts and accessories, maintaining self-instructional and reference information within the documentation set, maintaining and repairing equipment, and addressing opportunities for additional sales. Each of these activities is information intensive. Note that you have a significantly larger community of users in the support chain than in the supply chain. In the supply chain, you may have a significant number of users who benefits from content management. However, in the support chain, ten times that number will benefit. By focusing on the support chain, you are able to foresee the benefits of content management to customers, rather than only to your internal information developers.

Instructional materials, whether designed for classroom training or e-learning, require text, graphics, and rich media. Documents for customers, employees, and partners that explain how to install, configure, operate, troubleshoot, and repair products depend on technical content. Customer support personnel must not only be trained but must also have access to extensive libraries of information to support new inquiries from customers. Those responsible for generating sales for accessories and spare parts must be familiar with catalog descriptions, technical drawings, maintenance procedures, and more.

In many industries, the content created and used throughout the support chain ranges from several thousand pages of text and graphics to many hundreds of thousands of pages. In the aerospace, transportation, and telecommunications manufacturing industries alone, content can range in the millions of pages. Traditionally, most of the content in the support chain has consisted of text and graphics. With the advent of CD-ROM and Web delivery, we find more and more content migrating to rich media. Video, audio, and animation have become standard components of the support chain.

Pratt & Whitney, for example, produced over 50,000 pages of support information for its PW 4000 engine series, with the aid of Enigma's content management system. The information they published includes engine manuals, illustrated parts catalogs, service bulletins, and many other types of documents.

One of the wireless providers in the telecommunications industry supports a documentation set for a major switch system that has more than 500,000 pages of information.

These massive collections of information are not uncommon. But they are nearly impossible to manage effectively without a content-management solution.

Content management for Customer Relationship Management (CRM)

Content management easily supports the activities surrounding customer care. In fact, CRM has become one of the most active areas influenced by the concepts of content management. CRM systems typically include customer contact and opportunity information, but this information alone is often inadequate to provide a complete picture of customer transactions. Much of the content created during customer activities can be handled as images: order forms, invoices, correspondence, and notes. The information contained in these documents needs to come under content-management control, especially if they are to be made available, possibly through an enterprise portal, to everyone who interacts with customers. CRM crosses over between the supply chain and the support chain.

Content management for training

Much of the value provided by a training program for employees or customers comes from the value of the information represented in the training materials. We find, for example, that people who have attended training, especially on technical subjects, retain their training materials and use them as reference information long after they complete the courses. In fact, they retain and refer to training material long after it is out-of-date.

Content created for training, whether that training is instructor led or computer based, is an invaluable resource that should come under content management to be used most effectively. In a project for a training organization within a telecommunications company, we found that training materials were regularly recreated by individual trainers working in isolation. Even though many of the courses they developed shared subject matter, each trainer created unique materials. Even graphics were not shared among various courses.

With content management, the training organization was able to reduce its development costs significantly. They analyzed their course materials to identify modules and graphics that could easily be common to a group of courses. The "common to all" modules were created once and made available to all the trainers. Information that was unique to a particular course also became part of the repository so that it could be accessed by the individuals teaching that course. Reuse of training materials not only reduced costs and increased efficiency, it also enabled the trainers to spend more time interviewing customers and identifying specific training goals instead of spending time tweaking training materials and constantly developing new modules.

E-learning initiatives also provide a vehicle to make training modules more easily available to learners. By placing course materials in modular form in a content-management system, new and updated content can be quickly deployed to a Web-based learning environment. In addition, if the Web site is designed to handle content that changes dynamically, learners can assemble modules into personalized courses that fit their immediate needs. Learning Management Systems (LMS), combined with content management to support authoring by course developers, are capable of not only delivering static (author prepared) or dynamic (customized and personalized) e-learning content, but also providing course registration and tracking of learning completion and success rates.

Tom Kelly, vice president of worldwide training at Cisco Systems, reinvented training development and delivery at the company.*

Kelly cites an anti-learning bias as one of the major drivers behind the development of an e-learning environment. Like information-development, training has to keep justifying its existence. That often means that measuring the number of people attending classroom training is more important than measuring successful learning. Kelly notes considerable resistance to e-learning because people like the social interaction that comes with an instructor-led class. And, education is viewed as an event rather than an integral part of job performance.

To combat these biases, Cisco implemented a learning portal where employees track their own learning plan and automatically receive updates of time-critical information based on their job titles, interests, learning styles, and work areas. Through the learning portal, a salesperson downloads a 20-minute information chunk on a new product immediately before attending a customer meeting. If this immediacy of information access works as intended, the employee won't even label it "training."

As a training manager at Sun, Oracle, and Cisco, Kelly has long been fighting the paper glut and burdensome classroom time. He notes that Sun delivered a 5-foot box of training materials with the Solaris operating system. Distributing the information electronically saved millions and made access faster and updates easier. But just giving people faster access to enormous piles of information clearly wasn't a final solution. Accessibility is still the most important issue in information delivery.

At Cisco, Kelly's team created a Web site that groups content by audience and delivers a specific learning plan based on job titles, areas of work, technologies, and products. Searching this database of information is facilitated by a search technology they developed called INFO (Information Network for Field Organizations Locator). The Locator tool uses an XML-based metadata system that reads the metadata tags on every content unit in the database, including video, paper, spreadsheets, and PowerPoint presentations.

Because all the information is stored in a repository, content created for one audience can easily be directed toward another audience. In addition, Kelly's team has developed a method for employees to rank the quality of the content. The ranking system puts pressure on the content developer and helps to better match content with learning needs.

Kelly has also revolutionized content development at Cisco, an issue that should be of considerable interest to information-development managers. First, he gets content from its source (product developers, marketing specialists, technical documentation, and others who are willing to develop structured content using XML and metadata) as quickly as possible. Members of the training group are assigned to product-development teams from the beginning of a project. They record critical information by videotaping product experts, developing slides and audio tracks, and enhancing text with graphics, animation, test questions and answers, games, and simulations as needed. The information is made immediately accessible to the sales force, who prefer fast to polished.

Although content development is decentralized back to the product-development teams, the training organization controls its deployment. Using the e-learning infrastructure, the training team is responsible for getting the content to the people who need it, in the way they need it, as quickly as possible. Kelly believes that e-learning gives Cisco a competitive advantage by aggressively managing the company's intellectual capital.

Kelly informed me that they are working with e-publishing groups and the metadata framework team to establish corporate standards and guidelines. They are working hard to keep the momentum going. As we know from working with many in technical publications, the inertia of whatever people are comfortable with is difficult to overcome.

Tom Kelly has as many challenges as we all have in defining a new approach to disseminating vital information. It appears that he is trying to break down old thinking about training and turn it into learning by using the Web as a tool. Publications managers have the same challenge in moving away from books to deliver content dynamically.

* Cisco's program for providing education over the Internet to Cisco sales staff was originally described in the October 2000 issue of *Fast Company* (pp. 286–295).

Content management for information development and technical publications
Closely linked to training is information development used to support both internal activities and external customers. Formal information is developed to explain company policies and outline specific procedures to be followed in day-to-day activities in both the supply chain and the support chain. Policies and procedures manuals are developed in line with ISO (International Standards Organization) certification requirements and to establish best practices for the completion of myriad corporate tasks.

Federal Express, for example, provides manuals that direct the activities of employees in its ground-operations division. These employees are responsible for handling all the packages coming from and going to customers around the world. The policies and procedures manuals are organized by type of employee activity, which means there are separate manuals for couriers and station managers. Nonetheless, these separate manuals contain some of the same information. Some policies and procedures are common to all employees and some are specific to particular job functions. With a content-management system, individual policy and procedure modules are stored separately. When the authors are ready to publish, they can create specific manuals by assembling the modules appropriate to each job function. Because the modules are stored only once in the content-management system, they are written once, updated in one place, but reused in many different configurations.

Even more important to a global enterprise, the modules need be translated only once in each language. The some assembly process can be used to create individual collections of information in multiple languages.

Similarly, technical content directed toward the needs of external customers can be handled efficiently through content management. Modules of information are authored once, stored and updated from the repository, and assembled into appropriate publications. Not only is the same information available in every applicable publication, but variations on the information can be created and tagged for easy retrieval and assembly. For example, Dell Computer Corporation is able to create manuals for a wide variety of related products by creating inter-changeable modules. Variations in the information needed to support individual products can be tagged and selected. In this way, the author of a manual for a desktop computer uses the same core modules as the author of a manual for a lap-top computer. Where the information differs, the authors write unique modules or modify existing modules by labeling the details that are different. Find further discussion of reuse strategies in Chapter 9, *Developing a Single-Source Strategy*.

Instructional designers in the training organization and information developers producing technical and business information can share a repository. Much of the detailed information about products and processes is the same between training and documentation. Lawson Software Systems, a provider in the Enterprise Resource Planning (ERP) market, was able to design a process so that information was developed once and shared between customer training and technical docu-mentation. Costs were saved by writing once and using the information in two places, eliminating not only duplicate writing tasks but also reducing the amount of time needed for technical reviews and testing. Once a module is written, it can be reviewed and tested and readied for use in multiple documents. The cost reduc-tion associated with reuse is augmented by the ability to ensure that information is correct and complete and appropriate to the needs of the customer. In addition, the information in training materials and reference documentation is consistent.

Content management for customer service
As I have noted, significant information resources are created in the support chain by instructional-design and information-development professionals. The infor-mation resources they create should be shared and made widely available within the organization, as well as outside to customers and partners.

One of the primary users of much of the customer and business information created for training and documentation is customer service. Customer service is generally responsible for tracking a customer's purchase of a product throughout the life of the product. The staff in customer service needs information that is pro-duced by others in the organization. They also generate information of their own in support of customers.

Customers refer to customer service to check product availability, upgrade to new versions, purchase accessories, order spare and replacement parts, and so on. Customer service needs information about the customer's configuration of prod-ucts and information about versions and accessories. It should know what replacement parts match product configurations and whether they are available, where, and on what schedule. Service personnel must learn about products through a training program and consult technical information regularly. They have to update information about the customer, as well as use customer resource management databases. They generate information to support customers. All the information needed to support customers, upsell upgrades and accessories, and support parts ordering should be controlled through content management.

Content management for technical support

Technical support organizations in many companies double for customer service. However, technical support organizations in technical industries require additional information resources to support customers. Whenever new products are introduced, technical support staff require training that is instructor-led or computer- and Web-based. They need access to technical information resources produced by information developers, product development, and marketing. Depending on the industry, they may require access to regulatory information produced by government agencies and to interpretations of official documents provided by company specialists.

Technical support typically produces considerable information that should be available through a content-management system. They record customer problems and document the solutions. They track product bugs and report them to product development. They acquire information about customer concerns with the usability and functionality of products, documentation, and training. In many cases, they develop procedures, answer frequently asked questions, and provide supplementary information directly to customers.

Technical support systems have been designed to handle the information produced by the support organization. However, in many cases, these systems do not support general content management and may make linking to other information resources difficult.

An integrated content-management solution working throughout the activities in the support chain enables all of the support organizations to share and reuse information and provide that information directly to customers. One ERP provider, J D Edwards, provides its repository of technical information directly to its customers along with tools to add their own information to the repository. J D Edwards' commitment to self-service through the support chain has contributed to increased customer productivity and satisfaction.

Responding to the news and entertainment content-management challenge

In this discussion, I have pointed out how content management provides information resources for internal and external requirements. A content-management solution fulfills internal staff information requirements throughout the supply and the support chains. Content-management solutions support customers in a B2B relationship and consumers in a B2C environment. Through content management, information is authored once and reused many times, as well as made widely available through a single source.

An additional content-management challenge exists to support the information dissemination activities of news, information, and entertainment organizations, in particular those publishing through the Web. Web-disseminated information comes in all forms, from information resources created by the providers themselves to information that is drawn from outside sources. Syndication of content produced by one organization and made available to other organizations through the Web has become commonplace.

Content management has already made a significant difference in how information resources are managed by Web publishers. News sites like *The New York Times*, the *Washington Post*, and the *San Jose Mercury News* (one of the first of the online newspapers) publish information produced by their own authors and bring in information from many outside sources. The information is brought together in Web sites that allow users to pursue links from a current article to past articles on similar subjects and related resources that provide background, commentary, topic expansion, and more. Web-centric information organizations like AOL, MSN, and Yahoo provide millions of pages of information made available from thousands of organizations and delivered to one place. They enable customers to select and view only what is most important to them, to bookmark information they want to revisit, and to create their own information through newsgroups and chat rooms.

Weather.com, one of the ten most visited sites on the Web, not only produces its own information and provides myriad links to additional resources, but it manages data coming directly from the National Weather Service and similar weather-data-collection organizations worldwide.

Weather.com is one of the most visited sites on the Web, attracting weather aficionados as well as ordinary people who want to know if they should carry an umbrella or dig out the snow shovel by tomorrow. Each day, 12 million people look at the weather site, infinitely more than one would ever expect at a site featuring technical documentation. Nonetheless, we have much to learn from the information architects of weather.com.

Without content management, such news-oriented Web sites as weather.com, updated almost instantaneously, would be impossible. Information drawn from repositories and sent directly to Web servers through automated scripts, with format styles added only at the end of process, makes information management flexible and responsive to customer needs.

> **Twelve million people consult the weather.com site each day. Unlike other dot.coms, weather.com is growing rapidly and maintaining its profitability.**

Weather.com delivers over 300,000 pages of content, nearly a million pages if you count all the weather maps. Yet, the site makes all this content accessible so that people will keep coming back to find what they need. In the site's latest version, readers can customize their view of the site, creating a My Weather home page that presents reports for selected locations and six weather maps of their choice. In addition, access to additional information, such as airline schedules, is simply a click away.

To design the site, the information architects studied users: what they looked for, why they visited, and why they returned (or didn't). David Davila, the site's information architect, designed a hub-and-spoke model for the site's information. The users are at the center (the hub) of the model, surrounded by information resources related to their previous choices. The earlier site design used a more traditional hierarchical structure, one we frequently see with technical documentation, arranged in seemingly never-ending tree structures. Users were quickly lost in this model and found they had to shift to different hierarchies to find unrelated information.

At the heart of the site's success is a relentless customer focus. That customer focus is what is missing from so many high-tech companies. Publications organizations often are barred from interacting with customers. Just as often, technical communicators lack the desire to let customers lead the way. Following weather.com's example, we must develop user personas based on real in-depth information. We must track, as weather.com does, exactly which pages are visited every day (and which pages are not visited). We must hold focus groups, conduct site visits, and run surveys based on user visits to our Web sites. We must include links on every page that invite user feedback."*

* Weather.com was featured in the December 2000 issue of *Fast Company* (FC issue 41, page 186 or http://www.fastcompany.com/online/41/weathering.html) in an article, "Weathering the Storm," by Chuck Salter.

Developing continuous publishing as the key to frequent use

The news and information services available on the Web have upped the ante for content management among companies in the B2B and B2C world, especially those disseminating technical information for product evaluation and purchase and product support. Customers have learned that information should be current, linked widely to other related information, and easily accessible through well-designed navigation and search. Individuals have learned about collaborative filtering, in that they recognize that Amazon.com and other similar Web sites are able to assess their preferences in books, music, or other resources and deliver customized content. They become increasingly impatient dealing with Web-based information that is not focused on or responsive to their needs. If one Web site can open with a list of books that they are likely to be interested in, why can't the Web site supporting multi-million dollar products know what information is needed by a system administrator in contrast with an end user? Why can't information developers update information regularly and ensure that identical explanations and instructions occur everywhere they are needed?

Continuous publishing requires not only that information be updated in a timely manner but that new information be continually made available. It means that information created by users is fed back into the system and made available to others in the user community. The only possible way to accommodate dynamically changing information is through a sophisticated content-management solution supported by an Information Model that anticipates continually changing information resources.

Removing the Web production barrier

In a content-management solution, content is king. Having the right content in place, keeping it up-to-date, and removing content that is no longer relevant or timely ensures that the user community will find what they need. Unfortunately, organizations that started out developing Web sites by hand coding in HTML have learned that the process is incredibly slow. Even using HTML conversion tools requires that authors, information designers, and Web administrators must prepare information resources for inclusion in a site.

The preparation is as significant a barrier as hand coding. Hand coding or even conversion coding is by definition an individually controlled process. Some person must be involved. Once the information is coded and checked for presentation quality, the files should be posted to the Web site—again by an individual. The process is slow, tedious, and fraught with errors. Information is not updated in a timely manner. Out-of-date information is not purged quickly enough. Updates are missed, links are lost, or links go to the wrong places. Because the work must be done manually, problems are common. Wrong information or inconsistent information can be costly—in service calls, employee errors, or even lawsuits.

Existing content might have been directly coded in HTML or converted into HTML using tag-conversion software. Individual hand coding of documents by a Web-management organization introduces an enormous bottleneck into a content delivery that keeps content from growing in response to increasing needs for information resources. The only way to maintain a significant volume of information in a timely manner is by using a content-management system.

Dynamic content challenges traditional Web management practices

Preparing even static content and updating Web sites in a timely manner has proven difficult enough. Handling dynamic content and updating in real time is even more challenging. Content management provides a potential solution.

The process of updating content to the Web should be automated at two levels: posting and author workflow. Posting static content can be handled directly from a content-management system by creating scripts that draw modules from the repository, assemble them in an appropriate sequence or network of links, and add format styles in HTML, XML, or PDF (Portable Document Format). Automation of this final production step results in significant time savings. Compuware Europe B.V., developer of the UNIFACE software-development environment, notes that the time needed to deploy its entire technical documentation suite to the Web decreased from a week to an hour, once their content-management system was in place. Medtronic, manufacturer of implantable medical devices, is able to produce final output in minutes (or even seconds) instead of in days or hours.

Posting dynamic content is even more challenging because not only should content be updated regularly but the mix of content delivered to individuals and groups of customers must change in response to their requests or through tracking their progress through a site. Users whose experience with the Internet is tutored by Yahoo!, AOL, and Weather.com, have increasingly high expectations.

To respond, information architects must find ways to structure modular content. They must create rules to determine how information will be delivered and linked to other information, because they will find it increasingly difficult to know what information will be needed and how it should be structured. They will need to design Web sites that are placeholders for categories of content, based on a comprehensive Information Model. They will need to find ways to allow users to establish their own links and views of the information.

Maintaining a continuous information stream

Although designing interactive Web delivery is in itself a significant challenge, I believe the greater challenge is maintaining a stream of valuable information coming into content management. Some of the information coming into an organization's Web site will be syndicated from other sources. News and information developers have learned that their content has value if it is made available in the right places.

Just as companies are now creating mini-applications to streamline the process of developing numeric-data portals, we must develop applications that deliver content from outside sources.

Content produced by professional outside sources is much easier to incorporate than content produced by people inside the enterprise. The greater challenge is finding ways to encourage authors to produce and update information in a timely manner. Then, information developers must move information from authors to reviewers to approvers and to publication fast. That process requires workflow automation in addition to methods that simplify adding metadata to information resources.

Standard terminology for identifying information will allow authors to label information more consistently and make it easier to retrieve and deliver.

Automatically generating content often requires integrating information from multiple sources

As you work to enrich the content available to your community of users, you will need ways to integrate information coming from multiple sources and residing in distributed repositories. Technology like XML fosters the integration of all forms of content and provides the means to enhance delivery. The enterprise portal gives internal users a one-stop shop for information resources and numeric data coming from inside and outside the organization. The expansion of the enterprise portal to external partners and to customers brings targeted information to the individual.

Information architects and Web designers can work closely together to ensure that all users in the information communities that they serve get the information they need. Content-management systems are the enablers, allowing your business to create, manage, and publish content effectively. They must be supported by new processes, policies, and divisions of labor to address the requirements of large-scale operations.

Especially important is the need to negotiate the terminology used to tag information. If the terms are ambiguous or poorly defined, searching for tagged information may prove frustrating for all levels of user, both internal and external. Although terminology decisions require careful analysis and frequent compromise, they are critical to the success of information integration.

Developing your content-management solution: a phased approach

Once you're convinced that content management is in your future, you should follow a systematic process to plan your solution, understand and document your technology requirements, design your Information Model, and conduct a pilot project before implementing globally. The five-phase approach, as illustrated in Figure 1-4, gives you a process that is easy to follow and ensures a successful outcome. In subsequent chapters, I explain in detail how to accomplish each phase.

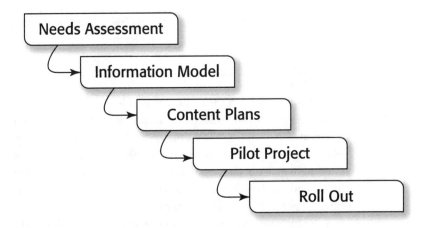

Figure 1-4 The model shows the five phases of a content-management project

As you plan, I advise you to think big. Content-management systems are not inexpensive. The more business needs that you are able to address, the more organizations can help to share the implementation and technology costs. When you begin an assessment, you should invite to the initial discussions representatives from all the potential stakeholders' organizations. Generally, that includes representatives of both the supply chain and the support chain. Explore in the initial meetings the opportunities for managing content and the opportunities for sharing information resources and reusing rather than rewriting. Paint the picture broadly and illustrate the possibilities of better serving the needs of the corporate community.

Usually a number of different organizations within the corporation have been thinking about a content-management solution. Some might even be fairly far along in defining a solution for their limited set of requirements. Unfortunately, the silo approach leads to a proliferation of technologies, many of which don't easily communicate with each other. If the teams begin to communicate, they can usually achieve a mutually advantageous solution and share the costs.

Although it is extremely important to think and plan big, it is also important to implement small. In the phased approach, I recommend that small, discrete pilot projects be selected for initial implementation. Work the kinks out on these pilots before implementing in the larger organization. Lessons learned will benefit subsequent rollouts, and people trained on the pilot will be available as internal consultants or project leaders for the next round of implementations.

Phase 1: Assessing your needs and developing a plan

Phase 1 of your content-management project must focus on a needs assessment. The needs assessment addresses four questions:

- Your users need information—what are their needs?
- You have information resources in your organization—what are they and how are they produced today?
- You have processes used by people who author content even if those processes are not formally defined—how and how well do these processes work today?
- You have technology in place—how effectively is it being used and how adequate is it to the task ahead?

You will find details to help you complete Phase 1 in Chapters 2, 3, and 4.

Purpose

You must understand the issues that currently make managing content a challenge in your organization, how the management and delivery of content must be improved, and how your solutions will improve the users' experience and enhance the organization's success and profitability.

Process

Your first step in assessing needs is creating a vision of your users' experience with information, both inside and outside your organization. That means gathering information on the current user experience by understanding the successes and failures of that experience.

After information gathering comes analysis. If your users' experience is not optimal today, define how it should change if your content-management solution is to succeed. The focus of your analysis is understanding the dimensions of your content-management solution—the point of view of each relevant group in the user community as well as that of the authors. Identify the many ways in which you might want to target information specifically to particular staff members, customers, and partners.

I find that many companies fail to appreciate the importance of defining the user experience. They approach content management only from the perspective of authoring and storing information. Although the savings achieved through information reuse and automatic publishing are easily quantified and can be used effectively to justify a content-management solution, more savings and significant quality increases are possible. Remember that the users are the victims of failures to deliver information effectively. By starting with the user experience, you ensure that your content-management solution contributes to meeting a critical business objective—increasing customer satisfaction and loyalty.

The second step in your needs assessment requires a complete inventory of your current information resources. Not only must you catalog and categorize the information you now produce, but you must compare what you have today with what you have discovered is really needed by your users or might be needed in the future. Remember that just because information exists does not mean that someone, somewhere, finds it useful.

The third step is to look closely at the processes that are used throughout your organization to produce, approve, and disseminate information resources. Find out who authors, who reuses information coming from other parts of the organization, and who reviews and approves information. Learn what tools are used to create information resources and how well they are used. Ask if authors use format styles in their documents. Identify how information resources are currently disseminated or published at present—in print, in HTML, on CD-ROM, in help systems, and the Web.

Finally, learn what technologies are used to author, store, retrieve, and publish information. Investigate systems that are already in place, especially if they are home-grown or specialized proprietary solutions serving the needs of one department. Understand how information is stored and accessed. Discuss with your Information Technology (IT) organization which database systems your company already owns and what their capacity might be. Find out if any other part of the organization is already investigating a content-management solution.

Deliverables

From your Phase 1 investigation, prepare a report and recommendation. The report should include your analysis of the business problem at hand and how its solution will improve the company's profitability. Your business case for content management must show what it costs to continue handling content as it is done today, what the short-comings are of the current approach, and what efficiencies and cost savings might be realized with a new and better solution.

Note that the kinds of skills and experience needed to do an effective analysis and design are unique and required only at the beginning of a project. If you have not been through several implementations, it is very unlikely that you will be able to anticipate the downstream implications of your design decisions. An experienced information architect with the assistance of an equally experienced integrator will likely save you considerable time and money.

Propose a time line for a project to implement a content-management solution and recommend who should be involved in the project. Be sure to include your most experienced people, those knowledgeable about the process, as well as new people who bring a fresh perspective. Note if additional human resources are needed or how people might be trained in the process.

Next step
Once your plan has been accepted, ensure that you have the funding and staffing you need to move to Phase 2.

Phase 2: Developing your Information Model and outlining your technology requirements

Phase 2 of your content-management project includes defining your information architecture and deciding upon the best technology solution to meet your needs.

- What are the dimensions of your Information Model and how do they define your requirements to categorize and label your information resources?

- What types of information are needed by your users and which ones are currently in use? Should you use everything you already have or create new information types to organize your information more effectively?

- How should you structure the content within your information types to support authors, maintain consistency, and facilitate optimal reuse?

- What technology components are needed to support the Information Model that you have defined?

You will find the details to complete Phase 2 in Chapters 2, 4, 5, and 6.

Purpose
In Phase 2, you develop your comprehensive Information Model, based on the needs of all your organization's content-management requirements. You also investigate technology solutions and develop a detailed technology requirements document.

Process
Begin by defining the dimensions you will use to identify the categories in your Information Model. These categories become the metadata you use to label the content and make it modular. At this point, you may find it advantageous to work with an information architecture consultancy and technology experts if you do not have such expertise inhouse.

First, your dimensions must be based on business information requirements. For example, you may categorize different product types and models, market segments, or subject matter.

Second, your dimensions must be based on author requirements. For example, you may categorize information by author, title, ID, editor, approver, original date, revision dates, version number, source, and so on.

Third, your dimensions must be based on user requirements. For example, you may categorize information by user job, skill level, experience, language, country, and so on.

You will find it useful to develop use cases or scenarios of use, narratives that describe how authors, business analysts, and users will interact with information in the future. The more use cases you are able to construct, the better your solutions are likely to be. Not only will use cases allow you to define author, user, and content requirements more precisely, but they will provide you with a valuable way to evaluate tools and technology.

Your Information Model provides the terminology (taxonomy) you will use to identify all the elements in your repository. Note that building your Information Model is best done with the help of experts. One of the unexpected benefits of the process is discovering additional opportunities to improve your content, workflow, and reuse. It is much easier and less expensive to discover these opportunities early than later in the process. An expert consultancy is likely to result in significantly lower future costs.

Then, move on to identifying your information types. Information types define the kind of content your authors create and how the details are organized. Each information type should be based on the needs of your user community. A typical set of information types for technical information includes concepts, procedures, and reference modules. More specific information types can be derived from these basic types. For example, your organization might need different information types for maintenance procedures and end-user procedures.

Finally, review your delivery requirements. What can be automated? What can be personalized or customized? What media must be supported now and in the future?

Once you have identified a minimal set of information types, go inside the types and identify the content units that authors will use to construct the types. The content units are the components of the subject matter that will guide the development of formal Document Type Definitions (style sheets in XML or SGML) if you plan to use structured authoring systems (see details of this process in Chapters 2, 5, and 6).

At the same time that you are defining the three-tiered structure of your Information Model (dimensions, information types, content units), you may begin to investigate technology solutions. However, I strongly recommend that you wait until after your Information Model is quite firm to define the technology you need. Until you know in some detail how you want to deliver information to your user community and formulate your Information Model, you are not ready to make a sound technology decision.

I find that too many organizations "jump the gun" and make technology decisions without adequate preparation. The technology specialists in an organization often feel that you can buy technology and "do what it says." Unfortunately, content-management systems don't say much. You have to specifically define all the interactions and outcomes you need; the content-management system will do only what you design it to do. If you select the wrong technology solution, the system will not do what you need. Without a clear Information Model, managers may come to rely upon templates provided by the system vendor and get locked into structures.

One organization I work with, a major telecommunications company in Europe, decided early to select a system that managed only large documents. Unfortunately, that decision has hampered their development of a single-source solution. They have to work with small chunks of information to reuse and restructure to meet customer needs. Their technology solution does not support this requirement.

Use all of the information you have gathered thus far to write a functional requirements document. Detail how you want to support your authors with authoring and workflow capabilities, what the content-management system must include so that you can store, manage, and retrieve modules from the repository, and, most important, how you should assemble and deliver information to your users.

Do not specify and design solutions. Stick to requirements alone. Identify and explain what you have to do. Let the vendors explain how they will accommodate your needs. Try not to place unnecessary limits on the technology solution. There will be new developments in the field that you have not anticipated. Don't close the door to these solutions by trying to prove yourself a technology expert.

Ask vendors to respond to your functional requirements (as a request for proposal). After you have analyzed the responses for completeness and clarity, ask for presentations. Use your requirements document to question the vendor representatives and be sure that you get satisfactory answers. Be aware that everyone exaggerates their capabilities to some extent. Ask for clear statements in writing about what is standard and what needs to be customized. Be very specific about compatibilities between your requirements and each tool you are considering. Ask about ease of integration between tools because integration problems can sink an otherwise sound specification.

At the same time, visit other organizations that are using the technology. Talk with people in the same roles as your team and find out about all the benefits and pitfalls they have encountered.

When you have selected a small group of final vendors, ask for a "proof of concept" in which the vendors prepare and present their solution with your own information. Recognize that you might have to pay fees for the "proof of concept," because the development process may be quite expensive for the vendors.

One effective technique is to write scenarios that you would like to test with the products. Know that some scenarios might be impossible to simulate without a good deal of customization work but be sure that you get to try out standard scenarios for authoring, storing and retrieving, content assembly, and possibly publishing. The assembly and publishing scenarios are likely to be the most difficult to simulate and are the areas in which technologies are most likely to fall part. If you don't test your assembly and publishing solutions, you may not discover the problems until you are deep into implementation (and your warranty period has expired).

Be comfortable with the people on the vendor's team. As you narrow your choices, ask to meet with the implementation team if they haven't already been involved. In many cases, you meet with the sales team initially, but they are often not involved with your implementation. Be certain that you communicate your requirements again to the implementation team. They might not be fully versed about your specific needs.

In many cases, you will find it advantageous to work with a system integrator and an information architect who are not part of the vendor's team. I don't want to suggest that the vendors cannot implement their own systems, but many of the solutions you will select will involve technologies from multiple vendors. If your delivery solution is complex, you will need considerable customizing.

For all but the simplest solutions, previous design, integration, and implementation experience is invaluable. Solutions that look promising in the design phase can be very difficult and expensive, or even impossible, to implement. If you don't have someone on your team who has been through several large-scale implementations, using a reputable system integrator can be the difference between success and a long, drawn out failure.

An information architecture team may also be valuable during Phase 2. Designing a sound Information Model is a complex task. You can save yourself many problems by consulting with professional information architects. They tend to ask the right questions and have the skills and experience to help you avoid the pitfalls.

I find, when our organization works with an internal team, that our information architects ask questions no one else has asked. Because we have experience with so many implementations—more than any individual company could have—we generally help people anticipate situations that they don't know might present problems.

Deliverables
From your Phase 2 work, prepare an Information Model (or several interrelated Information Models for your enterprise) that includes the metadata dimensions you will use to label modules in the repository, develop a minimal set of informa-

tion types that your authors will use to create modules, and define the content units that will make up your information types.

Prepare a guideline for authors for implementing the Information Model. The guideline should include descriptions of the model's components and instructions for their use. Typically, you will need instructions for using the metadata tags correctly, instructions for selecting the appropriate information type for a topic, and instructions for writing in an XML or SGML editor. Writing in an editor usually includes creating links and adding graphics or other media. A well-designed system should include guided editing features that encourage authors to implement the model.

You should prepare a complete draft of your guidelines for authors in Phase 2, to which you will revise and add during your pilot project in Phase 4.

Use the information types and content units to prepare your tagging system in the form of DTDs for XML and SGML authoring. Otherwise, set up forms-based writing or use systems that either allow unstructured documents to be included that are formatted for desktop publishing or use format-based styles to provide some structure for final formatting.

To guide your technology decision, write a functional requirements document that you send to vendors. However, be certain that your Information Model is firmly in hand before your make any decisions about technology. Even the simplest choices of technology can significantly influence your ability to implement your Information Model.

Next step

With your Information Model completed and your technology selected, you should work with your information architect, your Web designers, and your system integrator and other technology vendors to define exactly how the output from your content-management system will be delivered to your user communities. In all but the simplest solutions, the help of an expert team will save you time and money.

Phase 3: Creating your content assembly and delivery plans

Planning for content assembly and delivery is the critical activity of Phase 3. Content planning includes the manner in which you will assemble modular content into documents, often for paper and PDF delivery. But content planning also includes the design of information-rich Web sites, delivering in HTML or XML to browsers. The Information Model that you constructed in Phase 2 must become the organizing principle behind your navigation design for all interactive media.

The most difficult aspect of content planning is the assembly of modular components into compound documents. If the content is assembled appropriately, whether for static or dynamic delivery, it can be automatically rendered (attached style sheets) in any form.

Purpose

The purpose of Phase 3 is to link your Information Model to your assembly and delivery model. Because the intent of content management is to improve the user's experience, you should ensure that the way in which you organize the output of your content-management solution, especially on the Web, is governed by the Information Model.

Too often, we note problems with Web navigation that are the direct result of a flawed Information Model or a disconnect between the Information Model and its rendering on the Web. A complete Information Model includes not only the design of XML/SGML authoring, but also the assembly and delivery of content. Like the choice of a content-management system, your requirements for assembly, presentation, and delivery will have a significant impact on your Information Model. It is extremely important that your output requirement drive the model, as I discuss in Chapters 4 through 6.

In Chapters 7 and 8, I discuss in detail how to create content plans for both static and dynamic Web sites. These activities are the focus of Phase 3.

Process

If your only deliverables are static books, Phase 3 can be quite straightforward, although you may find it frustrating and time-consuming to reach agreement on standard formats for delivery. Content plans for static books are tables of contents enhanced with annotations that explain how the sequence of chapters and sections serves the needs of the users. The same content plan applies whether the book is printed or delivered in PDF or HTML.

If you are authoring in XML or SGML, you will have to create a presentation style for print production. In well-constructed XML or SGML, you do not have information about the typography or the page layout included in the tags. The presentation style for print is created as an output formatting specification, which defines how the SGML-tagged text will appear in print. Defining print output with a detailed output specification can be difficult and time-consuming, so plan early for this task.

A content plan, including assembly and presentation, for static Web delivery is more complex than a content plan for a book. Similarly, a content plan or information architecture for dynamic Web delivery is more complex than one for static Web delivery. In both cases, the content plan describes how the Web pages will be structured and how the navigation will work. The structure and navigation are guided by the Information Model.

When we look at Web sites that are guided by the Information Model, we find a firmly established structural and relational logic. Because the Information Model identifies the dimensions of the users' experience, the Web design enables the users to make decisions easily, from the home page, about how to find the information they need.

When we look at Web sites in which the Information Model either does not exist or does not inform the design, we see a site that is awkward and frustrating to navigate. The user is often confused about how to move through the links and has difficulty following links to a successful conclusion.

In Phase 3, concentrate on establishing a path from the user and business needs identified in your Information Model and the way that information will be presented in your Web delivery. See Chapter 8, *Developing Content Plans for Dynamic Web Sites*, for details about this process.

Deliverables

From Phase 3, prepare content plans for each type of deliverable you intend to produce. Content plans for books can follow a standard table of contents arrangement, or they can be dynamically generated to meet specific user needs and preferences (custom documents), or instantaneous system or operations needs. Content plans for static or dynamic Web sites are much more complex and should be developed using your Information Model as a base and employing techniques of User-Centered Design (UCD). For more information on UCD, see J. Hackos and J. Redish, *User and Task Analysis for Interface Design*.

Next step

After your Information Model and content plans are complete and your technology is at the early stages of implementation, it is time to begin your first pilot project.

Phase 4: Conducting and evaluating a pilot project

In your content-management project, think about planning big and implementing small. It is important that your system design address the entire problem domain, but initial activities should be kept small. That will allow you to minimize complexity and give users and support staff time to adjust to new ways of doing things. A good pilot can either be narrow and deep, exercising all aspects of structured authoring, or it can be broad and shallow, running a single, simple document through the entire process.

A pilot project provides you with an opportunity to roll out some functionality of your project quickly and get immediate results. You can use the pilot to train staff, work out the details of your Information Model and content plans, and test the technology solution.

Purpose

A pilot project allows you to ensure that you have adequate processes in place to implement your content-management solution. The pilot project should be selected to test your technology but also to identify process improvement opportunities and enhancements to your Information Model. What you learn from the pilot will help you hone your content-management solution to ensure its success. It's a critical phase that must not be skipped.

Process

The first step in Phase 4 is to select a suitable project. Here are a few guidelines:

- Choose a project that can be completed in a fairly short amount of time, between three and six months. A short project will give you a timely result that shows off the success of your process. It will also ensure that you can make course corrections and get immediate feedback. Finally, a short, small project improves the probability that adequate support will be available to deal with implementation problems as they arise and minimize the impact of serious design flaws.

- Select a project that has more new content than existing content so that you don't have a lot of tedious rewriting.

- Alternatively, convert a reasonably structured existing document(s) as a good exercise for your authors. Starting with an existing base can shorten the learning curve for authors. Beware, however, that you do not select an unstructured disaster that must not only be restructured but often rewritten from scratch.

- Ensure that you have an innovative and enthusiastic team assigned to the pilot project. This is not the time to bring the laggards along. This is not a time for second guessing and naysaying.

- Select a very strong project manager who wants to see content management succeed and who is an excellent communicator.

- Be certain that everyone involved in the project, including those responsible for final deliverables and translation, are brought into the planning early and are willing to work closely with the project team.

- Carefully discuss the potential risks of the pilot project. For example, what happens if the challenges of the new technology delay the delivery of the information and potentially delay a product release? Have each team involved in the pilot develop a risk-management plan that includes methods to mitigate problems if or when they occur. Ensure that the risk-management plan is approved by senior management.

The responsibility of the project manager is to establish the project goals, deliverables, and schedule as quickly as possible. It is especially important to include sufficient time for training the staff in the new processes and technologies. Usually, staff members will have to learn to write in a style suitable for modules that will be repurposed, think about creating topics that are suitable for multiple deliverables with multiple contexts, become comfortable with a new authoring tool, and learn to work collaboratively so that output will be consistent, well-structured, and reusable.

Realize that many more groups will be involved in a completely successful pilot project than ordinarily work on an information-centric project in your organization. You will likely include consultants, system integrators, and tools vendors, as well as your own internal information technologists, in the process.

Select a project manager who is an excellent communicator and who has a strong, clear vision of what the final result should be. Many groups will be curious about the progress of the pilot project, even if they are not directly involved. Some of those groups or individuals will hope that the project will fail, justifying their objection to changing the way information development has always been done.

During the course of the pilot project, use your project-management tools to track every activity. You will need this information to calculate cost savings and predict how long it will take to conduct subsequent projects. Maintain comprehensive progress reports that will provide a record of project activities to be used to guide the complete rollout.

Deliverables
The outcomes of Phase 4 include the pilot project deliverables and the project-management records. In addition, provide an updated version of the guidelines for authoring in your content-management solution. A training framework for authors, the support team, and managers should be an outcome of your pilot.

Next step
Once the pilot project is completed, you should write a project wrap-up report and hold a wrap-up meeting. At the wrap-up meeting, review with all team members and stakeholders what was successful, what challenges were encountered and solved, and what challenges remain.

Phase 5: Rolling out to the larger enterprise
Planning for a large-scale rollout of a content-management system should begin with the pilot project itself. Schedules, time estimates, process, and training should all be part of the pilot. You should also have completed your analysis of the risks, successes, and challenges of the pilot project and considered how you intend to improve the process in the next round.

You may decide, for example, to conduct another pilot project or decide on two or three next projects, rather than an enterprise-wide rollout. I strongly recommend conducting a series of phased rollouts so that you don't go beyond the capacity of your project managers and support staff members to assist with the new projects and help ensure their success. Additionally, the Information Model, processes, and outputs will evolve as authors discover what the new approach is capable of delivering.

Consider how the next projects will affect the existing infrastructure of information development in your organization. Will people need to be reassigned? Will current information have to be thoroughly revised if it is to be integrated into a single solution? How will new information be integrated into the growing implementation of content management? See Chapter 3, *Taking a Close Look at Your Information Resources*, for a discussion of what to bring under content management and what to leave out.

Consider assigning members of the pilot project to serve as project managers for the next phase. If you have selected team members well for the pilot, they should be capable of taking over as project leads with some additional training and support.

Purpose

The purpose of Phase 5 is to implement the content-management solution that you identified in the early stages of your planning. Your implementation might include your entire enterprise, using content management as a foundation for a workplace portal. Your implementation might include only those involved in the support chain or the supply chain. Your implementation, especially in large or global organizations, might include only a single enterprise function. For example, I have worked with companies that focus first on technical information development, training, or customer services, implementing a content-management solution for one of these functions on a global level.

Process

Complete your wrap-up report and conduct your wrap-up meeting to assess the success and challenges of your pilot project. Use your assessment to decide if you want a partial or a full rollout to occur. Once the new projects are proposed, develop a communication plan. As with any change-management effort, communication is the key to success. Meet with all teams that will have to adopt content-management solutions and openly discuss the positives and negatives that you have already discovered. Listen to their concerns and answer questions as fully as possible. Such efforts will help dispel doubts. Be prepared for concerns about stifling creativity and eliminating staff. Be prepared to explain the benefits that will result for customers and for staff members who have an opportunity to work with the latest processes and technologies.

Assign project managers to the new projects who have had experience in the pilot projects. Provide them with training and assistance to ensure their success. Continue to assign as many enthusiastic staff members as you can find to the new projects.

Deliverables

The Phase 5 deliverables are the completed projects. In addition, you will have new metrics as part of your project-management wrap-up reports to use to recalculate the Return on Investment (ROI). Although the pilot project gives you some indication of gains in efficiency and cost reductions, the full projects will be even more significant because you should be overcoming the problems inherent in pilots.

At this point, you are also probably considering technology upgrades and improvements or even moves to newer technologies. Attend conferences and seminars to keep abreast of changes in the field. Consider taking part in a benchmark study with other organizations that are at similar stages of implementation to judge whether your results are in line with others in your industry or those who are pursuing content-management in general. The Center for Information-Development Management <www.infomanagementcenter.com> regularly performs benchmark studies of content-development organizations.

Next step

Remember that no content-management solution is ever complete. As user characteristics, business needs, and authoring and delivery technologies change, you will have to update your Information Model as well as your processes. Mergers and acquisitions of existing businesses mean that you will continue to work on integrating additional departments into the process.

2

Implementing a Content-Management Solution

"Interesting, here are six groups…six different directions…six processes…six results. No communication between groups, yet they develop similar information…and not one of these processes works for the other groups!"

T he technology to implement a content-management solution consists of a collection of tools that support four critical components:

- content acquisition and authoring
- content management
- content assembly and linking
- content delivery, publishing information to a variety of user communities

In determining a technology solution, you must carefully consider how you want to implement in each of these four critical areas.

As an first step, I strongly recommend that every organization contemplating a content-management solution prepare a document that carefully and thoroughly defines requirements in each area. As a start, begin at the end of the process by first envisioning how you want to deliver information to your user communities.

Once you have carefully considered how you want to deliver information to your users and developed your vision of the user experience with your information resources, you are ready to build an content acquisition and authoring environment and a content-management solution that will allow you to deliver your vision.

Remember that delivering content to a wide variety of present and future customers, be they internal or external, begins with creating content that is appropriate and effective and kept continuously up-to-date.

In this chapter, you learn about

- the four primary components of a content-management solution
- the need to develop a vision of the users' future experience with information resources
- the requirements for your content acquisition and authoring environment
- the requirements for your content-management system
- the requirements for assembly and linking
- the requirements of a delivery system that draws information out of the repository and presents it to your users in multiple media

To deliver appropriate, effective, and up-to-date content requires a publishing and delivery solution that offers great flexibility. Consider that content might be delivered through print media; published to an intranet, extranet, or Internet; displayed on large-scale computer monitors or the small screens of Personal Digital Assistants (PDAs) or cell phones; and burned onto CD-ROMs. A content-management solution must enable multiple delivery methods, including new methods not yet developed but possible in the future.

The content-management solution

Managing content to meet the diverse needs of a large user community requires four primary components:

- an environment for creating and acquiring content
- a repository for storing and retrieving content
- a method for assembling and linking content
- a delivery mechanism for delivering content to your customers

Each of these components is supported by technology that enables organizations to deliver information in ways not necessarily anticipated by the original authors of that content.

As you develop your content-management requirements, start at the end. Develop a vision of the user experience with your future content. Describe how members of your user communities will access and use the information resources that will help them do their jobs and meet their goals.

Let's begin with an example. Consider the needs of an information architect for a hospital information system. Dan Palumbo, information architect for the hospital-information system software developer, anticipates only three types of delivery in the near future:

- printed documents

- documents available electronically in PDF

- documents available in HTML to be accessed through a Web browser

Dan is also considering additional delivery mechanisms in the future. He proposes that the company deliver information in the future to

- PDAs

- cell phones

- electronic books (e-books)

He wants to be prepared for these new ways of publishing in the initial implementation of his content-management solution. Technologies are evolving so rapidly that he wants to create a media-neutral repository, based on standards that will allow him to define new delivery methods in the future. In his most ambitious moments, he thinks about

- online learning systems

- help systems attached directly to software

- translations in several languages

In addition, Dan knows that others in his organization are considering more sophisticated methods to support dynamic delivery of content to the Web. Some information resources will appear in context-sensitive help to support the software systems in the hospitals. Other resources will be delivered on CD-ROM for those users who do not have easy access to the Web.

Build your vision of the future user experience

A vision of the user experience is a description of what the users will find when they seek to access and use your information resources both inside and outside your organization. As you begin to define your content-management solution, the essential starting point is this vision.

In considering the possibilities for delivery of information to staff, partners, and customers, Dan recognizes that his first step is to create a comprehensive vision of what the hospitals' user communities will experience in gaining access to and using their information resources.

Here is an example of Dan's vision statement describing the user experience with information that supports learning and using all the information resources available to them in their hospital.

A Vision of the User Experience accessing our hospital's information resources

Dan Palumbo

Our employees need information if they are to perform tasks effectively and find the information they need to work with their computer tools. Our hospital information system (HIS) software is used throughout the hospital. It is used by those responsible for accounting for patients, ensuring that information is available to support all the activities in the business areas of the hospital. The HIS is used by the doctors and nurses and other care-giving personnel to care for patients. Ancillary services like the diagnostic laboratories and the pharmacy use the HIS to record results and transmit them to those responsible for patient care. All these end-users in the hospital need information to learn and use the HIS software effectively and receive information relevant to their every day jobs and responsibilities.

Our vision of the future user experience with our information includes providing both training and ongoing reference information, as well as access to policies and procedures and care bulletins. Our employees need information to learn how to use their HIS software effectively. They need reference information to answer their questions and help them solve problems. They need specifications about how the system is structured for customization and troubleshooting. They need general procedures for performing their jobs effectively and access to the underlying policies. They also need up-to-date information about changes that affect their activities.

If we succeed in developing a content-management system, we will support our employees in learning and using their HIS tools and in their job performance.

Depending upon their name and password, employees will access only the information they need to learn and use in their job activities. For example, laboratory technicians in ancillary services will find only the information they must have to complete their tasks. If they are new to the hospital and our processes, they can log onto step-by-step procedures that will walk them through an entire process. Once they understand how the process works, they will access checklists and worksheets to increase their speed and accuracy.

In addition to text and graphic-based information, employees will be able to watch procedures being performed through a video feature. An instructor performs the procedure and explains exactly how it is done. The demonstrations are modular, taking 5 minutes or less to review. Employees will be able to follow the written procedures as they watch the video of the instructor.

When the employees want to perform the procedures themselves, they will be able to display quick reference cards on their screens. The quick reference cards (the help system) are always on top and always available. However, they can be rolled up and out of the way at any time.

By clicking on the online book icon on their screens, employees will be attached directly to our policies and procedures modular information. The modules will make available only the information resources specific to their jobs in the hospital. The online policy and procedure modules will be linked directly to our internal resource library so that they can be immediately updated as information changes.

Employees will be able to attach their own notes to their information and their training materials. The notes will be preserved through updates of the information in the system.

Troubleshooting information will be available as part of a diagnostic system. Employees will be provided with troubleshooting information in accordance with their responsibilities and levels of expertise. Different information will be provided to staff-level employees than will be provided to supervisors or technical experts, depending upon individual logons. Information will be specific to each hospital in the network, as necessary.

All the information provided, including training and reference, will be in modular form. Modules enable employees to find only what they must have to perform their jobs, mixing and matching modular information for their individual needs.

We will be able to update modules as soon as information changes rather than waiting for new releases of the software or monthly changes to the policies and procedures. We will combine modules into training and reference packages, identified by hospital, job function, and level of expertise. Modules will include

> both procedural and quick reference versions, including checklists and worksheets.
>
> We believe this new information resource will meet our employees' information needs as never before. Our planning must support these goals and our vision of the new user experience with our information resources.

Dan's vision statement, derived from an understanding of user requirements and discussions with those who have information to deliver, outlines the goals of the content-management solution he wants to build. The vision statement is the foundation on which the requirements for his content-management solution are expressed. Once the foundation is in place, he will be able to derive the requirements for authoring, repository, assembly and linking, and delivery.

The components of your content-management solution must be designed and implemented so that you can achieve your vision and reach your goals. Not only is the vision statement a foundation for your requirements, but, if properly articulated, it helps you prioritize seemly equal but competing requirements. If two requirements are at odds, the requirement that best supports the vision is more important. Similarly, if a requirement is articulated that does not support the vision, it should be given a low priority or even discarded.

Beware of beginning with only what you already have

You must start with a vision of the future users' experience with information. Your vision must be based on an analysis of the users and their information environment and an assessment of what will best meet their needs today and in the future. The vision must take into account the possibilities offered by new technology, but it should not specify the technologies to be used.

Too many organizations make the mistake of beginning only with the information they already have. They dive into legacy print documents, help systems, and HTML documents, information stored in flat files on servers, and information already in various databases. Too many badly designed Web sites (intranet, extranet, or Internet) contain nothing but legacy information. In most cases, very few people used the information when it was available to them in paper, even sitting on the nearest shelf or bookcase. It's unlikely that a burning need for this information will magically appear once it is available through an intranet, extranet, or the Internet.

Intranets, in particular, are often a dumping ground for timeworn information resources that never provided much value in the first place. As you evaluate your vision of the users' information experience, consider that the information resources you have in place might be inadequate to meet existing needs, much less new needs.

Begin not with what you have but with what your users need. Then design a process that you can use to produce the right information resources and make them widely available.

To evaluate your users' need for innovative information resources, consider finding answers to these questions:

> What information resources do you provide your users today? How do they use these resources at present? Do they use them at all?
>
> What are the most frequently visited resources? Why? What information do they provide? Is the information generally correct or accurate? Where does it come from?
>
> What additional resources do they have available to them in their work environment?
>
> What resources would they like to have that are not now available?
>
> How do they receive information most effectively at present? Do they experience problems with the accuracy, completeness, or appropriateness of the information they receive? What would improve their access to information?
>
> Do users have print documents available? If so, are they up-to-date and easily accessible?
>
> Do they use CD-ROMs in the workplace? If so, do they find the information on CDs to be accessible and useful? Are they updated in a timely manner?
>
> Do they have regular, timely access to a company intranet? a partner extranet? the Internet?
>
> Do users each have their own computers in the workplace and do they have convenient, high-speed access to intranets, extranets, or the Internet?
>
> Do they have access to the Internet or other electronic resources from home, while traveling, or in other work or leisure situations?

Do your users have laptop computers with Internet or intranet access when they are traveling? If so, is the access acceptable?

Do users carry copies of printed information when traveling to work sites?

Do they have other handheld devices such as PDAs or cell phones?

What types of information resources do they need on the road or at their home bases?

Do your users create their own information resources by assembling print or electronic documents from myriad sources? Do they create hand-written information resources such as notebooks, sticky notes, and others?

Do they keep these personal resources up-to-date? If so, what percentage of their time is spent updating information?

Do they depend upon other people for information? If so, what types of interactions occur? How effective are other people as information resources? How much time is spent interacting with people rather than finding the information independently?

Are there any resentments in a user work group toward people who frequently ask for assistance from co-workers?

Do users spend too much time calling the help line? Are they frustrated by the responses?

Do users have to sort through many versions of the information to find only those parts that address their needs? Is information about multiple products or processes mixed together in the same documents? Would users be better served if information were customized to their needs?

Do users often extract information and reassemble it to meet their personal requirements? Do they create their own cobbled-together documents based on information sources you have provided? How do they update their personal information resources? Are they updated at all? Would they be better served if they were able to personalize the content they receive?

Many more issues might be addressed as you turn to understanding the information needs of your users. The goal is to paint detailed pictures of their information needs and to use these pictures as a basis for your vision of the users' information experience.

Remember that your content-management solution must support fulfilling your users' needs.

To ensure that you have adequate answers to the questions, I strongly recommend that you schedule visits to your customers. The best way of obtaining realistic information is by observing what customers do with the information they receive. Surveys of customers never provide the depth of insight that you get from being there. Rarely would a customer tell you about all the information stored in sticky notes and stuck to the walls, nor would a customer mention the homemade collection of copies, notes, loose pages, and more that make up personal collections of reference information.

Surveys, however, can provide you with a broader view than the site visits alone. Once you complete some site visits, consider surveying more customers about their information needs based on what you have learned through observation and interview. You might want to include surveys on your Web site, asking customers to react to the information available.

In addition, pursue internal resources. Customer support, technical services, consultants, sales and marketing, and training might have information based on their customer contacts that will help complete the picture of information requirements. For more information on studying your customers, see J. Hackos and J. Redish, *User and Task Analysis for Interface Design.*

Once you have the information collected, you will need to analyze it and record your results. I recommend using user profiles, also discussed in detail in the *User and Task Analysis* book. User profiles are portraits of typical users, representing the interactions you want to address in your plan. You might find users with the same types of information-access problems that were portrayed in the scenarios of Chapter 1, *Is Content Management in Your Future?* From your user profiles, develop task scenarios or use cases that show how a customer might be searching for information or referencing information that you have provided. The profiles and scenarios are easy to review with others on your team or with managers from other departments. Their detail and realism help everyone to understand the needs. After your team reaches agreement on the goals of your information delivery, you are ready to develop a requirements list for content-management vendors.

The content-management components

Dan's next task and your next task as well is to define the content acquisition, repository, assembly and linking, and delivery requirements of your content-management solution (Figure 2-1).

Figure 2-1 The four primary components of a content-management system are authoring, the repository, assembly and linking, and publishing.

The authoring and content-acquisition environment is the source for the information that will reside in your content-management system. Information handled in the authoring environment might include:

- information authored by members of your organization
- information brought in from outside your organization (third-party)
- information licensed by your organization from external information providers (syndication)

The information you handle through your authoring and content-acquisition environment can take many forms:

- text of all kinds, both structured and unstructured
- links and relationships
- drawings, 3-D images, photographs, video, and other images
- voice, sounds, and music
- animation and interactive simulations
- slides
- Web pages
- imaged information such as forms, documents, correspondence, email
- financial and other data

Some of the information coming into your authoring and content-acquisition environment might be highly structured. Other information might be very free form. Some information might be created using traditional tools such as word processors, spreadsheets, slide developers, drawing tools, and HTML editors. Other information might arrive as digital images from still and video cameras. Still other information might be generated from numeric data sources and manipulated through programming before entering the content-management system.

No matter what the information source, all the information resources stored in a content-management system will have to be labeled in some way:

- file names in a flat-file system stored on file servers
- metadata attached to the files or objects stored in a database
- tags to identify the internal parts of each document or topic (proprietary style tags in standard word processing and desktop publishing software, HTML, XML, and SGML)

Once the information moves from the authoring environment, it must be stored for easy retrieval. The heart of the content-management system is a database or multiple databases, content repositories that help you keep track of

- the names of original authors and others who have interacted with any of the objects in the database
- workflow activities such as writing, editing, reviewing, approving, and archiving, including dates and times

- subsequent versions of the information resources as they are produced and supersede original versions
- the relationships of objects in the database to one another, including hypertext links and hierarchical relationships, such as tables of content
- other metadata

The primary functions of a repository are referred to as library services. These services include check in/check out, access control, and version control. Workflow is implemented in the content-management system but is generally not considered to be part of the library services.

Information objects stored in a content-management repository can be searched and retrieved by authors and others who need the information. These interactions are controlled by a layer of functionality called a content-management system. The content-management system monitors and controls all the interactions of users with the information objects:

- in standard ways established by your authoring community
- in customized and localized ways
- dynamically generated links
- user-defined assemblages
- system-defined assemblages

When the information objects are retrieved from the repository, they can be assembled and linked to one another.

They must finally be rendered in various formats and delivered in many ways:

- traditional print publications
- PDF facsimiles of print publications
- Web pages in HTML for the current generation of Web browsers (including cascading style sheets)
- Web pages using XML-based style transformations (XSLT)
- electronic books
- WAP for cell phones
- formats suitable for PDAs
- online help systems embedded in software products

In some cases, the objects are retrieved and assembled by authors or information architects directly. Authors create tables of content or other collections of topics to deliver to users, often in print, PDF, or HTML formats. The authors can insert output formats by assembling topics from the database into traditional word processing, desktop publishing, slide shows, or other media. The style sheets in these tools provide the formatting.

In other cases, authors assemble documents that contain standard SGML or XML tags that do not include format information. The format information is automatically attached as the assembled documents are printed or exported to HTML or other output media. The output component of the content-management system facilitates attaching output formats automatically.

In some cases, we want to deliver out of the repository in the same proprietary binary form that we used to create the information in the first place:

- Microsoft Word in/Word out
- Adobe FrameMaker in/FrameMaker out
- Microsoft PowerPoint in/PowerPoint out
- HTML in/HTML out

This process is called early binding, meaning that the assembly of the information and its format is defined before the information is checked into the repository.

In other cases, you want to deliver information to media types that are different from the authoring environment. For that reason, you may want to remove all output styles from the information in the repository, adding the output styles only when the modules are being assembled for delivery. This process generally means developing content in non-proprietary standard ways, such as SGML/XML and assembling them when them move out of the repository, a process called late binding.

Authoring and acquiring content

The process of authoring builds the components of content for your organization. Authoring starts with every business function that is responsible for documenting its activities and reporting on its work. Throughout the organization, people write memos, send emails, produce documents that are destined for short-term use, and produce documents that are designed to become part of the content store of the organization. In addition, many more documents come from outside the organization and are also designated to be preserved for future reference.

The content-management process begins with all sorts of information assets. Some of those information assets are likely to be acquired from outside your organization from third-party providers, through syndication, and through links to other resource sites.

I use the term information assets to refer to all kinds of information, including text, graphics, slide presentations, and other media. Information asset is an

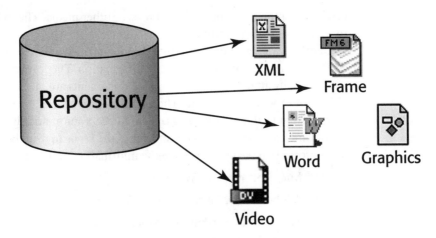

Figure 2-2 The authoring process begins with information assets of all kinds, including text, graphics, video, audio, and more.

appropriate shorthand to refer to all kinds of information resources without having to restate the list of possibilities each time.

When you look at the characteristics of authoring in most organizations, you find diversity. People use different applications to produce documents, including word processing systems, desktop publishing systems, presentation programs, spreadsheets, email systems, and more (Figure 2-2). You also know that organizations support a vast number of tools from a wide variety of application providers. Many organizations use the standard tools that come packaged with their computers. Others, especially those developing "official" information, use more sophisticated design and development tools.

As you develop plans for your content-management solution, you need to investigate the modes of authoring that occur in your organization. Each of them might have to be accommodated by your content-management system. When Dan Palumbo, the hospital information system developer, investigated his authoring environment, he found instances of

- unstructured authoring (no templates or style tags used), e.g., email

- forms-based authoring (forms completed in print or electronically with field-based content), e.g., content stored in databases

- format-based authoring (templates and style tags), e.g., Word, Word Perfect, FrameMaker

- structured authoring (content-based templates and content tags), e.g., XML and SGML

Note that there are major types of documents: information assets that have no overt structure added to the document either by templates and tags, information assets that have structure based on formatting alone, and information assets that have structure based on the content with or without style information included.

You can choose to support only structured authoring in your content-management solution, especially if you are implementing a system for a professional authoring group such as technical or procedures authors, or if you deal with content that must be delivered in multiple forms. Dan found that he needed to support at first a considerable amount of unstructured authoring, especially if he intended to include ordinary business documents under content management. However, he was eager to move to a more structured environment so that his information assets were more flexible in the future. That meant introducing a structured authoring environment using XML. It would definitely take some convincing, but Dan knew that without structured authoring, he would be limiting the future versatility of those assets to be delivered in new ways.

Unstructured authoring

Most of the authoring that takes place in organizations is unstructured. Authors create information in a loose, often idiosyncratic manner. Even though many of the tools they use allow some structure to be defined by using predefined styles or style tags, most individuals do not use them in a structured way.

Most authoring in organizations is unstructured for two reasons: first, authors do not believe they have any need for structure in the documents they create. They view the document as a whole; its subsections, if there are any, are created ad hoc. Whenever a new heading, a figure, a table, or a list seems appropriate, the author simply adds one. Second, authors do not want to take the time to learn to use style templates to create their documents. Templates for authoring are just another unnecessary complication, just one more thing to worry about that doesn't appear to add much value to the final document. Because the authors don't expect to reuse much of the information in their documents, why bother labeling it? You will find that certain transient (used once and never reused or accessed again) information in your organization might not be appropriate for content management at all. Primarily the information that has forward value in the organization comes under content management. See Chapter 3, *Taking a Close Look at Your Information Resources*, for a method of determining what to include in your content-management solution.

You also might address the typical way in which documents are produced in most organizations. Except for freely drafted emails and memos, many authors begin writing by finding a document that is similar to the one they want to create. For example, Dan finds himself developing a new business proposal for a customer. He knows that three months earlier she wrote a similar proposal. He finds that proposal, deletes sections that do not apply, adds new sections, and makes changes to others sections to match the needs of the customer at hand.

Forms-based authoring

Although unstructured authoring is the norm, a significant source of structured authoring occurs when people complete forms. Forms provide both consistent structure and content.

Forms require that information be completed in a highly structured manner and that content be presented uniformly. For example, a form might require that one uses separate lines to enter a first name and a last name. A form might also require that the name of a state be entered using the two-character postal code (e.g., CO for Colorado). Usually, the structure and content rules built into the form are required because of the database design that the forms support. A customer resource management database might, for example, require that first and last names be entered separately so that mailing labels can be printed and personalized letters addressed.

In short, the demands created by the output requirements govern the input requirements of the form. To make the information accessible in a database, people in the organization are required to enter information into forms (whether paper or electronic) in exactly the right way. Forms-based authoring can easily be transformed into an XML structure.

Format-based authoring

Aside from forms, however, the authoring landscape is quite bleak. Without forms to complete, many individuals authoring documents provide little structural information. Memos, emails, informal reports, slide presentations, and other commonly used information resources have little or no overt structure. At most, someone might provide headings that give some indication of the structure of the content.

When I review most documents people create, I find that even when tools are available to create structural or format tags, they are often unused. Standard word processors such as Word and WordPerfect enable authors to structure the format of a document by using format tags. Word styles can be used to label heading levels, body text, bulleted and numbered lists, and any number of additional format types used in a document. Nonetheless, I find that most documents contain no format tags at all. The ubiquitous "normal" style dominates. If a document has some formatting such as bullets, list numbers, bold or italic styles for emphasis, different fonts for headings, and so on, they are ordinarily added on an item-by-item basis.

Only in more formal documents, often created by professional authors, do we find attention to format styles. Word, WordPerfect, FrameMaker, Interleaf, and other desktop publishing applications encourage or require style tags that determine the appearance of the text.

For example, a typical FrameMaker document is based upon a style template. The template includes tags for headings, body text, tables, lists, figure captions, and many more template styles. A typical well-designed template for a complex document might contain 50 to 100 different style tags. The style tags, which are usually not visible on the screen, provide instructions used by printers to format the text. A heading might be rendered for printing as 18-point Helvetica bold, right justified to the margin. A similar rendering is provided for the screen so that authors can see what the document will look like before it is printed.

Unfortunately, the information in the tags focuses on the rendering only. The purpose of the tags is to define the appearance of a printed, PDF, or HTML page. the information is about the appearance of the information not about its content. Format tags of this sort have dominated the word-processing and desktop publishing technologies in your organizations, often to the detriment of content.

Why are format tags so popular among professional authors and other document designers? The format tags allow the style of the document to be easily changed. That 18-point Helvetica bold heading can be changed in one place to 24-point Times Roman. The change is made once and applied everywhere. In addition, by using the style tags designed for the template, the corporation can ensure that all the authors produce documents that look alike and are internally consistent. The tags also facilitate creating output for other media besides print. By using conversion programs, authors can easily create output that is appropriate for the Web, for a set of help topics, for an e-book reader, for a cell phone, and so on. The tags from one medium are simply converted to forms appropriate for other media.

Unfortunately, however, I frequently find that format tags are not used consistently, or authors override the standard tags to support their personal preferences for the "look" of a document. As a result, conversion programs fail. The conversion process ends up requiring considerable fixes and hand corrections, a process which increases conversion costs enormously. Conversion vendors often remark that they are able to automate the conversion of about 80 percent of the information resources they receive. However, the 20 percent remaining accounts for 80 percent of the total cost of conversion.

Generic markup languages
Generic markup languages were first developed to provide a standard for the style tags used by many professional publishers and to facilitate their translation into typesetting codes. The standard tag system makes it possible for the same document to be rendered in many different styles simply by changing the underlying style sheet. Generic procedural coding enabled a document to be printed on many different printers and, with the right conversion programs, to be rendered in many different media.

In most organizations, I find that policies and procedures, technical and business manuals, HTML-based Web pages (Hypertext Markup Language), and many other formal documents are prepared using format styles developed as cascading style sheets. Authors use the style sheets to apply the standard HTML formats to their documents. In fact, HTML tagging has provided an entry into style tagging for many individuals who had never previously tagged a document. HTML editors such as FrontPage or DreamWeaver make the procedural tagging less visible and obtrusive to authors who don't really want to learn the details.

Most format-centric templates provide little or no information about the content of the document except at the most rudimentary level. Format tags enable us to differentiate body text from headings, lists from regular paragraphs, and figures from tables, but they provide no information about the content of those style elements. However, format tags do provide a basic way for a content-management system to manage elements of text or other media inside a document. Any element in a document that has a tag can potentially be addressed by a content-management system.

If part of a document is to be stored and retrieved as a separate component in a content-management system, it must be tagged in some way. A completely untagged document can only be stored as a whole, without giving the authors or the users a view of what is inside the document unless they open the document.

Structured authoring

Structured authoring provides a method that is an order of magnitude more sophisticated and powerful for dynamic content delivery than format-based authoring will ever be. Although SGML and XML can be used (and even cost justified) to drive different print formats or even different HTML formats, that use does not come close to making use of the power and flexibility that SGML (Standardized General Markup Language) and XML (eXtensible Markup Language) offer in delivering dynamic content electronically (or in print, for that matter). SGML and XML are descriptive markup languages that can be interpreted and rendered by any presentation (publishing) system or by any business process.

Structured authoring implies that the author begin by using a tagging language to identify elements of the document based on their content rather than on their appearance. The tagging language is based upon a well-defined set of descriptive tags. Descriptive tags richly describe the content in a semantic way, enabling functionality far beyond simple formatting. In addition, SGML and XML provide authors with tools that reinforce the requirements that content be well-ordered, consistent, and reliable. Although structured authoring might seem daunting at first, many authors find that it is actually easier because they can concentrate on content rather than format.

Structured authoring is most effective when the content and the sequence of a document is controlled by a set of structure rules. It is possible to create SGML and XML documents by adding descriptive tags inside an information module, but to reinforce the structure and content requirements for a particular kind of document requires a standard set of rules. The rules for creating information modules for SGML and XML are called Document Type Definitions or DTDs.

A DTD is both a template for creating an information module and a set of rules that be can interpreted by a program called a parser. The parser ensure that the module conforms to the rules. Modules that conform to the rules (can be parsed), can then be processed unambiguously by many software processes, including formatting, presentation, transformations, business processes, dynamic and data-driven publishing, and so on. SGML and XML put intelligence and functionality in your content using standards and under your control, as opposed to building those processes into proprietary software applications over which you have little or no control.

The DTD provides the system of tags that is permitted in a particular type of document. For example, if you are authoring a policy statement, you might have to begin with tags for the title of the policy, its approval date, and its reference number. Each of these tags would be listed in the DTD. You might also want to ensure that all policy authors place the approval date before the reference number in the document. A DTD can specify the sequence in which tags must be applied and whether a tag is required or optional. If you want to ensure that reference numbers and approval dates are never left out, you would make them required elements.

The power of XML comes when it is used to tag information not by its format for assembly and delivery but by its semantic content. Semantic content refers to the meaning of the information, its significance for authors and users. For example, you might have a document that refers to a client contact by name ("We discussed the proposal with Jim Archuleta.") Using an XML tag <principal_client_contact>Jim Archuleta </principal_client_contact>, you will be able to search the document for the principal client contact without having to remember Jim's name. In another example, you might write a recipe list of ingredients that includes garam masala, a spice used in Indian cooking. By using an XML tag such as <Indian_spice>garam masala </Indian_spice>, you will be able to search the recipe content repository for all the recipes that contain Indian spices. XML is a powerful tool for labeling information according to the nature of its content rather than labeling it by its format.

The benefits of structured authoring using a DTD are that documents of a certain type are produced consistently, the information in the documents is labeled according to its content, and no format styles are applied to the document until it is ready to be published. The SGML and XML tags are style free, which means that new styles can be applied at publishing time to change the look of a document completely or to publish it to a new medium such as an e-book.

Structured authoring might seem more time-consuming to someone who has never used a template. It might also seem unduly restrictive to authors who are used to writing ad-hoc documents. However, for many authors, the structure inherent in the tag systems frees them from worrying about structure and formatting and lets them concentrate on the content alone. In fact, in the end-to-end process of developing multiple media, multi-language deliverables, structured authoring is considerably less complicated than "business as usual."

From the perspective of the content-management system, structured documents provide great flexibility because each tagged element in the documents can be stored as a separate object in the database and retrieved using the information in the tag, in addition to the actual content. Because each tagged element can be accessed separately, the content can be reused in other contexts.

Tagless authoring

Many authors do not want to learn how to work within an SGML/XML editor that shows the tags. If most of your authors have worked in an unstructured writing environment, they might very well resist having to use a tagging system for their writing. However, you can now find technology that allows authors to work in a seemingly unstructured environment, with Word, for instance, but still produce valid XML (valid means that the text follows a DTD). These tagless authoring systems hide the coding so that most authors creating standard types of documents are unaware that the tags are being put in for them.

Infrastructures for Information Inc. (i4i) developed its tagless authoring process for the US Patent Office. The Patent Office requires that patent application developers follow a set format and content, as discussed in the S4/TEXT vignette. For an illustration of the tagless authoring system, see Figure 10-3.

S4/TEXT-Tagless Editor

Infrastructures For Information Inc.

The *Tagless Editor* enables end-users to create and edit valid XML documents using Microsoft® Word as the interface. It is a full-function XML editor, not a conversion tool, and manages the XML instance and the Word image concurrently as the user works on the document.

One of the significant impediments to using XML in complex document applications has been the requirement that users of traditional structured editors understand the rules of XML and the particular DTD and actually apply markup to the content. Documents of this sort—technical specifications, patents, legal rulings, contracts, regulatory filings, and the like—are generally created by subject-matter experts. In order to capture documents in markup, organizations face the choice of either turning high-cost, high-value subject-matter experts into XML-markup technicians or adding an additional step where specially trained editors apply the markup.

The *Tagless Editor* eliminates this problem by concealing the XML and presenting help and options in terms of the document logic that the subject-matter expert already understands. An "out-of-the-box" editor cannot provide such guidance, but the *Tagless Editor* is designed to be customized for each document class. A Format Template defines the Word styles to be applied to each tag in context, and a Behavioral Instance provides a kind of script, in XML, which defines the behavior of the user interface and specifies all the behind-the-scenes processing needed to produce valid XML.

The nature and benefits of the *Tagless Editor* can perhaps be best understood in terms of a sample application. The United States Patent And Trademark Office (USPTO), like many government agencies, is seeking to reduce the cost and time delays associated with handling paper filings from their clients. To that end, the USPTO created an XML DTD for their primary input document, the Patent Application Specification, and developed a system whereby XML instances could be submitted via the Web directly into their automated workflow process.

However, Microsoft Word is the authoring tool on more than 85% of the desktops and its users showed little inclination to switch to one of the traditional XML authoring tools. If electronic filling was to become a viable option, the USPTO needed something to deliver valid XML from a Word environment, something that did not require the inventors and attorneys who create patent applications to learn XML. Working with the USPTO, i4i developed a custom version of the Tagless Editor, called PASAT (Patent Application Specification Authoring Tool) to meet this need.

The screen shot in Figure 10-3 illustrates some of the key features of PASAT: the Word interface provides a familiar authoring environment, without XML tags but with context sensitive help and options to guide the author. In the example shown here, the cursor is positioned in the claims section and the Office Assistant displays descriptive information and available options, not in terms of the underlying XML tags but in words understood by those who work with patents. This display changes appropriately as the cursor is moved, or as the context changes when an option is chosen. The more experienced user can turn off the assistant and display the options with a right mouse click. (Options can also be presented as toolbar buttons or on drop-down menus or implemented as control key actions.)

When the user enters text, the correct style and layout is applied by PASAT based on information in the Format Template for that context. The user can concentrate on the content while the form takes care of itself. The context sensitive options are specified in the Behavioral Instance (BI). In the example, if the user were to select "Insert New Claim," the BI script would tell the *Tagless Editor* to insert in the XML instance a new claim section element following the current claim section, within that new section, to insert a new claim-number element and a new claim-text paragraph element. The user would see the new claim number appear in the appropriate place in the Word image and the cursor move to the beginning of the line where claim text was to be entered.

When the document is finished, the user exports it as an XML file. This file can be re-imported and displayed in Word at any time for further editing. The Word file can also be printed directly, or saved separately, but when saved it cannot be reopened in PASAT since it is "separated" from the XML.

The underlying XML is maintained in a valid state by the *Tagless Editor*, such that an XML element cannot be in a position which violates the content model of its parent. However, authors need the flexibility to develop content in the order that suits their personal working style, so it is possible for elements to be left in an incomplete state; that is, for required elements to be omitted. Therefore, at export time (or from a menu option) the XML is validated and missing elements are reported to the user.

The authoring environment provided by the *Tagless Editor* is intentionally constrained. In order to maintain the validity of the underlying XML, it limits the user's ability to invoke Word functionality at will, though most of Word's features can be enabled in the appropriate context, and global functions such as Spell Check and Search and Replace are fully supported. On the other hand, the customized behavior for each document class provides a means to enhance ease of use and productivity while generating valid XML documents. The two main components of customization, the Format Template and the Behavioral Instance, can be produced by business analysts with minimal programming training, as long as they understand the XML and the users' needs. In addition, the *Tagless Editor* is designed to make it easy to add pop-up VBA forms for capturing highly structured data, or custom code in VBA, VB or C++, for specialized functions. PASAT is the result of such customization.

> In October 2000, the USPTO put PASAT up on their Web site for users to download and install in conjunction with existing Word 97/2000 software on Windows 95/98/2000 or Windows NT. Within twenty-four hours of its being made available, the USPTO received the first two patent applications submitted electronically from someone who was not a member of their test group. This fact alone is compelling evidence that subject-matter experts can create valid XML without becoming markup technicians through the capabilities provided by the *Tagless Editor.*

Adding metadata

The descriptive tags in a document are useful to control the content and to retrieve individual elements for reuse and reassembling. But descriptive tags are not sufficient, especially if a considerable portion of the information in your content-management system is unstructured. Both structured and unstructured information resources being prepared for content management have to be labeled at the document level to facilitate retrieval.

The information added to individual topics or even entire documents is referred to as metadata. Metadata means data or information about information. Some of the metadata might be related to the authoring and content-management processes, including the names of authors and others, dates of revisions and versions, security, and so on. However, metadata should chiefly be used to identify the subject matter of the content. For example, you might have procedures associated with a particular business process, product, product model, country, or even language. Metadata can be used to specify the subject matter inside the procedure, making it easier to retrieve by authors or by a publishing system.

Metadata can be added to unstructured documents using what might be called metadata wrappers. A metadata wrapper is much like a label on a can (Figure 2-3). The label provides information about the content inside. All information authored in your organization, as well as information coming from external sources, should be labeled with metadata. Detailed information on how to plan your metadata is found in Chapter 5, *Developing Information Types and Content Units.*

Metadata can be assigned directly by the author. Typically the author selects from a list of metadata that has been determined by the information architect. To simplify the process of assigning metadata, you should provide a set of default values that might be sufficient for most authors in parts of your organization. More than one set of default values might be needed for particular groups of authors.

Metadata can also be assigned automatically. Applications, such as Autonomy, are available that can analyze the content of a document and assign metadata from a predesigned set. Although such systems are not perfect and will need considerable tuning to fit your content, they might provide the best way of ensuring that

INGREDIENTS: TOMATO PUREE (WATER, TOMATO PASTE), HIGH FRUCTOSE CORN SYRUP, WHEAT FLOUR, SALT, SPICES, ASCORBIC ACID.

Nutrition Facts	Amount/Serving	%DV
	Total Fat 0g	0%
Serving Size 1/2 cup	Sat. Fat 0g	0%
Servings about 2.5	**Cholesterol** 0mg	0%
Calories 80	**Sodium** 710mg	30%
Fat cal. 0	**Total Carb.** 19g	6%
	Fiber 1g	4%
	Sugars 11g	
	Protein 2g	

Figure 2-3 A can of soup contains a label telling the user what ingredients are in the can. The nutritional label also describes the calories, fat content, and other information required by the government. The label contains the metadata used to categorize the content.

unstructured information is labeled and that information coming from outside sources is categorized in ways that will be useful to your authors and users.

Benefits of a tagging system

In the late 70s and early 80s, my company used a generic tagging system that pre-dated SGML, called GML or Generic Markup Language. IBM had developed this tagging system for use in a mainframe (IBM 370) environment to create IBM technical manuals. The tags were inserted by the authors and used to identify the format required for each content unit in the text. Tags used in this system were reminiscent of the tags we have used more recently in HTML. A typical tag set might consist of

```
<p> paragraph </p>
<h1> heading level 1 </h1>
<h2> heading level 2 </h2>
<ul> bulleted list </ul>
<ol> numbered list </ol>
```

and so on. The purpose of the tags was to establish the basis for formatting the documents for print. Each tag was associated with a command that told the type-setting system what to do with the content between the tags. For example, the <p> might be translated into 12-point Helvetica, first line indented 8 picas, left justi-fied, ragged right, line feed following for a typesetting machine or a computer printer.

Only occasionally did an author use a tag that provided some information about the content. For example, an author might use a tag for the part number of the document. However, the tag only provided information to be used to format the part number and place it in the correct place on the back cover.

The style sheet, which equated each tag with a print format, was developed separately. When the author was ready to print, the tags were converted to a print format understood by the printer software. Much later, with the advent of graphics terminals, authors were able to view the print output on the screen. This system worked great, as long as you wanted your output to look like an IBM manual. Changing the style for printing was difficult, but it was easier than retyping each individual document.

The benefit of the tagging system became obvious when graphics terminals made it possible for users to read the text directly on the screen in addition to having printed copies of the documentation. Although I'm sure a lot of clever programming was involved, from the point of view of the authors, the style sheet was simply changed to accommodate on-screen viewing. Instead of printing a Heading 1 as 24-point Helvetica bold, left justified, with 28 points of space before and 12 points of space afterward, the Heading 1 now appeared in a screen-readable font, left-justified on the screen, and displayed in blue or some other color. Without any work by the authors, the organization was able to create both print and online versions of the same input.

More recent technology has allowed us to convert text easily from one format to another. You can begin with Word and through various conversion routines and usually a fair amount of human intervention, output the same text as HTML, PDF, Microsoft Help, HTML Help, Java Help, and many others. The conversion tools translate one tag system into another tag system, many of them proprietary. Note that these conversion tools require people to complete the process.

XML and SGML provide us with a standard rather than a proprietary tagging system. You can author directly using XML tags. Or, you can convert from other authoring systems into XML/SGML, as long as you use descriptive tags of some sort in the original. You even have some conversion systems that will try to guess what descriptive tags you might have used by looking at changes in format within a document.

The early word processors like Wordstar or WordPerfect all required that tags be inserted into the documents to accommodate printing. In most cases, the tags were visible on the screen, but no formatting was visible until the document was printed.

With the advent of WYSIWYG (what you see is what you get) desktop publishing systems, authors quickly abandoned tagging technology. If an author used Word or FrameMaker or Interleaf (some of the more popular systems), the tags were still there if the author cared to use them, in the form of a style template. It was easy to select a style from a pull-down menu of the available styles. It was just as easy to add a new style as needed.

Authors could also choose to ignore the tags altogether and simply make the output "look right" by adding style elements such as type styles, emphasis techniques like bold or italic, spacing, and page positions like centering or left justifying. For authors not much interested in designing and using style sheets, WYSIWYG editors let them create attractive documents on the fly. Only when they or someone else had to revise the document did the absence of style tags present any difficulty. Idiosyncratic styling often meant that subsequent authors had to battle through countless tabs, spaces, and carriage returns to modify the text.

With the move to HTML and now XML, we have come full circle. Many of the first HTML systems required that the authors enter the tags with the text, until WYSIWYG editors became available. XML editors, and SGML in turn, also display tags on-screen to guide the author to use the predetermined tag system. Most of the more sophisticated XML editors provide some way for the authors to view a version of the output that has been formatted for the screen. Consequently, unordered lists have bullets and ordered lists have numbers rather than tags. However, the format viewed on the screen is usually only a temporary rendering. The actual presentation styles are associated with the tags on output. And, if you are storing your topics in a database, the styles for various platforms and media are associated with the tags only at the delivery stage of the process.

Summary of content acquisition and authoring

Content acquisition and authoring is the first part of a four-part content-management solution. Whatever solution you implement must support your methods of acquiring content. Remember, however, that content and documents are not one and the same. Without structuring and labeling your content, you cannot make it available for sophisticated manipulation, assembly, or even rendering for diverse outputs without a great deal of additional work.

Defining a content-management repository

The center point of a content-management solution is the content repository (Figure 2-4). The content repository is generally built upon a standard database, usually either relational or object-oriented. The database either stores the actual content or points to items in a flat-file system like those stored on a file server.

Relational, object-oriented, and XML databases all provide advantages and disadvantages in terms of database administration. They have no discernible effect

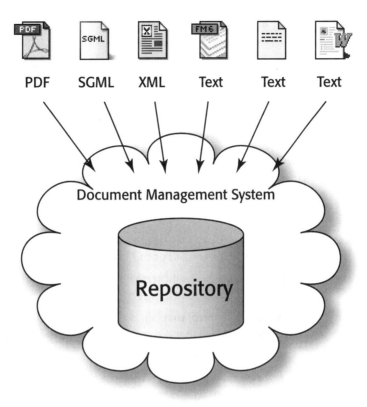

Figure 2-4 A content-management system is a software layer controlling a database-management system (like relational databases from Oracle, Microsoft, IBM, and Sybase and object-oriented databases like Poet and Object Store) that stores either the content resources themselves or references to those in a file-management system. Authors check modules of content into the repository and retrieve them from it through a content-management system.

on authoring. Choosing the type of database is often governed by the experience of your organization with database administration rather than on any characteristics that will affect authoring.

By storing your content using a content-management system, you ensure that they are

- more easily accessible to everyone in the organization

- available in one virtual location without having users search on multiple servers or individual hard drives

- a single point of access so that users can be confident that they have found the latest version of the information

- labeled according to when they were written and by whom

- tracked through a workflow process that records when and by whom they were modified

- managed under a security process that ensures they can be checked out and modified by certain individuals, read by other individuals, and not accessed at all by still more individuals in the organization

- made accessible through assembling, linking, and rendering to customers and others inside and outside the organization

To accommodate content management, traditional databases are overlaid with management software that provide a series of standard functions referred to as library services. These include

- a single point of access through a standard login procedure

- login security that ensures that content is accessible only by those with permission to read or modify it

- check-in/check-out security that ensures that a document cannot be edited by more than one person at a time

- version control that labels and stores the incremental changes made to a document so that older versions are accessible if needed

- standard information that facilitates search and retrieval

- optional workflow services that track a document through a number of individuals who are required to take some action such as review, edit, or approval

You should expect any content-management system either to include these standard functions or be able to add them as needed to meet your requirements.

In addition to the standard library services, you should consider the range of functionality you must have to support your authors and to provide the flexibility required by your vision of the users' experience with information resources.

Document management or component management

Content-management solutions are of two types: document management and component management. By far the most common solutions manage separate documents as objects in the repository. Component-management systems manage the individual elements inside the documents as objects in the repository.

Many organizations are well served with document management alone. Under document management, entire documents are stored in the repository as objects, often referred to by the "tongue in cheek" name of BLOBs, an acronym for Binary Large OBjects. Metadata wrappers assist in identifying the subject matter in addition to providing the standard identifiers of author, date, version, and so on.

In a document-management system, authors check documents into the repository so that documents come under security and version control. When the documents have to be changed, they are retrieved as whole documents from the repository, edited by authors who have permission to make changes, and checked back in. When they are ready to be published, they are assembled, linked, and rendered according to output definitions and published through a Web server, to print, or to a variety of other media.

Bursting configurations

With component-management systems, topics developed using structured content units with appropriate tags (either SGML, XML, or style tags) are burst apart or shredded for storage (Figure 2-5). Individual content units are stored as separate objects in the component-management system rather than stored as whole documents or modules. Consequently, the individual content units are available for reuse in different assemblies.

The level of granularity at which content units are stored depends upon the bursting configuration you have selected. Consider examples of different bursting configurations.

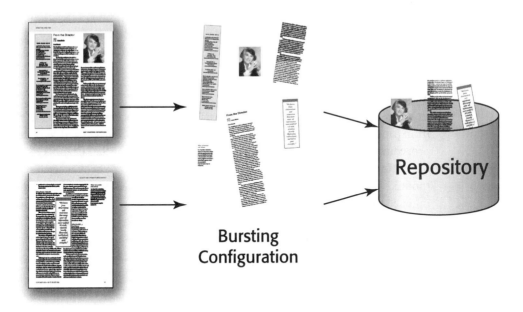

Figure 2-5 With a bursting configuration, tagged documents (using style or semantic tags) are burst apart upon check-in to the repository so that the individual chunks or content units may be managed separately.

You might begin with a large chunk like a chapter or a section of a document. The chapters or the sections might have been written as single pieces with lots of subsections and individual topics and content units. You might choose to separate the content in a chapter at the topic heading level, storing each topic separately in the repository.

You might begin with smaller chunks of information like topics and decide to burst them apart at the content-unit level, storing each content unit separately for potential reuse. The chunks, in this case, are much smaller or more granular than topic-level chunks.

For example, you might begin with a procedure in your maintenance manual as a chunk. Next, you decide that you want to chunk the content units of the procedure to include the purpose statement, prerequisites, steps, warnings, cautions, consequences, and alternatives. Because you have labeled these smaller chunks, the are now available for reuse.

The size of the information chunks depends on what is worth managing separately. The minimum size of a chunk depends upon the way you might want to assemble the content, especially when you want the content to be assembled in different ways depending on special conditions.

You might also decide to compromise, storing certain groups of content units at the topic level, rather than storing every content unit. Although bursting is a useful strategy when you begin with large documents, a different strategy may be more useful when you have complex information that will be assembled and delivered in many different contexts.

A modular strategy
In Figure 2-6, content for a set of maintenance procedures has been assembled from procedural modules stored separately. The authors have created separate procedures for Mounting the Bar and Chain, Tensioning the Saw Chain, Checking Chain Tension, and Checking Chain Lubrication and stored them as separate modules in the repository. When they are ready to assemble the maintenance manual, they select the modules in a particular order. The procedure for Mounting the Bar and Chain is followed by the procedure for Tensioning the Saw Chain. The same tensioning procedure completes the instruction for Checking Chain Lubrication and Chain Tension. The tensioning procedure is used in both contexts by referencing the same modules in the repository. If any of the tensioning modules, or any other module, is updated in the repository, it is immediately updated in all the contexts in which it has been used.

Although a bursting strategy often begins with large documents and breaks them into components, a modular strategy begins with the components and assembles them into compound documents for delivery or provides links between the individual modules in a network of information presented electronically.

Mounting the Bar and Chain

1. Unscrew nuts and take off cover.

2. Wear work gloves to protect hands.

3. Fit the chain—start at the bar nose—disengage the chain brake.

4. Fit the guide bar over the studs so that the chain cutting edges on the top of the bar point toward the bar nose.

5. ow turn tensioning screw clockwise until there is very little chain sag on the underside of the bar.

6. Refit the sprocket cover—and screw on the nuts only finger-tight

7. Tension the saw chain

Checking Chain Lubrication

The saw chain must always throw off a slight amount of oil.

1. **Never operate your saw without chain lubrication. If the chain is run** dry the **whole cutting attachment will be irretrievably damag**ed within a very short time. Always check chain lubrication **and o**il level in tank before starting work.

2. Every **new chain ha**s to be broken in for **about 5 to 10 minutes.**

3. Run **for 5 to 10 minutes at high** speed to break **in the chain. After br**eaking in chain, check chain **tension and adjust if** necessary.

Checking Chain Tension  Checking Chain Tension

1. Wear work gloves.

2. Chain must fit snugly against the underside of the bar. With the chain brake disengaged, it must be possible to pull the chain along the bar by hand.

3. If necessary, retension the chain.

1. Wear work gloves.

2. Chain m 1st fit snugly against the underside of the bar. With the chain brake disengaged, it must be possible to pull the chain along the bar by hand.

3. If necessary, retension the chain.

Tensioning the Saw Chain  Tensioning the Saw Chain

Retensioning during cutting work:

1. Shut down the saw and slacken the nuts.

2. Hold the bar nose up and tighten the tensioning screw until chain fits snugly against the underside of the bar.

Retensioning during cutting work:

1. Shut down the saw and slacken the nuts.

2. **Hold the bar nose up and tighten the tensioning screw until chain fits snugly** against the underside of the bar.

Figure 2-6 The two sets of maintenance procedures, Mounting the Bar and Chain and Checking the Chain Lubrication, reference the procedure for Tensioning the Saw Chain. Because each procedure is stored separately as a module in the repository, it is available for reuse in many different contexts. If the module is updated in the repository, it is immediately updated everywhere it is used.

If you have many legacy information sources that were originally composed as whole documents or chapters or sections of whole documents, you might find it useful to burst these components into modules to be stored and accessed separately in your content-management system. However, if you are going to move forward by structuring your information using XML or SGML, you might find it a much better solution to author individual modules and assemble them later. See the next section on assembling and linking for more information.

A reuse strategy

By creating individual modules, you make them available for reuse and for processing into a wide variety of outputs. You might further subdivide your modules by structuring them internally using descriptively tagged content units. You can then burst apart the modules and store individual content units or access the content units by searching on their descriptive tags. The individual content units might be reused in more than one module. They might be used across collections of modules in multiple locations.

Key advantages of such reuse, either at the module or content-unit level, are in updating, customizing, and translating. A module or content unit is written once and stored once in the repository. It can then be reused in as many different contexts as needed. If the module or content unit must be changed, every instance in which it is used can be changed simultaneously.

For example, an organization might have a warning message to ensure that maintenance technicians always wear grounded wrist straps when working on equipment that could produce an electric shock. The warning message is carefully developed to ensure that it meets government health and safety standards.

Consequently, it is important to the organization that the wording of the message not be inadvertently changed when it appears in many compound documents. If the warning message is stored in the repository and reused in numerous contexts, it will always be exactly the same.

The modules or compound documents in which the warning message is reused all refer to the same object in the database. That means if the warning message has to be revised or translated, it can be revised once and every compound document that references the message will display the new text instantaneously.

To secure the text against inadvertent changes, the content can be restricted. A security system attached to the repository and the authoring process includes the capability for a system administrator to restrict access to any document element. In the case of the warning message, it can be viewed and reused by many authors but only one author has permission to change the text.

For more information on reuse strategies, see Chapter 9, *Developing a Single-Source Strategy*.

A modified reuse strategy

In many cases, an authoring community might not always want to have a particular chunk of information changed everywhere when the content unit stored in the repository is changed. Consider again the warning message mentioned previously. The warning message might appear in hundreds of different modules and compound documents. If it is changed once in the repository, it can be simultaneously changed everywhere.

However, there might be a context in which you do not want to include the changed version of the warning message. For example, a warning message might have to be changed to reflect US laws but the change might not apply in the United Kingdom (UK). At this point, you might want to create two versions of the warning message, one for the US and one for the UK, using metadata to label the versions. Then, when you assemble the US document, you select (using a program script) only the US version. When you assemble the British document, you select the British version.

Workflow and notification processes

Workflow-management systems can be valuable additions to a content-management system. For example, you have decided to create two versions of a warranty statement, one in legal language and one in plain language to meet the requirements of different countries. Different authors are responsible for legal and plain language versions of the information in their own countries. However, the two versions of the warranty statement message are linked in a parent/child relationship. When the legal-language author attempts to change the message, she is warned that another version exists. At the same time, the plain-language author receives an email notifying her of the need for a revision. At this point, both authors can discuss the change or the second author can accept the change with another automatic notification to the first author, as illustrated in Figure 2-7.

Notification of this type is easily supported by a workflow process that functions between the authoring process and the repository. A workflow program can be designed so that individual authors are notified if a particular content unit or topic is being revised. The notification typically comes in the form of an email message alerting all the assigned authors to the change occurring to an element in the repository that they have reused in a topic or document.

The notification process might ask the authors either to accept or reject the proposed change. If the change is accepted, the information changes wherever they have reused it. If they reject the change, they can separate their content unit from reuse by establishing it as an independent content unit in the repository. In this case, there are two warning messages, a legal-language version and a plain-language version. The language dimension is labeled with metadata to make each version independently retrievable from the repository.

```
<warranty_info language="legalese">The              <warranty_info language="English">If you
Consumer shall have no coverage or benefits        buy this cell phone, we will not replace or
under this limited warranty if the Product has     repair it if you do something strange to it; if
been subject to abnormal use, abnormal             you drop it in a puddle or get it wet; if you let
conditions, improper storage, exposure to          your husband, brother, or friend try to fix it; or
moisture or dampness, unauthorized                 if you drop it, either by accident or on
modifications, unauthorized connections,           purpose. Even if a fuse blows or it breaks
unauthorized repair, misuse, neglect, abuse,       when we ship it to you, we will not replace or
accident, alteration, improper installation, or    repair it.
other acts which are not the fault of the          </warranty_info>
cellular phone company, including damage
caused by shipping and blown fuses.
</warranty_info>
```

Figure 2-7 These are two versions of a legal notice for a cellular phone: one written in "legalese" and one in plain language. If the first notice changes, the author of the plain-language version is notified so that she can modify the notice based on the first author's change.

Using notification and link management, a series of related but not identical topics can be effectively managed.

Workflow issues in large organizations

Large complex organizations often have difficulty tracking various workflow processes. In the case of the City of Las Vegas, the workflow process for developing, approving, and distributing policies and procedures was an issue that they had been trying to resolve for an extended period of time. Although they were making some progress, the City felt that they needed to take a more aggressive approach to finding and implementing a solution. The desired solution would need to assist them in notifying stakeholders (employees, management, general public, and other interested parties) and providing universal access to "current" documentation through a streamlined, standardized, and automated process. Las Vegas contracted with Governet, a specialist in workflow automation and Web development, to

- assist them in identifying current workflow processes and recommend optional solutions (both tools and processes)
- design and develop the approved solution

The solution was an Automated Policy and Procedure Approval Process, using "AuthorIT—Total Document Creation" as the content-management application, with Governet's Workflow Wizard tool customized to meet the City's specific workflow needs. (See Figure 2-8 and Figure 2-9.)

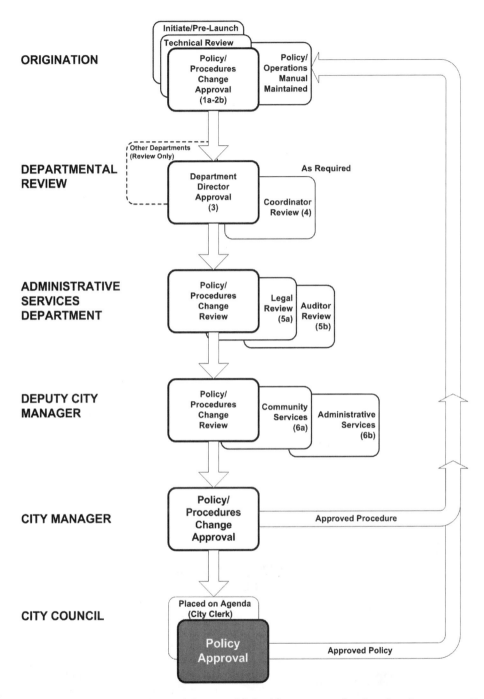

Figure 2-8 This diagram shows the workflow established by Governet for the City of Las Vegas. The process is used to facilitate the review and approval of proposed policies and procedures. (Governet, 101 Technology Drive, Idaho Falls, ID 83401, http://www.governet.net.)

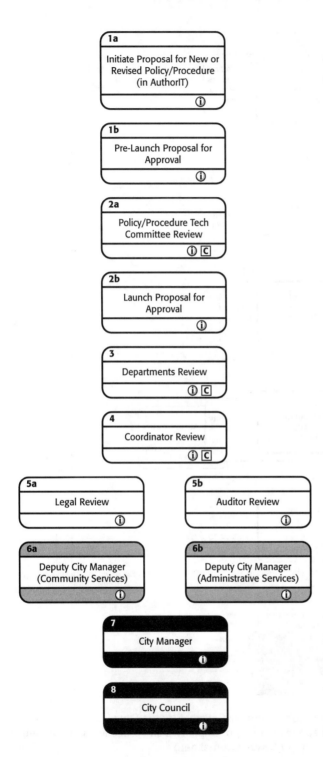

Figure 2-9 Stakeholders in the policy and procedure approval process for the City of Las Vegas check a Web site to view the status of the process. Green objects (white in the black-and-white image) indicate that a step in the process has been completed. Blue (gray) points the viewers to the current step. Black (black also) indicates a step yet to be done. Red (not illustrated) indicates that the proposal has failed or been disapproved.

By clicking on the small *i,* those with Web access can view a summary of the proposal, including the title, a brief description, who has to take the action, and what action is required. They can drill down to the proposal text itself. By clicking on the small *c,* reviewers view any comments that have been made and add comments of their own. (Governet, 101 Technology Drive, Idaho Falls, ID 83401, http://www.governet.net.)

Search and retrieval

Search and retrieval technology makes a repository useful. Without a way to find modules or content units quickly and easily, authors are more likely to write new content than reuse existing content. In many content-management systems, components are stored in a standard folder and file configuration, much like the Explorer view on your desktop. Authors find the modules they need by locating them in the folders in which they are organized. The file naming convention assists in finding the needed content resources. For small content-management systems, usually department-scale, such a folder and file storage system may be adequate. However, as soon as someone fails to understand the system, information assets become inaccessible.

With a file server configuration, you might search on the name of the file to find it. However, you might not have the capabilities of standard full-text search on the content of the files. Using full-text search, authors might be better able to find what they need, as long as they know which text to search. Full-text search frequently returns too many possibilities that must be individually opened and scanned to identify the information resource needed, a slow and laborious process.

In a content-management system with metadata and structured authoring, finding the information resource is greatly facilitated. Authors and users can search on metadata alone to identify the needed information. For example, if information is labeled by author and date, an author might be more easily able to find a module she wrote last year using a combination of title, full-text, and metadata search. "I want the module on support chain that I wrote about three months ago."

With structured authoring used to tag content units within modules, authors can locate particular content units that they want to reuse. For example, a search of metadata, element tags, full-text, and file name would help the author find the set of instructions she wrote within the last year on installing a frame relay and return only the instructional steps (if they are accurately labeled).

A strong search and retrieval mechanism is essential. Ensure that the content-management system you select supports a wide variety of search options. Beware of systems that support only full-text search or folder structures. These might be the least useful options.

Version control

How your content-management system handles versioning will also be a significant part of your analysis. A typical content-management system allows authors to maintain a history of changes they have made to individual documents, components, or modules as soon as they check them into the repository. With check-in capabilities, authors are asked what changes they made and why. For example, an author might annotate a change that he made to a module because of a functional change made to the product or because of an engineering change order. When the author checks the document in and writes the note, the content-management system stores the new version as the current version and records the note, as well as information about who made the change and when it was made.

Some systems store complete copies of each version (which rapidly increases the storage requirements of the repository). More often, the system stores the differences between the current version and earlier versions, minimizing storage.

Any system you select should make it easy for authors to view back versions of a document, module, or even a content unit within a module. It should also be easy for authors to promote an earlier version to the current version when a change is no longer applicable.

It is also possible to create modified versions of a module and maintain a relationship among them so that subsequent changes can be tracked. A parent/child relationship between a master version and the modified version assists authors in maintaining related but somewhat different information modules.

Link management

Links can be maintained in a repository to ensure that relationships among topics are maintained for future reference. In the warranty message example mentioned previously, the links are maintained to ensure that related information is updated at the same time. The most productive use of links is for reuse and customization. A "virtual document" may contain nothing but a collections of links that point to individual content modules. The links maintain the order in which the modules are to be included in the virtual document.

Link management is one of the areas of greatest variability between content-management systems:

- You are likely to require a system that supports one-way, anchored links. With one-way links, authors create cross-reference links in one module to content in other modules.

- You require that the relationship between linked items be exportable. If you might want to migrate from an initial content-management system to newer technology or another system in the future, you will want to maintain the links in your database. Unless the links are part of your modules and are maintained using a standard notation such as HyTime or XLink/XPath rather than a proprietary notation, you may lose the link information you have worked so hard to implement.

- You want links to be generated automatically to connect tables of contents and indexes in electronic documents to the corresponding topics within the documents.
- You want links to be established between topics in the repository and information that exists outside the repository, such as graphics or URLs.

The authoring community and the information architect both want to ensure that the links are maintained within the repository and are available when the information is published out of the repository. For example, a topic in one document might have a cross-reference link to content that appears in a different document. If the first document is published to the Web or to a CD-ROM, the information architect must ensure that the linked information is available to the users.

Content-management solutions must support link management to ensure that links are properly maintained. Link management includes providing reports of the links' current status, ensuring that notifications take place if links are about to be broken because of a deletion, and enabling publishing that includes or excludes links as appropriate.

Link reporting means that system administrators and information architects must be able easily to discover if all existing links are intact. A broken link in the repository might easily lead to a broken link and an error message upon publishing. If a published document has links to other documents or outside resources, the information architect must know that those links are all working properly.

Notification means that authors and others are informed when links might be broken. Consider when an author has established a link to another document in the repository. A different author decides to delete that other document or to change it in such a way that the link no longer applies. If such a change is about to occur, a workflow notification must go out to the owners of linked documents so that they might decide how the deletion should be handled.

Decisions upon notification can include eliminating the link, maintaining the link to an earlier version of the information, or revising the link so that it works with the revised information.

During publishing, the authors and information architects must ensure that broken links are never presented to users. When a portion of a repository is published to the Web, any potentially broken links must be noted and acted upon. If the information architect decides to publish a subset of the repository with some of the linked documents not present, the link should be hidden in the published version so that users do not receive error messages. In addition, the link should be preserved in the repository so that it can be acted upon in a future publishing round.

Multiple-language support

Link management is also closely related to support in the repository for multiple language versions of documents. In many multiple-language repositories, translated versions of documents are maintained through links. Each language version is linked to the original language so that changes to the original can be tracked in the additional languages. A typical solution is to start with the original language repository, in English, for example. When translations are prepared, the translated documents are brought into the repository with links to the English version. When a topic or content unit in the English version changes, the linked topics or content units in the multiple language versions also change into English. In this way, localization and translation managers know exactly what information must be retranslated to accommodate the changes.

Some repositories also allow you to store translation memory, indexes of previously translated words, phrases, sentences, and larger content units in each language. When new text or changed text appears in the original language, the translation memory is used to compare the new with already translated text in the memory. New information can thus be fully or partially translated in advance of its review by a professional translator. If a high percentage of the new text is very similar to existing text, very little new translation might be required. One organization using a repository to publish multiple language versions of user manuals finds that it translates less than 15 percent of its total text for each new product model.

Technical requirements for a repository

A document- or component-based repository must be designed to support the authoring and publishing processes in an organization. That means, in addition to the basic functionality of library services and the additional functionality involved in bursting, reuse, partial reuse, link management, and multiple language, the repository must be robust enough to support the development environment. These requirements include

- performance
- flexibility
- scalability
- remote access
- extensibility

A content-management repository must perform at a level that meets the needs of the authoring and publishing communities in the organization. In any investigation of performance issues, you should consider the number of people who will be regularly interacting with the repository by checking documents in and out, the timing of these interactions, and the size of documents to be handled. You have to consider not only the human interactions but the number and size of documents to be stored, especially if these documents include graphics, video, and audio files. The repository should be capable of handling current information resources and be expandable and extensible in the future.

Is the content-management system flexible enough to be adapted to your business processes, or must your staff change its process to meet the demands of the content-management system?

The content-management system not only has to be of sufficient size to perform well today, it must also be scalable to meet needs in the future. That means that check-in/check-out transactions should take a reasonable (to the authors) amount of time, that searches should be handled quickly and easily, and that retrieval and assembly should not bog down the system. If authors find it difficult to work with the repository, they are likely to find ways to work around it, often by failing to check topics and documents back into the repository as often as they should.

In one case, the check-in/check-out process was so slow that authors maintained files on their computer hard drives for weeks and months to avoid the delays inherent in a slow content-management system. The delays resulted because nearly all the authors tried to check in and check out documents at the same time of day. As a result, security was compromised and duplication of effort increased.

Remote access to the repository can present a significant challenge to your content-management solution. Be certain that a remote-access requirement is clearly stated when you assess the capabilities of various content-management systems. Authors are rarely in the same physical location. In many cases, individuals might be working at home with slow modems or working remotely at sites with uncertain communications connections. If you have a requirement for remote access, assess its impact carefully.

In some cases, it might be important to replicate a database in several locations so that it is more easily available. However, replication must also be handled carefully so that the authors in a particular geography find that they have access to the repository when it is needed. If authors are working on the same document collection from several different locations, the timing of replication will be critical to the success of the implementation.

In most cases, the information architects and business analysts interested in implementing a content-management solution should defer to the expertise of inhouse information technology (IT) specialists. These IT specialists also need to clarify their requirements and work closely with the content-management vendors to ensure that their needs are well understood and supported by the system capacity.

At the same time, IT specialists should ensure that they understand the requirements of the authoring and publishing communities. Then they will be able to represent their needs effectively to the vendors without the need for elaborate compromises from the authors as they try to work efficiently with the content-management system. In many cases, using an experienced product-independent third-party consultant and system integrator is the most cost-effective road to a successful implementation.

Multiple repositories

In many of the companies whose requirements I have managed and reviewed, I find the need for more than one repository. A single repository with one or two levels of "less managed" work-in-progress development areas is often a viable approach. In a multiple-repository solution, you might consider a working repository for authors, a publishing repository to handle Web interactions, a staging area for testing, and a cache to avoid excessive calls to the repository.

Working repository

A working repository must support authors during the development process, allowing for timely and easy search and retrieval, as well as responsive check-in/check-out functions. The working repository should be flexible and responsive so that authors can work effectively with documents.

Publishing repository

At the same time, an organization might also need a separate publishing repository, especially if dynamic publishing is to be supported. The repository that reacts to calls from the Web site must be robust enough to handle the volume of transactions without bogging down. It is unlikely that the working repository will also be able to function as the delivery repository.

Staging area

Finally, I have long recognized the need for a third repository in the system, one that accommodates testing before information is released for publication to the Web. This middle repository serves as a staging area in which the published information can be checked for errors before it is released to the public. A staging area repository holds documents or components that have been approved for publication, moving them to a testing ground from the working repository. In the staging area, the information architect's team can check for accuracy and completeness in content, presentation, and links.

However, a testing team should never make corrections, often referred to as "tweaking," in the staging area. All corrections must be made in the working repository and published again to the staging area until everything is ready for final release into the publishing repository.

Caching

Some solutions, especially those that must respond to frequent calls upon the database, also include a cache. Information that is requested from a Web client is pulled from the database, assembled, and delivered to the Web page. The information remains in a cache in preparation for the next request, thus avoiding frequent calls on the repository, a practice which often slows responsiveness and irritates customers.

Summary

As you can see, the repository part of your content-management solution allows you many options for storing and retrieving content. You might store content in many repositories throughout your organization to handle the particular needs of individual divisions or departments. You might build links between repositories so that information can be accessed between them and shared among many divisions or departments. You might create a working repository to be used by your content creators, a staging area in which to assemble, link, and test content before delivery, and a delivery repository that supports one or many Web sites.

You might decide to store information as whole documents with metadata wrappers to identify the content. You might choose to burst apart whole documents and store the parts as components for reuse in other contexts. You might decide to author individual modules, identifying them with metadata, and assemble them into compound documents or link them together in a network. You might decide to structure your modules into individual content units using XML/SGML descriptive tags so that you can search, retrieve, modify, link, and assemble individual components into still other contexts.

Many possibilities are available to you with a comprehensive content-management solution. However, you must have an information architecture that associates the repository that you need with your authoring environment. If the authoring environment does not provide structure, the documents are unlikely to be available for reuse, managed change, dynamic assembly, or linking. All the pieces of your solution must work together to support your vision of the user experience. Be aware that the whole problem domain must be understood and all requirements defined before the first tool is purchased.

Assembling and linking content

With individual modules stored in a repository or individual content units stored as separate entities, you have them available to create compound documents and linked structures. By creating compound structures from component elements rather than writing large composite documents, you assume greater control over your content and provide increased flexibility for its reuse and delivery in multiple media and multiple contexts.

Content assembly can occur from a repository in many ways, discussed in detail in Chapter 7, *Developing Content Plans for Static Web Sites*, and Chapter 8, *Developing Content Plans for Dynamic Web Sites*. Content assembly can be entirely under the control of the authors, it can be under the control of the information users, or content can be automatically assembled for different classes of users. In some content-management systems, compound documents are produced by dragging and dropping individual modules into a table of contents. The compound document references the component pieces in the repository so that if the components change the compound document also changes. Other systems allows authors to create compound documents by building references to the components inside of a master document. The master document presents a build list of components that are assembled from the repository. In many cases, build lists are established for standard compound documents that can be rendered and delivered whenever the components change.

Build lists can be simple lists of pointers to appropriate content modules (similar to a multi-level table of contents). They may also includes queries and scripts to enable custom to be assembled.

For example, you can create build lists that call for the US and the UK versions of your information to be separately assembled so that you have two deliverables of a compound document for two different audiences. You might define internal metadata in order to specify different versions of sentences or words within a text as part of a single-source strategy. In single-sourcing, you maintain a repository of multiple related content units and assemble them as needed to accommodate differences in your products, processes, and user communities. Find out more about single-source strategies in Chapter 10, *Authoring for Reuse*.

You can even create assembly systems that are user defined, allowing the user to create custom outputs of the information. However, your ability to assemble information in new ways depends upon the authoring processes and repositories you have included within your end-to-end content-management solution.

Linking

Links can be set into your information modules by authors who enter cross references between one document and another or one module and another. These links are maintained within the link management system in the repository. However, linking itself takes place as information is delivered through a Web browser or other rendering and publishing system.

As you will learn in Chapter 7, *Developing Content Plans for Static Web Sites*, and Chapter 8, *Developing Content Plans for Dynamic Web Sites*, not all your information modules should be placed in formal document structures through document assembly. Nor should all links be individually authored as cross references inside information modules. In a Web presentation of information, you might find your user communities are better served by a network of information in which links are logically defined.

A Web site is constructed with a navigation system based on linking. Navigation frames and tabs are typical structures included to allow users to understand the areas to which they can navigate. The relationships between navigation and the presentation of modules can be established through linking. For example, you might want to provide a hub-and-spoke model for your Web site in which users land on a particular module of information and are linked to related information. In this model, the link relationships are defined in terms of the metadata. For example, a user looking for information about installing frame relays might navigate to a module containing step-by-step installation instructions. From the installation instructions, the user uses links to navigate to related conceptual information, other related procedures, reference information about frame relay parameters, forms for ordering spare parts, and so on. All the interconnections are established using links. However, the links are not stored inside the modules as cross references. Rather than are defined as formal interrelationships in a link structure that is part of the site's information architecture.

Summary

Content assembly and linking are integral parts of the process of building both static and dynamic information resources. Modules of content can be assembled to produce compound documents that can be delivered as paper or in PDF or displayed as static pages on a Web site. Modules of content can be linked to one another internally through cross references added by authors or through relationships established using topics maps, metadata, and tags labeling individual content units.

Once the modules have been joined together in some relationship, they can be attached to presentation definitions to deliver them in forms that will appear attractive and readable to the users.

Delivering content

A system for delivering content to users is the fourth component of a content-management solution and often the most complicated to implement. In reviews of system proposals, I generally find that the greatest amount of customization, and thus the highest expense, comes on the delivery end. Customization is required because the needs of the user community are often unique. Detailed information about publishing options can be found in Chapter 7, *Developing Content Plans for Static Web Sites* and Chapter 8, *Developing Content Plans for Dynamic Web Sites.*

You can use a content-management system simply as an authoring repository. Documents are prepared, stored, and retrieved using the same authoring tools. A document begins as a Word or FrameMaker file, is stored in the repository under content management, and is printed as a Word document and distributed electronically as a PDF. All the styles used in the presentation of the document are provided by the same tool used to author the document. Word in, Word out, PowerPoint in, PowerPoint out, and so on. The styles used in the presentation of the document are controlled by the author.

However, one of the most important features of a content-management system is the capability to publish documents in multiple styles for multiple delivery media, regardless of the style used during authoring, as illustrated in Figure 2-10. The delivery mechanisms in content-management handle presentation styles in one of two ways: They either begin with an existing style provided by the authoring tool and convert that style into a style appropriate for another medium, or they begin with a neutral document without style tags and add the format during the publishing process.

Style conversion

Content-management systems are generally equipped to handle style conversion from one medium to another. They call on the capabilities of the authoring and publishing tools to perform conversions. For example, a document that begins in Word can be published as HTML by converting the standard Word style tags into HTML tags. A document that begins in FrameMaker can be converted to HTML or HTML Help or Microsoft eBook Reader. In this case, the conversion takes place through software that works with FrameMaker. The additional software converts each style tag in one system to a style tag in another system by using style conversion rules provided by the production editor or by using default values provided by the conversion software vendor.

The conversion process can be automated by programming the publishing process, often by using macros to apply the conversion software. In other cases, the conversion process is handled by the authors who run the conversion programs on the original documents outside of the content-management system.

Remember that no proprietary-to-proprietary conversion process ever provides exactly the results you want. Unless the input is absolutely predictable and consistent, conversions will always be less than perfect.

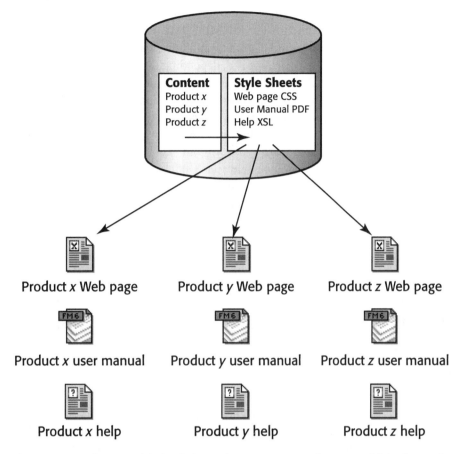

Figure 2-10 Styles are added to information resources as they are published out of the repository, providing great flexibility in the presentation of information.

Adding format styles

Presentation styles can also be handled by defining the published output required from the style-neutral tags of XML and SGML. The original modules do not include style tags; the tags describe the information in terms of its content rather than its presentation. As a result, the modules stored in the repository are format free. The presentation styles are added when the modules are ready to be published.

In this style-free environment, document and Web designers achieve the flexibility to change the presentation styles, add or subtract types of presentation styles, or even add new presentation styles as new delivery options become available.

To apply the presentation styles to the neutral XML tags, the information designer creates "style sheets" that are only applied upon publishing. More precisely, a rendering engine applies the formatting specified in a "style sheet" to the content contained in an XML/SGML document instance. For example, an original XML compound document might be rendered as a print version with one or more print styles applied, depending on the nature of the document, the printer used, and so on. The original document might be converted to HTML and displayed in one or more browsers. The document might be displayed using a WAP style set appropriate for some cellular phones or in a e-book for PDAs or similar handheld devices. The output might be prepared for Web delivery or placed on a CD-ROM to reach those without easy Web access. The output might be delivered as context-sensitive help attached to a software program in any of several different help styles, depending upon the platform.

The capability to add presentation styles at the end of the process rather than during the authoring process provides the information designer with great flexibility in redefining formats as needed by the user community. It also saves significant time and labor by automating traditional manual production processes.

Writing the requirements for your content-management solution

In this chapter, I have discussed many different ways of thinking about and planning for a content-management solution. I cannot emphasize enough the importance of creating a detailed requirements document before you approach vendors to learn about their products' capabilities. If you begin to look at products without an explicit definition of your needs, you are likely to become confused about the similarities and differences, strengths and weaknesses, of all the product combinations you will see.

With requirements in hand, you provide vendors with a well-defined way to respond to you. They are able to tell you which of your requirements are easily met with standard functionality, which must be customized, and which are not easily implemented with their solutions. You can use your requirements as a checklist, particularly if you have prioritized them (critical, necessary, nice to have).

Define your requirements according to the four components of a content-management solution outlined in this chapter: output requirements, linking and assembly requirements, storage and retrieval requirements (repository), and authoring requirements. Remember that authoring, storing, and retrieving are all specific in light of your vision of the user experience in finding and using information resources.

The checklist in *Appendix A: Content Management Requirements Checklist* offers some but certainly not all of the questions you should address and answer as you define your requirements. Expand or contract the list as necessary.

The issues and questions in this chapter are not exhaustive; rather they are designed to help your planning process. Some will not apply directly to your organization. Others may not reflect current practices but may suggest ideas about how you want to deliver information in the future. The rest of the chapters in this book expand upon these issues and questions and suggest ways in which you may want to organize your information to provide you with maximum flexibility in the future.

3

Taking a Close Look at Your Information Resources

"We need to figure out what our customers do and don't need to know. Dusty items to the left."

Too often, publishing to an enterprise-wide intranet or a business-related Internet site means little more than capturing facsimile copies in PDF of existing legacy print documents. The users are relegated to downloading hundreds of pages or trying to read long, scrolling browser-based text on the screen. The long files are often difficult to search effectively. Searches on the content of a site as a whole usually produce hundreds of hits rather than pinpointing the information needed by the users. Searches within individual documents often necessitate that the document first be opened in PDF on the screen. In many cases, the user gets the whole document or nothing. Information components within large, legacy documents cannot readily be reconfigured in new ways.

Web sites, intranets, and extranets that contain only facsimiles of existing print documents don't get used as much as they might be, simply because they are cumbersome. At the same time, new content entered manually as HTML and displayed on Web pages is often difficult to keep updated. The result is a great deal of legacy information that is infrequently purged and rarely updated. Often this legacy information was not widely or effectively used when it was originally in paper. When formerly inaccessible and unusable content is published to the Web, it becomes even less usable.

In this chapter, I discuss how to transform existing information into something more usable and relevant to users' needs, into corporate information assets. In some cases, I recommend leaving the information "as is" and simply linking to it with adequate warning for those users who need older information sources.

Still other legacy information might simply be archived for reference if needed but not included among newer, more up-to-date information.

One of the most important decisions you will make in planning your content-management project is to decide what information to include and what to exclude from content management. You might decide to manage the content that is most active. Such content might regularly change or might be in frequent use by some members of your user community. Other information might be infrequently used by only a few users, while some might be out-of-date and replaced by more recent content.

In this chapter, you learn how to

- decide if all your existing information should be accessible through your content-management system

- add existing print information to the content-management system through imaging

- label existing information for retrieval through the content-management system

- transform existing information into more Web-usable content

- take control of your information resources and publish them in a timely manner

To archive or not to archive

What information resources are most relevant to your business enterprise and to your customers both inside and outside your enterprise? What content should you manage in a content-management environment? What content should be made accessible to users through an information-rich browser environment? What content is used most frequently? What content is critical to business success? What content is most informative?

If your enterprise is like most, you have huge of collections of electronic and print documents that might or might not be useful to members of your user community. It is tempting to move all this stuff to any one of several Web environments so that anyone who might want to use it can find it more easily. In fact, once on an intranet or even an Internet site, much unused and often unusable information will be out of sight and out of mind. It's online; now, let's forget about it.

If you dig a bit deeper into our analysis of information needs, you often find that no one used the information before and that no one is likely to use it in the future. You might decide that, rather than preserving the past, it might be better to archive your legacy information, making it available only in extreme circumstances. It might even be possible, after legal requirements have been met, to discard information that is no longer relevant.

On the other hand, some companies have found it valuable to convert old print documentation to electronic format to make it accessible through the Web. Many manufacturers have to provide access to old documents, often documents that exist only in paper. Service manuals are an example of information resources that continue to be valued over many years. Consider that vehicles of all types are in use somewhere in the world. Caterpillar and Deere tractors, for example, might be 50 or 60 years old. People purchase and restore vintage automobiles. Otis Elevator asserts that many of its oldest elevators are still in use. Access to user and service information can be important to customers somewhere. As a result, a company with valued legacy information might find it useful to make such information available electronically.

In most cases, however, legacy information no longer needs to be easily accessible. Enterprises might keep paper records for some years and discard them when they are no longer legally required. But, in most cases, information needed by employees or customers is either regularly updated or has a designated end-of-life date when it no longer applies. Information changes frequently; products go out of production and out of use; business practices change; procedures are updated or made obsolete by new information.

In some cases, however, you might have to retain archives of information for legal purposes. Some organizations retain information forever. Others set a time limit of a certain number of years. You might have to prove that certain information was available on a Web site at some time in the future. For this reason, you should retain archives of files distributed through the Web, whether internally or externally. Some organizations decide to save images of entire sites for archive purposes.

If you decide to archive information and not include it within your content management system, consider how to handle the archiving and how the information in electronic archives will be available in the future. Sometimes it is important to save copies of original software used to create documents or to save facsimile copies in formats that will be readable in the future.

Once you've decided what you must move into content management, you have other issues to consider, one of which is preserving print information through imaging.

Adding existing print information through imaging

Many organizations have an enormous collection of information that remains in print form:

- legacy information produced on earlier word processing systems
- completed forms including handwritten information and annotations or signatures
- information created prior to electronic processing

These information types and many more can be brought into a content-management system through imaging. The imaging process creates a facsimile picture of the original document without making the information inside the document accessible electronically.

To include images of print and handwritten documents in your content-management system, you must provide an XML-based index (or metadata wrapper) of the information resources. You use metadata to identify the content of the documents so that they can be retrieved.

In most cases, you begin the identification process by analyzing the type of information contained in the documents. For example, you might have documents containing customer information. Each document might be indexed by

- customer name
- customer identification number
- document identification number
- type of document (form, graphic, report, correspondence, and so on)
- references to other key information used to identify the document

The process of deciding upon the metadata will depend both on the content of the information resources and how you might want to manage the information and deliver it into the hands of users.

The process for labeling imaged information is the same as the process for labeling any information within the content-management system. The labels, or metadata, depend upon how the information is going to be used. The more you know about how the information will be used, the better you will be at deciding how the imaged information should be categorized.

Labeling existing electronic information for storage and retrieval

In content management, the process of attaching labels to existing information is referred to as attaching XML metadata wrappers around the information.

Think of existing information, especially imaged information and information saved as whole documents, as content inside an envelope. See Figure 3-1. The information resource inside the envelope is hidden from view. Only the address on the outside of the envelope can be read. The more complete the address, the more information is known about what is inside the envelope, the more capability is available to store the information in a content repository and retrieve it as needed.

Figure 3-1 The envelope contains existing information. That information is labeled by writing identifying information (metadata) on the envelope.

The metadata wrapper in XML can consist of as many labels as appropriate to identify the content of the envelope as specifically as possible. The goal of all search and retrieval systems is, of course, to return one unique item that is exactly what the user is looking for. The more specific the labels, the more likely that the information inside the envelope will be uniquely retrievable.

Using automatic content classifiers

Software applications exist that can help you identify the contents of otherwise inaccessible documents. By evaluating the content based on probability algorithms, such systems provide possible labels that identify what information is contained in the document. Using automated content classifiers might provide a significant time advantage for bringing existing information into your content-management system, especially if you have a large volume of information to categorize.

Be aware, however, that the more automated the process, the more likely that you will not get the results you want. Your goal should be to label information in sufficient detail so that it is uniquely retrievable by authors and users of the content-management system.

The capability of the automated applications to identify the content adequately depends upon the specificity of the content and the degree to which it is recognizable in the text. Most of the identification software use probability formulas, word frequency, or linguistic analysis of text strings to identify what is most significant in the content. If the content is very well structured, the software is more likely to provide meaningful labels.

Using people skills to label information

Professional cataloguers who understand the requirements of your user community might be the most effective way of determining how to label existing information that is not structured. In all cases, people are much better than software at identifying content. You might need professional information architects to establish the context in which information might be retrieved and to frame the appropriate metadata for the XML wrapper. Consider working with a team of professional cataloguers, especially if you have a significant amount of legacy information to categorize. Work with the cataloguers to determine a scheme that will be most useful for search and retrieval.

When you work with an imaging vendor, you will be asked to designate unique identifiers for every piece of information imaged and brought under content management. However, not all imaging vendors make use of XML standards to identify documents. Your best resources for including imaged information in your content-management system will be human beings who will analyze and categorize the resources.

Ask authors of new information to provide an analysis of existing information that is also under their control. The authors of related information are most able to identify unlabeled content accurately and completely. Existing authors might also be able to set up hyperlinks between new information and information that will not be modified or tagged when it is moved into content management.

Attaching XML metadata to existing or legacy information is the most direct way of labeling the information for storage and retrieval. However, it might be advantageous in terms of space and file type to store some legacy information in its original file management system or simply on existing servers. In this case, you might find it necessary to store the metadata outside the original documents and use pointers to the location of the documents in other systems. Although they are not strictly part of your content-management system, the documents are nevertheless accessible through the search tools of the content-management system.

Transforming existing content

Existing content that is already in electronic form can be managed through your content-management system in several ways:

- You can import the content "as is" by simply attaching metadata to the existing files.

- You can save the content in PDF (a facsimile copy) and attach metadata to the PDF file.

- You can store existing HTML content, again with the appropriate metadata.

- Finally, you can decide to transfer existing content in an XML-structured resource so that the content inside the existing documents is reusable and stored as individual objects in your content-management system.

Note that in many organizations, the electronic files of documents prepared for print delivery might have already been converted to electronic delivery using PDF. PDF preserves the original book structure and is often most suitable if the expectation is that the user will print a complete copy for reference. You will also be able to deliver PDF documents on CD-ROM to users for whom CD-ROM access is more convenient than access through the Internet.

PDF is also useful when you want to provide HTML-based versions of the same content as your print publications on a Web site. HTML-based content is often awkward to print, especially if the content is long. You see many Web sites that provide the same documents in PDF for download and print purposes only.

When you import entire unstructured files into your content-management system, they are typically stored as BLOBs. BLOBs can be labeled with metadata to identify them, but the information inside the files is inaccessible for publication as separate components. Text, graphics, and other forms of information embedded within BLOBs are not accessible for reuse by authors unless the components are cut out of the existing document and stored separately in the content-management system.

Leaving your legacy information "as is"

You might decide to leave your legacy information in its existing, unstructured form even though you want to manage it through your content-management system. In most cases, you should attach metadata to the existing file structure. In such cases, the extended file name, including the entire folder structure, should be appended to the document. File names alone, especially if they are abbreviated to accommodate older operating systems, might be insufficient for authors to find information that they might want to reuse. In addition, if you decide to output information to a Web environment dynamically, you will need a mechanism to find and retrieve information based on the nature of the content rather than the file name.

For example, you might want to retrieve information by the author's name, the last date of revision, or especially by the nature of the content. To do so, all the information you maintain in content management must be adequately and carefully labeled.

Restructuring existing information

Restructuring existing information is the more time-consuming and expensive solution for managing your existing information resources, but restructuring ultimately leads to more uniform, reusable, and accessible content. To restructure means biting the bullet and deciding to make the effort. It can mean

- starting with existing semi-structured content and using that structure as a guideline for restructuring
- creating entirely new structures and rewriting content

If existing content is already well-structured, the existing templates can become a guide to developing an XML-based structure. If existing content is not well-structured, it might have to be reorganized, rearranged, or even rewritten according to the new structures you develop.

Be aware that the task of restructuring existing content can take as long as writing new content into the new XML structures. The outcome, however, will be significantly more usable and more reusable.

Restructuring existing content also gives you the opportunity to evaluate the usefulness of the content. You might decide to eliminate content that has little value to users. You might develop a more modular style for the information, rather than delivering long narrative text. You might decide to abandon existing book structures, such as chapters, sections, and so on, in favor of modules that can be delivered dynamically in whatever contexts are most appropriate to the users.

Restructuring also provides an opportunity to conduct a comprehensive user and task analysis. This analysis often reveals significant problems with existing information. Information that describes tasks from a system point of view might not be useful to users who have their own goals to reach. A user and task analysis will provide a foundation for a restructuring that will benefit users more than converting will. When I applied a single-source strategy to the documentation for a large-scale printing system, I first conducted a user and task analysis. The subsequent restructuring was as significant as the single-source strategy in providing users with more effective and usable information.

One caveat—users are not always pleased when information is restructured. They had learned to find topics using the old structure, even if it wasn't especially usable. In one case, when information was rewritten into topics and presented in a information center online, users complained that they couldn't find their old standbys—chapters and sections. The authors revised the topics to include notes and pointers for those long-term users back to the original structure.

Normalizing existing content

In the restructing process, you might find considerable duplication of content throughout existing libraries. In fact, repetition of the same or very similar content throughout an organization's information resources is highly likely and extremely common. Few organizations, without the benefit of content management, are able to avoid repetition and near repetition among their information resources.

The process of restructuring existing content can, more than likely, lead to a process called normalizing. In any database design, you try to have information in only one place to avoid having to update it many times and to avoid the problems that occur when some instances are updated and others are not.

All databases must be constantly monitored for duplications or near duplications. Whenever duplications or near duplications are found, they must be normalized. That is, the content must be examined to ensure that it is indeed the same and not intended to be different.

I have found that the normalizing process is very important to the initial development of a content-management system. If information is developed and stored as modules, duplication corrupts the database. You should institute a process, in transforming existing information, to search for and normalize repetitive information sources. By doing so, you clean up the database and make the information vastly less expensive to maintain.

Removing repetitive information can take time and require special attention to accuracy. In projects I have developed, I find that information that is nearly the same presents the most problems. In many cases, I have had to research the differences, often by contacting technical experts or finding experts in the subject matter to ensure that I am not removing necessary distinctions.

Sometimes it is possible to tell that information is identical simply by noting that the major differences in two texts are stylistic rather than substantive. Note that the text in Figure 3-2 is nearly identical but reflects the different styles of two authors.

In other cases, it is difficult to tell if the content should be different or is actually the same. The text in Figure 3-3 appears more different between the two versions than it actually is.

Consider whether the differences, although accurate, should be preserved in the database. In many cases, I've found that differences are maintained that are not materially significant to the user community. Yes, it might be nice to know, as was explained to me by the writer of my original cell phone's manual, that one holds the power button on the cell phone for 0.4 seconds to turn on the phone and 0.5 seconds to turn off the phone, but no one in the user community might care or even be able to act on this difference. As a result, you would be better served to eliminate the differences and store only one, more simplified version.

Transforming existing content provides many opportunities for improving its quality, if you have the time and resources to do so. You can introduce a consistent

Creating a Comfortable Work Environment

Lighting, furniture, posture, and other work conditions may affect the way you feel and how effectively you work. By arranging these elements to meet your needs, you may be able to minimize fatigue and discomfort. While setting up your new computer, take time to evaluate your work environment.

This chapter offers tips on the following topics:

- Placement of the keyboard, mouse, and other input devices
- Viewing angle of the display
- Furniture and posture
- Lighting
- Vision care
- Work habits

Promoting a Safe and Comfortable Work Environment

Introduction

Lighting, furniture, posture, and other work conditions may affect the way you feel and how well you work. By adapting your work environment and personal practices, you may be able to minimize fatigue and discomfort and reduce the risk of resulting strains that some scientists believe can lead to injury.

This chapter offers recommendations on the following topics:

- Placement of the keyboard, mouse and other input devices
- Furniture and posture
- Hand and arm position and motion
- Viewing angle of the display
- Lighting
- Vision care
- Work habits
- Health habits and exercise

Figure 3-2 These two texts discuss the same subject in the same way. The authors have chosen slightly different words and some minor content differences for the same subject. To be reusable, this text must be normalized. Instead of maintaining two versions, the author community must decide on one. Reprinted with permission. © 1994 Compaq Computer Corporation

style across all parts of the library of information that you're maintaining. You might want to maintain consistent organizations of information as well as consistent terminology and writing styles. Consistency across your database of information will increase the value of the information to the user community and reduce your costs of maintaining the information in the long run.

In one case, a system administrator book had not been modified for so long that the authors found that they were still telling users to press F1 for help in step-by-step procedures. Context-sensitive help had for years been accessible using a question mark (?) icon. The instructions for accessing help were different across the book because it had only been updated rather than rewritten. When the information was put into modular form, the inconsistencies were corrected and references to F1 were removed.

Removing and Installing the Hard Drive

The removable hard drive is a fragile computer component and must be handled with care. It is important to perform a tape or diskette backup of your hard drive information before removing the drive. Failure to back up the hard drive can result in loss of information if the drive is improperly handled. Refer to the online *User's Guide* for information about creating a backup.

 CAUTION: To prevent damage to the hard drive and loss of information, observe these precautions when handling the hard drive:

- Remove the hard drive only when the computer is OFF, unplugged, and the battery pack is removed. Do not remove or install a hard drive while the computer is ON, in Standby, or in Hibernation.

- After removing the hard drive from the computer, immediately place the drive into the hard drive carrying case which was provided with your computer.

- Handle the drive carefully. Do not drop.

- Avoid exposing the hard drive to temperature extremes.

- Avoid exposure to products that have magnetic fields such as monitors or speakers.

- Electrostatic discharge can damage electronic components. Before handling the hard drive, ensure that you are discharged of static electricity. When handling the hard drive, always grasp the outer metallic case and avoid touching the connectors. For more information, refer to Appendix E, "Electrostatic Discharge."

- Do not spray the hard drive with cleaners or expose it to liquids.

- Compaq recommends not mailing the hard drive. If the hard drive must be mailed, ship it in its carrying case in a bubble pack mailer or another suitable form of protective packaging. Place a mailing label with the wording "Fragile—Handle With Care" on the mailer.

Caring for a Removable Hard Drive

The Compaq LTE Elite Family of Personal Computers comes equipped with a removable hard drive. A removable hard drive is a fragile computer component and must be handled with care. It is important to perform a tape or diskette backup of your hard drive information before removing the drive. Failure to back up the hard drive can result in damage to the hard drive and loss of information if it is handled improperly.

To prevent damage to the hard drive and loss of information, observe these precautions when handling the hard drive:

 Remove the hard drive only when the computer is OFF, unplugged, and the battery pack is removed. Do not remove or install a hard drive while the computer is ON, in Standby, or in Hibernation.

 After removing the hard drive from the computer, immediately place the drive into the hard drive carrying case which was provided with your computer.

 Handle the hard drive carefully. Do not drop.

 Avoid exposing the hard drive to temperature extremes.

 Avoid exposure to products that have magnetic fields such as monitors or speakers.

 Electrostatic discharge can damage electronic components. Before handling the hard drive, ensure that you are discharged of static electricity. When handling the hard drive, always grasp the outer metallic case and avoid touching the connectors. For more information, refer to the online *User's Guide* or the *Beyond Setup* guide included with the computer.

 Do not spray the hard drive with cleaners or expose it to liquids.

 Compaq does not recommend mailing the hard drive. If the hard drive must be mailed, ship it in its carrying case in a bubble pack mailer or another suitable form of protective packaging. Place a mailing label with the wording, "Fragile: Handle With Care," on the mailer.

△ **CAUTION:** Failure to comply with these cautions may result in damage to the hard drive and loss of information. For additional information on installing, removing, and locking the removable hard drive, refer to the online *User's Guide* included with the computer.

Figure 3-3 At first glance, these two texts look completely different. On closer examination, it is clear that they are very similar. The author of the text on the right added icons to illustrate the points about handling the hard drive carefully. More investigation is needed to decide which text is most appropriate for reuse. Reprinted with permission. © 1994, 1995 Compaq Computer Corporation

Using conversion tools to create structure

Software is available that will assist you in converting existing documents into XML-tagged content. Most of the available conversion tools require that some format tags be in place in the source files. For example, you might have files that are already tagged in Word or FrameMaker or any other application that supports the use of templates. Source files that have not already been constructed using a style template will be more difficult to convert.

The XML tagging tools use the format tags in the original files to guide the conversion process. For example, if you have developed a standard template in Word or FrameMaker, an XML converter will pick up the existing tags and restructure them as XML. The problem, of course, is that unless you have created templates that identify content by more than its page format, there will be little information in your template to create meaningful, content-focused tags during the conversion process.

Some of the XML conversion tools can be guided by the designer to put more intelligence into the conversion. If your source documents have meaningful structures that are simply not expressed in the format template, you will still be able to map the original item to a new XML tag in your DTD. Figure 3-4 shows an example of original text in Word mapped to an XML DTD.

If your original procedure template calls for a "purpose" paragraph to follow the title, you can map the original paragraph tags to a purpose tag in XML. As long as the structure is consistent within the original documents, you can guide the conversion tool in translating format tags to meaningful tags.

If your original documents are not structured by the meaning of the content units and you use a format template only, you might have much more difficulty converting to XML tags. The format tags, such as heading level, paragraph, bulleted list, numbered list, and so on, do not provide information about the nature of the content. They only describe how the text is to be formatted for output as print, PDF, or HTML.

When you convert format styles to XML, you do not get additional information. Your conversion process results in a document that is tagged for presentation, not for search and retrieval or reuse.

If your information is not governed by a format template, your conversion process will be much more difficult. Some conversion tools will attempt to find a structure in an original document based on cues such as capitalization, spacing, emphasis techniques like bold or italic, list types, font size changes, and so on. Depending upon the consistency with which the original authors used format tags to correspond to content structure, you can get acceptable results on the first tries. In these cases, you will have to use trial and error to focus the conversion tool on your information types and attempt to map styles to new XML tags.

Heading 1	**Starting Crystal Ball and Loading the "Vision Research" Spreadheet**
Normal	The Crystal Ball disk you received includes the Crystal Ball program and the "Vision Research" spreadsheet. Use this spreadsheet as you follow the tutorial instructions in this chapter. Later, as you become more familiar with Crystal Ball, you will use your own spreadsheets, as described in Chapter 3. Be sure to make a copy of your Crystal Ball disk before you do anything else. Then, begin by starting Crystal Ball and loading the "Vision Research" spreadsheet into the program.
Normal	To start Crystal Ball and load the spreadsheet:
Steps	1. Turn on your Macintosh.
Steps	2. Insert a copy of the Crystal Ball disk into the disk drive.
Steps	3. Click the Crystal Ball icon.
Steps	4. Choose Open from the File menu.
Indent	A dialog box appears with a directory of the files and folders on your disk. An example of this dialog box is shown in Figure 1-1.
Figure Placeholder	
Figure Caption Heading	**Figure 1-1**
Figure Caption Text	A dialog box listing the files and folders on your disk
Steps	5. Click the "Vision Research" file name.
Steps	6. Click the Open button.
Indent	The "Vision Research" spreadsheet is loaded into Crystal Ball and appears on your screen as shown in Figure 1-2.
Figure placeholder	
Figure Caption Heading	**Figure 1-2**
Figure Caption text	The "Vision Research" spreadsheet.

```
<?xml version="1.0" encoding="UTF-8"?>
<?xml :stylesheet href="Starting Crystal Ball.css" type="text/css" charset="UTF-8"?>
<XML>
<TITLE></TITLE>
<Heading-1><A ID="pgfId-998202"></A>Starting Crystal Ball and Loading the &quot;Vision Research&quot; Spreadsheet</Heading-1>
<Normal><A ID="pgfId-998203"></A>The Crystal Ball disk you received includes the Crystal Ball program and the &quot;Vision Research&quot; spreadsheet. Use this spreadsheet as you follow the tutorial instructions in this chapter. Later, as you become more familiar with Crystal Ball, you will use your own spreadsheets, as described in Chapter 3. Be sure to make a copy of your Crystal Ball disk before you do anything else. Then, begin by starting Crystal Ball and loading the &quot;Vision Research&quot; spreadsheet into the program.</Normal>
<Normal><A ID="pgfId-998204"></A>To start Crystal Ball and load the spreadsheet:</Normal>
<StepsList>
<Steps><A ID="pgfId-998205"></A>Turn on your Macintosh.</Steps>
<Steps><A ID="pgfId-998206"></A>Insert a copy of the Crystal Ball disk into the disk drive.</Steps>
<Steps><A ID="pgfId-998207"></A>Click the Crystal Ball icon.</Steps>
<Steps><A ID="pgfId-998208"></A>Choose Open from the File menu.</Steps>
</StepsList>
<Indent><A ID="pgfId-998209"></A>A dialog box appears with a directory of files and folders on your disk. An example of this dialog box is shown in Figure 1-1.</Indent>
<Figure-Placeholder><A ID="pgfId-998210"></A></Figure-Placeholder>
<Figure-Caption-Heading><A ID="pgfId-998211"></A>Figure 1-1</Figure-Caption-Heading>
<Figure-Caption-Text><A ID="pgfId-998212"></A>A dialog box listing the files and folders on your disk<Figure-Caption-Text>
<StepsList>
<Steps><A ID="pgfId-998213"></A>Click the &quot;Vision Research&quot; file name.</Steps>
<Steps><A ID="pgfId-889214"></A>Click the Open button.</Steps>
</StepsList>
<Indent><A ID="pgfId-998215"></A>The &quot;Vision Research&quot; spreadsheet is loaded into Crystal Ball and appears on your screen as shown in Figure 1-2.</Indent>
<Figure-Placeholder><A ID="pgfId-998216"></A></Figure-Placeholder>
<Figure-Caption-Heading><A ID="pgfId-998217"></A>Figure 1-2</Figure-Caption-Heading>
<Figure-Caption-Text><A ID="pgfId-998218"></A>The &quot;Vision Research&quot; spreadsheet</Figure-Caption-Text>
<Body><A ID="pgfId-998197"></A></Body>
</XML>
```

Figure 3-4 This test sample shows the original structure of a Word document mapped to an XML DTD.

Format tags

Format tags are most frequently used to ensure that the output (print, PDF, or HTML) is consistent throughout a document. The format tags detail information in property sheets or other similar devices to govern the development of output.

In Figure 3-5, you see an example of typical format tags used in a pull-down menu in Word.

Figure 3-5 These are typical format tags in Word.

The format tags in Word, for example, govern the choice of font and the placement of the element on the page. The Heading 1 tag in the example tells the printer and the on-screen rendering (WYSIWYG) that this text must appear as 16-point Arial Bold with 18 points of leading above and 14 points of leading below. The text should begin at the left margin and be left justified.

Format tags are used most often in word processing or desktop publishing applications to determine the appearance of the text on output. Format tags are also the focus of HTML, determining how the text element will appear in a browser.

Semantic or meaningful tags

Semantic tags provide information about an element of text that is quite different from its output format. Semantic tags label information according to the nature of the content rather than its appearance. For example, what might be a tagged as a paragraph in Word would be tagged as a purpose statement in a procedure in XML. Figure 3-6 provides an example of semantic tags. With semantic tags, the author is guided to create the specified content, often in a required sequence, such as immediately following the title of the procedure. With semantic tags, an author can refine a purpose statement written for procedure and use it in other contexts. In addition, with semantic tags, the user can search for a procedure with a particular purpose by searching for the "purpose statement" text in a procedure.

It is possible to put semantic tags into Word or other desktop publishing programs. However, the word-processing program generally compels you to specify the format requirements for the text. In addition, programs like Word require you to use standard tags, such as Heading 1 and Heading 2 if you want to use the automated Table of Contents process. Your ability to provide meaningful tags is limited.

If you are in the process of moving from a desktop publishing environment to a content repository, begin changing your templates to be semantic long before you

Figure 3-6 This example of semantic tags demonstrates how the tags are used to describe the content rather than the format of the text. For example, instead of using a tag labeled "numbered list item," the tag is labeled "step," referring to a step in a procedure.

begin to use an XML editor. However, without an XML editor, you will not be able to specify a sequence or require that some tagged elements be included in your document.

With XML, you can both predetermine a sequence of tagged elements and specify which are required and which are optional. You will find more information on creating semantic tags and labeling the content units in your information modules in Chapter 6, *Using Content Units to Structure Information Types*.

Adding format upon output

Format tags require that the author apply the format to a document as it is being written. If you are using a standard template in Word, for example, you write with a format in place. Each time you label a paragraph or a heading or a bulleted list, you are adding information about the presentation format to the text.

If your output is always the same, be it print and PDF or HTML, adding format tags to the original document or module is appropriate. WYSIWYG (What You See Is What You Get) was originally designed for just this purpose. Desktop publishing systems enable you to see pretty much what the text will look like when it is published. Web composition programs do the same. You can see approximately what the text will look like in the browser as you are composing.

If you have to output the same content in different collections of information, the presence of format information in your authoring environment can be a hindrance. Both SGML and XML were developed to enable format-free tagging. The authors work in a presentation-neutral environment. The format information is added only when the information is about to be published. As a result, you will find it easier to adapt the same content to different formats, including more than one print, HTML, or help format. You will also be able to move your content to WAP, e-Book, and other electronic formats, including ones that are not yet available or not even in the planning stage. Adding format at the end of the process rather than the beginning provides a flexibility that is especially significant to dynamic Web publishing. You often do not know how the user will need the output until very close to the publishing event.

Format-free tags do not, however, have to be semantic tags. With format-independent tags, you simply label information by its role in a document layout without specifying how that layout will appear. You label information elements as headings, paragraphs, lists, tables, and so on. Then, when you are ready to publish, you map the tags to one of several style sheets.

Semantic tags must also be mapped to style sheets upon output, just as you would map format tags. In many cases, semantic tags and format tags are mapped to HTML tags for output to a browser.

Insisting on meaningful tags

Remember that information is most retrievable when it is clearly labeled according to its content rather than its format. If your goal is to send information to a browser in a variety of environments, meaningful tags will best support that end. The more information is retrievable by the metadata associated with its content, rather than its format, the more quickly and specifically retrievable that information is likely to be. Format tags provide no information about content and do not add, in most cases, to information retrieval.

Many implementations of XML or SGML tagging fail to include meaningful tags. You might wonder whether it is worth so much work tagging information in these systems only to end up with format information. I see many DTDs in which the tags are the standard sets (paragraphs, lists, tables, headings, and so). I also see many cases in which non-XML templates are converted into XML with no additional information added to the tags. The only purpose, then, of the tags is to maintain a format-free repository and add style information at the time of publication. That purpose is certainly worthwhile but it fails to take advantage of the full capabilities offered by an XML or SGML tag systems.

To gain the most benefit from either restructured or newly written information, you are going to have to find a way to ensure that the content is tagged semantically with a set of tags that adds value to the information content units. Without such tags, you end up with format only.

To add semantic tags to existing text requires that you analyze the content in considerable detail, a task made easier if the original information has been structured in the first place. Often, however, you find the original information to be only loosely structured with much confusion about what content should be provided. Because authors are unclear about the purpose and value of the recommended structure, many of the resulting documents are very inconsistent.

The most straightforward way of tagging modules is to use XML or SGML editors, applications that add the tags for the authors and guide them through the text composition. With these editing tools, authors work within the tags, concentrating on content rather than on format. Most of the editors allow authors the choice of displaying full tag sets, partial tag sets, or no tags at all. In most cases, the authors are able to view the text in an on-screen rendering that resembles what might be a typical paper or browser-based presentation. If the number of tags is kept to a minimum, many authors find tags easy to work with after some training in the new editors.

Nonetheless, you are likely to have many authors in your organization who are initially uncomfortable working with tags and templates. Many of these authors have never used templates with the standard word processors and can be very confused and frustrated if they suddenly find themselves having to work with tags.

As long as you have templates with simple information structures, you might want to find tools that hide the tags from the authors and simplify the process they must use to produce standard modules of information. A solution offered by some organizations is to develop forms that contain the tags but keep them invisible to the authors. The authors simply insert their text into the fields in the form, thus developing content modules that have standard structures. The tags are added to the information through programming connected to the fields. Forms accommodate required sequences and can handle required and optional fields as well.

The forms can also be set to insert standard default metadata associated with the modules (also possible with XML editors) or with variable content in the text. The author might have little or nothing to learn about the tagging process. If author-specified tags are required, they can be handled through dialog boxes which allow the author to identify attributes of the text simply by checking boxes.

Other tools are available that provide even more flexibility than using forms. These tools allow authors to begin writing by making a virtual copy of an existing document. The author can use the existing text, change or delete the parts of the text, or even "cut and paste" modules or content units from other sources. Each of the modules or the content units within the modules comes pre-fitted with XML tags. The authors insert the tags into new modules without being aware that they are doing so. In these tools, the changed modules become new instances in the database.

You will find many opportunities to add value to existing information by transforming it into structured content. Once the content is structured, it becomes more easily managed for reuse in a content-management system. Structured information is not only categorized and labeled as a whole but also contains content units that are themselves categorized according to the information they contain.

See Chapter 6, *Using Content Units to Structure Information Types*, for more information on developing structured information types and embedding semantically labeled content units.

Using standard metadata from external information resources

I am beginning to see more and more attempts to standardize the categorization of information. Many of the efforts have focused on industries in which information must be shared among institutions or companies. For example, the human genetics field has been attempting to institute standard metadata to identify information. In chemistry, bibliographers have long used standard keywords to categorize information that has been published. Now those keyword systems are being converted to XML metadata for use through the Internet.

Johns Hopkins University School of Medicine and leading medical societies have formed the MedBiquitous Consortium to create technology standards for online communication of information. Their goal is to create a comprehensive XML framework for sharing medical information. They will focus on developing XML standards to facilitate communication. They will also work to develop standard terminology in the medical field.

The telecommunications manufacturing industry is preparing to standardize at the metadata level, an effort being driven by the telecommunications customers who want to be able to access information from multiple manufacturers in common ways. In industries like telecommunications, where products from many manufacturers are used together, standardization of metadata can be very valuable for the information users. They need learn only one system of accessing information rather than separate systems for each manufacturer.

In most cases, the efforts at standardization are being led by industry consortia rather than individual companies. Representatives of the companies take part in the decision-making, of course, but the standards are published by industry associations.

If you are in an industry in which an external body is attempting to set standards for metadata, you would be well served to participate in the standards effort. Not only would the use of standard metadata contribute to making your information more accessible to the user community, you would be saved the time and trouble of developing all the metadata categories independently.

One of the best known of the standard systems has been developed to support searching across the Internet. Called the Dublin Core, it has been developed by the Online Computer Library Center (the OCLC) in the US. The OCLC conducts workshops on the Dublin Core and how it should be implemented. They assume that authors from many different organizations will use the standard metadata categories, rather than only trained cataloguers.*

The Dublin Core consists of 15 core qualifiers, which might be organized into the following three groups: content, intellectual property, and instantiation. Each element is defined and guidelines provided for creating metadata using each element.

---

* For more information about the Dublin Core and details about the elements and their qualifiers, see http://www.dublincore.org.

The content group contains seven elements: coverage, description, type, relation, source, subject, and title. These elements serve to describe the content of a information resource. For example, title is used to give a name to the resource, while subject is used for the keywords or phrases that describe the content of the resource. Source refers to a second resource from which the current resource is derived.

The intellectual property group contains four elements: contributor, creator, publisher, and rights. The creator or author refers to the primary individual or organization responsible for developing the resource, and contributor refers to additional creators besides the primary one.

The instantiation group contains four elements: date, format, identifier, and language. Date refers to the date that the resource was made available in its present form. Identifier refers to a string of text and numbers that uniquely identify the resource, such as an ISBN number, for example.

Developing your own standards for third-party suppliers

You might also find your own organization becoming a provider of standards. Today, much information comes from outside individual organizations. Consider, for example, all the companies whose products are assemblages of hundreds of systems developed by sub-manufacturers. Each of these subprojects has its own suite of information that must be incorporated into the complete system being sold to another organization. Consider, for example, the aircraft manufacturers who are responsible for providing operations and maintenance information to their customers, but much of the information is developed by secondary manufacturers that are providing parts of the plane. They require that the secondary manufacturers submit their information using standard SGML metadata and tags. This standardization ensures that the information will be compatible as a whole and vastly decreases the manufacturer's costs for assembling and disseminating its documentation.

Many organizations that are handling third-party information resources or the documentation produced by Original Equipment Manufacturers (OEMs) should consider providing standard XML metadata, information types, and content units so that the total body of information delivered to the end customer is consistent and compatible. Standards ensure that users can search across information sources and find what they need more quickly than if all the information is produced differently.

Standardizing the use of metadata and tags within your organization

In addition to the task of ensuring that information resources coming into your organization from outside are standardized and capable of becoming part of your content-management system, you must find ways to ensure that similar standards are maintained inside your organization. Part of your task in building an Information Model, as described in Chapter 4, *Creating an Information Model,* is to arrive at a standard set of words to describe your information. The standard set of words becomes the metadata and the tags that will be used to describe all the information under content management in your organization.

If individual authors attempt to add their own tags and metadata to documents or parts of documents, your content-management system will become more and more unmanageable. The same problems would occur in any database if individuals were allowed to put information into the repository without regard to the data model. New information entered without the appropriate labels would not be accessible by anyone who didn't know the original authors' intent. In addition, downstream automated processes, such as those for dynamic Web delivery, can break as unexpected tags are encountered.

Agreeing on the categorizing and selecting the right words (the taxonomy) to label them will be the most difficult task you are likely to face in creating a comprehensive content-management solution for your organization. The more broadly based the information resources that you want to come under content management, the more difficult the task is likely to become. The rewards, however, are considerable. Once information is well labeled, it becomes accessible by more and more people inside and outside your organization. The information resources under content management can be regarded as the knowledge assets of your enterprise. These information resources are just as critical to the success of an enterprise as the data in the financial systems.

Recognizing that determining metadata is an ongoing process

Users change, products change, new opportunities for the interchange of information present themselves. The Information Model you develop today will not be the Information Model you will need five or ten years from now. In some organizations, today's model might not be sufficient to accommodate next year's organizational structure. With mergers, splits, acquisitions, and sales adding to the complexity of product and service solutions, I find that the metadata needed to describe information assets will continue to change.

One of the clear advantages of a content-management solution, in comparison to keeping information in isolated, incompatible file systems, is that a repository structure is changeable in the future. With file systems resident on servers, changes in the organizational and information structures often lead to duplication of information resources. A document created and stored in one place, by one group, is needed by another group in another location. Most often, the document will be copied and stored in more than one place. When one document changes, the other copies of the document can easily be overlooked and remain unchanged.

In a similar manner, when a particular module of content is needed in more than one output context, that module of content is copied and duplicated, adding to the difficulty of maintaining the consistency and integrity of the information resources. A content-management solution must ensure that one module of information exists in only one place for updating, while at the same time it is available to be published in many contexts. As the contexts change, due to organizational changes, customer changes, product changes, and so on, the metadata labeling the information modules must also change.

I have described situations in which metadata tags are directly entered as part of your individual modules of information. To change the metadata by adding new tags or new values for a particular tag means going back to the original information modules and entering the changes, a time-consuming process. For this reason, do a thorough job of thinking about and organizing your plan for your metadata during the planning stages of your content-management project.

In addition, however, you might want to consider a process by which metadata can be stored externally from the information modules. The metadata would be part of the database but would point to the appropriate modules of information rather than being embedded within them.

Use technology, such as topic maps, that externalizes the assembly process rather than requiring that authors, or the content-management system itself, embed the assembly information into the module. When assembly information is externalized, it can be more easily changed without having to change it in each affected file.

Investigating your users, your business, and your authoring environment

In Chapter 4, *Creating an Information Model*, you will find details about how to analyze your user and author communities and your business environment. The Information Audit, which is the basic planning stage for content management, must include this investigation and the subsequent analysis. As part of your Information Audit, you must include existing information. From the discussion in this chapter, you have seen that existing information can be brought into your content-management solution or remain separate. You can incorporate unstructured information resources as well as structured. The effectiveness and usability of your content-management solution will greatly depend on how you make these decisions.

One of the goals of your Information Audit is to discover the categories that you will use to build your Information Model. Only with a thorough knowledge of and analysis of your users, authors, and business perspectives, will your Information Model succeed. Success means making information easily accessible to both authors and users. With careful planning and decision-making, you will produce a content repository that will support communication, collaboration, and business effectiveness at many levels.

4

Creating an Information Model

"Funny. Here is what our customers need to know and not one group even comes close to this!"

An Information Model provides the framework for organizing your content so that it can be delivered and reused in a variety of innovative ways. Once you have created an Information Model for your content repository, you will be able to label information in ways that will enhance search and retrieval, making it possible for authors and users to find the information resources they need quickly and easily.

The Information Model is the ultimate content-management tool.

Creating your Information Model requires analysis, careful planning, and a lot of feedback from your user community. The analysis takes you into the world of those who need and use information resources every day. The planning means talking to a wide range of stakeholders, including both individuals and groups who have information needs and who would profit from collaboration in the development of information resources. Getting feedback requires that you test your Information Model with members of your user community to ensure that you haven't missed some important perspectives.

In this chapter, you learn

- what an Information Model is
- why an Information Model is critical to the success of your content-management system
- how to create an effective and usable Information Model

It's very easy to tell when a Web site you're trying to navigate has no underlying Information Model. Here are the tell-tale characteristics:

- You can't tell how to get from the home page to the information you're looking for.
- You click on a promising link and are unpleasantly surprised at what turns up.
- You keep drilling down into the information layer after layer until you realize you're getting farther away from your goal rather than closer.
- Every time you try to start over from the home page, you end up in the same wrong place.
- You scroll through a long alphabetic list of all the articles ever written on a particular subject with only the title to guide you.

Sound familiar? What does it feel like when a well-designed Information Model is in place? Oddly enough, you generally don't notice a well-conceived Information Model because it simply doesn't get in the way of your search.

- On the home page, you notice promising links right away.
- Two or three clicks get you to exactly what you wanted.
- The information seems designed just for you because someone has anticipated your needs.
- You can read a little or ask for more—the cross-references are in the right places.
- Right away you feel that you're on familiar ground—similar types of information start looking the same.

Did all of these pleasant experiences happen by accident? Not in the least. Finding the information you needed quickly and easily requires a great deal of advance planning. The basic planning and design tool is the Information Model.

What is an Information Model?

An Information Model is an organizational framework that you use to categorize your information resources. The framework assists authors and users in finding what they need, even if their needs are significantly different and personal. The framework provides the basis on which you base your publishing architecture, including print and electronic information delivery.

An Information Model might encompass the information resources of one part of an organization. For example, your Information Model might provide a framework for categorizing your corporate training materials or the technical and sales

If an Information Model is clearly defined and firmly established, users will be on a fast track finding and retrieving the information they need.

information that accompanies your products. Your Information Model might include engineering information produced during product development, policies and procedures used internally in the day-to-day conduct of business, information about customers used in your sales cycle or about vendors used in your supply chain. Some of the information resources you bring under content management might be available across the corporation for internal use, such as human-resources information. Other information resources might be specific to the needs of one department or division of your organization.

As you plan what to include under content management and what to exclude, you must consider a wide range of dimensions through which you will categorize and label your information. Some of the dimensions will be specific to the needs of information authors. Others will meet the requirements of your products and services. Still others will explicitly meet the needs of internal and external users of information.

As you design your Information Model, consider how large an information body it must encompass. Some Information Models are very small, specific, and limited in scope. Others stretch across entire organizations, encompassing thousands or millions of pages. In the next section, you start with a small, personal Information Model. In subsequent sections, you consider larger, more complex models for larger bodies of information.

The three-tiered structure of an Information Model

The Information Model you build will have a three-tiered structure. At base, the first tier of the Information Model consists of the dimensions that identify how your information will be categorized and labeled for both internal and external use in your organization. The second tier sorts your information assets into information types. The third tier provides structure for each information type, outlining the content units that authors use to build information types. Figure 4-1 illustrates the three-tiered structure. In this chapter, you learn how to determine the basic dimensions of your Information Model. In Chapter 5, *Developing Information Types and Content Units*, you learn how to identify your information types. And, in Chapter 6, *Using Content Units to Structure Information Types*, you learn how to identify the content units that provide the internal structure for each information type.

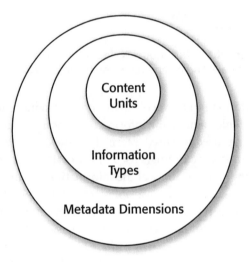

Figure 4-1 The three-tiered structure of an Information Model

The dimensions you identify as the foundation of your Information Model become the attributes and values of the metadata you will use to label your modules of content in your repository. The information types will provide your authors with the basis for creating well-structured modules that represent a particular purpose in communicating information. The content units will describe the chunks of content that are used to construct each information type.

In the next section, you will look at an extended example of the process one might use to begin the development of an Information Model. Throughout the core design Chapters 4, 5, and 6, I refer to this extended example to provide you with a model for developing the Information Model for your organization.

Starting with a personal view of an Information Model

Here is a typical example of how an Information Model might be applied. At home, I have a large collection of cookbooks and cooking magazines, plus lots of recipes cut out of newspapers or sent by friends and relatives. Yet, every time I want to find a particular recipe I remember having used or look for a new recipe for a dish I want to try, I'm stymied by the very books that are such a valuable resource. Where is that recipe? Which book or magazine was it in? Was it last year or ten years ago? Is it in the small green file box or the large cookie tin?

When a sound Information Model is in place, it assists users in finding the answers to their questions.

The cookbooks I own are organized in various interesting ways. Some are organized by month, based on the original magazine issues. *Sunset Magazine*™, for example, publishes a cookbook annual in which each chapter contains a month's worth of recipes from its magazine. Other cookbooks are organized alphabetically by ingredient or by country of origin. Still other cookbooks are organized by the main ingredient or a part of a complete meal. Several books I own have sections focusing on chicken, pork, beef, or vegetables. They also have sections on soups, desserts, and appetizers. All these different organizations are interesting and effective individually. However, as a complete collection, they fail. They fail because they lack a comprehensive Information Model to support the organization of their content.

How might I improve the organization of the recipes in the cookbooks? First, I would need to understand how I or another amateur cook might search for and use the information. If I'm organizing the content for myself, I might want recipes organized by ingredients, parts of the meal, country of origin, and time to complete. I might also want to organize them by recipes already tried, successful recipes, unsuccessful recipes, new recipes that look interesting but remain untried. All of these categorizes would facilitate searching for just the right recipe for an occasion. In fact, by assigning one or more categories to each recipe, I would be building an Information Model to fit my conceptual view of the cookbook world. If I wanted to include others in my Information Model, I'd need to know something about the categories that would be interesting to them.

The Information Model also assists authors in retrieving information for reuse and revision. It helps us answer questions like

- Where is that explanation of what cornstarch does in a recipe? (See Figure 4-2.)

- Where are the recipes for pasta with asparagus?

- Don't you have an instruction for cutting a chicken into pieces for frying?

An organizational Information Model

Several years ago, I conducted an interesting and significant test of an organization's informal Information Model. A state department of vocational rehabilitation needed to answer questions from its constituencies, which included disabled individuals seeking job assistance and companies inquiring about hiring and supporting the disabled. Much of the information to answer these questions could be found somewhere in the large volumes of government regulations and policy statements maintained in the organization's library, in the offices of staff members, and in the heads of key employees. Unfortunately, the right person with the right information to respond to a question wasn't always available. Or, the person taking the question would not always know whom to ask. As a result, some customer questions were not being handled as well as management wanted. They needed a content-management system to support their goal of being responsive to their constituencies. I conducted an Information Audit of their responses to provide a design concept and cost justification for the new system.

The audit was simple and interesting to conduct. Based on a well-researched list of typical questions developed by the experienced managers, members of my staff called at random with requests for information. They recorded how long it took to obtain the right answer. Most of the time, the department staff was very effective. Calls were answered promptly; often the person taking the call could

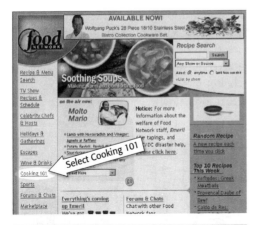
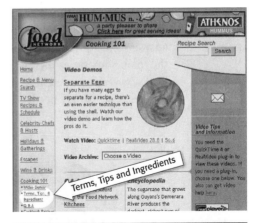
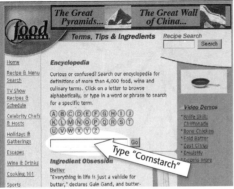
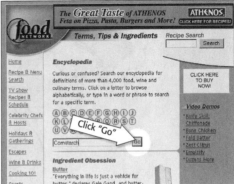

Definition: Cornstarch is a fine, powdery flour ground from the endosperm, or white heart, of the corn kernel. Lacking gluten, it is used as a neutral-flavored thickening agent in such preparations as sauces and fillings and to give baked goods a delicate texture. It is also known as cornflour.

Figure 4-2 Just what is cornstarch and what is it doing in my recipe? By following a link from Cooking 101, the amateur chef locates an explanation in the Ingredients Encyclopedia on a well-organized Web site. A comprehensive Information Model underpins the Web site design.

provide the correct answer immediately or within a few minutes. But, at times, callers were shifted around to several individuals without obtaining a satisfactory answer to the questions. In other cases, the promised materials never arrived in the mail. Sometimes the materials received weren't the right ones. Although the staff was very competent as a whole, better internal access to information resources was sorely needed (see the cartoon below).

People use many sources to find the information they need: other people, the library, books nearby on office shelves, sources in other organizations. A sound Information Model ensures that the sources of information are effectively categorized according to the users' conceptual model of the information.

An Information Model could be built so that it facilitated ease of access and accuracy of response. In this instance, much of the information needed to answer questions was available, although not always quickly available. In cases where the correct information was not available at all, the gap meant that new information assets should be developed.

The investigation showed that a content-management system was needed. To be effective, the content-management system needed to be based on a sound Information Model, one that would become the eventual framework for a content-management system. The immediate goal was to make the information resources readily available to the staff members. The long-term goal was to make the information resources available to the outside customers through an Internet site. If it was well designed, the Web site would allow the agency's constituents to find their own answers even more quickly and easily than by calling in.

A place for everything

One way to think about an Information Model is as a large filing system—a place for everything and everything in its place. In fact, you have the real life example of the library as a content-management system that embodies a particular Information Model. Through familiarity, people learn to make effective use of a common and consistent Information Model to find what they need.

At university, I learned how to use the graduate library which was organized according to the Library of Congress' Information Model. I knew exactly where to find the books I needed, often without using the electronic catalog system that had recently replaced the old paper card catalog system. I knew which floor the eighteenth century history books were on and where to find the art history as well. In fact, I could walk into any university library and pretty much find my way around. The Information Model on which these libraries are based is quite uniform among higher-education institutions. It gives you a nice, comfortable feeling of continuity. The books are where you expect them to be. Each book has a number that identifies its place on the shelves, and experienced users who have learned how the system works feel very much at home.

Unfortunately, not all libraries are the same. Going to a different kind of library is as disconcerting as venturing into a new Web site.

In recent years, I have used the local community library far more often than I use the university library. My local library was at first really confusing; nothing was where I expected it to be. The reason—they manage their content using a different Information Model, a different arrangement of categories, based on the Dewey Decimal system, which is often used to organize community libraries. I was frustrated to discover that the books *by* my favorite author were in one location while the books *about* the author were in quite a different location. Eventually I figured out the system but I have never felt quite at home with it.

Information Models not only facilitate fast search and retrieval, they also create a sense of familiarity and belonging for their users. As experienced users of a content-management system based on a sound Information Model, you know where to find what you need. It's right there in the same place it was last time and exactly where you expected. As a library user, the Information Model underlying the library's content-management system allows you to manage the content effectively for yourself.

Even familiar models are challenging for newcomers

Unfortunately, Information Models that are quite understandable by experienced individuals are often equally obscure to newcomers. The vocational rehabilitation department could create an organization for their information resources that would be easily accessible to trained personnel working on the inside. But would the same organization of information work for the outsiders, the people with the questions? Most likely, the answer would be "no."

The problem is that the content-management system that is useful for the authors of the information is not usable by users of the information who do not understand the underlying Information Model.

Take the case of the library. The typical catalog makes information available in several ways, typically by the name of the author, the title of the work, and key-words and descriptions associated with its subject matter. If you know the author's name or the title of the work, the search can be reasonably quick and easy. But lacking that critical information, the opportunities for frustration abound. How do you find information when you have no title and no author? How do you, for example, find out about the insect that bit you in the jungle of Guatemala and is causing you excruciating pain? Is it listed in a guide to Central American entomol-ogy? What about a book on tropical diseases? Just where do you begin? If you were an expert on insects or tropical diseases, you would know where to look. But with-out an expert's knowledge of the underlying Information Model, the solution would probably be too long in coming. If you were on a Web site, you would be tempted to click out before you wasted any more time becoming frustrated.

To be usable by a wide range of individuals with different experiences and expectations, an Information Model must be designed by those who take the time to study and understand the prospective users. By organizing information resources through our analysis of the users and envisioning the user experience you expect for the future, you have a chance at being successful in helping your users reach their goals quickly.

Information Models based on static categories can be difficult to learn

The problem with the libraries is that to gain familiarity with their Information Models, you need help and experience. In fact, you even need to have some train-ing in school about how to find things in the library. The libraries employ quite sophisticated help systems, often in the person of reference librarians, to help naïve users find what they need. The reference librarians are taught methods of asking the right questions of the users in order to point them in the right direc-tion. Unfortunately, when your customers visit your Web sites, there are no help-ful librarians—so all the assistance has to be immediately obvious to them. The Information Model you design provides the framework for that assistance.

An Information Model is based upon the categories you select to label and organize your information resources. These categories must emerge organically from your analysis of user requirements. Otherwise, your users will experience some of the same problems that occur in the library—a set of formal categories that is based more on the categorizer's view of the nature of the information resources than upon the users' needs.

The information architects of the public and university libraries made decisions based on a formal categorization of the material in the collections. The primary organization follows academic, classical subjects —history, art, music, literature, science, and so on. The secondary and tertiary organizations are based on author's name or time period (centuries) or geographic locations and a host of other possibilities, depending on the nature of the subject. The organization appears to mirror the organization of the academies, especially in the university libraries. The people in the History Department are sure to find much of the information they need in the history category. For novices to become experts, they have to learn the system. The system doesn't change in response to the users' needs.

The more the Information Model reflects the way that users think and work, the more effective it will be in delivering the right information to them.

Just think—what if the library could be rearranged depending upon the users' profiles? I will consider this possibility when I demonstrate what a dynamic Information Model can do for you—and your customers.

Why do you need an Information Model?

Designing an effective, comprehensive Information Model is a critical and sometimes formidable step in developing a resource that will provide answers to your customers' most arcane questions in their search for information. A content-management system that will make information accessible must be built upon a sound Information Model.

Otherwise, what you will have is a loose collection of files with cryptic names, inaccessible except to the experts. It's what you now face when you try to access a company's information resources. Where is the information stored? How are the files named? What about information inside the files? What if you don't know the exact titles and content? What if the people who know the file system leave the organization?

The evidence that the existing systems of storing information fail is quite massive. Everyone has stories to tell of the impossibility of finding the information they need, whether the resources are in printed volumes or in online systems. Where did you put that government document that lists the requirements for employers of the disabled? That policy document is 800 pages long, and the table of contents and the index do not include the words you are using to find an answer to your question. If you don't know what the author called it, you can't find the information you need. If you don't know where the author put it, how are you to find it and use it yourself?

A strong, effective Information Model solves the problems described when it is designed in the context of a content-management system. The model labels information according to the ways it will be accessed. In fact, the information can be reorganized in many ways, depending upon who is doing the looking. Most important, the model provides the framework needed to make information accessible to experienced and inexperienced seekers alike. It reduces frustration and enhances productivity. It means that people spend less time searching and more time using information resources. It helps to ensure that resources are not rewritten or recreated through an author's sheer frustration at not being able to find them.

Static Information Models

As you begin to construct your Information Model, you will be tempted to use the various logical (or illogical, for that matter) categories that others originally used to set up their files in the file servers. I find, for example, technical information that is organized by product line. All the information associated with Model A is organized inside file folders labeled Model A. A similar structure might be in place for Model B of the product, or the structure might be entirely different because the people in charge of Model B don't communicate about organizational schemes with the people in charge of Model A. Note that Figure 4-3 illustrates a typical hierarchical arrangement used in a file-management system. A hierarchical Information Model, using a system of folders and files, works well as long as everyone in the organization understands the design.

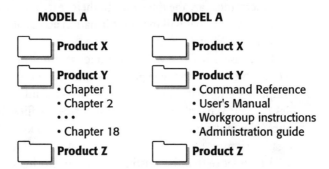

Figure 4-3 A hierarchical information structure is typically used in a file-management system, such as the hierarchical view of folders and files in Windows Explorer. This static organization is useful as long as its use is restricted to people who understand the information and the organizational logic of the Information Model embodied in the hierarchical design.

Functional departments within companies use categories and organize them in ways that reflect the ways in which the resident experts conduct business. The

Human Resources Department, for example, might organize its information resources into categories such as employee benefits, employee demographic information, and so on. The electronic filing system reflects how the experienced people in the organization think about the information. Introduce just one newcomer, and confusion results.

In devising an Information Model for dynamic Web delivery, you need to resist the temptation to create a static system where there is only one way to find a particular piece of information. Although the system is usable by experts, newcomers and outsiders will be defeated.

Dynamic Information Models

The solution to a static representation of your information resources is a dynamic Information Model, one that changes in response to the needs of the users. Take the library, for example; what if a library patron could wave a magic wand and the library would rearrange itself in response to a particular set of needs. Let's say that a patron wants to find not only all the books written *by* Steven King but also all the books and articles written *about* Steven King. In addition, the patron would like to know more about mystery and horror writers in the second half of the twentieth century living in North America or in the United Kingdom. Once the patron's need is known, all the books in the library and the articles in all the periodicals fly around rearranging themselves into an optimal solution. Sounds a bit like a magical library; rather messy, I'm afraid. But it would be a godsend for the individual user.

The books and other materials in the library rearrange themselves to suit the needs of each individual user.

For those of us delivering information through electronic media, the danger of being hit by flying books and periodicals ripping apart can happily be avoided. If you have studied your users and worked hard to anticipate their needs, or put in place systems to continually monitor their searches, you can quite literally rearrange the library. The Information Model is the mechanism that makes dynamic updating of the information possible. But the Information Model is only as good as your analysis and creativity can make it.

Defining the components of the Information Model?

The Information Model consists of information resources that you have categorized so that they can be effectively searched and retrieved. The categories reflect your understanding of the dimensions that represent the points of view of each relevant group in the user community. For each of the dimensions you establish, you assign labels (most likely in the form of XML metadata tags) that describe each information resource in terms of the relevant categories and subcategories.

Look at how the cookbook information designer might develop an Information Model for a cookbook content-management system. Table 4-1 consists of two columns: the first describes the primary dimensions and the second lists the individual instances of the category—the subcategories—that might be found in your information resources. Because the Information Model is based on an analysis of how users might want to find the information they need, the more comprehensive the user analysis, the more successful the dimensions will be. The dimensions become your XML metadata attributes and the subcategories are the values associated with the metadata attributes.

The metadata attributes and values that are embedded in each information module make it possible for the person searching for a felicitous menu to come up with a Chinese main course featuring fish and accommodating a low fat diet. Another person searching for a Vietnamese soup would also be successful.

Not only would users be able to gather and rearrange the information to suit their requirements, but the information developers would also have many ways to organize the information. A developer wanting to produce a low-fat Chinese cookbook would be able to find all the appropriate Chinese recipes and arrange them by meal or primary ingredient or Chinese region and so on. Table 4-2 illustrates how a database table might be organized to represent the dimensions identified for the recipe database.

While you are gathering information that will guide the development of your Information Model is the best time to consider many possible organizational schemes. For example, the technical documentation supporting a company's hardware products might be organized by product model number. Or, the techni-

Table 4-1 Recipe metadata attributes and values

Metadata Attribute (Dimension)	Value (subcategory)
Primary recipe ingredient	Beef
	Lamb
	Chicken
	Fish
	Shellfish
	Vegetables
Ethnicity	Italian
	Mexican
	Chinese
	Irish
	Thai
	Vietnamese
Role in a meal	Starters
	Soups
	Sandwiches
	Salads
	Main courses
	Side dishes
	Desserts
Special diets	Low fat
	Low salt
	Low calorie
	Low cholesterol

Table 4-2 This table illustrates how a database might be organized to accommodate the recipe metadata attributes and values that were identified in Table 4-1.

Title	Ethnicity	Special Diet	Role
Spring Rolls	Chinese	Low fat	Starter
Canneloni	Italian	Low salt	Side dish
Taco Salad	Mexican	Low calorie	Salad
Shepherds Pie	Irish	Low cholesterol	Main course

cal documentation might be arranged according to the basic sets of tasks from installation through configuration, standard use, troubleshooting, and maintenance. Still other organizational schemes might reflect the job skills required to install, use, and maintain the equipment or the level of expertise of an individual within a particular job classification (expert, journeyman, beginner).

The primary categories that describe your information resources will be related to specific information types and content units. An information type might be a procedure consisting of step-by-step instructions for installing a hardware device. Content units for the procedure might list the tools required for the installation, the warnings about taking proper safety precautions, observations on handling typical installation problems, or recommendations for setting up the workplace for safe and efficient use.

Analyzing user requirements

Information architects at Nortel Networks decided to organize its information according to three interrelated primary dimensions: workflow, product model, and information type.

They began by analyzing the types of work done by the end-users of their products. They learned that people planned for the installation of the new equipment they needed, wrote specifications and evaluated products, installed and configured their new hardware and software, upgraded existing hardware and software with new versions, monitored error reports, engaged in troubleshooting activities, and repaired and replaced components and software applications.

The Information Model that they developed began with a dimension that allowed them to label information topics among their information modules with values that represented the end-user's workflow. Superimposed upon the workflow dimension was the product model that the end-users were working with. That meant, for example, that one topic developed in the information resource would have two initial labels: one for the place in the customer's workflow and another for the product model. A specific topic might be concerned with hardware installation for computer model A.

The third dimension involved the types of information to be found among the topics in the information resource. Some topics described background reference information that users could read to understand how the particular product model worked. Other topics contained procedures for installation or configuration or monitoring. Still other topics described tools required, troubleshooting recommendations, or safety warnings.

The basic categorization and labeling they defined in a comprehensive, corporate-wide Information Model is illustrated in Figure 4-4.

If this Information Model were used simply to store or find a module in a content-management system and always used in the same context, you would attach

Category	Customer Support	Technology Fundamentals	About the Product	Plan and Engineer	Install Hardware	Install Software	Commission	Configure	Administer	Manage Performance	Manage Accounting	Manage Faults	Manage Security
Category Definition	Contains information that facilitates customer interaction with the company.	Contains information about telecommunications and computer fundamentals that are the foundation of the product technology.	Contains information about specific technology fundamentals that apply to the product.	Contains information about planning the implementation of the product to meet requirements and specifications.	Contains information about installing and removing hardware.	Contains information about installing and removing software.	Contains information about bringing the product online and verifying that it operates according to specification.	Contains information about setting up the hardware and software functionality.	Contains information about controlling access to and managing the hardware and software.	Contains information about managing resource usage.	Contains information about managing the measurement of resource usage for the purpose of billing.	Contains information about managing the detection, isolation, and correction of abnormal operation.	Contains information about managing the protection of resources from unauthorized or detrimental access and use.
What's New	Understanding what's new in customer support.		Understanding what's new in the product's release.	Understanding what's new in planning and engineering.	Understanding what's new in hardware installation.	Understanding what's new in software installation.	Understanding what's new in commissioning.	Understanding what's new in configuration.	Understanding what's new in administration.	Understanding what's new in performance management	Understanding what's new in accounting management	Understanding what's new in fault management	Understanding what's new in security management
Fundamentals		Understanding safety requirements. understanding industry terminology. Understanding computer fundamentals. Understanding networking fundamentals. Understanding data communications fundamentals. Understanding telephony fundamentals.	Understanding the management system user interface. Understanding the product's basic capabilities and characteristics. Understanding product terminology. Understanding how to find and use product information. Understanding the product's architecture. Understanding how the project works.	Understanding planning and engineering fundamentals.	Understanding hardware installation fundamentals. Understanding safety requirements.	Understanding software installation fundamentals. Understanding the software installation user interface.	Understanding commissioning fundamentals.	Understanding configuration fundamentals. Understanding the configuration user interface.	Understanding administration fundamentals. Understanding the administration user interface. Understanding the file structure and database.	Understanding performance management fundamentals. Understanding the performance management user interface. Understanding performance data.	Understanding accounting management fundamentals. Understanding the accounting management user interface. Understanding accounting data.	Understanding fault management fundamentals. Understanding the fault management user interface. Understanding fault data.	Understanding security management fundamentals. Understanding the security user interface. Understanding security data.

Figure 4-4 This telecommunications company devised a comprehensive Information Model for its technical information across the corporation and encompassing a wide variety of products. The model is organized according to the functions performed by users of the equipment and software, including activities such as software installation and installation planning. The dimensions are further organized according to information types, from conceptual information through task and troubleshooting information. Source: Nortel Networks, Inc. Permission to use granted by Nortel Networks, Inc. All rights reserved.

one label to the topic for each category. For example, a procedure for trouble-shooting a problem with Computer B would be given three labels as illustrated in Table 4-3.

However, the same procedure might be applicable to more than one product model. In that case,

<product model = "computer A, computer C, computer F, and so on">

A particular safety warning might be applicable to workflow activities involved with installing, replacing, and upgrading a hardware component. As a result, the workflow dimension of a particular information topic would include the following:

<procedure workflow = "installation, replacement, upgrading">

Table 4-3 Metadata attributes and values for the workflow dimension

Metadata Attribute (Dimension)	Value (subcategory)
Workflow	Planning
	Specification
	Installation
	Configuration
	Monitoring
	Troubleshooting
	Maintenance
	Replacement
	Upgrading
Product model	Computer A
	Computer B
	⋮
	Computer X
Information type	Safety warnings
	Hints
	Procedures
	Background information
	Concepts
	Tools required

By labeling information in multiple ways, a particular topic of information will appear in more than one context, depending upon the needs of the users of the information.

Assessing authoring requirements

To be most effective, an Information Model is first focused on the users of the information. However, other dimensions of the information emerge when you study the requirements of the authors.

Information authors also need to create, store, find, and reuse information topics as they develop information resources. In general, the authoring community wants to know

- Who first authored a topic?
- When was it first written?
- Who edited the information topic and when?
- What changes have been made to the topic, by whom, and when?
- Why were the changes made?
- Are there many versions of the information topic, reflecting a series of changes?
- Which version am I viewing at this time?
- When was it created?
- Who approved the information topic for publication to the Web?
- When was it approved?

These questions reflect the work processes of the authoring community. They can be expressed as dimensions and values associated with each information topic created and stored in the content-management system. Authoring requirements mean that you have additional labels to attach that support creating, storing, searching, and retrieving information from the system.

A table of authoring workflow requirements might look like Table 4-4.

Many authoring dimensions can be automatically assigned to an information topic. For example, you know that John Jones is the author of a particular topic because John logged onto the content-management system using his password. You know the date that he first authored the topic based on the date stored in the system. You also know that John is the author, not the editor of the topic. However, the only way you can tell why John revised his information topic two weeks after he first created it is by looking at the notes he included when he made the change and checked the topic back into the content-management system.

Other information that tracks the authoring processes is based upon a workflow system that can be configured to route information topics from author to

Table 4-4 Dimensions of an authoring workflow Information Model with values

Metadata Attribute (Dimension)	Value (subcategory)
Author	Individual name
Editor	Individual name
Activity	Initial creation Editing Approval Revision
Activity date	Date
Version	Number Date
Reason for changes	Notes

editor to approver. The individual's role in the process is defined in the workflow system, and the workflow system automatically selects the appropriate category and label to use.

Version and release control requirements

Keeping track of versions of the information is a standard part of a content-management system. Each time an author makes a change and checks a topic back into the database, a new version is created. If the author explains what change was made and why in a note, then even more information is available to anyone tracking the changes.

Version information included in the Information Model helps the development community ensure that the latest version is being released to the users and that earlier versions are available whenever they need to go back. This practice adds up to straightforward version control.

However, you have learned that, in many organizations, information changes in ways that are not always neatly predictable by simple versioning. Companies have multiple versions of products available to customers at any one time. Information related to earlier models might all need to be available simultaneously. For example, many heavy equipment manufacturers makes available on their Web sites the maintenance manuals for 25, 50, or even 100 years of products. Somewhere, some place, someone might need to repair one of those original pieces of equipment.

Even more complicated for your Information Model are topics that are associated with interim product releases. A new release of your products might be planned for the end of the quarter. But during the development life cycle, it isn't always clear which version of the product and which functions will end up included in the final release. Sometimes small, interim releases are made to test functionality; these require documentation. However, the information in the topic modules continues to change as feedback comes from the customers, the test team, and the developers. I've learned of groups that maintain as many as nine different versions of the information during the development process. Some changes can affect all versions, while other changes affect only some of the versions. Handling multiple versions of the same or nearly the same information modules is a challenge to your Information Model.

Product developers, particularly software developers, have opted to release updates to product functionality more frequently than ever before. Some companies release information every three months, others every few weeks, still others weekly. In addition, these same organizations maintain multiple versions of the product and the information during development. Only when release decisions are made is it clear which versions of the many topics will actually be released to the customers.

Multiple streaming releases have caused considerable stress to information-development organizations because the changes in information are difficult to track. However, you can use your Information Model to bring some semblance of control to the release process through the use of categories and labels and through the relationship of parent-child topics to one another.

When you need to keep track of versions of information, you might want to split off a particular version and add new labels. Let's look at an example illustrated in Figure 4-5.

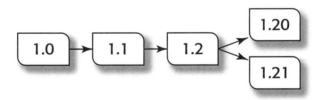

Figure 4-5 During the development of a procedure, several interim versions are produced. Eventually version 1.2 splits into two related versions that reflect two ways in which the produce might work. Authors must track the related sub-versions to ensure that subsequent changes in the information are reflected in both instances.

These two versions are related to version 1.2 but have differences that reflect two possible methods of talking about a product. The first method reflects one possible way the product can work; the second method reflects another possible way. One of the methods will be released eventually but during the authoring process, you need to keep track of both. You need a process of categorization that allows for a relationship among the sub-versions. You want to keep track of the changes to the primary version (Version 1.2) that can affect both the sub-versions. But you also want to maintain the distinctions between the sub-versions, at least until a decision is made about which one to release.

To handle this relationship, you need a system of categorizing versions that links the sub-versions to the primary version but continues to track changes to the sub-versions as well as changes to the primary one. By developing a series of dimensions and values that allow us to label the sub-versions and track the relationships, you can provide a way to handle potentially complex interrelationships among topics.

The architect of a comprehensive Information Model, in this case as in others, must be aware of the requirements both of the user and of the authoring communities. Both communities have roles that will influence the design of your Information Model.

Building an Information Model

The process of building an Information Model starts and ends with the intended users of the information. If you begin with the users' needs for information, you are said to construct a *top-down model.* However, if you begin with the information resources that you already have in your library, you are said to construct a *bottom-up model.* In most cases, you do a combination of both, beginning with your user profiles and also inventorying your information resources to understand the information you already have and how you might deliver it to particular members of the user community.

Note—Despite the temptation to create an Information Model that matches your current information resources, be careful. In most organizations, many have created information resources that no one actually appears to need. In one case, when the authors tracked the hits on the online policies and procedures for several months, they discovered that no one ever accessed them. Information resources like these provide answers for which there are no questions. They once might have met the information needs of someone, often a business analyst or a product developer, but now they have lost even that limited purpose. Sometimes it is better to abandon your legacy information or simply store it *en masse* for occasional retrieval in case it is ever requested, rather than attempting to categorize and label the information. In other instances, you might prefer to put minimal dimensions and values on the information, creating basic wrappers, without spending time unnecessarily trying to understand and restructure the information.

Deciding on the scope of your Information Model

As you begin the task of building your Information Model, consider once again the scope on which you will work. Is the Information Model to be restricted to your department's information? If your responsibility is training material, you might want to begin with an Information Model that identifies all the training text, graphics, and rich media that you include in instructor-led and computer-based courseware. Your Information Model should provide a framework for categorizing all your training information resources so that they can be used to construct new courses, packaged for e-learning and instructor-led training, or even mixed dynamically to form personalized courses based on the results of online user assessments.

If your Information Model encompasses all your product information resources to be used in marketing and literature, in catalogues, and in technical manuals, your framework is likely to include a wide range of information categorized by dimensions of product model, user profile, language, country, and others.

If your Information Model accounts for internal information spanning multiple organizations, you need to involve all the various organizations in the modeling exercise. An Information Model that is designed to support customer care might need to take into account the dimensions of use of sales, marketing, account management, order fulfillment, pricing, training, documentation, policies and procedures, customer support, field engineering, and more. Such a model will involve gathering input from many different author communities within and outside the organizations, as well as information about the customer requirements.

If your Information Model encompasses an entire corporate body of information, you will need to include multiple information providers and information users in your investigation. One Information Model for an entire corporation is a significant undertaking, requiring multiple levels of information gathering. It requires coordination among many individuals and agreement on the dimensions needed to describe author, information, and user requirements.

A project of such large scope as a corporate-wide Information Model requires a strong project plan, a very capable project manager, and a set of team members who have decision-making responsibilities. The team members will need to identify the dimensions of use, agreeing on a common descriptive language (a taxonomy) that will be used to categorize and label the dimensions.

In some cases, information resources will be used across the organization and by a wide range of customers and partners. In other cases you will want subsets of your Information Model to address the requirements of specific parts of the organization, even at the division or department level. Specific information can be restricted for use among a few individuals or by those in one organization. Other information might be visible more widely. One technical information organization, for example, wanted to maintain a dimension that categorized the source from which they had received an information resource. However, they did not want the source to be identified to customers or to others in different departments. They selected some dimensions that were for internal use only, even though most of the dimensions they used to categorize information were available corporate-wide.

Identifying the dimensions of your Information Model

The first step in building your Information Model is to identify the dimensions that govern your users' need to access the information resources. To understand the concept of dimensions, consider the following user scenarios applied by the manufacturer of a chainsaw.

Product model

A chainsaw manufacturer has several closely related models of its basic consumer chainsaw that is designed for casual suburban users with little experience. They are likely to use the chainsaw infrequently. The manufacturer wants to provide user guides in print and on the Web to support the customers. The user guides will include safety instructions and procedures that are the same for all the consumer models and some procedures that differ from model to model.

In developing an Information Model, the authors of the user guides want to categorize and label their information topics by the model of chainsaw that they support. In this case, the consumer product model is the metadata dimension (see Table 4-5) and the values are the various individual models of the chainsaw. The authors will be able to create individual user guides, plus PDF files for online delivery, that contain both information common to all the consumer models and information specific to an individual model.

Consumers looking at the Web site will be able to find a unique set of information for their model of chainsaw without having to wade through the information topics for many different models. The authors will be able to write common information once and reuse it among all the consumer manuals, as illustrated in Figure 4-6.

Consumer target language

The chainsaw manufacturer has another issue that can be addressed through the Information Model; the consumers need the information on using the chainsaw in many different languages. Because the manufacturer sells this consumer product worldwide, the user guides are translated into several different languages. Thus, consumer's target language is another essential dimension for managing the information resources.

Table 4-5 Dimensions of a product-oriented Information Model

Metadata Attribute (Dimension)	Value (subcategory)
Product model	Model 21
	Model 23
	⋮
	Model 25

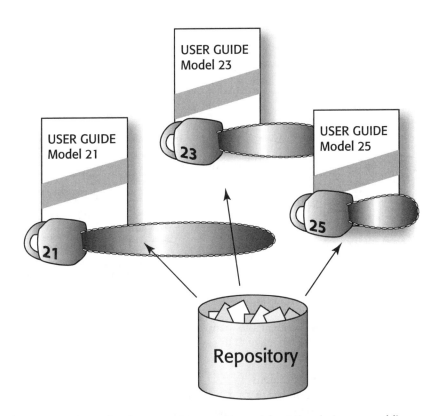

Figure 4-6 Information is targeted to specific models of the chainsaw, enabling customers to find only the information that pertains to their model and their needs.

If the information topics are labeled by the consumers' target languages, then the authors can create print, PDF, and Web versions of the information in all the languages. When the consumers goes to the Web site, they can retrieve the information for the appropriate model of the chainsaw in their language of choice. The manufacturer will also be able to include the correct language version of the user guide in the chainsaw package, as illustrated in Table 4-6 and Figure 4-7.

Table 4-6 Dimensions of a multi-language Information Model

Metadata Attribute (Dimension)	Value (subcategory)
Consumer language	English
	Latin American Spanish
	Spanish
	Dutch
	Italian
	French
	German
	Japanese
	Brazilian Portuguese

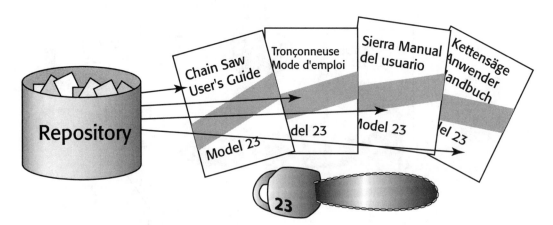

Figure 4-7 Not only does the chainsaw manufacturer produce custom manuals for each model, it also provides the manuals in the language of the users.

Information delivery

In addition to creating individual paper, PDF, and Web versions of the chainsaw user guides, the chainsaw manufacturer also wants to provide information for training. The company wants every consumer to have training on basic chainsaw use and safety before leaving the store. For this purpose, the manufacturer employs local sales representatives who also serve as the trainers. To ensure that all the training is delivered in exactly the same way and to reduce its liability, the chainsaw manufacturer would like to produce training topics. Fortunately, some of the information included in the user guides is also appropriate for training. By labeling some information only for the user guides, some information only for training materials, and some information for both, the manufacturer avoids considerable duplication of effort, as illustrated in Table 4-7.

Table 4-7 Dimensions of a delivery-oriented Information Model with values

Metadata Attribute (Dimension)	Value (subcategory)
Information delivery	Training
	Manual
	Web only

In addition, the manufacturer wants to include video clips and animation on the Web site so that the consumers can access self-paced training and actually view how a task is performed. This information cannot, of course, be used in the paper-based training materials. That means the information delivery dimension should also include a label for Web only. Figure 4-8 shows information available for a variety of instructional and reference media.

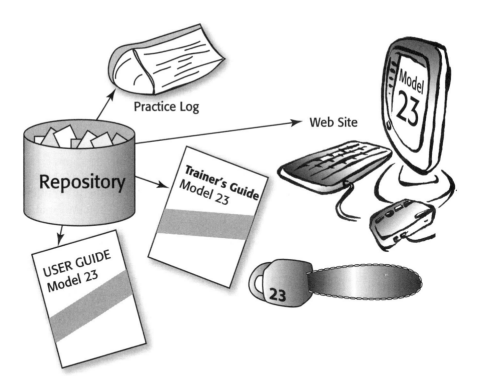

Figure 4-8 Chainsaw information is available for training by an instructor, for delivery over the Web, and a user guide. Each deliverable contains information targeted specifically for how the deliverable will be used.

Customized user information

Recently, the technical authors who develop the manuals, training, and Web-based information for the chainsaw manufacturer learned that they have a very high percentage of customers who are complete beginners using chainsaws. They would like to offer customized versions of the user guides and training materials depending upon skill level. To be able to reuse some information that is needed by all users and create other information in experienced and novice flavors, they want to label information topics with a user profile dimension, as illustrated in Table 4-8.

Table 4-8 Dimensions of a user-oriented Information Model with values

Metadata Attribute (Dimension)	Value (subcategory)
User skill level	Beginner
	Experienced

As a result, the company will be able to produce beginner and advanced versions of the manuals and the training without having to write everything twice. The sales representatives can decide which paper-based versions to give to particular customers, and the Web site can be designed to deliver the appropriate level of information based on a set of questions asked of the site visitors.

User country

Language is not the only geography-dependent dimension that the chainsaw manufacturer has to worry about. Specifications are different from country to country in which the chainsaw is sold. In the US, the information has to be provided using English units; in other countries, information is provided using metric units. Other country-specific requirements dictate changes to safety warnings, copyrights, and other issues. The manufacturer needs a country-specific dimension, as illustrated in Table 4-9, to control the information that differs and to deliver the appropriate information topics to print and to the Web.

Most of the information in the user guides and training materials will be the same, but the country dimension is important to keep track of specific regulatory requirements.

Analyzing a customer user community

The dimensions that are listed for the chainsaw manufacturer are derived from an analysis of the user community and of the way the product is designed and delivered to the users. Without a good analysis of the needs of the user community, an

Table 4-9 Dimensions of a country-specific Information Model with values

Metadata Attribute (Dimension)	Value (subcategory)
Country	US
	UK
	Brazil
	Argentina
	Germany
	France
	Spain
	Italy
	Japan

Information Model will tend to reflect the organization of the product, the interests of the host company or the internal organization of the departments, or the untested assumptions of the author. Analyzing user information requirements is essential to a successful Information Model and to its implementation in a dynamic Web environment.

In analyzing your customer user community, you need to examine multiple characteristics:

- Are your customers in different countries? Are their information needs different because of special country requirements or cultural characteristics?

- Are they most comfortable reading and listening in their own languages?

- Are your customers likely to be working with one model of your product at a time? Do they need exclusive information about that product, unmixed with other models' information?

- Will they need information that bridges multiple products?

- Do your users bring different levels of experience and expertise to their use of your product and its information?

- Do they need to practice skills learned through instructor-led or self-paced learning?

- Do your users perform very different jobs with your products? Are some of them supervisors? Others technicians? Still others clerical workers? Just how do their information needs differ?

- Do your users have different information needs because they use your products in different industries? For example, do the people using your information in a hospital differ from those using the same information in a warehouse?

- Do your users need different information because of age, disability, or other special situation?

- Do they need information based upon where they live or what they do?

- Are they most comfortable with print material, or do they prefer information to be online? Will a mix of information in a variety of media be most appropriate?

One user community might have information needs primarily based on job functions or role in a workflow. Other user communities might find that their information needs are strongly influenced by their level of expertise. Still other communities might prefer to read about broad concepts while their counterparts prefer task-oriented information. Some users want short synopses; others are more focused on in-depth analyses. And, all of these user communities might have individuals with all of these requirements at different times.

By understanding your consumer user community and how its members relate to the information you can provide, you will be more successful in evaluating the dimensions of your Information Model and making the most effective choices in the categorization of your information resources.

Analyzing an employee user community

The same process of user analysis applies when you are building an Information Model of your internal information. Once again, you need to address a series of questions about the information needs of the users in your organization:

- What information needs to be accessed by each user community in the organization?

- Does everyone need human resources information or basic information about corporate policies and procedures?

- Do some users need information that is specific to the department in which they work?

- Do other users need information that crosses departments?

- What training needs do you want to accommodate with information resources?

- Do your salespeople need access to information about your products? Do your customer services people need access to development information as well as customer support resources?

- Are information needs associated with particular company workflows? For example, what are the needs associated with the payroll system? Does everyone need access to information about personal deductions and benefits? Do clerical personnel need information about payroll practices for their jobs?

Each of these information needs can lead you to a dimension and a set of values for your Information Model. For example, you might have dimensions associated with workflows inside your organization. You might have dimensions associated with general managerial functions. You might have dimensions that concern only people in certain departments, like your product developers. You are most likely to discover that information needs occur throughout the organization instead of being isolated to one group.

Let's take the example of a software product-testing organization. The people responsible for testing need information that is part of the software development life cycle and is produced by the programmers. They might also need information that is produced by the technical communication organization that explains how the product is supposed to function. They produce information about their test plans and test results that is used by other organizations. In some cases, they might need information that comes from outside laboratories that test aspects of the product and issue reports. These reports might need to be made available to the sales organization for use in new business proposals.

By understanding the network of information needs, you can build an Information Model that enhances information access and retrieval among work groups rather than one that restricts access only to a particular work group.

Analyzing users' goals and tasks

Much information presented through the Web ignores the dimension of user tasks. Yet, you know that users often are looking for information to support successful task performance. Because so many Web sites are focused on the product rather than on the users, the emphasis has been on categorizing information by formal hierarchical systems in which users progressively drill down from high-level to low-level topics by following a logical progression of groups, topics, and subtopics.

By focusing on users' goals and the tasks they need to perform to reach those goals, you can provide a means of navigation that might be more closely related to ways in which the users need to look for and use information. Although traditional hierarchical categorizations might address tasks, the tasks are most often framed from the point of view of the system or the author rather than the user. In such cases, you find system tasks such as "Accessing the serial port" rather than a user-oriented task such as "Printing a file on your nearby printer."

Authors often complain that, when they try to associate information with job skills, they quickly learn that different customers often assign tasks to different people or job skills. Different organizations have different job titles for work that includes the same tasks; other organizations group the tasks differently among job areas. A clerk in one company might perform the same tasks reserved for a supervisor in another company.

By linking information to job tasks and workflow within organizations, you provide a significant way of allowing users to navigate through information. You also provide a mechanism for responding to differences among organizations.

Let's look at a typical workflow for tasks centered on preparing a monthly payroll, as illustrated in Figure 4-9.

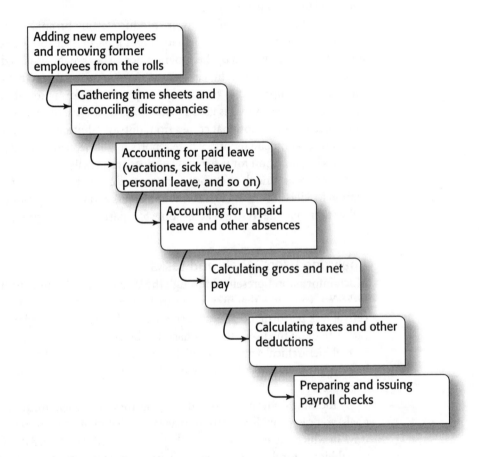

Figure 4-9 The table reflects a typical workflow in a payroll department.

Each of these tasks might be supported by a number of information topics. Some topics will address the responsibilities of supervisors to establish sound business practices. Other topics will provide procedures for ordinary and unusual tasks. Some topics might explain why and when special issues need to be addressed. Still other topics might explain the overall concepts needed to understand how the payroll system is supposed to work. Finally, topics might address typical errors or mistakes that are easy to make and include advice on recovering from them.

By categorizing information according to typical workflows and labeling information according to the tasks being supported, you can enable users to access the topics they need to perform their jobs. Even if different companies assign the tasks differently, user profiles can direct individuals to the information that supports their tasks rather than to all tasks. If one individual is responsible for adding new employees and changing employee information, that individual can generate an individual set of topics and instructions (the proverbial "my book") to support day-to-day tasks.

Customer organizations will also be able to designate information by internal user profiles that they construct. You might give customers the facility to build profiles of each of their users of your system or product and assign information resources accordingly.

The dimension of a user task can be handled by drawing the particular task from the title of the topic. For example, task-oriented information might instruct a payroll clerk on "How to calculate gross pay." The information type might be a procedure and the data used to identify which procedure it is might be taken directly from the task title supplied by the author. The author might associate the particular task with a larger grouping of tasks using a dimension and a value. For example, the task to calculate gross pay might be part of a larger group of tasks called "Completing the monthly payroll."

Analyzing the authoring community

Even though your user community is the primary source for your Information Model, you cannot neglect the authoring community. Users will want to access your intranet or extranet sites according to many different dimensions to find information resources to support their needs. Authors will need to locate information topics that they can reuse in different contexts for delivery to customers or employees or produce a new topic based on an existing topic by establishing a relationship between the topics so that most of the details are the same but some are unique.

In analyzing the authoring community, you should address these issues:

- What is the workflow now used to move information through the information-development life cycle?

- What roles need to be explicitly identified in the workflow? Writer? Editor? Translator? Approver?

- Do the authors need to keep track of the schedule on which information must move through the workflow? Is it important to know when something must move to the next step?
- Are authors handling multiple versions of the information at the same time during the life cycle? How do they currently keep track of the versions?
- Are the authors handling multiple releases of the information versions during the life cycle? How do they currently keep track of the releases?
- Do authors need to be able to identify where information is being reused by other authors?
- Do they need to know about multiple topics that are related to a primary information topic?
- Do the authors need to categorize by dimension any information that is created outside the organization, for example, by third-party providers or through syndication?
- Do they need to keep track of where the information originated outside the organization?
- Which dimensions do the authors want to control and which dimensions can be accounted for automatically?

Returning to the chainsaw scenario I mentioned earlier in this chapter, you learned that the authoring community consisted of technical authors preparing the user guides and the Web-based instruction, instructional designers planning the instructor-led training, marketing authors developing sales collateral for print and the Web, engineers developing the product specifications, and translators developing multiple language versions of the information. All their roles need to be identified through the dimensions of the information-development life cycle. In addition, the authors want to know where the information is in their workflow so that they can ensure that the information is ready to be released with the product.

Because many of the topics can be reused within the same documents or among different documents, the authors want to be able to track the history of reuse, which requires that another dimension be created with which to label the information modules. They hope that most of these dimensions can be automatically controlled by the content-management and workflow systems rather than require their input. They are busy enough tracking the user dimensions.

Many authoring dimensions need not be exposed to others in the organization, nor to external information users. They are there to meet the requirements of the authors' working environment. For example, one organization might want to code information about its products by the batch number used by the manufacturer. The batch number would be available internally, but would not be available to external customers going to the Web site to place orders.

Inventorying existing information

I strongly believe that a top-down Information Model is the best choice to ensure that you are organizing information to optimize user accessibility. However, I also understand that many organizations start with a considerable amount of existing legacy information. In inventorying existing information in preparation for integrating it into an Information Model, you need to consider

- What information should be transformed to meet new design and labeling standards?
- What information should be added specifically to support dynamic Web delivery or better information reuse?
- What information should be delivered in existing formats such as print, HTML, or PDF?
- What information should not be included in the new Information Model at all?

I have worked with a number of organizations that have decided that some information, especially legacy information associated with older products, should not be included in a new Web delivery strategy. They have decided to orphan that information and make it available only on special request.

I also believe that it can be a practical solution for dealing with some existing information to create metadata dimension/value wrappers that describe the content in terms of the major metadata dimensions already identified but leave the information in whatever format it was originally created. For example, groups might decide to produce Word and Adobe FrameMaker documents as PDFs and simply identify them for retrieval through full-text search or using the dimensions of the Information Model.

Still other information needs to be transformed to meet the needs of the Information Model. Chapter 5, *Developing Information Types and Content Units*, explains how to transform information so that it meets information needs more effectively and provides more opportunities for repurposing.

Identifying existing Information Models

Much of the existing information you need to review will be organized into hierarchical groupings or unique Information Models, depending upon the preferences of the author community. For example, you might find information collected into books so that the topics can be easily published and shipped to users.

For instance, you often find corporate policies and procedures collected into volumes of information. Your human resources department might produce an employee benefits manual or a manual for new employees. Your payroll organization might have a manual on handling the payroll. Each department might have its own procedures.

In a study for Federal Express, I found policies and procedures for ground operations (the people who pick up and deliver your packages) collected in a series of manuals. The information was organized by geographic area. One manual addressed procedures for the United States; another manual addressed international procedures; a third manual contained international procedures used in the US.

Other information might be organized according to job functions. Federal Express, at the time of my study, produced a manual for ground operations supervisors.

Public Service Company of Colorado produced a series of 18 manuals for the various stages of inventory control called the Storekeepers' Manuals.

A technical communication organization is likely to have a large set of information collected into various hierarchies or tables of contents. The hierarchical relationships are reflected in the tables of contents of an entire library of documentation. Some documents are organized according to the parts of a product; others are organized by job function like system administration and end-use; others represent stages in a typical workflow like installation and maintenance; still others represent different collections of information presented in print, HTML, and help systems.

As you inventory existing information collections, as illustrated in Figure 4-10, be careful that you do not assume that the existing collections or packaging solutions are effective. You might find that information is collected together because of convenience or tradition. I found, for example, one technical communication organization that had divided information topics among books depending upon the likelihood that the information would change. Information that changed frequently was placed in one book; information that rarely changed was placed in another book. This arrangement was convenient for the authors but presented considerable problems for the users because they had no idea how changeable a particular piece of information might be.

In most cases, the information was collected for the convenience of its authors rather than for the convenience of the users. Your task is to relate the information in the resource to the top-down Information Model that you are building. To understand the relationships to the user requirements that you have identified, you will most likely need to decompose the collections, take apart the existing hierarchical relationships, and look for opportunities to identify topics that might be delivered in new ways to individual users.

Return to the dimensions you identified during your examination of the user and author communities. Consider the possibilities of task-oriented workflow, user goals, and job functions and think about product models, geographies, languages, industries, and so on.

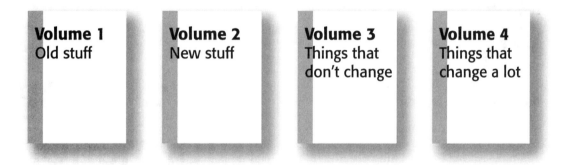

Figure 4-10 As you inventory current collections, consider if the existing organizations are effective or ineffective. Developing a new Information Model should encourage you to rethink existing hierarchical structures and discover more flexible models for collecting and packaging information resources.

Evaluating new information relationships

As you review existing Information Models, you must be alert to the possibilities for redefining and redesigning your information. The new Information Model you are building is likely to supersede existing models. You will remove information from existing collections or books and use the topics to develop new means of delivery that are more responsive to user needs. You will also return to many of the existing contexts for the information once you decide that those contexts remain effective.

The dimensions that you have identified as you construct your Information Model will become the metadata that you use in your content-management database to label your topics. Each topic will have one or more dimensions associated with it and one or more values associated with each dimension.

The metadata will be used by search engines to find the topics for new and existing authors who will want to modify the topics, create new versions of the topics, or place the topics in new contexts and relationships for users. The metadata of your Information Model will also facilitate the dynamic delivery of the information topics to users who have identified their information needs.

Not only will the metadata system of dimensions and values facilitate search, it will also provide Web designers with insights into the creation of navigation schemes on the Web sites. Navigation ought to be supported by the underlying Information Model even if the Web interface is not simply a reflection of the Model.

By creating a comprehensive Information Model for your information resources, whether it is for a specific part of your organization or the organization as a whole, you have built a tool that will aid both authors and users.

5

Developing Information Types and Content Units

"Now the users can tell what the information can do for them, not just which organization wrote it."

Your Information Model provides you with a framework for categorizing your information in terms of the dimensions you have identified in your user and author communities. However, another critical dimension is needed to categorize your information, based upon the nature of the information itself. That is the information type. If the first tier of the Information Model consists of the dimensions of use, the second tier identifies the range of information types used to produce content in your organization.

Dolores has to write a new procedure for the team members in the customer support center. She opens Arbortext's Epic Editor and selects the DTD for a procedure topic. The XML tags are part of the DTD, which helps Dolores to create the required information at the beginning of the support-center procedure. After she completes the procedure, she checks it into the content-management system. The workflow system automatically sends it to Kelsey, Dolores' supervisor, for approval. Kelsey decides that they need to link the procedure to a new policy statement. Kelsey uses Epic Editor to create the policy statement, using another DTD for the policy information type. She adds a policy link to the original procedure and checks it back in. Using two distinct information types allows the staff and supervisors to ensure that the content is consistent, follows the prescribed structure, and will be available to all the team members as soon as the director signs the approval form.

Information types are subject-matter-related categories of information that authors use to create a consistent, well-structured topic. An information type consists of a set of required and optional content units. A topic is any stand-alone chunk of information that does not require another topic to be understood. A topic can be any size, as long as the content is self contained.

Because topics rather than books (chapters, sections, and so on) are the key to sound information design for content management and Web delivery, a principal dimension of every Information Model is the information type. Information types provide the structure and content guidelines you use to author individual topics or transform existing topics so that they can be reused and repurposed.

Every topic of information you author and manage through your content-management system and every topic of information you bring into your content-management system from outside your organization should be assigned an information type and given a label for that type. In the example from the customer support team, Dolores selects a DTD that automatically labels her topic as a procedure. Kelsey's policy is also automatically labeled once she selects the policy DTD. By creating topics according to the rules established for the information type, authors can ensure that their information is consistent, well-structured, and reusable in a variety of different contexts. The information types are typically designed by an information architect who understands how the topics will be assembled into many different contexts. By defining information types explicitly, the information architect ensures a higher-percentage of reuse than if topics are written in an ad-hoc manner by individual authors.

Typical information types might include conceptual overviews, procedures, product descriptions, business benefit analyses, training materials, and so on. You need to encourage the authors in your organization to create specific topics according to the guidelines and standards you have provided for well-defined information types. Their topics will be better structured and more understandable than if they write long, rambling narrative accounts. The topics will also be more easily developed into an inventory of reusable parts and delivered out of your content-management system in unique ways.

In this chapter, you learn

- ■ what information types are
- ■ why they are important to developing your content-management solution and completing your Information Model
- ■ how to create usable, well-structured information types
- ■ how to add specific content units to each information type

You will know how to decide what information types are needed to deliver your content to your user community and how the information types that you develop should be used to create topics of content. In addition, I provide examples of many information types for reference.

What are information types?

As readers and users of information, you are all familiar with the concept of information types. You turn to our cookbook collection expecting to find many instances of the information type, recipe. You expect the recipes in a particular cookbook to be organized in exactly the same way. You are confident that you'll be given a list of ingredients before you see the step-by-step instructions. You know that you'll find the instructions for putting the ingredients together in the same place each time. Within a particular cookbook or family of cookbooks, you look for and are rewarded with consistent content and presentation (see Figure 5-1).

Figure 5-1 This collage of pages is from a diverse collection of cookbooks.

Although all recipes have some features in common, they might also have special features that distinguish the author or the collection. For example, one magazine usually includes wine suggestions at the end of the recipes. Another cookbook includes the history of the recipe and anecdotes about its origins. Still another names the individuals who contributed the recipes to the collection.

Cookbooks are not the only areas in which you expect to find consistent information types. Travel guides typically give us a consistent set of information about hotels, restaurants, museums, and so forth. Web sites such as Weather.com provide a standard presentation for each local weather report. Amazon.com has a consistent set of descriptions and reviews associated with each book it features. Magazines and newspapers typically include standard content in each issue, in addition to the changing content of the news stories and major articles. Even the news reports and feature articles follow a standard format. You've all heard of the concept of the inverted triangle, in which the most important information in a news article occurs at the beginning of the article with more detailed but perhaps less critical information coming at the end.

Information types become even more ubiquitous when you look at business and technical information. Companies publish standard operating procedures that attempt to follow a consistent structure and include consistent content. Law firms and real estate offices have standard contracts, deeds, and forms of all kinds. Companies develop standard forms for myriad transactions either in paper or electronically. Policies take on a common look and feel within a single organization.

When users find recognizable information types, they bring a set of expectations about what information will be included.

Widely reusable topics that can be delivered in new and dynamic ways depend on well-formulated, clearly defined information types. To assist authors in writing consistently and enable users consistently to look in the right place to find what they need, you need to create a unique template for each information type. The template might be as undemanding as a standard template in Word or FrameMaker, or it might be developed in XML or SGML. It might be defined by a Document Type Definition (DTD) in XML or SGML. It might also be constructed as an XML schema. Find more information about templates in Chapter 6, *Using Content Units to Structure Information Types.*

Information types can be strictly defined by exacting templates or loosely defined by guidelines. For example, a newspaper reporter does not write a news article using a template. Nonetheless, the article has a predictable structure because the sequence of elements in the article is a professional standard in journalism and is rigorously enforced by experienced editors who have internalized the "template."

Why do you need information types?

Technical information is often written according to standard information types such as procedures, concepts, warnings, specifications, and others. In developing training materials, instructional designers use standard ways of organizing information into lessons with objectives, exercises, procedures, concepts, and examples.

Having a standard information type makes the author's job easier because the structure of the content is predetermined. The author is free to concentrate on the details and nuances of the information content. Of course, the author is also free to choose which elements of the structure to implement when writing a particular topic.

Standard information types also make the users' tasks easier by producing a reliable content source in which the users come to expect the same types of information with the same structure each time. Such consistency enables the users to recognize the kinds of information they are looking for. When users click on a hypertext link to view information that is well structured using information types, they are rewarded by a consistent presentation of information, whether the information is contained in a news article, a weather report, a policy statement, a procedure, or many other possible types. Information types provide not only a consistent look and feel to the information available to them but also provide consistency in the content and structure of the information.

Inconsistencies invite confusion

Sometimes, however, Web sites and even more traditional print or on-product information collections suffer from the absence of clear, coherent information types. When inconsistency is the norm, every click is a surprise. Nothing ever looks the same from page to page. The users have little chance to develop a set of expectations and see them upheld. Although diversity is the spice of life, too many spices can give users a stomach ache.

Information types provide labels for the many categories of content that you intend to deliver through the Web. By assigning every information topic to an information type, you provide a method for organizing the information and assisting the users in locating and understanding that information. Standard information types reinforce consistency guidelines for authors, making authoring easier and faster.

Consistency within and across information types makes it easier for users to recognize the kind of information they are looking for. Information types provide not only a consistent look and feel to the information available to them but also provide consistency in the content and structure of the information.

Let's look at a Web site that could profit from developing a consistent set of information types. Ohio State University has a typical university Web site with lots of diverse information and little if any central control of the content or style of the site. The goal during a recent informal usability test of this site was to find out if the university offers a degree program in technical communication.

As test participants navigated through the Web site, they were engaged in a continuous decision-making activity. They wanted to make good decisions and resented having made bad decisions that forced them back to the beginning or made them continue to pursue a path further that already should have given them success.

One route test participants followed was to navigate to the specific Web pages of the departments that might offer programs of this type. Every department's Web pages not only looked completely different but contained different types of information. The users were continually surprised by what they found after each click.

The home page of the English department is illustrated in Figure 5-2. That home page contains

- an introductory statement about the mission of the Department of English
- a table of contents leading to other pages in the department's site
- a search button that searches only the department site
- the department's address and phone numbers

The home page of the Computer Science department looks entirely different and contains different information, as illustrated in Figure 5-3.

- Although the department is named and you are given its address and phone numbers, there is no mission statement on the home page.
- A table of contents in the form of buttons is available.
- Links are available to go back to the university's home page, the diversity program page, and the home page of the College of Engineering.
- No search button is available.

Other departments have equally unique home pages. Philosophy shows a picture of a campus building, presumably where the Philosophy Department is housed. The French and Italian Department has a picture of a stained glass window and a table of contents. Certainly the appearance of each page reflects the particular sensibilities of the departments. However, the absence of standard content is discon-

Figure 5-2 The Ohio State English Department's home page differs from the home pages of other departments at the university.

Figure 5-3 Notice the differences between the Ohio State Computer Science department's home page and the English department's home page in Figure 5-3.

certing. This lack of consistency in the information type "department home page" persists throughout the site. The inconsistency makes the information resource as a whole completely unpredictable. Most of the people who participated in our informal usability test quickly became frustrated and generally declared themselves anxious to quit the site in under five minutes.

I could present many other examples. The university Web site is typical of sites in which the layout of each Web page or grouping of pages is under the control of the people who author the information. The lack of an overall authoring and development strategy leads to the inconsistency. The addition of a set of information types would greatly contribute to improved access to the site's information resources.

To build a coherent Web site and provide a consistent set of information resources to users, think about standards. You need to develop standard information types as well as standard ways to develop a topic using an information type as a guide. Information types are important components of your Information Model, whether for a Web site or through more traditional print or on-product presentation of information.

Supporting the Information Model

At its base level, the Information Model spells out the primary dimensions that represent the point of view of each relevant group in the user community as well as the point of view of the authors. At its second level, the Information Model defines the standard information types that authors use to create topics. The information types help you organize and define the content that you want to manage, even if you do not define the content units that make up the information type. However, the most comprehensive role of information types in the Information Model occurs when the components of the information types are well defined. These components are called content units.

What are content units?

Content units are the smallest chunks of information you deal with in your Information Model and are, therefore, the basic building blocks of information types. They specify each category of content that might be found in a particular information type and guide the author in writing a particular instance of the information type.

Some content units are unique to an information type; others are common across information types within an enterprise; some might even be common across an industry if standardization is promoted industry-wide. They are most effectively designed when they identify the nature of the content rather than its appearance on the screen or on the page. However, some content units will be more specific than others. You will find that you most likely need a combination of specific and more general content units to build your information types.

Take, for example, the information type, News Article, that you find on so many news content Web sites, as illustrated in Figure 5-4. At the very least, a news article might be defined as a summary of a particular day's event. The information type might contain the content units listed in Table 5-1.

Table 5-1 Information type for a news article

Information type	Definition	Content Units
News article	A summary account of a particular day's event	Title Author Date Source Lead paragraph Detailed paragraph Subhead Conclusion

Although news articles appear to be rather free form, they have underlying structures that guide the authors in their composition. For example, a typical news article will begin with general information about the event and become more specific and detailed toward the end. The standard of the inverted pyramid style (most important information at the beginning, less important at the end) enables the editor or compositor to cut text at the end to make the article fit the page.

A marketing description of a new book is an information type that is routinely produced by book publishers. You find such statements included in Web sites that sell books, as illustrated in an excerpt for the Amazon.com site in Figure 5-5. Typically the description includes the title of the book, the author's name, the publisher's name, the date of publication, the ISBN, and a few paragraphs that describe the content and focus of the book, as listed in Table 5-2.

A different example comes from guidebooks like the *National Geographic's Field Guide to the Birds of North America*. Each bird description is written according to a strict structure. The description begins with the common name of the bird, its Latin name, and its length in English and metric units. The text that follows contains a narrative description, often comparing the selected bird with other similar birds. The call is then described, followed by the range and notes on the general habitat in which the bird might be found. To the left of the description is a map of the US showing the bird's general location in summer, winter, and during migration. See Figure 5-6 for an example of a page from the *National Geo-*

Date
Title
Author
Source
Dateline
Lead paragraph
Detail paragraph

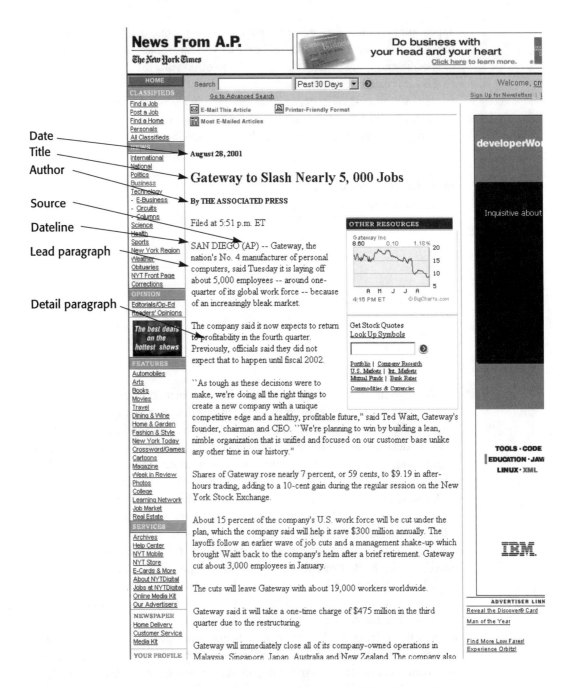

Figure 5-4 A typical news article from the Associated Press's Web site displays the standard structure of the news article information type.

Table 5-2 Information type for a book description

Information type	*Definition*	*Content Units*
Book description	An account of the focus and content of a book offered for sale	Title Author Date of publication Publisher ISBN Description

graphic's Field Guide. Table 5-3 lists the content units for a bird description in the *National Geographic's Field Guide.*

An even more structured example of an information type is a corporate policy statement, as illustrated in Figure 5-7. The policy statement generally consists of a title, several dates, a group responsible for authoring and updating the policy, a policy number, those to whom the policy applies, and several paragraphs that explain the policy. Table 5-4 lists the content units of a typical corporate policy statement.

Policy statements should be constructed consistently so that there is no confusion about what is intended or how the policy is to be applied.

Technical information contains many examples of structured information following standard information types. I might, for example, refer to the information types of a standard How to… help topic. For example, Figure 5-8 is a procedural help topic in Quicken. Table 5-5 lists the content units for the procedural help topic information type.

Each of these information types guides the authors in producing a consistent topic that users can rely on to present the information that they need. Without information types as a guide, any content is likely to become increasingly inconsistent. Whenever you have different authors, with different points of view, or even the same authors working over extended periods of time, information types provide a mechanism to ensure that information is developed and presented in the same way.

Supporting reuse

A free-flowing narrative almost never contains elements that can be reused in different contexts. Unstructured text is often unique in context as well as content; it is characterized by the often idiosyncratic style of the author. Except for the occasional quotation or definition of a term, almost nothing is reusable.

Title

Author

Date of publications

Publisher

ISBN

Description

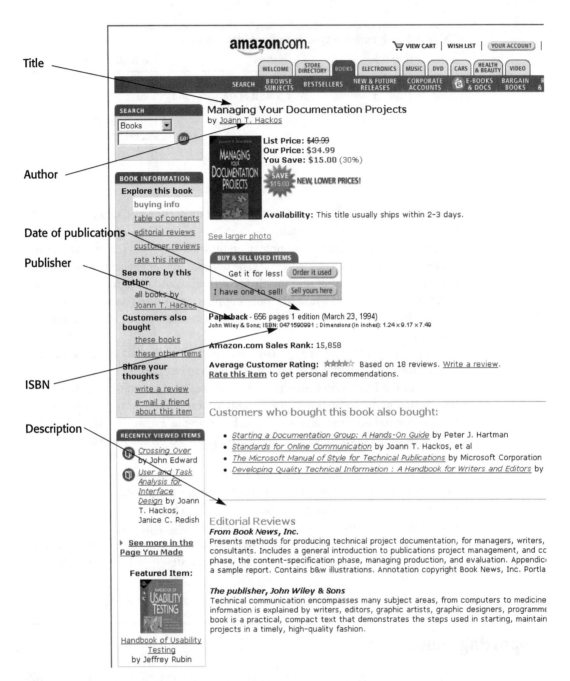

Figure 5-5 This is a typical book description from amazon.com.

Table 5-3 Information type for a bird description

Information type	Definition	Content Units
Bird description (National Geographic)	Description designed to assist the birder in locating the bird and distinguishing it from other related species	English name Latin name Length in English units Length in metric units Comparative description Call Range Habitat Range illustration

For an organization to foster reusable content, that content must be structured. The most straightforward way to encourage structure is to provide for a small number of information types.

Consider an example from *National Geographic's Field Guide.* In the print version of the guide, the description of the Mourning Dove is placed with descriptions of other doves from the Family Columbidae (the cuckoos). The guide is organized by the categorization of bird families favored by ornithologists. However, in another version of the guide, the designer might want to include the description of the Mourning Dove in a section on common birds of the United States. The same description might also be included in a section on birds that frequent backyard feeders and prefer feeding at ground level. In an online version of the guide, the user might find the Mourning Dove in a search of large mostly light brown birds, or that coo, or even among birds that prefer sitting on power lines.

Because the standard description follows a strict information structure, it is reusable in many different contexts.

The same might be true of the troubleshooting procedures in the online help system. In Quicken Help, entire sections are devoted to "What if something goes wrong?" However, the same troubleshooting information is also referenced in the "How to ..." context-sensitive topics available from inside the program interface, where the troubleshooting information is specific to the topic on the screen. The same troubleshooting topic is used equally well in more than one context because the troubleshooting topics follow a structured form and contain basically the same content.

As you build your Information Model, consider how information might be used in a variety of contexts. Such contexts might include user skill, workflow, task, industry, system, department, product, and many more. If you are able to maintain a standard set of information types as an integral part of your Information Model, you will be able to maintain consistency at the same time that you promote information reuse.

English name

Comparative description

Call

Habitat

Range Illustration

Latin name

Length in English units

Length in metric units

Range

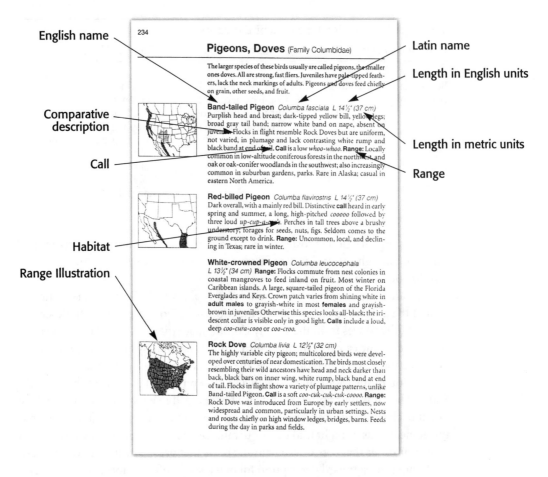

Figure 5-6 An example from *National Geographic's Field Guide to the Birds of North America,* illustrating the use of highly structured information types. Reprinted by arrangement from the book *Field Guide to the Birds of North America* by the National Geographic Society. Copyright © 1983, 1987, 1999, National Geographic Society, Washington, D.C.

Table 5-4 An information type for a corporate policy statement

Information type	Definition	Content Units
Corporate policy	A statement of a corporation's business rules	Title Initial date Revision date Policy number Policy application Authoring responsibility Statement of business rule

3-40 Meal Break Policy

Policy

The company provides meal periods for eligible employees.

Scope

Domestic Ground Operations hourly employees.

Management Responsibilities

Management is responsible for including a meal break and specifying the amount of time to be taken in the employee's work schedule.

Employees may be scheduled for meal breaks of 30–60 minutes. Meal breaks taken near the beginning or end of a shift are discouraged unless required by an operational emergency. The meal should normally occur between the third and sixth hour as the work load permits.

Meal breaks should not normally be scheduled to exceed 60 minutes. However, meal breaks up to 90 minutes may occasionally be scheduled if required by unusual circumstances.

The meal break requirement does not apply to employees working split shifts. The extended break between shifts is to be used for meals.

Employee Responsibilities

Employees are required to take scheduled meal breaks. Prior management approval is required for an employee to work instead of taking the normal meal break. The approving manager must indicate approval by signing the employee's time card.

In all cases, employees must enter the correct codes on their time cards to indicate the length of their meal break.

State Laws

In states where specific laws mandate meal breaks, employees are provided meal breaks in compliance with the law.

Date of Last Review

Last review of this policy was July 1992.

Figure 5-7 This example of a corporate policy shows a standard structure that is repeated in every corporate policy.

Table 5-5 Information type for a procedural help topic

Information type	Definition	Content Units
How to... help topic	Provides instructions for performing a task	Title Task description Numbered steps Screen illustration Definition of terms Tip Note Related topics

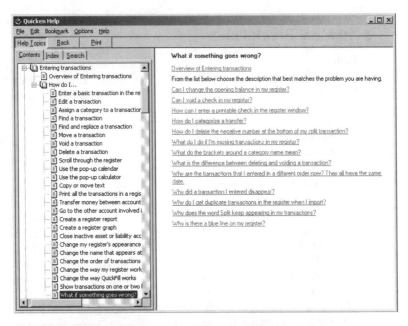

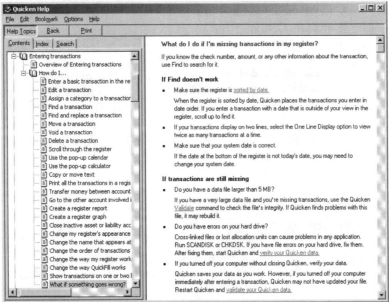

Figure 5-8 The example from Quicken Help shows that the same help topic can be accessed through different contexts. One point of access to the list of problems is under the heading "What if something goes wrong?" in the main help table of contents. A second point of access to the list of problems is a Troubleshooting link accessible from the "How do …" pull-down menu inside the Quicken program. These troubleshooting help topics are context-sensitive, relating specifically to the program function that the user wants to troubleshoot. (Copyright © 1985–2002 Intuit Inc. All rights reserved.)

Assisting authors

Information types help authors select the appropriate details to include in a topic and help them structure the detail in a consistent manner. Information types help ensure that important information is not omitted in some topics and included in others. Likewise, information types ensure that extraneous details are omitted when they are unnecessary or make the content more difficult to understand and use.

What if, for example, the authors of the bird descriptions, having no content or structural guidelines, wrote the descriptions differently each time. In some cases, the length and height data, which helps us distinguish large birds from their smaller cousins, may be missing. In another case, there might be a description that contains interesting information about behavior, only to find that behavior information missing in the next description. By writing the descriptions differently, the authors confuse their readers, who never know exactly where in a description to look for a particular fact or indeed if the fact will be found in the description at all.

This problem comes to light quite dramatically when you compare one bird guide with another; because the books are different, with different authors, publishers, and imagined audiences, the descriptions vary considerably.

A rather different guide, for example, is the *Stokes Field Guide to Birds of the Western Region*, as illustrated in Figure 5-9. In this guide, the information type that equals the bird description is not only organized differently, it also contains different content.

In the *Stokes Field Guide*, the identification information still includes the English and Latin names and the length, but the length is in English units only rather than English and metric units. Information is provided about the bird's appearance but where there were complete phrases in *National Geographic's Field Guide*, in the *Stokes Field Guide* you have brief identifiers separated by semicolons such as "long pointed tail; shorter outer tail feather broadly tipped with white." The content unit, "feeding," indicates that the bird eats weed, grass, and grain seeds, as indicated before, but the National Geographic authors told us nothing about the Mourning Dove's nest and eggs, nor anything about its courting displays, as does the *Stokes Field Guide*. Both authors provide information about habitat and voice, but *National Geographic's Field Guide* has a bit more about the bird's range besides the ubiquitous range map. The differences are sufficient to make the descriptions unique and require that a dedicated birder own both books rather than just one. Nonetheless, if the content of each book is put on a birding Web site, the users would be confused. Some information available from one source would not be available in the other source.

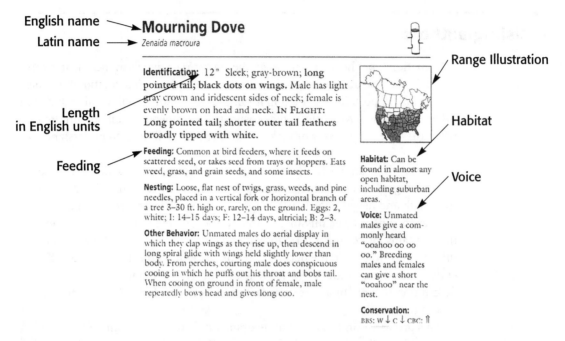

Figure 5-9 An example of a bird description information type from the *Stokes Field Guide to Birds: Western Region* by Donald Stokes. Copyright ©1996 by Donald W. Stokes and Lillian Q. Stokes. By permission of Little, Brown and Company, Inc.

If the information type = bird description were standardized, each author could still provide a unique range of details and observations. However, the same categories of detail would be available in both instances.

If authors write in idiosyncratic styles, it will be difficult from an organizational editing and review perspective to know if information is complete. Some descriptions will include some details and leave out others. How are the reviewers to decide what is complete and correct and meets the needs of the users of the information?

What happens when new authors join the team? Will they write their content in entirely different ways from the existing authors? If the information continues to differ or vary, it will become more difficult to find and reuse.

Structured information types provide assistance to authors in the following ways:

- All authors include the same content within each information topic.

- Authors are confident that they have included the necessary information and excluded extraneous or irrelevant information.

- Experienced and inexperienced authors write more quickly.

- New authors know what is expected of them when they begin to create their topics.

- Editors and reviewers know how to determine what is complete and correct.

- Authors are able to find information topics that meet their needs in a new context without having to rewrite.

- Information that is intended to be reused across media, products, and context is available for reuse without being rewritten or substantially revised.

In each case, information types are designed to make the authors' jobs easier.

Deciding not to use information types

Some information is meant to be idiosyncratic. Some authors are so clever and interesting that readers want to listen to their voices in everything that they write. Unfortunately, as interesting as the writing might be, it can rarely be reused and often can be difficult to categorize. The more unusual the content, the less likely that anyone searching for information about a subject will be able to find this piece of information.

If you want information on your Web sites to be accessible, you have to be certain that you can categorize and catalog it. If the content is so original and distinct, you might be unable to find it. In fact, you might have to work very hard to find ways to characterize the information content. So, you still need information types, even though you might have some information types that will only include labels surrounding the information as a whole rather than the purpose and structure used to create the information in the first place.

Deciding when to use information types

Your analysis of the information types you need in your Information Model should be based on two important perspectives:

- the user community
- the business and product requirements

The users' information requirements are the most important perspective needed to create a successful Information Model. If the users cannot find the information they need to perform successfully and reach their goals, then the content-rich information resource would be judged unsuccessful. Without an understanding of the users' perspectives, the authors will write what they happen to know about—which might be a great deal—rather than what is needed and necessary.

In Chapter 3, *Taking a Close Look at Your Information Resources*, I discussed in detail how to analyze the information needs of your user community. If you have not gathered your user requirements, it is highly likely that the information you provide will neither meet the users' needs nor fit the users' conceptual model of how information should be organized and retrieved. Your selection of information types should first be determined by the way your users think about the information.

Information types in the birding guide

In studying the approach of the birding guide authors, you might gain insight into how they believe birders will use the information. The information type, bird description, suggests that the people using the information might both see and hear the bird, hence information about appearance and voice. The authors also note that most birders are likely to see or hear the birder in its ordinary habitat so that they describe the typical conditions where the bird is most likely to be seen. They also note that the bird has regular ranges, often depending on season (winter, breeding, and migration). The information about places birders might see the bird, depending on the time of year, will be helpful in differentiating a commonly seen bird from one that is only passing through. Knowing whether a bird is common or unusual in a particular place is also helpful. A birder is more likely to scrutinize a bird that is unusual than one that is common to a location. If I'm not likely to find a Greater Roadrunner in New Jersey, I'd better take a really careful look at a strange bird before announcing to the world that I've found a rarity.

By knowing a great deal about the audience, the authors of birding guides determine how much and what kind of detail they should provide in the information type = bird description.

Information types in the cookbook

Cookbooks or cooking magazines use a strictly defined information type in communicating recipes even though the recipes they present come from a wide variety of sources. For example, the recipes in *Food and Wine* magazine have the following content units:

- title of the recipe
- quantity served
- list of ingredients
- instructions for preparation

Figure 5-10 shows a typical recipe from the Food and Wine Web site, containing the standard content units.

As long as these standard content units are included in each recipe, a few variations are permitted. Some recipes conclude with the name of the chef. If the chef is famous, the recipe title might be preceded by the chef's name. Some recipes include a note about wine or beer, identified by a small wine or beer glass icon.

In a recipe for Fried Oysters with Pancetta and Leeks, you are informed that "Lager beer—such as Heineken—is one way to balance the bite of cayenne, vinegar and arugula here; another is bubbles. California brut sparkling wine, such as Domaine Carneros or Scharffenberger, would be ideal for the purpose."*

In some cases, the recipe may begin with a a content units that is a serving note or a caution. For example, in the recipe for Blackberry-Polenta Bread Pudding, the magazine writer notes that "At Nana's [his restaurant], Scott Howell [the chef] serves this rich dessert with a lemon curd sauce; he often uses blueberries in place of the blackberries."†

The health-conscious, low fat recipe Web site from the US Department of Agriculture takes an entirely different focus. The healthy recipes begin in the traditional way, as illustrated in Figure 5-11.

Each recipe concludes, however, with a content unit that contains nutritional data. The nutrition table (as a content unit) lists calories, fat grams, cholesterol, fiber, and sodium per serving, plus all the vitamins.

In each case, the cookbook authors have determined what details their particular users want to know.

Developing technical information types

The advantage that the birding guide and cookbook authors have, in comparison with authors of complex technical information, is the relative simplicity of their information types and the traditions that dominate the markets for this information. Standards evolve when information is used by similar audiences everywhere. Standards, like the standards for presenting recipes in cookbooks, are somewhat culturally specific, with different styles in different countries.

Technical information is not only more diverse but also has fewer traditions to govern the selection and development of information types. How then should an information architect select the appropriate information types to define?

The answer to this question must be grounded in knowledge of the users' information needs. The answer must also be informed by an understanding of research done in technical communication. This research suggests that certain

* *Food and Wine*, September 1995, pg. 94.
† *Food and Wine*, September 1995, pg. 66.

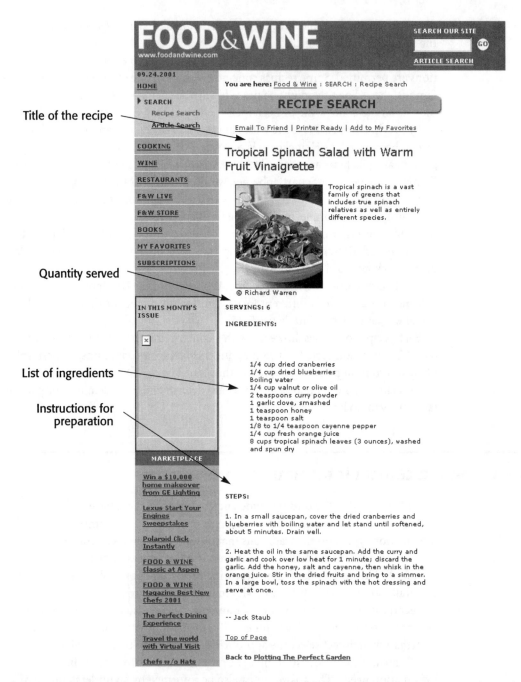

Figure 5-10 An example from *Food and Wine* magazine Web site, www.foodandwine.com, shows the standard content units of a Food and Wine recipe.

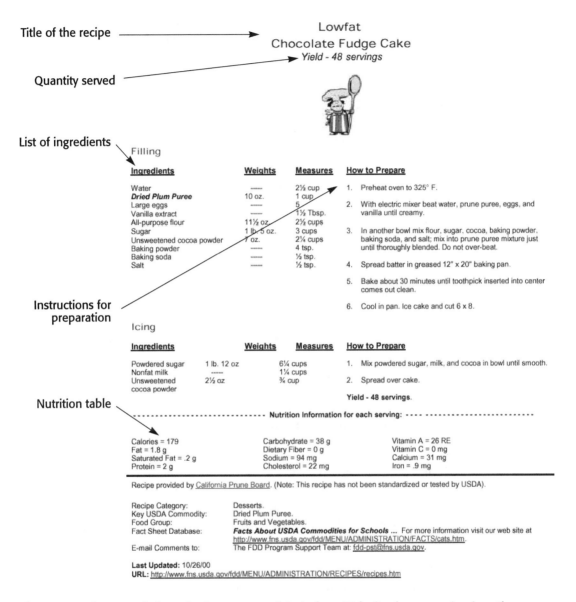

Title of the recipe ────────────────▶ Lowfat
Chocolate Fudge Cake
▶ *Yield - 48 servings*

Quantity served

List of ingredients

Filling

Ingredients	Weights	Measures	How to Prepare
Water	———	2½ cup	1. Preheat oven to 325° F.
Dried Plum Puree	10 oz.	1 cup	
Large eggs	———	5	2. With electric mixer beat water, prune puree, eggs, and vanilla until creamy.
Vanilla extract	———	1½ Tbsp.	
All-purpose flour	11½ oz.	2½ cups	
Sugar	1 lb. 5 oz.	3 cups	3. In another bowl mix flour, sugar, cocoa, baking powder, baking soda, and salt; mix into prune puree mixture just until thoroughly blended. Do not over-beat.
Unsweetened cocoa powder	7 oz.	2¼ cups	
Baking powder	———	4 tsp.	
Baking soda	———	½ tsp.	4. Spread batter in greased 12" x 20" baking pan.
Salt	———	½ tsp.	
			5. Bake about 30 minutes until toothpick inserted into center comes out clean.
			6. Cool in pan. Ice cake and cut 6 x 8.

Instructions for preparation

Icing

Ingredients	Weights	Measures	How to Prepare
Powdered sugar	1 lb. 12 oz	6¼ cups	1. Mix powdered sugar, milk, and cocoa in bowl until smooth.
Nonfat milk	———	1¼ cups	
Unsweetened cocoa powder	2½ oz	¾ cup	2. Spread over cake.

Yield - 48 servings.

Nutrition table

- - - - - - - - - - - - - - - - - Nutrition Information for each serving: -

Calories = 179	Carbohydrate = 38 g	Vitamin A = 26 RE
Fat = 1.8 g	Dietary Fiber = 0 g	Vitamin C = 0 mg
Saturated Fat = .2 g	Sodium = 94 mg	Calcium = 31 mg
Protein = 2 g	Cholesterol = 22 mg	Iron = .9 mg

Recipe provided by California Prune Board. (Note: This recipe has not been standardized or tested by USDA).

Recipe Category:	Desserts.
Key USDA Commodity:	Dried Plum Puree.
Food Group:	Fruits and Vegetables.
Fact Sheet Database:	**Facts About USDA Commodities for Schools ...** For more information visit our web site at http://www.fns.usda.gov/fdd/MENU/ADMINISTRATION/FACTS/cats.htm
E-mail Comments to:	The FDD Program Support Team at: fdd-pst@fns.usda.gov.

Last Updated: 10/26/00
URL: http://www.fns.usda.gov/fdd/MENU/ADMINISTRATION/RECIPES/recipes.htm

Figure 5-11 The example from the Department of Agriculture Web site shows a recipe from the California Prune Board. The recipe includes complete nutrition information, as do all the recipes on the site.

presentations of information are more effective than others in responding to users' information needs.

Most technical authors would acknowledge that their information is dominated by the information type procedure. Procedures explain, in step-by-step fashion, how users must proceed to complete a task and reach a goal. For example, consider a procedure for finding a word in a document with the elements or content units labeled as in Figure 5-12.

This procedure is very simple. It consists of just three content units: a title, action steps, and a feedback statement. The information architect might add additional content units such as an illustration of the Find word dialog box, an introductory paragraph that explains the purpose of the procedure, or a definition of a key term embedded in the introductory paragraph.

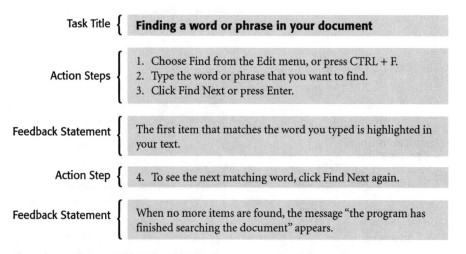

Task Title { **Finding a word or phrase in your document**

Action Steps {
1. Choose Find from the Edit menu, or press CTRL + F.
2. Type the word or phrase that you want to find.
3. Click Find Next or press Enter.

Feedback Statement { The first item that matches the word you typed is highlighted in your text.

Action Step { 4. To see the next matching word, click Find Next again.

Feedback Statement { When no more items are found, the message "the program has finished searching the document" appears.

Figure 5-12 The example shows a procedure with the content units labeled.

A typical set of information types for technical information

Procedures are an integral part of any Information Model that addresses how users are to perform tasks. Other information types emerge when you focus on users who need to reach task-oriented goals. Information types that support task-oriented users might include a

- conceptual overview
- warnings and other consequences
- statements of fact
- definitions of terms
- reference or background information

Each of these information types must have a definition that explains under what circumstances it is used and for what purpose. The information type must also consist of a series of content units arranged hierarchically if necessary.

Agilent Technologies, at the corporate level and with cross-organization representation, created a modular approach of integrated editorial guidelines, page designs, and screen designs for post-sales customers using print and electronic documentation about products. This approach is a refinement of Hewlett-Packard's Editorial Design System. Agilent's approach is described in the Agilent Identity System's Document Design Standard.

The design guidelines recognize that people prefer to read technical information in small, self-contained chunks, called modules. Modules are self-contained units of information that a customer can understand by themselves, without reference to other information. A modular design accommodates those who want to move quickly to a topic they need and easily find related topics. A modular design also facilitates the working of learning-product developers. By writing discrete, well-structured modules, they are able to reuse content in many different output media, including printing, help, CD-ROM, and Web.

The design standards recommend that information modules be divided into four information types:

- Task modules, which help a user get comfortable and learn new tasks
- Solution modules, which help a user solve problems
- Concept modules, which help a user understand background
- Reference modules, which help a user explore details of a product

In addition, the design standards provide for overviews that introduce the structure of the other modules to the reader. An overview might be used to introduce a compound document. It provides orientation, explains concepts, or outlines logical categories that a user might need to navigate an information collection.

The design standards include more detail and examples for writers who need to decide which modules to create for their users.

Figure 5-13 illustrates the guidelines for building a Solution module in *Agilent Identity System's Document Design Standard*.

Developing your information types

It's very tempting, especially when you already have thousands, hundreds of thousands, or even millions of pages of existing technical information, to tap the existing information as your source for information types. Nonetheless, it is more important to ensure that the information types you establish meet the needs of your users into the future. Otherwise, you will be preserving a legacy of information development that might have never been focused on customer needs or might no longer meet customer needs today or in the future.

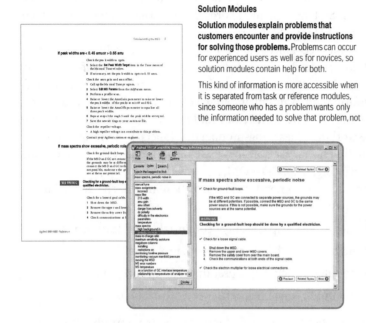

Solution Modules

Solution modules explain problems that customers encounter and provide instructions for solving those problems. Problems can occur for experienced users as well as for novices, so solution modules contain help for both.

This kind of information is more accessible when it is separated from task or reference modules, since someone who has a problem wants only the information needed to solve that problem, not

information about a related task or component. However, be sure to provide links and references between solution modules and related task or reference modules.

If the module heading is not sufficient to describe the problem precisely, begin a solution module with brief text or illustrations providing detail, such as the specific symptom or instrument reading constituting the problem.

Follow with steps, which can take the form of a list containing:

• checksteps ("Check that . . .")

• messages (displayed errors or states)

• symptoms (set of characteristics)

Order the steps in a logical sequence. For checksteps, this usually means the solutions are in the order of frequency. For messages, alphabetical or numerical order often allows quick access.

Follow each step with an explanation—text, substeps, or illustration—that helps a user find the remedy quickly.

Figure 5-13 Guidelines for building a Solution module in *Agilent Identity System's Document Design Standard.* (©Agilent Technologies, Inc. 2001)

The other difficulty that occurs when you try to develop information types from your legacy information is that, in most cases, the legacy information does not follow a standard. In many organizations, legacy information has been developed with only very loose standards in place and, even when standards were observed, the legacy information has been developed by different groups or individuals who have had their own ideas about what information to include.

If you examine much legacy information, especially technical information that makes up the bulk of information needed on intranets or Internets, you find information written in many different ways. It's extremely difficult to analyze for the type of content it contains. Much of the content appears to have little or no value to the potential user communities.

In one case, I was reviewing information that had been developed for users of a complex system. As I expected, I found many procedures for installing, configuring, troubleshooting, and repairing the system. Some of the procedures, especially those for troubleshooting, were quite well organized according to a standard structure. Other information, especially non-procedural information, was another matter.

Much of the conceptual, background, overview, or reference information presented in introductory sections of the documentation were almost impossible to classify. I found system overviews in more than one place, ostensibly describing the same system but written very differently with different content. I found lists of system components, but some lists contained one set of components and some lists contained other sets with some overlapping. I found numerous definitions of subsystems with no explanation of why those subsystems were being defined. I found even more pieces of information for which there was no context. The information just seemed to appear out of nowhere.

When I asked the authors why particular pieces of information were included in the text, the authors first responded with logical rationalizations for the content and only when pressed came to the conclusion that they did not know. Many of the pieces of information had been added by other authors, many of whom were no longer with the company and so were not present to explain their no longer obvious choices. Other information, equally puzzling, had been added because a customer had asked an odd question or an engineer or programmer decided that the information was important and should be included. In fact, there seemed to be little planning or rationale for what got included, and much of if was randomly inserted into the document.

In this case, it would be easier to start over rather than try to elicit structure from the legacy information. The information was not well structured to begin with; new information, following a predefined structure as illustrated in Figure 5-14, would be easier to write from scratch. The structured text can be rendered according to a style sheet as illustrated in Figure 5-15.

As you begin to review your existing information, be careful about trying to force labels onto badly structured or even unstructured legacy information. Rather, define what your users need to know about concepts, overviews, background, and reference. Begin with the requirements of your user community, rather than the legacy. You will often discover that a great deal of the information that has been included in the past is poorly organized and rarely used. You might decide that it is more effective to leave it out or to make it available only under special circumstances.

If your user community would profit from a strong overview, develop a way to define and structure that overview. If you define an information type = overview, as illustrated in Table 5-6, then determine what kind of content ought to be in an overview, rather than looking at overviews and trying to figure out what kind of content they contain. Although existing information can serve as a guide, it should not be the determination of structure.

An overview, for example, might describe an entire process flow. The process flow will allow the user to place the individual procedures that follow into a chronological context. An overview might provide examples of what the user might gain

```
<task_title>Retrieving Network Alarms</task_title>
<task_summary>Retrieving alarms is the first step in locating and clearing a fault.
Filtering and sorting helps you identify specific alarms and determine which ones
you must clear first. After you've cleared an alarm, retrieve the alarm list again to
find out if your troubleshooting has uncovered additional problems.
</task_summary>
<steps>
<step_item>Choose Alarms from the Search menu.</step_item>
<feedback>The Alarm dialog displays the alarms for every network element you
are logged in to.</feedback>
<step_item>Locate a specific alarm.</step_item>
<left_table_header>If you want to</left_table_header>
<left_table_list_item>Change the order of the alarms.</left_table_list_item>
<left_table_list_item>View alarms on a specific network
element.</left_table_list_item>
<left_table_list_item>View a subset of alarms.</left_table_list_item>
<right_table_header>Do this</right_table_header>
<right_table_list_item>Select a Sort button.</right_table_list_item>
<right_table_list_item>Select the element in the network element filter
list.</right_table_list_item>
<right_table_list_item>Choose Filter from the view menu. In the Filter dialog box,
select the network elements to Include or Not Include. Select the severity level
and Click On/OK.</right_table_list_item>
<step_item>To view alarm details, double click an alarm.</step_item>
</steps>
```

Figure 5-14 The example illustrates the new standardized structure for creating a troubleshooting procedure.

from a particular function; for example, an overview of networking might explain what a user might be able to do once a computer is connected to the network.

Two overviews, defined according to user requirements, might contain the content units shown in Table 5-6.

In a case in which your users need more than one type of overview, you might want to define the content units for a typical, generic overview before defining the specifics of different types of overviews. In the situation above, the process and functional overviews are subsets of a general overview information topic.

Information type definitions

Once you have identified the information types for your Information Model, you will need to create a guide for their use. Without a guide, the various authors in your organization might find it difficult to decide which information type is most appropriate for what they want to write. The guide should explain the purpose of the information type and quote instances of its use in the organization.

Retrieving Network Alarms

Retrieving alarms is the first step in locating and clearing a fault. Filtering and sorting helps you identify specific alarms and determine which ones you must clear first. After you've cleared an alarm, retrieve the alarm list again to find out if your troubleshooting has uncovered additional problems.

1. Choose Alarms from the Search menu.

    The Alarm dialog displays the alarms for every network element you are logged in to.

2. Locate a specific alarm.

If you want to	*Do this*
Change the order of the alarms	Select a Sort button.
View alarms on a specific network element	Select the element in the network element filter box.
View a subset of alarms	Choose Filter from the view menu. In the Filter dialog box, select the network elements to Include or Not Include. Select the severity level and Click On OK.

3. To view alarm details, double click the alarm.

Figure 5-15 The new standardized structure for a troubleshooting procedure is rendered for presentation in print.

Table 5-6 Example of overview information types and the content units they contain

Process overview	*Functional overview*
Title of overview	Title of overview
Purpose of the following the process	Summary of reasons for using the function
Typical starting point	List of advantages in using the function
Conditions affecting the starting point	List of disadvantages in using the function
Illustration of complete process flow	Illustrations of the function in use
Explanation of complete process flow	
Statement of where to go next	

A typical guide to information types might have the information illustrated in Table 5-7.

Table 5-7 Guide to the purpose and use of information types in an Information Model

Information type	Purpose	Instance of use
Procedure	To provide instructions that enable the targeted user to complete a task and to reach a goal	Turning on the Power PC Entering your personal information Adding contacts to the contact database
Conceptual overview	To enable the user to form a mental model of the process or task so that it can be completed successfully	The importance of battery conservation Why you must install the synchronization software first Why synchronizing is useful
Definition of terms	To enable the user to understand the meaning of a term in its context of use and relate the term to the conceptual model of the system that he or she is creating	What is synchronization? What are contact categories? What is the Startup menu and how does it appear?

Your authors will need to decide which information type to use for their content. The information type, in an XML-based Information Model, will be identified by metadata so that authors can search for particular information types in the database. In addition, if you define content units for each information type, by selecting a particular information type to begin authoring, the author will be supplied with a standard template of the appropriate tags.

One high-tech company has developed a set of definitions for its nine information types:

- concept
- procedure
- process
- glossary entry
- fact
- example
- figure
- assessment
- exercise

The following description explains how authors are to work with the concept information type:

Concept

(Product Description, Benefit, Overview)

When to use:

When you need to communicate a group of objects, symbols, ideas, or events which

- are designated by a single word or term
- share a common feature

You generally use a Concept when the content module can be written as:

- What is …?
- What are the types of …?

Sequence:

Typically, Concepts are sequenced before Process or Procedure content modules in the content module map. Concepts might include embedded Example, Statement, Glossary entry, and Media Objects modules.

Structure:

Concept information types contain the following elements:

- Introduction (required)
  - establishes the purpose of the content module and orients the user/learner to what they can expect
  - short and concise
  - no dependencies with other content modules

- Definition (required)
  - Clearly identifies related characteristics, optionally using bulleted list
  - industry specific
  - short and concise
  - emphasizes the term/concept being defined

- ■ Process (optional)
- ■ Example (optional)
- ■ Statement (optional)
- ■ Figure (optional)
- ■ Assessment (optional)
- ■ Glossary entry (optional)

Avoiding the proliferation of information types

In most cases, you will find that the information types you decide to create will be unique to the business and products of your company or organization. In fact, you are unlikely to define all the information types needed at first. Authors will request new information types to define information as they discover what users need. The information types you define are likely to grow.

The more information types you create, the more difficult it will be for authors to decide which one is most appropriate to their needs. I strongly recommend that you keep the number of information types as small as possible. Authors will attempt to get an information type defined for everything they have ever written in the past, leading to the proliferation of types that are not really unique.

Begin with a small set of information types that are clearly different from one another. Then, as authors want to add types, consider first if they can be accommodated by the more general types. If not, decide if the new information type is a particular instance of a general type. If it is, create a subinformation type based on the general type.

In the previous example, I created two subtypes for an overview. Some of the content units are common to both subtypes. In creating a template or DTD for the overview type, I would first create the general set of content units, then add the specific subset to each subtype definition.

Considering industry standards for information types

Unless an industry is required to follow standards, usually because of government regulation, companies organize their information in widely different ways. One company's method of writing a troubleshooting procedure might be completely different from another company selling almost exactly the same product. Companies in competitive positions with one another might believe that information quality presents a competitive advantage. As a result, they encourage their authors to be different. More likely, people in the information-development organizations are unaware of how information is presented by their competitors.

The differences are usually neither a problem nor an advantage—that is, unless the information resources are being used by the same customers. Customers often use products from competitors in their workplace. Related products are placed side by side and are often used by the same individuals. In the telecommunications industry, for example, an operator of a telephone system might combine equipment from numerous companies. Although the equipment can often be integrated successfully, the operators find that the information resources provided to them are organized and written differently.

One manufacturer might organize information according to tasks, another according to functions. Each manufacturer includes procedures, but the procedures include different levels of detail, are organized differently, and have different terminology for the same equipment and tasks. The operators would prefer that the information has common information types.

Movement toward common information types in companies with related products has been discussed in some industries, begun in a few, and effectively accomplished in some, in most cases because of regulatory requirements. The aircraft manufacturing industry organizes operations, repair, and maintenance information very similarly because the same personnel operate and repair planes from different manufacturers. Having information organized differently would likely increase repair time and cause mistakes.

Although common information types and content unit organization is a desired characteristic among customers, little progress has been made toward standardization in the high-tech industries. More standardization occurs in accounting practices and in electronic data exchange processes for business to business transactions. Perhaps this standardization takes place because accounting practices are more standardized than are high-tech operations and service practices. However, the customer is not served by the confusion. I have urged organizations in competitive and related industries to work together to institute common terminology and common information types. Perhaps this cooperation will increase as content management and Web delivery of information become more widespread.

Web delivery highlights differences in approach to information development and dissemination. It is easier to hide differences in books than on a Web site. An individual company's lack of standards is also more obvious on a Web site because information users can easily experience differences in design and organization as soon as they click and open different documents. On some Web sites, every click on a different document results in a surprise. None of the information is organized uniformly or written consistently.

Because the Web reveals poor information-development practices to the buying public, an individual company is best served by increasing the amount of standardization, especially by developing standard information types. Among companies, the lack of standardization is also more obvious than ever before—a good reason to increase communication and collaboration among information developers throughout an industry.

IBM's DITA standard

In an effort to promote the development of standards around information types and develop a consistent XML architecture for technical information, IBM information developers constructed the Darwin Information Typing Architecture (DITA). The intent is to create an open source standard that others can use to specify more detailed information types based on the global type called the topic. The IBM team has specific three specific technical information types, derived from the topic and named concept, procedure, and reference. In the following vignette, Michael Priestley and David Schell describe the conceptual model underlying DITA. For more information and the XML DTDs use the URL at the end of the vignette.

The Darwin Information Typing Architecture

Michael Priestley, Dave A. Schell

The Darwin Information Typing Architecture (DITA) is an XML-based architecture for authoring, producing, and delivering technical information that promotes reuse of content, design, and process. It consists of a set of design principles for creating information-typed topics and for using that content in various ways, including help, Web portals, and books.

DITA simplifies the creation of audience-specific content, DTDs, and processes. It is based on principles of modularity and reuse that allow not only the fast deployment of customer solutions but also the painless evolution of those solutions as customer needs, and our understanding of them, evolve. It is based on the following basic principles:

Topic orientation

DITA focuses on the topic as the smallest independently maintainable unit of reuse. This allows authors to focus on writing topics that efficiently and completely cover a particular subject or answer a particular question without dwelling on the various places the topic might end up being read.

Information typing

DITA focuses on information types as a way to describe content independent of how that content is delivered. Instead of creating chapters and appendixes, authors can focus on writing concepts, tasks, and reference topics using structures and semantics that remain valid regardless of how the information reaches the reader.

Specialization

DITA allows authors to create more specialized information types, so that the structures and semantics of the information are as specific as they need to be for a particular audience.

Inheritable processes

DITA-aware processes, such as publishing and translation, work automatically on more specialized types and can also be specialized themselves.

Embodied in architectures

These principles are embodied in two architectures:

Information architecture

The information architecture describes what a topic is and what the three core information types are (concept, procedure, and reference). This provides a basic level of consistency across all DITA content, which allows for reuse of infrastructure and interchange of content across the entire range of possible information types.

Specialization architecture

The specialization architecture describes how new types of topic are derived from more general types of topic, and it describes how specialization-aware processes can access topics at whatever level of specialization they require. For example, a generic print process may treat all types as just topics, and a task-indexing system may treat all task types as just tasks.

Affecting content, design, and process

Topics can be authored as context-free chunks that can be reused by reference in multiple contexts without affecting the topics. Control of reuse is moved out of the topic and into the context, making both topics and contexts easier to maintain. By contrast, large documents that are conditionally processed to produce multiple outputs quickly run into problems of scalability: with each new output, new conditions must be added to the source, and ultimately the source becomes unmaintainable. Without the separation of content from context, reuse does not scale: your source becomes less maintainable with each additional reuse context or condition, and contexts can collide or accumulate as they compete for space in the topic content.

Topic types can be designed as specializations of more general types, reusing the general type design by reference. This makes it faster to create new types and requires less maintenance because there is no duplication of shared declarations. And since the new types can be processed just as if they were the more general type, content in the new types can be deployed immediately, giving customers immediate access to the more specific content categories and structures.

Topic transforms can also reuse code from more general transforms by reference. The new process can be created faster than if there were no model and requires less maintenance than if it were created from scratch. And since the new process reuses the more general process, it can even handle less specialized information, or otherwise specialized information, as well as more specialized information. In other words, a type-specific transform will automatically process unknown content in terms of the lowest common denominator between the transform hierarchy and the content's type hierarchy.

Reuse by reference lets DITA solutions be deployed quickly, maintained centrally, and improved cheaply.

Gives us focused content, design, and process

As a result, we can afford to provide customer-specific solutions (delivering the content our customers need, sorted and categorized according to their priorities) without compromising portability or flexibility: meeting the needs of users today, but not at the cost of meeting their needs tomorrow.

Where to next?

For more information, including DITA DTDs, transforms, papers and a discussion forum:

http://www.ibm.com/developerworks/xml/library/x-dita1/index.html

Michael Priestley is a writer and XML developer with IBM Canada and DITA's specialization architect

D. A. Schell, PhD, is Strategy and Tools Lead, IBM Corporate Information Development Leadership Team

Common XML standards enhance cross-company collaboration

Standardization, using XML as a mechanism, increases the opportunities for intra- and inter-company collaboration on information development. The development of information types as part of a comprehensive Information Model provides an opportunity to institute standard XML metadata tags throughout a particular industry. If companies could agree upon which information types to use, they could increase the uniformity of the information they deliver. For example, an industry might agree to label their information types as the following:

- hardware description
- software description
- hardware diagnostic
- software diagnostic
- hardware replacement procedure
- software error-correction procedure

With such labels, at the very least, all customers could identify the basic components of the information library across manufacturers.

By using XML metadata and tags in common, each manufacturer of a product would add to the standard presentation of information.

However, information types alone will not provide enough standardization for highly technical information delivery. The information developers must go inside the information types to standardize the content units that are the building blocks of the information types.

6

Using Content Units to Structure Information Types

"And all of our procedures will look like this..."

Each information type needs a semantic map that shows what components it contains and in what order they need to appear. For example, a product data sheet is typically well organized in many product development organizations, containing content units in a predictable order. Every time customers review a data sheet, they can depend upon finding the same content units they need, most often in the same order they have become used to.

The same can be said for other types of highly structured information like procedures. A corporate procedure might contain a standard series of content units designed for internal use. An instructional procedure provided with a product might contain a series of content units that define what the users need to complete the task successfully.

In this discussion of structure, I emphasize using XML as an important tool for creating templates and guidelines that ensure that structural elements within modules are reusable and variable, depending upon the dimensions that the content manager decides are required by the customers.

Relating information types to content units

Let's look at descriptions in Table 6-1 of the information type identified as bird description from two different field guides.

Table 6-1 Different content units support a common information type

Publication	Information Type = Bird Description
National Geographic's Field Guide to the Birds of North America	Drawing English name Latin name Length in English units Length in metric units Description Call Range Range map
Stokes Field Guide to Birds of the Western Region	Photograph English name Latin name Length in English units Description; male; female Feeding Nesting Other behavior Range map Habitat Voice Conservation

The content units provide a standard structure inside each information type, but the standard differs depending on the author's intention and the publication. Either structure guides the author within each publication to produce the appropriate content in a uniform way, and the standard structure provides an opportunity for the reader to find specific information quickly and easily. Once the reader shifts from one guide to another, some of the details change.

Given the differences in approach, the user's task of finding discrete pieces of information is still enhanced by the way the content units are organized and labeled. What if the same structure were written as a narrative? Consider this example of the bird description written without the standard structure in place.

> Bewick's Wren — Thryomanes bewickii L 5 1/4" (13 cm) Long, sideways-flitting tail, edged with white spots; long white eyebrow. Subspecies differ mainly in dorsal color. Eastern T.b.bewickii, is bright reddish-brown above; south Texas criptus duller, but still tinged with red. Widespread eremophilus of western interior is the grayest; western coastal races grow browner and darker as one travels north. Northwest calaphonus is dark, richly colored, with a rufous cast. Song variable, a high, thin buzz and warble, similar to Song Sparrow. Calls include a flat, hollow jip. Found in brushland, hedgerows, stream edges, open woods, clear-cuts in the east. Sharply declining east of the Rockies, especially east of the Mississippi. (National Geographic *Field Guide to the Birds of North America*, 1999. Third Edition, Washington, DC: National Geographic, pg. 334)

If the narrative were also written somewhat differently each time, readers would have considerable difficulty finding the details they need.

In the cookbook examples in Figure 6-1, I showed the differences from one cookbook publisher to another, even though the recipes contained the same basic information.

In the communication of consumer information about high-tech products, you would find similar differences among content units in information types. In the next example, note how a cell phone manufacturer explains how to use the same function in two different user guides for two different models in Table 6-2.

Granted the functionality is slightly different in the two examples. Model A uses a key called Talk while Model B labels the same key SND. However, that difference provides little justification for changing the basic information this much.

In each case, the information for one model appears to be written nearly independently of the other model with no corresponding improvement in usability. Because the users are likely to have either Model A or Model B, they will never know the difference. However, the manufacturer would have been better served and could have reduced information-development costs by using a single source for the same information for both models. If the functional description were written once and stored in a content-management repository, that description would be available for use in the documentation for both phones.

Consider the changes in the language in each of these paragraphs in Table 6-3 from the same manufacturer.

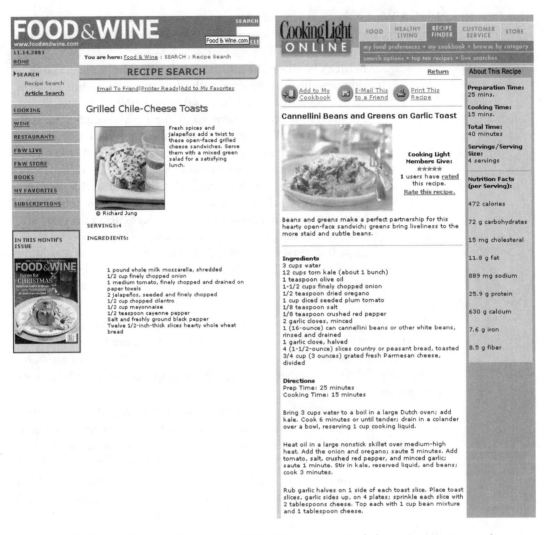

Figure 6-1 Similarly designed recipes show slightly different structural elements or content units.

The differences in wording are trivial; in fact, it's obvious that both authors began with the same source paragraph. However, the differences require that two paragraphs be independently composed, updated, reviewed, and translated, significantly increasing the cost of development and production over time. Both of these statements are labeled Important. It would be wise to ensure that they are both equally correct and equally readable, a goal better served if they were the same.

Table 6-2 Functional descriptions in two models of one manufacturer's cell phone

Model A	Model B

Emergency calls
 	
    Before attempting any emergency calls, see "Emergency Calls" on page 82 for important safety information.
 	
1.   If the phone is not on, switch it on.
 	
2.   Key in the emergency number for your present location (e.g., 911 or other official emergency number). Emergency numbers vary by location.
 	
3.   Press Talk
	To Make an Emergency Call
	
	    Before attempting any emergency calls, see "Emergency Calls" on page 65 for important safety information.
	
	1. Switch your phone on and make sure service is available.
	
	2. Press and hold CLR to clear the display. Enter the emergency number (e.g., 911) and press SND. Give your location and do not end the call until permission is granted.

Table 6-3 Different emergency call information in two manuals from the same manufacturer

Model A	Model B

IMPORTANT!
    Official emergency numbers vary by location (e.g., 911). Only one emergency number is programmed into your phone to be dialed automatically by Emergency key 9, which might not be the proper number in all circumstances.
	IMPORTANT!
	    Official emergency numbers vary by location (e.g., 911). Your phone has an emergency number programmed into your phone that can be dialed automatically with Emergency Key 9. However, this might not be the proper number in all circumstances.

Defining the content units for each information type

Content units, like information types, should be defined organically, depending upon the needs of the users of the information and of the subject matter itself. Some organizations would like to depend completely on a set of predefined content units because their developers claim that the predefined structures are found often in technical and business information. Although such "standard" content units might be reasonably ubiquitous, they are less likely to meet the needs of a particular audience and subject matter.

To decide upon content units to include in an information type,

- understand the background, education, and prior experience the users are likely bring to the situation of use.

- determine what information must be present for the user to complete a task successfully or understand a key concept, process, description, and so on.

- designate some content units as required for the information type and some as optional. The required content units are those that make the information type recognizable and understandable in and of itself. An optional content unit supports some users at different experience levels.

Let's review the tutorial information type designed by Autodesk for its AutoCAD Learning Assistance. Figure 6-2 shows an example of a tutorial for Placing Raster Images in Your Drawing Files.

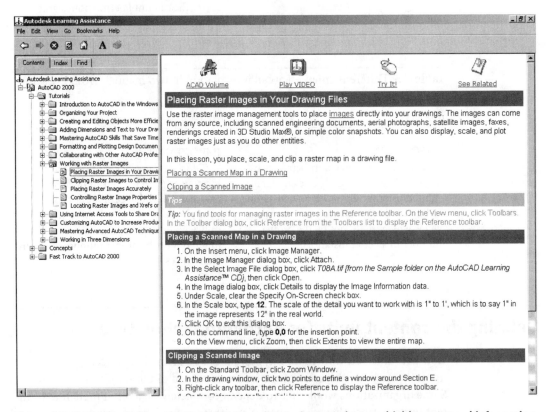

Figure 6-2 An example from the AutoCAD Learning Assistance shows a highly structured information type, the tutorial. (Image provided courtesy Autodesk, Inc. Copyright 2001. All rights reserved.)

This information type consists of the following content units:

- title of the tutorial task
- purpose statement containing an example and definitions of terms
  - hypertext link to command reference
  - hypertext link to concept topic
- introduction to the lesson sentence
- subtitles of the individual lessons with hypertext links
- tip noting the location of tools in the Graphic User Interface
- subtitle of the first lesson
- step-by-step procedures for completing the lesson
  - hypertext link to a command reference
- subtitle of the second lesson
- step-by-step procedures for completing the lesson
  - hypertext link to a command reference
- tip containing a selection short cut

The only optional content unit in the tutorial is the tip; all other content units are required. This same structure is followed for every tutorial in the Learning Assistance. The tutorials are identical in structure except for the tips.

Creating a uniform structure allowed AutoDesk instructional designers to produce tutorials quickly with more than one writer and ensure that they were all written in exactly the same way.

An XML structure for the tutorial information type would look something like the one in Figure 6-3.

The structure for the content units was determined before the tutorial was written, rather than the other way around. The structure was developed from an analysis of the user's needs rather than derived from an existing tutorial.

In general, I recommend analyzing and designing the structure of the content units in an information type through information analysis and design, grounded in user analysis. This practice produces more usable, consistent, and minimalist information types and content units than does either the practice of deriving content units from existing unstructured information or adopting a generic set of information content units from outside your organization. The only exception to the rule is when the structure is required by an outside regulatory agency.

The AutoDesk Learning Assistance has only two information types, the strictly defined tutorial and the free form concept. The concept is loosely defined, consisting of only a title and one or more paragraphs of text. The Raster Files concept, illustrated in Figure 6-4, is typical.

```
<tutorial>
<tutorial_title>Placing Raster Images in Your Drawing Files</tutorial_title>
<tutorial_purpose>Use the raster image management tools to place <hypertext
link="concept">images</hypertext>directly into your drawings. The images can come from any source,
including scanned engineering documents, aerial photographs, satellite images, faxes, renderings created in
3D Studio Max&#x00AE;, or simple color snapshots. You can also display, scale, and plot raster images just as
you do other entities.</tutorial_purpose>

<introductory_statement>In this lesson, you place, clip, and scale a raster map in a drawing
file.</introductory_statement>

<tip>You find tools for managing raster images in the Reference toolbar. On the View menu, click Toolbars.
In the Toolbar dialog box, click Reference from the Toolbars list to display the Reference toolbar.</tip>

<lesson_title>Placing a Scanned Map in a Drawing</lesson_title>

<numbered_action_steps><step>One the insert Menu, click Image Manager.</step>

<step>In the Image Manager dialog box, click Attach.</step>

<step>In the Select Image File dialog box, click<emphasis>t08A.tif [from the Sample folder on the AutoCAD
Learning Assistance&#x2122; CD]</emphasis>, then click Open.</step>

<step>In the Image dialog box, click Details to display the Image Information data.</step>

<step>Under Scale, clear the Specify On-Screen check box.</step>

<step>In the Scale box, type <emphasis>12</emphasis>. The scale of the detail you want to work with is 1"
to 1', which is to say 1" in the image represents 12" in the real world.</step>

<step>Click OK to exit this dialog box.</step>

<step>On the command line, type <emphasis>0,0</emphasis> for the

insertion point.</step>

<step>On the View menu, click Zoom, then click Extents to view the entire
map.</step></numbered_action_steps>

<lesson_title>Clipping a Scanned Image</lesson_title>

<numbered_action_steps><step>On the Standard Toolbar, click Zoom Window.</step>

<step>In the drawing window, click two points to define a window around Section E.</step>

<step>Right-click any toolbar, then click Reference to display the Reference toolbar.</step>

<step>On the Reference toolbar, click Image Clip.</step>

<step>On the command line, type <emphasis>|</emphasis> and press <emphasis>ENTER

</emphasis> to select the last object place in the drawing.</step>

<step>Press <emphasis>ENTER</emphasis> to accept the New Boundary option.</step>

<step>In the drawing window, click tow points to define a rectangular boundary around the Section E
geometry.</step></numbered_action_steps>

<tip>You can select an image by using the shortcut menu. Right-click the image, then click Properties. Select,
copy, and paste the complete image URL address into the File Name.</tip>

</tutorial>
```

Figure 6-3 An example of the AutoDesk tutorial converted into XML tags.

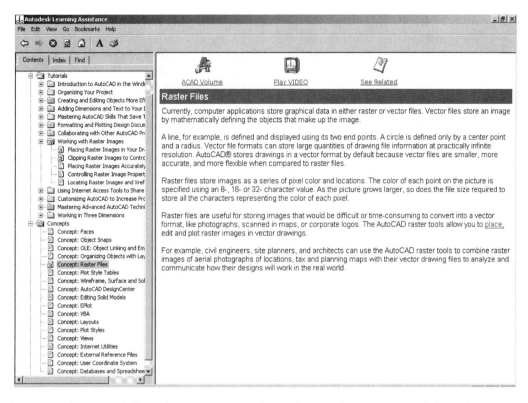

Figure 6-4 This example from the AutoCAD Learning Assistance shows a concept information type. (Image provided courtesy Autodesk, Inc. Copyright 2001. All rights reserved.)

The structure of this information type consists only of the following content units:

<concept_title>
<concept_description>
    <paragraph>
    <definition_of_term>
    <consequence>
    <example>
    <hypertext link = "concept link">
    <hypertext link = "tutorial link">
    <hypertext link = "command reference">

In most instances, I have labeled the content units according to their meaning rather than their format on the page. The exception is the <paragraph> tag, which is both semantic and indicates a generic format. You will find that you need both purely semantic tags that identify the type of content they label, as well as format tags that identify a more general structural element like a paragraph or a bulleted list.

Although it might not be possible to avoid all use of general structure tags, analyze the content required and label it in a meaningful way. Meaningful content tags identify information in a way that will be useful to the users who are searching for information and to the designers who want to provide an effective presentation of the information. For example, if you tag the <definition_of_term> in the concept information type, the presentation designer might be able to format the term in a way that makes the definition stand out. In addition, the search system will be able to hone in on the point at which a key term is defined rather than every instance of the term.

Content units should identify meaning not format

As the examples in this chapter indicate, content units should be designed to identify meaning not format. Unfortunately, you will find many organizations developing XML structures based entirely on the format tags already present in their style templates. A typical Word or FrameMaker unstructured template, for example, is likely to consist of style tags such as

> heading 1
> heading 2
> body text
> bulleted list
> numbered list
> header
> footer

These style tags indicate how the content is to be formatted for output to print or converted to HTML or other presentation styles. The style tags typically identify the font and font size, the line length and line spacing, the amount of indention, the spaces above and below a chunk of text, and so on. They tell almost nothing about the significance of the unit of content, nor do they tell the author what to include or exclude when writing a topic.

To move toward an XML-centered Information Model, you need to develop what are called "semantic" tags—tags that describe and specify the *type* of content you intend to include in the content unit. For example, a typical set of semantic tags for the content units in a specific information type might include the following:

> task title
> action steps
> purpose statement
> warning
> consequence

feedback statement
definition
process overview

You need to use semantic tags for two purposes: to guide authoring of the information topic and to assist in accessing the information for search mechanisms that target the content of the information. Semantic tags enable more focused and intelligent searches because information is categorized by its meaning rather than by its presentation.

NCS Pearson, a provider of applications, services, and technologies for the education and testing market, has created a set of information types to accommodate both print and Web forms of user assistance. One example of a user-assistance type is the Procedure Web Page. A Procedure Web Page displays when a user requests online assistance for a specific task, as illustrated in Figure 6-5.

Procedure Web Page

Subtype	Reusable Subtype	Components	123	Multiple
		Web Page Heading		
Procedure				X
		Procedure Heading	X	
		Introduction	X	
		Prerequisite	X	
	Step-by-step			X
		Guideline		X
		Tip		X
		Caution		X
		Reusable Table		X
		Image – Web		X
		Callout		X
		Troubleshooting		X
		Example (reusable subtype)		X
		Message		X
		Hyperlink		X
	Related Topic Links			
		Group Heading	X	
		Hyperlink	X	X

Figure 6-5 This diagram illustrates the content units that comprise the Procedure Web Page. Subtypes and content units in bold are required; other content units are optional.

Does that mean that you should never use style tags for your content units? Not at all. In some cases, you might feel there is no need to add specific details about content that is specified in a more open-ended form. In these cases, you might resort to stylistic tags such as paragraph or bulleted list. But in most instances, I strongly urge you to look for opportunities to add semantic-based metadata to your information resources. The more structural information you provide about the content through the use of the XML metadata, the more likely that your authors will find information they can reuse rather than rewrite. The more information you provide in semantic tags, the more likely that you will enhance the abilities of your user community to find the precise information that they need.

Avoid automated tagging engines that deliver only stylistic tags

Several tools are available that will convert unstructured documents or modules, usually those authored in Word or FrameMaker, into structured documents or modules using XML tags. In most cases, the tags inserted through the conversion process will be stylistic tags. Because the original text rarely contains semantic tags, neither will the automatically converted text.

Nonetheless, you might find it possible to map your original tags in the unstructured documents to semantic tags through customizing of the conversion tool. If your original documents have a meaningful structure, even if that structure is not reflected in the format tags, you can use the format tags and their relationship to one another to derive a semantic and often hierarchical structure.

With regard to our recipe example, each recipe in a particular collection of recipes is likely to be organized systematically and consistently. However, it's likely that only stylistic tags have been used to label a series of title, paragraphs, subtitles, and numbered lists. A typical Word version of a recipe would look like Table 6-4.

Such a recipe has a repeatable structure than can be formalized by converting the stylistic tags to semantic tags. The semantic tags label the content rather than the style of the content units.

The recipe with semantic tags is illustrated in Table 6-5.

The presentation style is defined at output, not during the authoring process.

A more questionable practice, however, is to take existing information and reformat it as XML without analysis and restructuring. Instead, the information is labeled primarily according to format structures like paragraphs, bulleted lists, numbered lists, and so on. Because the new XML structure contains no information about the nature of the content (semantic tags), fewer opportunities exist to deliver the internal content dynamically or to reuse the content in different contexts according to a variety of user dimensions. It might be possible to repurpose the content to different media types but not to leverage the content in different contexts without semantic tags.

Standard content units support consistency and usability

A standard structure for your information types lets authors come up to speed quickly and produce useful information that supports the content-management

Table 6-4 A recipe tagged with typical Word style tags

[heading 1]Marinara Sauce

[paragraph]My grandmother always made a very mild tomato sauce to serve with pasta. She avoided strong flavors like onion and garlic, preferring a more herb-based sauce with basil and parsley as the primary flavors. She also used a food mill to turn the tomatoes into a smooth sauce with no tomato pieces. The food mill also removed the seeds from the sauce, an important step because tomato seeds are bitter and add a bitter flavor to the sauce when they are not removed.

[heading 2]Ingredients

[list item]2 28-oz. cans of Italian tomatoes without basil

[list item]2 tablespoons basil

[list item]2 tablespoons parsley

[list item]2 teaspoons salt

[list item]2 teaspoons pepper

[list item]2 tablespoons sugar

[list item]Water as needed

[heading 2]Preparation

[paragraph]Puree the tomatoes in the food mill until nothing is left except skin and seeds. Be careful not to grind the seeds into the tomato puree. Add water to the food mill if needed to moisten the tomatoes during the processing.

[paragraph]Place the tomato puree in a large sauce pan over low heat.

[paragraph]Add the herbs and seasonings and cook for 2 hours, adding water as needed to prevent the sauce from becoming too thick.

[paragraph]Serve over hot pasta.

Table 6-5 The same sauce recipe with semantic tags

[recipe title]Marinara Sauce

[Introduction]My grandmother always made a very mild tomato sauce to serve with pasta. She avoided strong flavors like onion and garlic, preferring a more herb-based sauce with basil and parsley as the primary flavors. She also used a food mill to turn the tomatoes into a smooth sauce with no tomato pieces. The food mill also removed the seeds from the sauce, an important step because tomato seeds are bitter and add a bitter flavor to the sauce when they are not removed.

[Ingredient]Ingredients

[Ingredient Item]2 28-oz. cans of Italian tomatoes without basil

[Ingredient Item]2 tablespoons basil

[Ingredient Item]2 tablespoons parsley

[Ingredient Item]2 teaspoons salt

[Ingredient Item]2 teaspoons pepper

[Ingredient Item]2 tablespoons sugar

[Ingredient Item]Water as needed

[Preparation]Preparation

[Action Step]Puree the tomatoes in the food mill until nothing is left except skin and seeds. Be careful not to grind the seeds into the tomato puree. Add water to the food mill if needed to moisten the tomatoes during the processing.

[Action Step]Place the tomato puree in a large sauce pan over low heat.

[Action Step]Add the herbs and seasonings and cook for 2 hours, adding water as needed to prevent the sauce from becoming too thick.

[Action Step]Serve over hot pasta.

goals of the organization. Standard content units help ensure the information produced throughout your organization is consistently written and keeps experienced authors from wasting effort by inadvertently creating new information types ad hoc, time and time again. Standard content units enable new authors to produce information according to the goals of the organization rather than placing the training burden on editors and reviewers.

Users also know what to expect every time they look at information new to them. Procedures, concepts, and reference information, for example, have their own individual look everywhere they appear.

You will find that you need to constrain some information types very strictly with very rigid structures and many rules about the content units within them. In other cases, you can be more accommodating, encouraging the authors to design what needs to be communicated about a particular topic. The instructions on how to implement a content unit within an information type become an integral part of the author guidelines you need to produce.

Standard content units support reuse

Without standard structures for a variety of information types, you are unlikely to achieve sufficient reuse to make your content-management strategy more cost effective. The more variable and free form your information is, the less likely that components can be reused. If topics are written individualistically, rather than following well-designed information types, they will be too individualistic to be reused in different contexts. If information types contain widely different content units, they are less likely to fit into alternative content plans (tables of contents for print output, Web navigation, or CD-ROM design).

The more idiosyncratic and unique to context the writing becomes, the less likely that it can be reused in another context. The more structured the information, the more likely it will be and can be reused.

Standard content units speed development time

Standardizing the writing process by providing structure significantly speeds the time spent developing information. Authors who follow the standard structures report that they write topics more quickly than if they have to consider how to write in addition to what to write. Authors can concentrate on content rather than concentrating on format and structure. They spend time ensuring that information is correct, up-to-date, and relevant. They are also considerably less likely to insert irrelevant or extraneous content that might occur if they are unfamiliar with minimalist methods of information presentation. The structure presented by the content units enables authors to focus on the content that is critical to meeting user needs.

7

Developing Content Plans for Static Web Sites

"One for you…two for you…and one for you…"

Creating modular information and storing it in a repository is only half of the content-management solution. You must be able to publish the information—extract it from the repository and present it to users. To extract and assemble your modules to create complete documents, Web pages, or entire Web sites, you need to develop a content plan for your information resources. The content plan contains the instructions for assembling the modules into a navigation structure that users will be able to follow to find the modules of information that meet their needs.

Many, if not most, Web sites contain only static content. The information architect and information designer create a structure for the content that is created and assembled by authors. The content might include information presented in HTML or information presented in PDF, typically representing information that was prepared for traditional print output. The content is presented in only one way on the Web site. Users navigate through the site or use search tools to find the information they need. They can either read the information on screen or print it for reading away from the screen. The information on the Web site changes only when it is changed by the authors.

Content plans provide a method for describing the content and its organization for a static Web site. Content plans for static Web sites might address the organization of the entire site, might be limited to subsections of the site, or might be further limited to the organization of entire collections of information accessible through the site.

Content plans might represent individual collections of a subset of the content modules in your repository. Each collection might be tuned to the needs of one user community, one workflow, one product, or even one medium. Content plans provide the context and arrangement for the modules that make up the collection. Content plans for static Web sites become, when extended, the information architecture for the entire site or for portions of the site that present subsets of your information resources.

No matter what your technical or enterprise business applications, your content plans for a site or a subset of a site must be based upon the dimensions that you have already identified in your Information Model. For example, you might want to build a content plan for a Web site based on

- user roles in relationship to your products, services, or internal activities
- process workflows expressed through policies, procedures, and best practices
- subject-matter relationships based on any number of content categories
- information organized along product lines or service categories
- time-related information

Some of the output you make available through a static Web site might take traditional forms associated with print information. You might find yourself publishing to the Web:

- books and articles
- technical manuals
- white papers
- product specifications
- data sheets
- news articles
- press releases
- service bulletins
- policies and procedures manuals

Each of these individual documents is organized according to the hierarchy established by individual content plans. The content plans prescribe the sequence in which modules from your repository will appear in the document or on the static Web page. In many cases, the sequence established in the content plan is revealed through an expanding and contracting online table of contents.

The content plans are not, however, simply standard tables of contents. Although the plan for an individual collection might include a table of contents, the plan also describes the organizational rationale of the content and explains how that organization will support users' access to the information.

Despite the dominance of the book metaphor in the past, I strongly recommend that you consider using content plans to design more versatile ways of presenting content on static Web sites. Consider moving toward solutions that present information on the Web in more modular and accessible forms than long, hierarchical tables of content. You might want to present content in modular form in HTML, supported by a rich network of related topics through hypertext links. The relationship of the information modules to one another can be defined using a content plan.

Your Web site itself requires a content plan, commonly referred to as the Web site's information architecture. The information architecture outlines how, where, and when information modules will be made available and how they will be linked to other modules of information. The content plans for information-centric Web sites describe how static, browser-accessed content will be organized, assembled, displayed, and linked.

Defining the static content published to the Web is much like producing a content plan for traditional print output, although the table of contents is replaced with a map of the site showing how topics will be linked to one another and how they will appear in relationship to the navigational of the Web page.

In this chapter, you learn

- why content planning is important to your information design
- how content planning encourages you to build a context around otherwise independent modules of information
- what information a content plan should include
- how to develop content plans appropriate for static Web content, as well as traditional book-like documents

You also learn about publishing coherent, well-organized information by relating individual topics of information to one another. By establishing useful relationships among information topics, you present a more comprehensive and complete view of a subject and present the users with a context that supports and enriches the information topics they need.

Why is content planning important?

In developing a content-management repository that is flexible and supports the reuse of information in a variety of ways for your authors, you are likely going to develop a repository that contains many individual modules of information. A policy statement, an instructional procedure, the catalogue description of a product, graphics of a product or a part, a training exercise, and a section of a specification or the description of a completed project for a customer should be stored as separate and distinct modules within the repository. These separate modules of information become most valuable when they are presented in a rich context of supporting and related information. Content planning is the method I recommend to define those relationships and promote their efficient access by your users.

In some cases, authors and users will need to access an individual module out of context. An end-user of a telephone system might, for example, need a procedure for setting up a multi-company conference call. One of the hallmarks of well-written procedures is that they are often usable as stand-alone modules.

Stand-alone modules, however, have their limits. More often, a user will want access to information in a context. Consider, for example, the task of setting up that conference call on the new phone system. If you have never set up a conference call before, you want information right away that will help you complete the task. However, you might not know that several different methods are available for making conference calls. If the procedure you are looking for is presented in the context of alternative methods, you might decide that another method is more appropriate for the conference call at hand. The context, in this case, informs you that several related procedures exist and allows you to choose among them.

And what happens if the conference call procedure fails to produce the desired results? (For some of us, that happens most of the time.) Where do you find the relevant troubleshooting tips? Who is available to help solve the problem? If a carefully selected set of related topics is available, as illustrated in Figure 7-1, then the information user has an opportunity to search further for answers as problems arise or circumstances change.

Figure 7-1 A network of information modules enables a user not only to find the information needed to perform a task but also to access background information, additional related procedures, and troubleshooting hints.

In other cases, users might need to know about more complex interrelationships among information resources than might be required to complete a difficult technical procedure successfully.

The user might experience a typical scenario like this one in which the user is slowed down while trying to get the needed information from diverse sources.

User scenario for locating information on an intranet site

"I'm ready to install the new frame relay into our network. Where do I find the installation instructions for Model 7.1946? The instructions say I need to ensure that the network is synchronized after the installation. Where is the instruction for synchronizing the network?

These synchronization instructions are very complex. I better read a overview of synchronization first before I get started. I wonder where I can find that? What is something goes wrong with the installation and the synchronization? Where do I find the troubleshooting help? If I need to call customer support, where is the phone number? Or, can I send them an email?"

Getting answers to these questions can not only involve several different procedures, but the user must also understand the concepts behind network synchronization and troubleshooting frame-relay problems. The user might also need the phone number of the support person assigned to helping set up custom relays or might find it useful to enter a chat room with other people performing similar tasks.

By creating content plans that organize information for a variety of user needs, the information architect establishes relationships among the topics to be drawn from the repository. The architect also accounts for alternatives in the selection of information to be included in a content plan, depending upon the circumstances of use.

Building a context for your information

Why bother with content plans? Why do you need to present information in context? Isn't it enough to deliver the right module at the right time to the user? Why can't the user just use the search mechanism on the Web site? Don't they prefer to search rather than navigate anyway? Under what circumstances would a user be interested in more than a single module of information?

The problem with disembodied modules is just that. They have no body of information in which to exist. They lack a context, a place to go next. The user searches for a specific topic but has no idea where to go next or what information might be valuable in understanding the topic itself.

So—do you present a disembodied module to a user? What if the single module of information is not sufficient? Where does the user go next? What information is related? What comes before? What follows? What else is relevant? What more should he or she know about this subject matter? What additional information resources are available?

Some years ago, a group of researchers conducted an interesting experiment with a group of people who were experts in tracking down legal information. The researchers asked the legal research experts to find all of the relevant information pertaining to a particular question of law. Then they sat back and watched. The experts were able to find only about 15 percent of the relevant information on the topic, even though they were trained to investigate legal problems. The researchers were themselves aware of the 100 percent of relevant information that was available in the database.

Even more interesting, when the legal experts were asked what percentage of the total relevant information they had discovered, they responded with estimates of from 80 to 85 percent. They believed that they had found a much higher percentage of the relevant information than they had. If experts can't do better than 15 percent, what hope is there for the rest of us who are novices at searching or are unfamiliar with the subject matter? How do you find the help you need?

Legal experts are able to extract only a small amount of the available information from a large and difficult-to-access repository. Even though a high percentage of the information they need remains inaccessible, they are unaware of the limited results of their search.

In this case, the total body of available and relevant information would have provided the needed context for solving the legal problem. Even though the expert legal researchers knew a great deal about constructing queries and searching in a variety of ways, they had failed to identify the entire body of information within which the problem should have been solved.

You have probably encountered similar problems in searching for information on the Web. Have you found all the available information? Is there anything critical that was missing? No wonder that most people rely on several, not just one, Internet search sites. You try your queries again and again, hoping that more relevant information might turn up. Unfortunately, most of the information you find is not relevant at all. In fact, most searches return high percentages of irrelevant information and low percentages of relevant information.

Content planning, in the hands of the information architect, provides a mechanism for addressing the accessibility problem. If an information architect, working with users and subject-matter experts, constructs one or many sets of relationships among information topics, then particular users, if their needs fit the contexts available, will be more likely to find the sets of relevant information that they seek.

What is a content plan?

A content plan is a description of the organization of information and the rationale that drives the organization. It draws together modules of information from the content repository and presents them as a coherent whole. In its simplest form, a content plan describes a sequence of information arranged in a table of contents. The table of contents presents the modules of information in a linear order, with a logic that should represent the points of view and needs of the users and the nature of the information itself.

Content plans are used to describe more than simple tables of content. On a Web site or in an online help system, the modules of information are organized into a network of related topics, some clustered around particular subjects areas, other set in a pattern of linked modules that might represent a step-by-step sequence, a logical information set, or other patterns appropriate for the users.

Finally, content plans can be used to structure the relationships among individual modules. One module might become the hub of an information network, with other modules related to it through relationships identified by your Information Model.

The content plan at its best represents the view of an information architect who is familiar with the users' point of view and the context in which the information modules are best presented. The content plan represents how users will navigate through and link to information modules.

Content plans for collections of information topics

Content plans for static collections of information on a Web site might be represented by an electronic form of a table of contents. The electronic table of contents lists the interrelated information that has been collected and the order in which it has been structured for ease of access.

The information architect has wide latitude in determining the order in which the modules are represented. The order can be based on a variety of principles of structure. For example, a typical table of contents for technical information is organized according to one of these principles:

- chronological order of tasks to be performed (workflow or taskflow)
- functional order related to the design of a product
- tasks that range from easy to difficult to perform
- conceptual order to best facilitate the learning process

Many additional structures are, of course, appropriate for a variety of content. For example, you might organize internal policies and procedures according to the functional areas of the organization. A company might have its policies and procedures organized by department, such as human resources procedures or computer operations procedures.

The most effective organizational structures respond to the needs and points of view of the users of the information. Business and technical information structures will be most successful if they are based on an analysis of user goals and tasks.

Chronology

A chronological order, following a task flow from the beginning of a process to its end, is typical of business technical information. A technical manual that informs a user how to get started using a new product might begin with installation instructions and move through a sequence of events from configuration, first tasks to be performed, subsequent tasks to be performed, and so on. A business procedures manual might follow the order in which tasks should be performed to complete a process from beginning to end.

This part of the table of contents of my 1994 book, *Managing Your Documentation Projects*, is primarily chronological (Figure 7-2). It describes the information-development process from beginning to end. The chronological sequence describes the workflow to be used by the project manager.

If I were to organize a Web site around the topic of managing documentation projects, I might use the same chronological sequence in a navigation frame. The users would be able to access the individual topics directly from an expanded table of contents or by moving from one topic to the next topic in the chronological sequence.

Part Two: Starting the Project—
The Information-Planning Phase

Starting Projects on Time
    When does a project start?
    Getting publications in the communications
        loop
    Participating on cross-functional design teams
    Getting an early start
    When is early too early?

Defining the Need for Information
    The tradition of needs analysis
    When do we *not* need technical
        publications?
    Taking a minimalist approach
    The project manager's role in needs analysis

Creating the Information Plan
    Defining the purpose of the Information Plan
    Understanding the purpose of the development
        project
    Determining the publication goals and objec-
        tives
    Analyzing the audiences for the publications
    Developing a high-level task inventory
    Selecting media

Creating the Project Plan
    Timing early planning activities
    Setting up the planning team
    Finding early indicators of project scope
    Using page-count metrics
    Making a preliminary estimate of required
        resources
    Estimating project costs
    Creating a resource spreadsheet
    Creating a preliminary schedule of milestones

    Assigning roles and responsibilities to team
        members
    Selecting publication tools
    Planning for translation and localization
    Planning for testing
    Planning for maintenance
    Summary

Managing the Phase 1 Review Process
    Presenting alternative plans
    Communicating tradeoffs
    The quality/scope tradeoff

Part Three: Establishing the
Specifics—
The Content-Specification Phase

Creating the Content Specifications
    Understanding the purpose of the Content
        Specification
    Determining goals and objectives
    Analyzing product, audience, and environment
    Performing a detailed task analysis
    Organizing the publication
    Estimating pages and graphics
    Downsizing the publications
    Combining the Information Plan and Content
        Specifications

Revising the Project Plan
    Reviewing the Content-Specification
        estimates
    Estimating revision projects
    Revising resource requirements and
        schedules
    Leveling resources
    Scheduling the next phase—Implementation
    Planning for production

Figure 7-2 This is the chronologically ordered table of contents from *Managing Your Documentation Projects* (Hackos, 1994)

Task activities

Another typical sequence for technical information represents user activities that are not sequential but might be performed in any order. If you look at the manual that comes with your cellular phone, you will likely find that it is organized according to the tasks you might want to perform with the cellular phone. Figure 7-3 shows a typical task-oriented organization of topics. By clicking on a topic, the user is hyperlinked to the appropriate module. In addition, users can easily move from topic to topic using the browse sequence.

Introduction
Safety Information

Getting Started
Introduction to Batteries
Installing Batteries
Charging Batteries
Overview of your Phone
Using the Key Button

The Basics
Turning Your Phone On
Reading the Indicators
Placing and Ending Calls
Receiving Calls
Redialing Numbers
Basic Tone Controls
Taking Shortcuts

Using Memory
Introduction
Making the Best Use of Memory
Storing
Recalling
Pause Dialing
Using Calling Cards

Using Messaging
Introduction
Receiving Messages
Viewing Your Caller IDs
Checking Your Voice Mail
Reading Your Messages

More Information Resources
Introducing the Menu Features
Your List of Phone Numbers
Learn how to store and recall numbers
Using Call Timers
Learn how to monitor the length of your calls
Setting Tone Controls
Learn how to adjust your phone's tone controls
Lock/Security Features
Learn how to control access to your phone
Phone Options
Learn how to personalize your phone's operation

Reference Information
Accessory
Troubleshooting
Glossary

Figure 7-3 Task-oriented information is used in the manual for using a cell phone.

Easy to difficult

Training materials are often organized in order of the difficulty. A training sequence might begin with information about concepts and tasks that are easy to understand and perform. At the end of the sequence, the customer might learn more difficult concepts and perform more complicated tasks. A similar sequence might be helpful in a technical manual that will be used by the customer as a self-instructional text. Figure 7-4 shows a typical set of topics for a training manual.

Classified Document Control

Lesson 1: Introduction to Document Control
> What You Will Cover
> Getting Started
> Using the *Student Workbook and Classified Document Control Handbook*
>
> Module 1: Understanding the Classified Document Control System
>
> Module 2: Identifying and Verifying the Markings of a Classified Document
>
> Module 3: Accepting Custody of and Protecting a Classified Document

Lesson 2: Getting Started with Document Mark-Up
> What You Will Cover
> Looking Back at Lesson 1
> Getting Started

> Module 1: Preparing a Document
> Module 2: Marking a Correspondence-Type Secret Document
> Module 3: Completing a Document Accountability Receipt
> Module 4: Copying a Classified Document
> Module 5: Completing a Document Transaction Receipt
> Module 6: Physically Transferring a Classified Document
> Module 7: Consolidating and revising Classified Documents
> Module 8: Destroying Classified Documents

Lesson 3: Advanced Document Mark-Up
> What You Will Cover
> Looking Back at Lesson 2
> Getting Started
> Module 1: Completing a Document Accountability Receipt for Various Documents
> Module 2: Protecting a Classified Document

Figure 7-4 A content sequence is used for an e-learning program.

Conceptual

Many tables of contents are organized according to a logical structure suggested by the subject matter and the author's conceptual model of the subject matter. They usually begin with conceptual overviews of purpose and goals and end with details for action and implementation. Many types of structure are available to authors. The purpose of the traditional document-oriented content plan is to explain the design being proposed for the tables of content. See Table 7-1 for an outline of a document content plan and descriptions of the information required in each section.

If you intend to present collections of information on your Web site, then you need to write content plans that describe the sequence and explain the rationale you have used for your design.

Table 7-1 The recommended content plan for a static organization of information modules

Section	Description
Purpose statement	Summarize the user requirements that you are meeting in the design and development of the content for your static Web site.
Audience	Describe the audiences for whom the content is being assembled. Include references to the user profiles that you have already established for your audiences. Divide the descriptions into audience groups.
Tasks	Describe the goals and tasks for each audience group outlined above. Explain how the design of the site's content will meet the needs of each audience group and support its goals.
Usability goals	List the usability goals that you have established for the static Web site. A typical usability goal might include the time it usually takes users to find the information they need. Usability goals might also describe the performance goals for the users. In stating a user performance goal, describe how the user will be more able to reach a goal and perform a task if the Web site is well designed.
Use scenarios	Provide the use scenarios that describe in detail how a particular user with a particular goal will find the required information resources. Begin with the primary use scenario for each user group. Then, as needed, include the secondary scenarios and explain exactly how they are intended to function.
Architectural rationale	Describe the organizational plan you have for the content including how the various collections will be structured. For a collection, describe how each topic or set of topics relates to the needs of the audience groups and their tasks described above. For the individual topics, explain how your organizational structure for the individual topics supports the goals and tasks of a particular audience.
Taxonomy	Describe the categories you intend to use to label information. Describe how the word choice matches the user's words for describing functions and tasks. Describe how the category names (headings) will relate to the specific information types that you have designed for your topics. Explain how users will find particular information types.
Outlines	Provide individual outlines for each collection that you are including in your content plan. Annotate the outline by detailing the modules you will create, the information types you will use for each module, the user objectives you will meet, and the metadata you will use to access and assemble the individual topics in the repository.

A typical content plan for a collection of topics contains the following information:

- goals and objectives of the users with respect to the information
- brief descriptions of the subject matter, the intended audience, and the environment in which the information will be used
- the tasks likely to be performed by the users (if the information is task oriented)
- an explanation of why the author has organized the information into a particular sequence
- the topics to be addressed, annotated with notes about what will be included (information types) and why (user objectives)

For more information on content plans for static information resources, see Chapter 10 of *Managing Your Documentation Projects* (Hackos, 1994).

In the sample content plan in Figure 7-5, the subject matter is related to a particular technical product.

The content plan allows the authors to identify the appropriate modules in the database and organize them into the predetermined structure. The author assembles the modules into a virtual structure that helps the user navigate the information on the Web site. If the assembly process is automated, drawing the modules directly from the repository, the modules will refer to the content in the Web server repository. Because you maintain an active relationship between the working repository and the Web repository, if the content in any of the modules is changed, the collection will reflect the changes immediately.

With a content-management system, authors can easily assemble new collections by developing content plans and creating lists of modules in which the module name is linked to the modules of information in the repository. The HTML-based modules on the Web site might be read on screen, printed, or saved in PDF and made available electronically for download and printing.

You will find considerable information distributed through the Web that began as traditional books and has been made available to users in modular form. The expectation is that most users will download the all the individual modules intact and print them, using the paper copy as a primary reference. An increasing number of users will read some portions of the text on screen or will attempt to print one or a few pages.

Creating a set of recipes

Our database of recipes provides a good illustration of how modules of information stored in a content-management system might be assembled into compound Web-based documents. For example, an information architect might want to design a new online recipe site offering only healthy recipes (low fat, low cholesterol, and so

Content Plan—Small Business Phone System

Client company/project: Small Business Phone System
Writing project manager: Jim Brown
Tentative start date: January 19

Please review this content plan and return your comments to the project manager by 2:00 p.m., February 2. Please contact Jim Brown at 555-7586 if you have any questions about the content plan.

Audience Profile

System managers in small businesses where SBPS is installed are those responsible for maintaining the telephone system in the company. They are probably among the following:

- owners of the small businesses
- office managers
- administrative assistants
- secretaries
- receptionists

In addition, switchboard attendants may sometimes serve as system managers.

These infrequent users know few, if any, telephony terms. However, they need to learn some telephony terms so that they can communicate with maintenance technicians.

They know nothing at all about what is involved in programming a telephone.

Because most small businesses will not require modifications to the system more than once a month or once every two months, managers will probably not program the system often. They might, therefore, have to relearn some of the programming tasks each time they modify the system. In addition, there is apt to be a relatively high turnover among system managers. The *System Manager's Guide* will be used frequently as a training tool.

Overview by Section

Introduction to managing your telephone system

The Introduction to the *System Manager's Guide* briefly explains the customer's role as manager of the system and why the management tasks are important. It explains how information is structured in the Guide and where the manager should like to find specific topics.

Getting Started

This section introduces system managers to the SBPS telephone system and to the *System Manager's Guide*.

Figure 7-5 This typical content plan is for an individual volume in a technical library.

Section Objectives

After reading this section, users will:

- recognize the installation form
- know which features the system manager can change and which features the SBPS technician must change
- recognize special terms used in the *Guide*
- understand the kinds of telephone equipment available with the system
- understand what they need to know before they can begin modifying the system
- understand the basic steps for modifying both telephone and system features

Section Organization

Section 1 includes the following topics:

What features can I change?

This section explains in general terms the system-wide features and the individual features affecting only one telephone that the system manager can change.

Understanding this guide's conventions

This topics explains the terms used to identify the people who are involved in setting up and using the telephone system.

Equipment

This topic lists the five kinds of telephone equipment available in the SBPS system and explains how to use the telephone to modify features.

Before you begin modify'ng features

This topics describes

- the feature sections
- how to use the ON-OFF lamps
- how to change feature values
- how to use the keys, buttons, and feedback tones

Modifying telephone and system features

This topics provides two tutorials with annotated step-by-step instructions for modifying

- a telephone feature, including logging on, targeting a station, identifying the feature, changing the lamp setting, exiting the management code, and logging off
- a system feature, including logging on, identifying the feature, setting a multiplier, changing the feature value, exiting the management code, and logging off.

Figure 7-5 This typical content plan is for an individual volume in a technical library (continued).

on). The information architect decides to organize the site in two ways: the primary ingredients and the place in the meal. She begins the online information with an introduction that includes nutrition guidelines and ideas for modifying other recipes so that they are healthful as well. The collection of topics is listed below:

- creating healthy meals
- appetizers
- soups
- sandwiches
- salads
- breads
- breakfast
- pasta and grains
- beans
- poultry
- fish and seafood
- meat
- vegetables
- desserts and cookies
- sauces and dressings

If the information architect were using a content-management system, she could assemble the recipes from the repository based on the metadata that identifies each recipe according to meal order and major ingredient. She could add introductory material and store that in the repository. She might allow users to print the modules as a book or offer users an HTML-based version on the Web site. The information architect might specify to the Web designer a navigation frame and a search mechanism based on the metadata.

A majority of organizations publishing significant amounts of information on the Web are creating their compound documents in just this way, especially if they are already using a content-management system. Information modules are collected and assembled into traditionally structured compound documents and delivered as document collections.

The shortcoming of this method is that much of the information assembled into collections might be more usable if the collections were tailored to the needs of particular users. For example, technical and business-oriented collections that contain information intended for use by people who have very different roles and responsibilities. A technical manual might include information intended for the technical specialists who install and repair the equipment as well as information for those who use the equipment on a daily basis to run an operation or accomplish a specific objective. Individuals might find the information more usable if it were tailored to their work roles.

Similarly, some individuals want to know how to perform only one particular procedure, such as filling in a time sheet. They don't want to search through a mass of information that includes every one of the company's payroll procedures and policies. A Web site that delivers only the required procedure will be much more usable than an entire collection of procedures and policies that have not been separated into individual modules.

Content planning is the method you use to design how information will be displayed on an intranet, extranet, or the Internet for employees, customers, and business partners alike.

Topics maps are excellent tools to implement content planning, either for static or dynamic content, as described in the following vignette.

Topic Maps

Eric Freese, Isogen (division of Datachannel, Inc.)

The concept of topic maps takes content planning to a new level. The topic map model allows information architects and users not only to create topics and connect them but to provide information about why the topics are connected and in what circumstances the connections are valid within a given set of information. It is also possible to define mechanisms that can create new topics and relationships based on a set of rules.

A well-designed topic map can serve multiple functions at the same time. It can help users find necessary information by following a defined set of links. It can also provide the ability to see information related to the topic that can then be browsed whenever and however the user wishes. It allows a user to query the information within the topic map to locate more accurately the desired pieces of information. These actions are all possible because a topic map is built as a layer of topics and the relationships between them. The topics and the relationships exist separately from the information being described, allowing them to be modified without having to modify the source information.

As the user browses through a topic map, any given topic can act as the hub of the entire information network. When a link between topics is followed, the view of the network changes slightly because a new topic is acting as the hub. It is still possible to see the previously browsed topic, but a new set of information is also available.

The information within the topic map can be presented in any format, be it in an expandable table of contents or a set of links on a web page. The format is largely controlled by the use case requirements for the information being presented.

The topic map model is made up of three main building blocks: topics, associations, and occurrences. A *topic* is an anything a user might want to describe or model. Topics can be organized into a taxonomy by defining types, which are themselves topics. Topics can be related by defining *associations*. Associations consist of two or more member topics that play a specific role within the association. Associations can also be typed using topics. *Occurrences* allow topics to point to content, such as web pages or metadata.

We will use the recipe example discussed previously in this chapter. Consider a recipe for a grilled ham and cheese sandwich. Possible topics that could be defined include: recipe, ingredients (ham, cheese, bread, mustard, mayonnaise, etc.), classification (appetizer, soup, dessert, etc.), utensils, nutritional information, calories per serving, and preparation method (grilled, baked, sautéed, etc.). Recipes could be organized into a taxonomy using the topics of type "classification." By defining an association of type "recipe," the ingredients could be grouped together. In fact, another topic called "main ingredients" could be defined to divide the ingredients further and provide more intelligent access to the information set. The recipe association would then consist of topics playing the role of "main ingredient" (ham, cheese) and others in the role of "ingredient" (mustard, mayo, etc.). Possible occurrences of the recipe could include pointers to a Web page showing the complete recipe and/or pictures of the prepared dish. Occurrences can also include metadata about a topic such as preparation type (grilled, in this case) or calories per serving. If specific rules have been defined, it would also be possible to imply that the sandwich is served hot because it is grilled.

Association for a Recipe

Member Topics	Role
Ham	*Main ingredient*
Cheese	*Main ingredient*
Bread	*Ingredient*
Mayonnaise	*Ingredient*
Grilled	*Preparation method*
Ham & cheese sandwich	*Dish*
Knife	*Utensil*

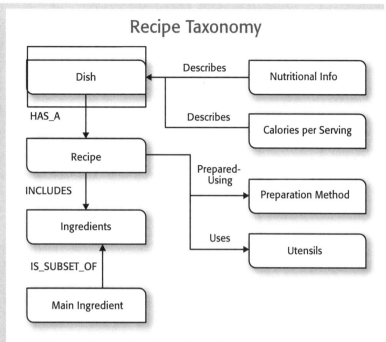

This diagram shows the relationships that you can establish using topics maps, including associations and occurrences.

Topic maps also provide the ability to provide filters for information being presented. Filtering is done through a mechanism known as *scope*. Common examples of scopes include language and user permission. By defining scopes on topic characteristics and associations, it is possible to mask the existence of some of the information within the topic map and within the information set as a whole. An application of scopes within the recipe model might include personal taste, so that a person who dislikes liver is not presented with a recipe for a pâté.

Building and using a topic map to assist access and navigation to a set of information allows the actual content pages to be left static. The browsing and presentation of the topic map information can then be done dynamically. As a result, access to a Web site can be filtered based on specific parameters such as user preferences or rights, while allowing the core information to remain the same. Only the path to the information is different.

Content plans for Web sites

Many information-centric Web sites include considerable information that is presented in book-like tables of contents. On a complex Web site, you will find a wide variety of information types:

- new product catalogues
- product specifications
- sales literature for downloading
- white papers
- monographs (concerning a particular narrowly defined subject)
- instructional manuals
- training materials

The information represented by these information types is organized to be read and used in a particular sequence. That sequence is predetermined by an author and remains static, much like a traditional table of contents. Most of the time, the original organization of the print documents is preserved in the organization of the online version of the information.

More interesting is the possibility of using the Web for information that does not fit neatly into books or for which books are irrelevant. Static information, which is information that does not change on a Web site unless it is updated by the authors, does not have to be presented in static structures. Nor does all the information need to be static. Some information can be updated automatically as it changes in the database. Other information can be reassembled according to the users' specifications. Still other information might change in response to the users' actions in searching for information resources. I discuss dynamic assembly and presentation of information in Chapter 8, *Developing Content Plans for Dynamic Web Sites.*

Planning static content for the Web

Despite the attraction of dynamic content, most content-rich Web sites are developed with static content defined by the information architect and the authors. The content is produced by authors either inside or outside the organization. When it is ready to be released, it is delivered to a webmaster who posts it to the site. The information on the site changes only when new content is delivered and deployed.

Such static content can conveniently be stored in a content-management system so that the Web pages can be generated automatically. This process saves the time required by individuals such as webmasters to post the content manually. Scripts that direct particular content to the Web site are developed so that the content is deployed when it is ready. In many organizations, deployment also means that content is moved from a working repository inside the firewall to a Web server outside the firewall.

The content plan provides the design for the Web site and is created by the information architect. The plan has its foundation in the Information Model originally created for the information resources stored in the repository. The content plan associates modules of information in the repository with appropriate Web structures. The plan also describes the architecture by means of which the information modules will be navigated, searched, and displayed and how they will be linked to one another.

Two planning issues relate to the presentation of content on a Web site: the overall navigation of the site and the context in which individual information modules are presented.

Navigation design

One of the primary responsibilities of the information architect is to design the navigational structure of the content-rich Web site. Overall navigation of a Web site is not in the scope of this book. For additional resources on Web navigation, see *Information Architecture for the World Wide Web* (Rosenfeld and Moreville), *Web Navigation: Designing the User Experience* (Fleming), *Designing Web Usability: The Practice of Simplicity* (Nielsen), and others listed in the bibliography. However, several issues affect the static delivery of content to the Web:

- delivering documents in PDF
- creating traditional linear structures (tables of contents)
- navigating using hierarchical structures (drill down)
- navigating using the search function

Each of these methods of delivering static content provides advantages and challenges to users.

Delivering documents in PDF

Many content-rich Web sites are designed to deliver documents solely in PDF. These electronic documents are facsimile copies of documents originally designed for print and are readable on-screen through the Adobe Acrobat™ reader. If the documents are prepared properly, the reader will find an expandable/collapsible table of contents in the left frame. By selecting an item on the table of contents, the reader navigates to the selected text in the right frame. The original book structure with chapters, sections, modules, and page numbers is preserved.

PDFs can be designed to be used and read on screen. In such cases, the page size is proportional to the size of the screen on which it will be viewed and links are placed within the text or navigation buttons are created on the pages. These replace the hierarchical tables of contents that usually appear in a frame on the left.

Although PDFs can certainly be read on a screen, they are typically designed to be downloaded to the user's own workspace and printed. They permit books or other similar long documents to be delivered electronically.

Despite the advantages of PDF, the format presents problems for many users. Downloads are often time-consuming, especially for long technical manuals. Searches are often difficult because, in many cases, PDFs must be searched one at a time. The PDF interface is often awkward to navigate, in part because the page structure is maintained, requiring users to scroll past margins at the top and bottom of each page.

PDF is a great format for printing extended text. As an alternative to providing only PDFs on a Web, organizations provide HTML based modules for on-screen reading and PDFs in background for downloading and printing. In this way, the user is able to print an effectively formatted page rather than an HTML page.

Creating traditional tables of content

Tables of content (TOCs) provide a context for information in a basic linear form. Many content-rich Web sites make the original documents available in forms that are more easily read online. Such documents are converted to HTML or other browser-compatible formats and presented with a full TOC. In most cases, TOCs appear in a separate frame and are expandable and collapsible much like they are in PDF. In other cases, the TOC is available within the Web page, allowing the user to navigate through the linear structure to find the needed topics. Because most Web-page TOCs require that the page be refreshed as the reader moves among sections, the process of navigating through the TOC to find a required topic can be tediously slow.

Navigating through a TOC online presents other problems to the user besides slowness. The user has to pursue a linear path to find a particular heading before opening and reading the text related to the heading. If the currently displayed TOC heading is a second-level or third-level heading, many topics are or might not be accessible except from inside other topics.

The user selects a heading and reviews the text for relevant information. Not finding the required information means traversing the TOC once again or many times in search of the appropriate topic. The navigation process is slow and awkward because the user must wait at each step for the page to display. No wonder that most users resort to searches. However, most Web sites offer only full-text search, searches that address only headings, or keyword searches that rely on indexes of terms. As a result, the search process might also fail to bring the user to relevant content quickly.

Some electronic books also provide additional access to the content through traditional back-of-the-book indexes and search functions to use within an individual volume or across several volumes in a library. Users who are familiar with the terminology used in the book or are familiar with the terminology generally used in the subject matter might find traditional indexes useful. The index items should, of course, be hyperlinked to the accompanying content.

Some online solutions also provide indexes in which individual index items refer to more than one topic, much like the index in a book refers to more than one page number.

However, you will find that many online indexes decrease in usability by referencing too many topics. Research on indexing shows that users are best able to use indexes that refer to no more than two or three topics, not 10 or 20. The more specific and carefully designed the index, the less time is required for users to find information.

Traditionally organized content-rich Web site

Look at any number of content-rich Web sites, particularly those that present thousands or hundreds of thousands of pages of technical content. These sites show the information architecture focused predominantly on traditional TOCs. Reviewing technical documentation on sites like IBM, Hewlett-Packard, Cisco Systems, Apple, and others reveals nearly identical structures.

Docs.sun.com is an example of a traditionally organized content-rich Web site. This site presents all the technical documentation for Sun Microsystems' products. The Welcome Page (Figure 7-6) divides the resources into several broad categories:

- New Information (What's New)
- Subject Categories
- Collection Titles
- Product Categories
- Frequently requested information
- Related Information on other Sun sites

Hierarchical structures

Hierarchically presented categories are designed for browsing, leading the user through a deep hierarchy of subject matter. The variety of starting points reflects the dimensions with which the information resources have been categorized. The primary dimensions used for the information in the Sun Microsystems' technical documentation library are the subject matter that is covered in a particular book, the titles of sublibrary or individual books, or the Sun product to which the information refers.

The three categories—subject matter, collection titles, and products—represent the most complete views of the documentation libraries on the site. The same

Figure 7-6 The Welcome Page of the Sun Microsystems' documentation Web site is found at www.docs.sun.com.

documents are listed in each of the categories and might also appear in the New and Frequently Requested categories as well.

Subject Categories groups the collections and document titles into five subject groups as illustrated in Figure 7-7.

- system administration
- programming
- desktop manuals
- hardware
- manpages

The first two groups represent user roles, the second two represent types of equipment, and the last is a reference to UNIX operating system commands. Each of these subject groups is expandable with four, five, or even six levels of titles before reaching the table of contents of a particular book in the documentation library.

Collection Titles presents the collections of books in alphabetical order by the name of the collection. The names are primarily product names, so that the Solaris 8 documentation collections titles are listed in sequence under the name, Solaris 8, as the initial text.

Figure 7-7 In the category, Browse Documentation by Subject, the user finds five areas in which documents can be located: system administration, programming, desktop manuals, hardware, and manpages. www.docs.sun.com

Product Categories groups the collections by the type of product, beginning at the highest level with two groups: hardware and software. If you know the product you're looking for, you probably come closest to finding the appropriate book title using the product categories.

Although the three dimensions selected to organize this extensive library are reasonable, the navigation designed for the site is likely to prove daunting for all but the most knowledgeable searchers. The user following the navigation paths must click through a complex, multi-level hierarchy of subjects, collections, and products and all their subcategories before reaching an individual title. If the hierarchical path pursued happens to be incorrect, the user must begin again, often several levels up in the hierarchy. Faster computer systems, which produce faster page refresh rates, help to improve performance. Even better would be to reduce the depth of the hierarchy, eliminating several levels of clicks between the user and a goal.

Navigating using the search function
The search functions on content-rich sites present a similar challenge to the user needing information. In most cases, the searches are difficult to limit. The default approach searches everything on the site. Search limits rarely offer options beyond selecting the product name.

The IBM site allows the user to navigate by book, command, programmer's reference, and task/topics. The tasks appear to be organized according to possible workflow or user role.

The docs.sun.com site offers an interesting alternative method of reaching desired content, although the options might be too limited to assist searches effectively enough.

At each level of the information hierarchy on the Sun site, the search function changes, enabling the user to focus the search on fewer documents. At the highest level of the site, the Home Page, the search includes all the documents on the site in all of the collections. However, when you reach the page, Browse by Product, the search can be limited to a particular product category, such as hardware, thus eliminating all the documents that are concerned with software products.

Even with the improved search function, the path to the right information is still strewn with boulders. In one instance, a full search on all documents resulted in 161 hits. By limiting the search to programming information in the subject category, one still receives 41 hits. To reach the information you might want from the page titled, Browse Documentation by Subject, requires eight clicks and this only when you know exactly what you are looking for and when you are reasonably confident that the information you are seeking actually exists in the library. It's even more useful when you know what the subject is called in the documentation, a luxury not often available to the average user.

The navigation and search design of the Sun technical-documentation Web site is typical of the design of many content-rich Web sites. In fact, the Sun site is one of the better implementations. However, the categorization of the subject matter limits the ability of the user to pinpoint needed information quickly. The content plan or information architecture underlying the site design is limited by an absence of metadata and modular construction that might help the user find what is needed. The three major divisions of information lead almost immediately to collections and titles. At this point, the users search for data in the form of the words in the titles, rather than searching for categories. As a result, the users finds too many topics, many of them irrelevant to their information goals.

Missing relationships

In many content-rich technical Web sites, you will find a frustrating lack of hypertext links. The primary linking mechanism appears to be an inline cross reference. The cross references originally appeared in the print documents and are simply transformed into hypertext links in the HTML or PDF versions. Most of the cross references refer to the same volume or, less frequently, to other volumes in the collection.

The linking structures rely on the traditional book paradigm, directing the user to another chapter or section for related information. Provisions for navigating the larger libraries of information or for linking to other information resources on the site are rare or non-existent. Technical support information, e-learning modules, marketing information, and others sources are almost never linked to one another. These information resources are created by different people in different parts of an organization without considering what the customers want to know. The customers do not care which organization created the information. They know only that information resources are not linked for their benefit.

Once users have managed to arrive at a topic with some of the information they need, it is virtually impossible to find other relevant resources that would perhaps better assist in answering the question or solving the problem.

How might better content planning have improved the navigation of the static content on a typical content-rich site?

Presenting information in context

The typical hierarchical Web site presents information in the context of the dimensions into which the information has been divided by the information architect. Typical dimensions become metadata categories such as subject matter, product, and task or become data categories expressed through the titles of collections and individual books in the library. Once the user arrives at a topic, few resources are presented to create a context for the information except for the traditional linear structure of the TOC.

However, you will find many examples of content plans for Web sites that do provide a rich context of information resources associated with individual topics. In most cases, however, the topics are not presented as chapters and sections of books but are presented as individual modules of information. The most common information type is the article. An article might be

- a news story
- a product data sheet
- a feature article
- a white paper
- a service or information bulletin

The "article" information type has been designed to be reasonably brief (little more than can be read in five minutes or less), addresses a single topic with a sense of completeness (a beginning, middle, and end), and can be read for information independently of any other topic.

Despite the relative completeness of the article, the information architect rarely stops at that point. Associated with the individual article are links to a network of related information.

The New York Times on the Web

A good example of a Web site that does provide rich content is the *New York Times* Web site (www.nytimes.com). The primary articles on the site correspond to the issue of the newspaper. They are categorized by subject matter into several content areas:

- arts
- business
- health
- international
- national
- New York Region
- obituaries
- politics
- science
- sports
- technology
- weather
- Op-Ed (opinion pieces by noted commentators)

Once readers find an interesting article, they are directed to a page that highlights the category in the heading. In this way, the readers know the relationship of the article to the category. In addition, the readers are directed to additional information that is related to the subject of interest. For example, a typical set of links (Figure 7-8) takes the readers to

- multimedia presentations about the topic
- related articles from earlier editions of the newspaper
- reproductions of other publications, typically government documents
- a Readers' Opinions area that serves as an idea exchange, much like an ongoing "Letters to the Editor" section

On this page, the center article, "Decline in Hitting Coincides with Change in Baseball's Strike Zone," is part of the Sports Section of the paper. The Multimedia link presents a discussion by the sports reporters of the dismal Mets season. One related article provides an expansion of the sidebar of statistics about runs and strikes that already appears on the right side of the page. The second link leads to a page that summarizes and links to many earlier baseball articles and additional links to a wealth of baseball information from game scores to classic photographs. The readers can link to the Readers' Opinions and go directly to lots of statistics.

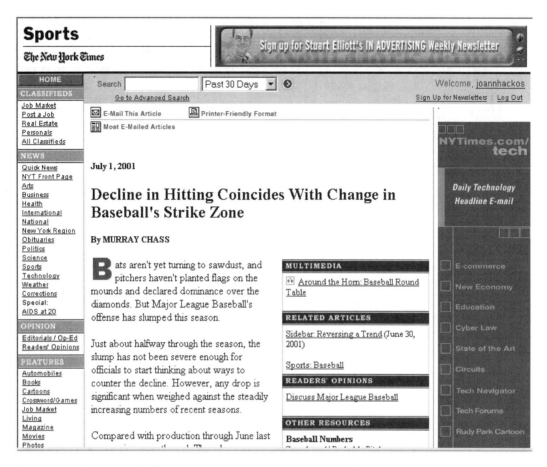

Figure 7-8 *The New York Times* Web site contains a set of related-information links at www.nytimes.com.

Searching the New York Times archives

The search page (Figure 7-9) presents a variety of methods for finding any of more than half a million articles in the paper's database (all the articles since 1996 are available either free or for a small fee). Readers can limit their searches by the sixteen categories by which the information in the database is categorized.

The readers search by entering key words (the site supports a full text search), but the keyword search can be extended to the full article text or be limited to the title or a summary. In addition, readers can search for the articles by a particular writer. Searches are sorted by the closest match, the latest article first, or the oldest article first. Further limits can be placed on the age of the article from today back through 1996. Even more search options are detailed on the Search Tips page.

The New York Times home page presents the lead articles for the day and then lists the articles according to the categories. Remarkably enough, the entire news-

Figure 7-9 *The New York Times'* advanced search function is shown on the site's search page.

paper is available on the Web site, including all the classified ads, the cartoons, crossword puzzles, book reviews, and more. Readers can link to breaking news from the AP and Reuters news services as well.

All of this content is static, but the overall site architecture reflected in what I have termed the content plan, organizes the information into rich contexts. The readers are continually provided with links that take them into additional topics that expand their understanding of a subject. The information is organized by subject matter, author, media, and date, with full-text search provided for the words in the titles and, ultimately, for any word string in the text. A particular article or topic of information is often no more than one or two clicks away from the home page.

Another well-linked news source is *The Industry Standard* Web site (Figure 7-10), www.thestandard.com. On this site, business articles are linked to the company's stock price and to related content categorized by the terms company, article, topic, research, and insight. The research category links to research reports related to the article at hand and is usually available for a fee from one of the major business research organizations.

Figure 7-10 The Industry Standard Web site (www.thestandard.com) contains links to related content.

Using the Information Model as an organizing principle

Andersen Windows sells a variety of windows and doors for residential and commercial construction. They have provided a Web site that is closely related to the design of their paper catalogs. Although many of the pages on the Web resemble the catalog pages, Andersen Windows' information architect has created a Web site that is based on the company's Information Model.

The Andersen Corporation Web site displays all the earmarks of a well-developed Information Model, some of which have been expressed directly in the site's structure. Examine the most important elements of the design.

The very first splash screen (Figure 7-11) embodies the primary dimensions of the model and relates two complementary points of view: the organization of the company by marketing division (Andersen Windows, Andersen Commercial, Andersen International); and the user point of view by the customer's role (home owner, commercial building owner, contractor, architect).

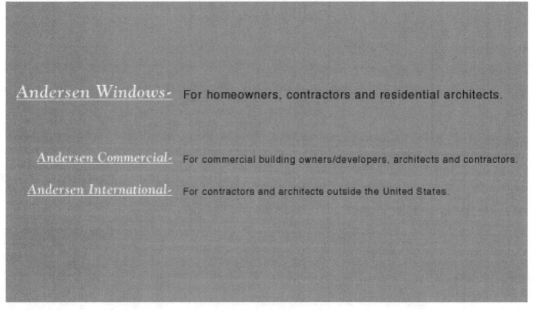

Andersen Windows- For homeowners, contractors and residential architects.

Andersen Commercial- For commercial building owners/developers, architects and contractors.

Andersen International- For contractors and architects outside the United States.

Figure 7-11 The Andersen Windows home page (www.andersenwindows.com) illustrates the primary dimensions of the underlying Information Model.

Notice that the text for each point of view helps define the other. Although Andersen Windows, which include a lighter-duty grade window best suited to residences, and Andersen Commercial, a heavier grade best suited to commercial buildings, have both architects and contractors as audiences, they are differentiated by association with home owners or commercial building owners, and architects (in general) or residential architects. These mutually reinforcing categories make it more likely that a customer will make a suitable choice on the first try.

Clicking Andersen Windows opens the next screen. Here a customer is offered the choice of role to assume before moving on (Figure 7-12).

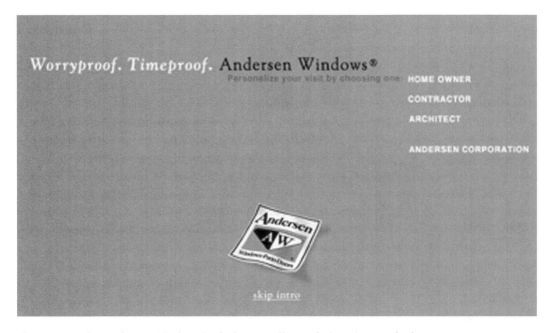

Figure 7-12 The Andersen Windows' splash page offers a choice of user role: home owner, contractor, or architect.

The Home Owner Welcome page demonstrates the relationship between the content plan and the information types relevant to the plan. At the top of the screen, the first level of navigation tabs allows customers, if they wish, to requalify themselves as architects or contractors. The second level represents the content plan—individual collections of information drawn from the information repository that have been clustered in coherent categories that home owners can recognize as embodying their interests. The body of the screen is the Home Owner Welcome information type. It might be defined as the homepage for home owners, briefly defining categories of interest and providing an orienting base from which to enter each of them. This information type is composed of content units as shown in Figure 7-13.

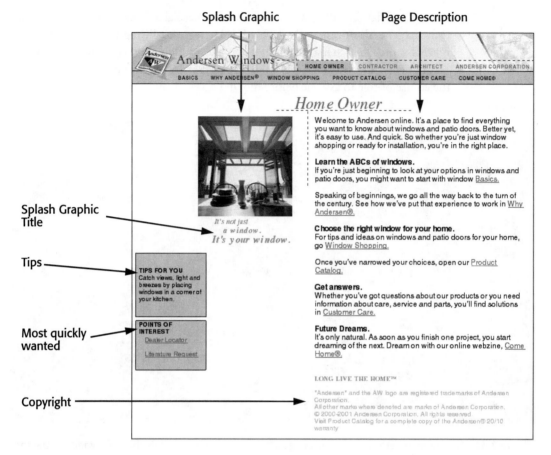

Figure 7-13 The Andersen Windows' Home Owner Welcome page contains content units appropriate for the target users.

- Page Description: A brief blurb about the area. It should identify the type of content so users know what to expect. Each description has a text link to other pages on the site.

- Splash Graphic: An attractive image for the intended audience. Visually differentiates this area.

- Splash Graphic Title.

- Tips: A box with the text "Tips for you" and a hint about window design.

- Most Quickly Wanted: A box with the text, "Points of interest." The box contains text links to information often wanted quickly and so should be available with the fewest clicks.

- Copyright: Copyright and trademark information.

The corresponding Contractor Welcome information type has many of the same elements as the Home Owner Welcome page. Notice in Figure 7-14 that three of the content plan categories are the same—Basics, Why Andersen, and Product Catalog—while the remainder are different—Window Shopping, Customer Care, and Come Home target home owners. Service and Parts, and Upper Story aim at contractors. The content units are the same, except that Tips has been omitted.

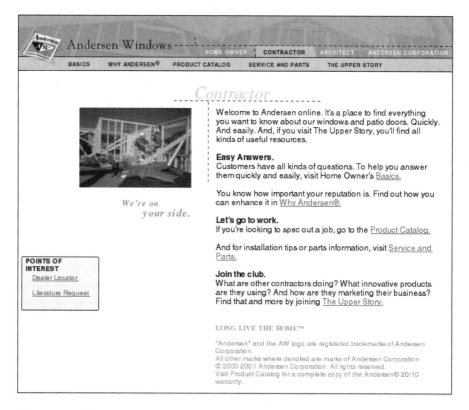

Figure 7-14 The Contractor Welcome page contains content units appropriate for a different group of target users.

Only one collection of information called Catalog is available to all three audiences. Users reach the Catalog by clicking the tab on the Welcome page for each audience (Figure 7-15). Catalog is not an information type: it is a collection of modules represented in the content plan. The content plan specifies the styles of available windows in the three rows of tabs at the top of the screen, and for each style of window, lists the relevant issues of interest in a table of contents at the left. The catalog opens by default, displaying the leftmost set of tabs (Hinged/Casement/Basic) and the top item in the table of contents (Welcome/Introduction) for the product line. Introduction is an information type with content units specified as they were for the Home Owner Welcome page.

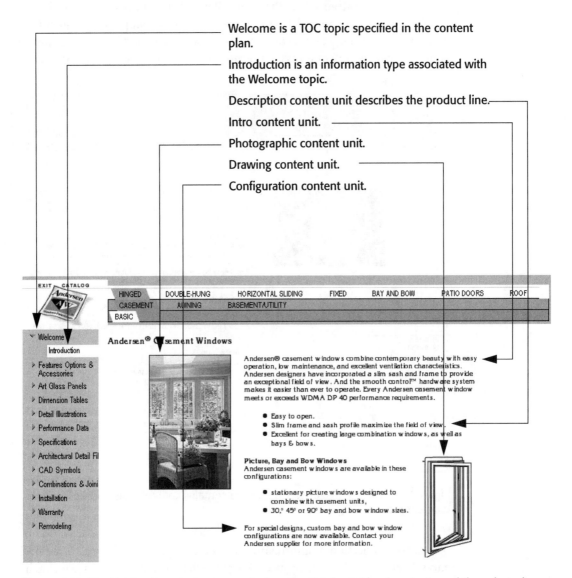

Welcome is a TOC topic specified in the content plan.

Introduction is an information type associated with the Welcome topic.

Description content unit describes the product line.

Intro content unit.

Photographic content unit.

Drawing content unit.

Configuration content unit.

Figure 7-15 The Catalog introductory page displays the Catalog table of contents and the selected information type.

Clicking the Patio Doors, Gliding, and Andersen Gliding tabs opens the Patio Doors/Gliding/Andersen Gliding Introduction for that product line with the same set of content units (Figure 7-16).

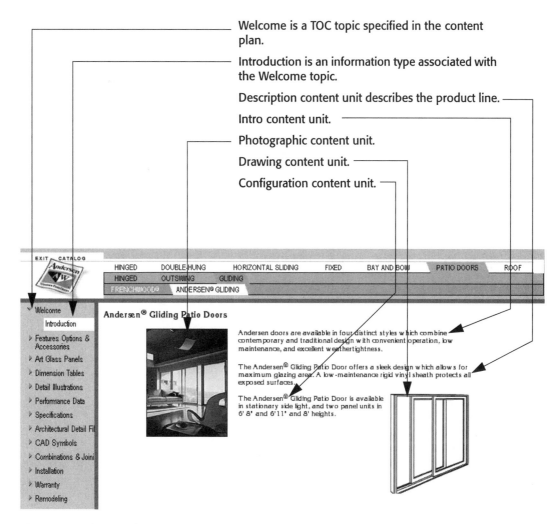

Welcome is a TOC topic specified in the content plan.

Introduction is an information type associated with the Welcome topic.

Description content unit describes the product line.

Intro content unit.

Photographic content unit.

Drawing content unit.

Configuration content unit.

Figure 7-16 The introductory page for Gliding Patio Doors shows the same set of content units.

Each topic in the table of contents is composed of one or more information types. The Dimension Tables item, for example, has two information types: Size Tables and Clear Opening Specs & Glass/Unit Area (Figure 7-17). The content units for the Size Tables information type could be chunked in different ways. The most likely method is shown in the illustration along with the metadata attributes.

Title: The name of the product line [Metadata attribute = product name]

Product: Dimensioned elevation drawing for one product in the product line [Metadata attributes = product number, size table]

Dimension ID: Labels the relevant dimensions [Metadata attribute = product number, height]

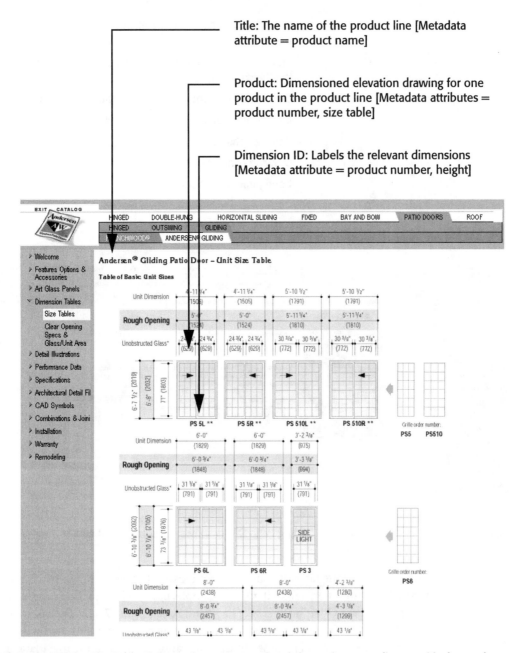

Figure 7-17 The Size Tables information type organizes information according to critical metadata dimensions.

Developing a content plan for static content

The content plan for a Web site will have some of the same primary components as the content plan for an individual book or a collection of book titles. The focus in both cases must be on the needs of the user. For that reason, the content plan begins with a statement of the user's information goals and requirements.

The standard information you need to include in a Web Site content plan is illustrated in Table 7-2.

Table 7-2 A content plan outline for a static Web site

Section	Description
Purpose statement	Explain the business requirements that you are meeting in the design and development of the content portion of your Web site.
Audience	Describe the audiences for whom the content is being assembled. Include references to the user profiles that you have already established for your audiences. Divide the descriptions into audience groups.
Tasks	Describe the goals and tasks that you expect for each audience group outlined above. Explain how the design of the site's content will meet the needs of each audience group and support its goals.
Usability goals	List the usability goals that you have established for the Web site. A typical usability goal might include the time it usually takes users to find the information they need. Usability goals might also describe the performance goals for the users. In stating a user performance goal, describe how the user will be more able to reach a goal and perform a task if the Web site is well designed.
Performance goals	Describe how the Web site must function if it is to meet the user requirements for speed and functionality.

(continues)

Table 7-2 A content plan outline for a static Web site (continued)

Section	Description
Architectural rationale	Explain why you have designed the arrangement of the content as you have. Describe the organizational plan you have for the content including how it will appear to the user, what types of links will be available from each topic of content, how the navigation is intended to work, how searches will function.
Paper prototype	Include a paper prototype (can be a rough sketch) of how the pages of the site will be structured. The paper prototype should support and illustrate your architectural rationale for the site.
Use scenarios	Provide the use scenarios that describe exactly how a particular user with a particular goal will find the required information resources. Begin with the primary use scenario for each user group. Then include the secondary scenarios and explain exactly how they are intended to function.
Taxonomy	Describe the categories you intend to use to label information on the site. Describe how the word choice matches the user's words for describing functions and tasks. Describe how the labels on the site will map to the dimensions you are using in your metadata to provide access to topics in the database.
Site Map	Provide a rough sketch (at least) of the organization of topics on the site. A graphic representation of the navigation should assist you in clarifying the organizational and navigational plan for the information topics.

The following content plan, illustrated in Figure 7-18, describes the organization of an information Web site that centers on technical product information. The information architect's intent is to guide the users quickly to a specific topic and then lead them to related topics. The topic that emerges as the result of navigation, index, or search becomes the hub topic. The spokes emanating from the hub direct the users to additional related information.

Lion-DF 2.0 Information Plan

Client company/project: Lion Company
Project manager: Kathy D
Start date: February 6

In this Information Plan, we describe our understanding of the Web site to be designed and produced, the users, and the high-level tasks they will be performing with the Web site. We then describe the implications of these factors on the design and propose our design for the site.

By March 20, Lion should review this revised plan, write all remaining comments on this copy of the plan, and sign below to indicate approval of the plan with changes as marked.

Please contact Kathy D at (000) 000-0000 if you have any questions about this plan.

Site Organization

Lion has two main types of customers for this product: commercial and technical. Commercial customers are banks, financial institutions (like Wall Street), and retailers. These customers are "data driven"; they need the operating system to process batches quickly. They do online transaction processes (OLTP) and want no down time, since every minute can cost them vast amounts of money. A commercial customer might have only 10 to 15 servers to transition, with lots of clients.

Technical customers, on the other hand, make money designing and manufacturing products. They include industry segments like transportation, aerospace, semiconductors, and discrete manufacturing. These customers are "application driven"; they need the operating system to support the applications they use, and they expect their applications to run faster on the new operating system than they did on the old. Down time for these customers affects their time-to-market. They try to avoid down time by moving to a new operating system only if it supports the applications they use and makes their applications run faster and stronger. Unlike a commercial customer, a technical customer might have hundreds or thousands of workstations to

transition. The sheer numbers of machines they have to transition contributes to their relative sluggishness in moving to new operating systems.

The Web site described in this plan is targeted at Lion technical customers at large, replicated sites. The large technical customers need information to be delivered quickly and effectively through the Web.

At the home page, customers will immediately decide which type of customers they are: commercial and financial or technical customers in transportation, aerospace, semiconductors, and discrete manufacturing. As soon as the initial decision is made, each customer will be directed to a special Welcome page describing the organization of information using a hub-and-spoke model. Conceptual, task-oriented, and reference information will be carefully outlined on the Welcome page and targeted to the specific conceptual model of the selected customer

If the customer selects a concept topic, for example, they will be immediately presented with the concept and provided with links to closely related tasks and reference information. Tasks will be categorized according to customer task models and reference information will be grouped according to specific categories determined through usability testing with members of each customer group.

Task Description

This section describes the high level tasks that technical customers at large, replicated sites perform to move from their current operating system to Lion 2.0. Lion's technical customers want to move to the new system by performing a cold install and then loading patches rather than by upgrading, because most technical customers are using the 1.0 operating system and upgrading to 2.0 requires them to first upgrade to 1.1 and then upgrade again to 2.0. Lion also feels it will be easier, especially with the new installation tools they have created, for technical customers to transition to 2.0 using a cold install. Therefore, this section summarizes the high-level tasks involved in a cold install.

Figure 7-18 The content plan for a technical-information static Web site describes how the information on the site will be organized.

Each high-level task is further linked to relevant conceptual and reference information at each conceptual page on the site. Once a particular customer staff member selects a task to perform, all relevant conceptual and reference information will be displayed and linked following the hub-and-spoke content plan for the site.

Deciding Whether to Move. The impetus to transition to a new operating system usually comes from engineering managers' demands for better, faster hardware and software, which in turn comes from the end users' demands. However, engineering managers' demands are of course not the only factor to be considered. A prospective customer's technical computing/information systems group also specifies its requirements for the new operating system and sets up an evaluation. In the evaluation, vendors (like Lion) create "solutions" based on the customer's requirements and compete on the basis of product availability, performance, ease of use, price, and other factors. Lion routinely assigns Technical Representatives to such "shoot outs" to make sure the prospective customer has all of the information needed to make a decision. If the customer decides to purchase Lion's products, the Service Organization is assigned to handle the details of the account. In this way, Lion always has real people tending to the needs of large, replicated sites; Lion does not leave these massive customers to get what they need from Web sites alone. Nevertheless, making sales information available to prospective customers via the Web means that at any time, the key decision-makers can get general information they might need to make a decision.

At a high level, **deciding** whether **or not to** move to Lion 2.0 is a **three-part** process. First, **the Site Planner decides** whether or not the site should even consider moving to the new operating system. For **this reason, the Site Planner is the "gate keeper" to a new account. Second, if the Site Planner thinks it's worth considering, he or she involves the other kinds of administrators to evaluate the business case for moving, from their respective angles. Initial meetings with prospective customers usually involve the customer's Site Planner and Technical managers, who can approve the purchase. Third, if this group is convinced of the business case, then the Site Planner (with input from other administrators) determines how to make the transition.

Evaluate new features and price/performance claims. In this step, the Site Planner and other managers who have the authority to make a purchase learn the business reasons for transitioning. If effective, the audience is impressed by the features and price/performance claims and wants to know more.

Verify whether applications are available. Because the technical customers that Lion is targeting use the operating system to support their applications, prospective customer's Site Planners are very concerned with whether or not the ISV applications and public domain software that their company needs have been qualified and/or ported to the new operating system. The Site Planner also wants to know how well and how fast these applications perform on the new system.

The Site Planner is also concerned about whether internal applications have been qualified and/or ported to the new operating system, but this is not information that Lion can provide.

Figure 7-18 The content plan for a technical-information static Web site describes how the information on the site will be organized (continued).

The technical Web site for Compuware Europe B. V.'s UNIFACE product is a good example of a hub-and-spoke information design. The Welcome page, illustrated in Figure 7-19, of the UNIFACE 8.2.01 Library, describes the information types used to structure the modules: conceptual information (what is), procedural information (how to), reference information of various kinds, and a glossary of terms. The instructions suggest three ways of accessing the modules, through navigation from the table of contents, by using the search mechanism, and by referring to the related-topics links at the end of each Web page.

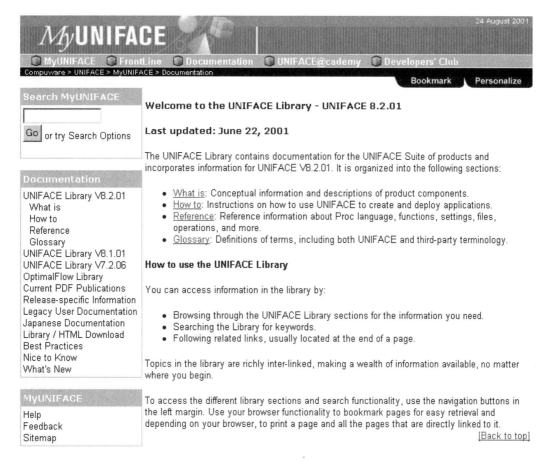

Figure 7-19 The four information types are described on the UNIFACE 8.2.01 Library Welcome page. Compuware is a registered trademark of Compuware Corporation and UNIFACE is a registered trademark of Compuware Europe B.V.

The four information types represent four values assigned to the metadata attribute, information type. A primary metadata attribute is the product name, in this case the 8.2.01 UNIFACE version. Other product names can be selected from the navigation pod to the left.

Each of the information types is further described in its own Welcome page. The Concepts Welcome page (Figure 7-20) includes several content units. The page begins with an introductory definition that explains what a concept topic is and includes a definition of the audience and an explanation of the structure of the "what is…" topic. Next come a series of links to specific conceptual topics organized by subject area, function in a possible workflow (for example, installation and configuration), and user role (such as application programming).

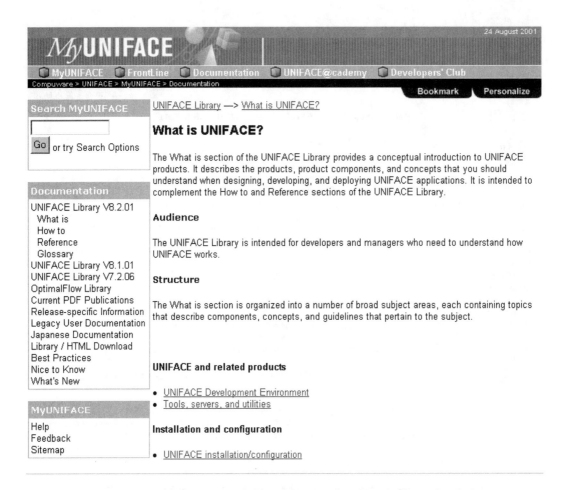

Figure 7-20 The Concepts Welcome page explains the concept topic to facilitate the choices users must make. Compuware is a registered trademark of Compuware Corporation and UNIFACE is a registered trademark of Compuware Europe B.V.

If the users are programming applications with UNIFACE, they might select the Application Programming link. Within application programming, many different conceptual topics are available, including one that explains the three-tier architecture. In three clicks, the programmers have found a useful conceptual topic. From the top-level topic of the three-tier architecture, additional links take the programmers to advantages, requirements, and further conceptual information about the presentation, business logic, and data-access tiers. At this level, the conceptual topic is not linked to task or reference topics.

The UNIFACE information developers have gotten off to a good start with their information architecture. The content plan for the UNIFACE Web site begins with strong organizational principles focused on four basic information types described on the initial Welcome page. However, as the information developers have discussed with me, the content plan must go farther in defining optimal and easily understood navigational paths through the topics. The topics themselves need to be more clearly categorized, which suggests that additional categorization of the dimensions of the Information Model at the top level is required.

Moving from static to dynamic delivery

Most of the technical information Web sites you encounter are static. That is, the content plan is developed by the information architect and the authors. The topics are well-organized to support navigation, indexes, and searches, but the structure does not change in response to differing user needs, nor is the content dynamically updated with changing information. The organizational architecture remains the same, and the information delivered is usually not variable. The only typical exception on static sites is to deliver the content in multiple languages. The user selects a language from a list of available ones, and the site content is immediately delivered in the selected language. To extract different languages from the repository means that the topics are identified with language-related metadata.

In Chapter 8, you learn how to design content plans for dynamic delivery of information.

8

Developing Content Plans for Dynamic Web Sites

"Look at that...it works! He's smiling!"

M ost of the content you find on Web sites is static, especially among sites that present detailed technical information about products. The content is planned, developed, and organized by authors and delivered in traditional TOC structures in PDF, HTML, or help files. Primarily on Technical Support Web pages do you find technical content that is updated regularly, especially in areas called FAQs (for Frequently Asked Questions). Regularly updated technical content is often limited to news releases, technical bulletins, new information about bugs, and downloads.

On content-rich sites that focus on current events, you find static content as well, designed and organized by content experts. The information on these sites is updated more often than on technical sites. New articles are added each day to news sites. Some sites feature late-breaking news coming directly from sources like the international wire services.

The updated information is prepared quickly and added to the site, but—more important—it is still prepared directly by an individual responsible for the integrity and usability of the content. Dynamically changing content is much rarer, in part because it is more difficult to design and implement, but also because many information developers don't know enough about creating dynamic content to include it in their information architecture.

Nevertheless, presenting content dynamically has great potential to make Web-based content-rich resources more valuable to users. Users appear eager to work with resources that are "customizerized" to their needs and respond to their queries effectively. Users also appear to prefer personalizing information resources that they use frequently. I have seen, for example, a considerable interest in centering enterprise content management around the e-workplace portal.

To realize the promise of delivering information dynamically, you need to explore the possibilities and design an Information Model that supports making changes automatically.

In this chapter, you learn about

- the prospects for dynamic delivery
- the processes you need to implement in your content design to support dynamic delivery
- the issues to address in your content plan for a dynamic Web environment

Planning dynamic content for the Web

Content planning plays a significant role in delivering content dynamically, especially when the intent is to publish customized or personalized information. Customized information refers to the practice of developing subsets of information directed toward particular user communities to meet the needs of one company or particular group of users within the customer's organization. For example, Ericsson Telecommunications publishes customized versions of technical documentation based on the functionality and data requirements of each customer that uses its equipment. By including customized content requirements in a content plan, an organization can develop and publish multiple custom versions of its content using a single database and avoid the cost of rewriting and relocalizing the same content multiple times.

Content planning also has an obvious role in personalization—the practice of allowing individual users to develop their own view of the information so that they access only what they need, not everything available on the site. The type of personalization that you want to support should be fully defined and its implementation detailed in your content plan. You might, for example, want to allow individuals to select the content they want to display, creating a "MyWebSite" capability on your Web site. You might also want to track user activity and deliver increasingly personalized content, much like Amazon.com does in collecting data about the buying patterns of its customers. Such a direction for delivering individual and changing content requires a detailed strategy that should be described in a content plan.

Producing a sound content plan for dynamic content delivery begins, as usual, with an understanding of the users' requirements:

- Do users need some information that is updated frequently and regularly?
- Do users want information to be customized according to their circumstances?
- Do they want information that is specific to their roles in the workflow, the products they use, or the companies they work for?
- Do they want to be able to personalize information to meet their own needs?
- Do they want to be able to manipulate information in ways that make it more valuable for them?
- Do they want to know about others who use the same information resources?
- Do they want to know how others evaluate the usefulness of the information resources?

These are just a few of the questions to address as you consider your users' needs in relationship to dynamically changing information. Some needs will help you focus on adding small amounts of dynamic content to a basically static Web site. Other needs will move you toward customization and personalization processes. Still others might lead to dynamic assembly of information resources into new collections tailored for the individuals who specify them.

Building a user community through dynamic delivery

One of the primary functions of Web sites that has emerged in recent years is building communities of people with similar interests. Chat rooms, for example, have emerged for thousands of special-interest groups. Web sites that cater to the needs of special interests seem to spring up daily (and disappear just as quickly). Sites that deliver specialized technical content, such as information on XML at www.xml.com, build communities of specialists interested in the subject matter.

Companies developing information in support of product sales and the effective use of these products have a more difficult time promoting a community, in part because they bombard visitors with all of the information about all of the products all of the time. The same is true for many company intranets. Users must slog through pages full of information they don't need to find what they do need.

Both customization and personalization support the goal of building communities of users. Communities are, of course, better served with information as their needs become better known. Communities are often eager to share information among colleagues, thereby enhancing the knowledge base. Communities provide resources that change with circumstances and can be selected by subgroups within the community as necessary. In all, information designs that respond to user needs provide the starting point for community building.

Developing dynamic content within a static architecture

The simplest way to explore dynamic-content delivery is by adding a small element of changing content to your Web site. Many personal Web sites already include elements like live video to enable visitors to witness a changing event. I spent several days a few years ago tuning in to a site that had a video camera inside the nest of a Peregrine falcon. The image changed every hour or so, allowing me to watch the birds hatching and growing up. When the young birds finally fledged and flew off, the camera was removed.

Sites like *The New York Times* include elements of dynamic content by providing late-breaking news stories with alerts sent by email to subscribers. The Web site, www.nytimes.com, illustrated in Figure 8-1, also includes a graphic of the stock prices of a company being discussed in a business news article. The graphic is tied into the stock exchange and the prices are changed every 15 minutes during the trading day. Note that the newspaper site designers selected a moderate rate of change for the dynamic information. It would be easy to decide incorrectly and annoy the reader with information that changes too frequently.

The Wall Street Journal includes changing information on stock prices, commodity prices, currency exchange rates, and other dynamic information as an integral part of their Web site, www.wallstreetjournal.com, as illustrated in Figure 8-2

An even more interesting use of dynamic content appears on the site www.weather.com, as illustrated in Figure 8-3. This site is one of the most visited on the Internet and makes extensive use of dynamically changing content.

The weather site offers content that changes frequently based on source changes from the National Weather Service and others. The weather maps on the site change every 15 minutes. In addition, the site has a cache of several weather maps that allow the user to animate the images and watch weather changes progressing over a set period of time.

In addition to the basic weather maps, other information based on weather data also is changed periodically. The site offers links to local, regional, national, and continental weather forecasts and information that assists hobbyists. Data and maps are available displaying

- current weather conditions
- local, regional, national, and global forecasts

Figure 8-1 *The New York Times* Web site regularly changes stock-price graphics.

Figure 8-2 *The Wall Street Journal* site changes information frequently.

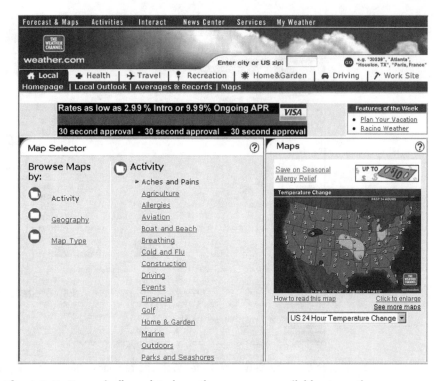

Figure 8-3   Dynamically updated weather maps are available at weather.com.

- gardening outlooks—precipitation
- boating outlooks—wind, rain
- golfing outlooks—wind, rain
- skiing outlooks—snow conditions, snowfall predictions

Information provided in the weather maps is handled automatically, rather than through the control of content developers or editors. As soon as the live weather map information is available, it is displayed to the consumer.

Updating data based on user queries

Rather than present the same dynamic information to all users, other data types provide up-to-date information customized for particular users. Consider, for example, a typical catalog that displays price and availability to prospective buyers. In a business (B2B) environment, this type of information changes rapidly and can be affected by who is looking for it. A dynamic Web site providing pricing and availability data to customers through an extranet or through the Internet might determine what data is presented to customers by their relationship to the company. A best customer might qualify for lower prices and faster availability than a new or infrequent customer. The catalog information changes based on customer, quantity of the order, frequency of purchase, and so on. The information being fed to the Web page comes from many databases, including the repository that holds the text descriptions and graphic images of the products, in addition to a database that stores the user profiles. Other data, such as

- prices
- availability of products

come from databases that hold transactional information, such as manufacturing, pricing, inventory, and others. Figure 8-4 shows two examples of the introductory page of Amazon.com. The first example shows the home page for an unregistered visitor. The second example shows a home page customized for a registered user.

Developing customized content

The examples of dynamic content you have seen have been based on drawing data from traditional financial and enterprise databases and moving the information to the Web in the appropriate context needed by the user. Information can be further customized by drawing information topics from a content-management system and delivering the topics based on the needs of users in particular circumstances.

Customization addresses several potential issues involved in dynamic content. The connection between *customization* and dynamic delivery is that static customization refers to variations that are preassembled by authors. These variations are published and are available to the customer who navigates or searches the site according to the customization parameters. Dynamic *customization* refers to variations that are assembled on the fly from the repository. If the customer is identified through a logon, the content is assembled dynamically and presented according to the customer's profile. If the customer selects a particular variation of the information based on a search or navigation path, the variation is again assembled on the fly. Dynamic assembly is most appropriate when there are more variations than are practical to store on a static site.

You might need to prepare variations of the content being delivered based on a variety of customer requirements:

- product models
- user profiles
- workflow roles
- local environments such as business, country, and region

Standard new user greeting

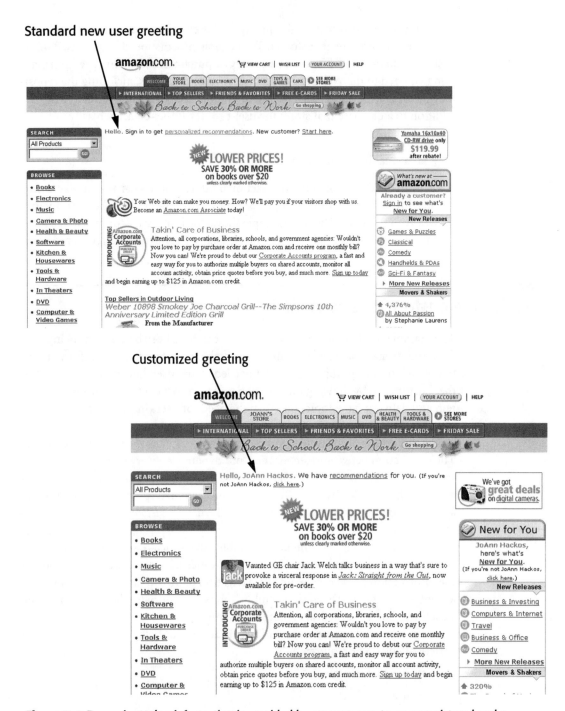

Figure 8-4 Dynamic catalog information is provided by amazon.com to an unregistered and a registered user.

Some telecommunications vendors, for example, produce different versions of information topics based on the needs of specific customers. In one case, the company modified the data in tables in technical manuals and changed how tasks were to be performed based on specific requirements coming from key customers. The customers wanted their own data in the tables (not generic data). They wanted their own internal procedures represented (not generic procedures). The vendors accommodated such requests for their most valuable customers.

Tweddle Lithography Company of Clinton Township, Michigan, producers of technical manuals for the automotive industry, creates custom versions of the documentation and instructions depending on the car model, the language, and the country. For one model of vehicle, user manuals were produced depending on language and country (a Brazilian Portuguese manual for Brazil and a European Portuguese manual for Portugal). In addition, a version of the documents for a second brand name were produced with nothing other than branding changes, because the second model is nearly identical to the first.

In the case of print documents like the user manuals for automobiles, the content that will be assembled into customer manuals is prepared in advance for the users and produced out of a single-source repository. Other information is dynamically delivered to a Web site, depending upon the user's profile (as determined during logon), the product line selected, the language preferred, the customer represented by the user, and so on. Rather than storing the content in static but interchangeable Web pages, it is predesigned, housed in a database repository, and delivered to the users on demand.

Product models

Accommodating differences among product models is one of the best ways to use a single-source repository. Information that supports different models of a product will usually have a high percentage of content that is identical for each model. At the same time, a smaller percentage of the information changes to accommodate model differences. Single-source strategies allow you to create a database of interchangeable modules that can be delivered according to the specifications associated with a particular product model or according to a myriad of other specifications associated with platforms, operating systems, industries, countries, and others. In Chapter 9, *Developing a Single-Source Strategy*, I discuss in detail planning and implementing a single-source strategy.

By identifying the differences and labeling the variable components carefully, the information architect can deliver custom versions of the product information and manuals to the appropriate customers. The customers benefit from not having to sort through information on models they do not own.

In a single-source project I managed a few years ago, the authors were able to separate out 32 distinct versions of the product and deliver documents that had

Five children are eating identical ice cream bars. One says, "mine is chocolate." Another says "mine is strawberry." Here are five identical ice cream bars where the only difference is the flavor. A single-source strategy enables an organization to deliver specific configurations of its information resources to accommodate the needs of different user communities.

fewer than 25 percent of the pages of the original documents. The original documents contained references to all 32 versions mixed together. The customers were constantly forced to decide whether or not a particular paragraph, illustration, or table was related to the version of the product they owned.

Decreased product liability
Single sourcing to produce custom versions of the documents decreases product liability. Customers trying to sort out which product models they were reading about were more likely to make mistakes in their use of the products. In the case of products that can cause bodily harm, consumers' mistakes caused by using the documentation are likely to lead to lawsuits. The more versions of the product the documents describe, the more difficult those documents are for consumers to navigate.

Web-centric versions of product information and user documentation can easily be customized so that each product has a unique set of documentation. Solving this problem when documents are printed and shipped is more difficult because companies want to avoid the higher inventory costs that can result from having multiple versions of the documentation.

The automotive industry, however, is looking at using print-on-demand technology to customize manuals that are delivered in print. The concept under consideration is to create a database that allows the manufacturer to generate a custom manual for each car coming off the assembly line. The manuals would contain only the features that the customer had purchased and would be assembled automatically and printed at the point of assembly. The owner would find a custom manual, perhaps even personalized (Deborah Jones' Manual), in the glove compartment.

As the automotive industry turns toward in-car electronic devices, they also might want to include electronic versions of the owner's manuals. If the original components in the database are developed in XML so that a format is attached to the modules at output stage, then it will be simple to automatically publish both print and electronic versions of the information at the end of the assembly line.

User profiles

User profiling provides yet another opportunity for customization of information. For example, users of information typically fall into one of four stages of use:*

- novice
- advanced beginner
- competent performer
- expert performer

Table 8-1 summarizes ways in which information needs differ based on stages of use.

By investigating your community of users in terms of their stages of use, you might find opportunities to customize information further. The information delivered on your Web site for novices will differ considerably from the information you would deliver to competent or expert performers. Novices and advanced beginners are most likely to look for one solution to a problem or the simplest way of performing a task. More competent and expert customers will want greater numbers of links to additional information resources. They might prefer a direct link to engineers or customer service to ask questions of the experts. They might prefer a facility to exchange information with others of a similar bent.

Customizing information by stages of use has occurred frequently in traditional print documents. Note the popularity of the various print series for less

---

* For more detail about Stages of Use, see J. Hackos and J. Redish, *User and Task Analysis for Interface Design*.

Table 8-1 Information needs based on progressive stages of use

Stage of use	Summary of information use
Novices	Novices are completely focused on solving their problems. They are concerned about making mistakes and looking foolish because they don't know what to do first.
	They want to get started quickly and focus on performing tasks and finding answers to their questions. They do not want to spend time on concepts that someone else tells them they are supposed to learn first.
Advanced Beginners	Advanced beginners have gotten over the fear of using a new product or making a new decision. Nonetheless, they are solidly task focused. How do I ... is their primary interest. They still don't want to spend time learning. They want only enough information to be successful at reaching an immediate goal.
	Most users of products or information never progress past the Advanced Beginner stage.
Competent Performers	Competent Performers are far enough along in their task-based doing that they begin to get curious about how the product really works. They are willing to spend more time learning, but only for those products that are important to them. For most products, they remain Advanced Beginners.
	However, for a small number of products with a strong relationship to work or avocation, they are now willing to learn. Much of the learning focuses on troubleshooting, understanding what went wrong and how to fix the problems.
Expert Performers	Expert Performers are willing to invest considerable time and energy learning all there is to know about a product or subject. They want to spend time on details and concepts because they find themselves performing tasks for which there are no simple solutions in the documentation. They are interested in talking with subject-matter experts and appreciate ways to interact with other experts. They want all the connections to all the information that is available. They are often willing to pay to learn more or to have preferred access to information.

sophisticated consumers of Windows, XML, Wine, and so on. Technical manuals are often designed for novices (the getting started guides) or expert performers (UNIX MAN pages). Given the flexibility of providing custom content on the Web, customers can select the level of information they want about a topic. Some of this customization is most easily handled by allowing customers to selectively link to additional information. You can create a design so that customers can choose a particular path through the information based on their own preferences for a particular stage of use. One customer might decide that he or she needs only the Advanced Beginner version while another customer is interested in the detailed information and more complex explanations of the Expert version.

Workflow roles

Users can also be profiled in terms of the work they do. For example, most computer operating system developers provide separate information resources for end users and system administrators. The tasks performed are different and the level of previous knowledge and experience is also likely to be different. Authors generally, although not always correctly, assume that administrative tasks will be performed by more computer-savvy individuals.

Most accounting and similar transactional systems divide information by workflow as well. Supervisors might get information about tasks that only they are authorized to perform. Much less information about the inner workings of the systems is available to end users. System administrators might also need information on background tasks that no one else in the organization will perform.

Many static Web sites already have an array of work roles covered in the information resources but finding and using them is often up to the user. With customized dynamic delivery, the user's work role can be established in advance (by logon or through security restrictions) so that only appropriate information will be delivered to the user.

It is important to remember, however, that role assignments themselves are not static. Jobs are reassigned, split among different roles, joined together to span responsibilities, and so on. The Web site should be designed so that users themselves can adjust the information modules they choose to deliver to particular role assignments.

The e-workplace portal, customized for a particular work role, is a good example of workflow customization. If the information accessed through the portal is updated regularly and includes both data streams for financial analyses and information resources that are constantly changing, then the portal benefits from dynamic updating and assembly.

Other environments

Many other opportunities for dynamically building content to meet particular needs will likely present themselves to your business environment. You might want to develop country-specific information for different markets, information in various languages that differs in style and content, or information specific to particular types of businesses. One company decided that it wanted to make customized examples and illustrations available to different market segments for its product. These differences affected the details rather than the core of the information delivered. As such, its reassembly on the fly to the Web was a more workable solution than building numerous static subsets of the information.

Tagging information for dynamic delivery

Remember that information that you intend to delivery dynamically must be appropriately tagged. With labels to identify the modules or submodules of information, the information cannot easily to directed to multiple outputs. Figure 8-5 shows a model of information labeling that allows modules of information to be directed to different versions of a product.

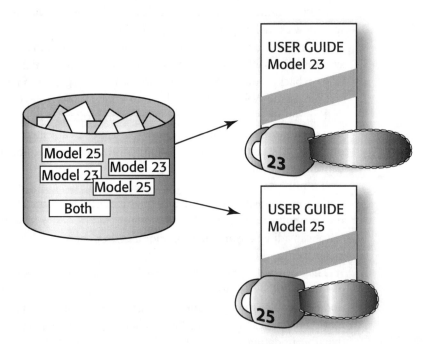

Figure 8-5 A single source of modules in a repository directs information to build two different versions of the chainsaw user's guide, one for Model 23 and another for Model 25.

Tracking customers

E-commerce Web sites regularly track users' navigation and buying patterns to deliver custom content. Customers returning to a book seller's site receive pages related to books they might have purchased previously. Sites that sell apparel often remember the style, size, and clothing type preferences of registered buyers. The users' buying patterns are recorded and used to reconfigure the initial page viewed and sometimes the types of links available from that page.

The practice of tracking users' moves is rarely seen in content-rich sites, but tracking could easily be used to deliver information that is targeted to specific users' needs.

One way of implementing tracking is to trace the navigation and search paths of the users. Users who go immediately to technical information about a particular product might be first presented with that product's information the next time they visit the site. Of course, it's difficult to know if the users found what they needed without asking. Many sites already have a mechanism to find out about usefulness of the information. They have designed forms that ask the user to rate the usefulness of a particular page. Amazon.com, for example, asks customers to rate the usefulness of a particular book review. The data is then used to score the information's usefulness on a scale of one to five stars.

Similarly, some content-rich sites have asked users to provide ratings, as illustrated in Figure 8-6 and used the ratings to revise navigation paths or rank query results.

User rankings might also be used to construct links to related topics. Links could address the questions of usefulness. A group of related-topic links, might read:

"Most other users who read this piece of information also found these topics useful."

Keeping search statistics

Tools are also available to track search inquiries and how customers ask their questions. The customer asks a question through a Boolean search system or a natural language query. The text of the question is saved, and the customer is asked to rank the usefulness of the returned topics. The topics found and used are associated with the original query, helping the information architects to further customize the search categories and lead the customers more reliably to useful information.

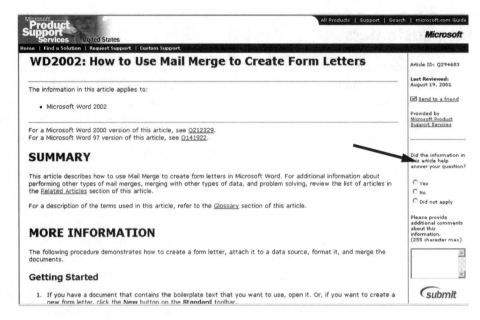

Figure 8-6 Microsoft's Web page asks customers to rate help articles.

Assembling content dynamically

In this discussion of delivering content dynamically from a repository, I have so far only alluded to the process of assembling topics in unique ways that meet the needs of users.

Dynamically assembled content based on user selections is an exciting possibility that extends the capabilities of content-rich Web sites. Take another look at the cookbook example.

Scenario 1: Planning a dinner party

The Web customer has been clicking through recipes and related information on the Web site. Finally, he decides to create a menu for a dinner party. He has selected a primary recipe for his entree and would like to add recipes for other parts of the meal that would complement his selection. He uses the metadata categories to assist his search. He is planning dinner for five and decides on the following courses:

- two appetizers
- a spinach salad
- the pork tenderloin main course

- some sort of rice dish, possibly wild rice
- asparagus because it's in season now
- a cheesecake for dessert

He finds a spinach salad right away plus a wild rice combination with lots of herbs and lemon juice. He locates the recipe for Hollandaise sauce for the asparagus, and he already has the pork recipe picked out.

The Web site includes a menu maker that suggests accompaniments for a main ingredient. He uses the menu maker to find two appetizers that fit with his emerging menu. Unfortunately, both recipes are designed to serve ten. He uses a quantity calculator on the site to cut them both down to five servings. Finally, he locates a cheesecake recipe that looks interesting but he doesn't know what one ingredient, ricotta cheese, is. The glossary of terms gives a description and suggests that ricotta will be found near cottage cheese in the market.

Finally, he requests a total ingredients list to use for shopping. One of the ingredients for the wild rice comes with an alternative herb to use if he can't find fresh tarragon. He also gets a list of suggested wines with the various courses he's outlined.

The Web site, backed by XML metadata and algorithms that calculate greater or lesser quantities, has allowed the customer to assemble a custom cookbook for his dinner party. When he downloads the personal cookbook, it includes video instructions for making the Hollandaise sauce so that it doesn't end up as scrambled eggs.

This scenario could be designed into standalone cookbook software. However, all the functionality can also be powered by XML. With XML, the recipes have appropriately tagged lists of ingredients and the quantities (cups and tablespoons) have tags that permit calculations. The ingredients can be combined into a single list and the quantities added together to produce a shopping list. Links refer to preparation instructions, glossary definitions, alternative choices, and wine accompaniments.

Each recipe has metadata tags that associate it with a course, an ethnic group, nutritional information, quantity, and so on.

Scenario 2: Delivering command reference information

One company I worked with delivered a command reference manual to its customers containing thousands of commands in alphabetical order. Users found the reference manual difficult to use because most of the commands did not apply to the equipment and software they were working on. They needed a small subset of the commands. So the Web site design included a form for customers to complete that allowed each one to obtain a personalized command reference manual. Users listed their hardware and software configuration. Then, accessing the XML metadata, the system returned from the repository of commands only those commands that corresponded to the users' environment. Instead of thousands of commands to wade through, most users received a subset of fewer than 500. Technical information lends itself to dynamic assembly.

Scenario 3: Extracting information for technicians

A heavy-equipment manufacturer had posted an 800-page maintenance manual in PDF on its Web site. The service people complained that it was too large and took too long to download. They argued that they only wanted the sections of the manual that applied to their task at hand. As a result of the customer complaints, the company adopted a tool that allowed them to build personalized versions of the maintenance information.

The users scanned a list of topics on the Web page. The list had been created by the technical authors who had analyzed the way subsections of the information tended to be used. The users checked boxes on the page to indicate the sections they wanted. Then, the software extracted the appropriate pages from different parts of the document, assembled them into a new document, added a table of contents and page numbers, and applied a cover page identifying the technician, date, and subject. The extracted pages were then published in PDF for downloading. The technicians received their own personalized mini-versions of the service information.

Scenario 4: Creating customer user guides

A manufacturer of custom personal digital assistants (PDAs) used dynamic assembly to supply custom user guides with the devices. The dealer indicated the functions the customer needed from the PDA hardware and software by going to a Web form and checking off the functions on a list. Each function's description and operating instructions had been stored in the repository. In addition, the dealer could decide what kind of display the customer wanted and how the external controls on the hardware would be activated. Alternative text and illustrations for these variations were also stored. Once all the choices were made, the system collected all the relevant topics and illustrations and assembled them into a pre-set table of contents order. The page breaks were added automatically, following a complicated print publishing algorithm, and the entire file was delivered in Post-Script form to a printer selected by the dealer from a pre-arranged list. The printer made the required number of print manuals and arranged to have them shipped to the dealer for distribution to the customers.

In each of these scenarios, the topics stored in the repository are labeled with XML metadata for ease of retrieval. Depending upon the scenario, additional XML metadata is included to allow for calculations. In the PDA scenario, the style information needed for the creation of print output in PostScript is only added after the topics have been assembled. The tags in the source topics do not specify format. They refer only to the content of the topics.

Personalizing content

People personalize content all the time, especially for products or tools they use frequently. The ubiquitous note stuck to the computer monitor, taped to the desk, or pinned to the bulletin board is an attempt by people to create their own personal information resources.

A colleague once described to me what he considered to be the best manual he had ever had. He was working as a technician and used information constantly about the products he handled. Consequently, he assembled a collection of pages copied or cut from books, materials brought back from training courses with notes included, little colored sticky notes, printed copies of tables and graphs, penciled notes, and pictures and put them all into a three-ring binder. His personal manual grew as he gained experience and delved into other subjects related to his work. He had created what he called My Book.

When he left for another position, he gave My Book to the person taking over. Yet, he told me that he was certain the new technician had thrown the "whole mess" away as soon as my friend was out the door. The new technician was unable to use the idiosyncratic collection—he would have to create his own.

Charlie has developed a personal information resource, a contraption referring to a bulletin board filled with diagrams, charts, spare parts hanging from cords, etc.

Personalized content in a Web environment provides customers with the capability of building My Book. Regular site visitors who use the information about products, processes, or services are able to create their own collections.

In the scenarios describing dynamically assembled content, users selected from among author-determined subsets of the information. With personalized content, the users make more decisions about the content they want to access regularly.

Bookmarking has been the most obvious tool for users to return to information they found useful. Bookmarking, however, has had severe limitations because bookmarks are made to particular Web pages rather than to categories of information. Bookmarks have also been associated with PDF, but when the information is updated, the topics to which the bookmarks referred are often lost.

Personalization processes need to be more robust than simple bookmarking. They need to make it easy for users to select categories of information they find valuable. Once they have selected the categories they want, the users receive updates, bulletins, or even warnings that enhance their knowledge of the subjects.

Many Web sites already provide opportunities for users to personalize the content delivered. Two well-known examples are *The New York Times* and Weather.com

- *The New York Times*, as illustrated in Figure 8-7, allows readers to personalize the email news summaries they receive by deciding among categories of news articles.

- Weather.com, as illustrated in Figure 8-8, lets users choose their home city and six other locations to receive daily weather reports and allows them to select six weather maps to appear on the personal pages.

In each case, the customer selects from a list of options, checking ones that are to appear on the personal page and ones that should be omitted. Sites that provide content in multiple languages encourage users to select the language that they want immediately from the home page. Figure 8-9 shows the Compaq Web site in two languages.

Fortunately, much more can be handled through personalization than typically occurs among Web sites, especially Web sites featuring highly technical content. If you develop a user-centered Information Model, you can provide users with relevant categories of information that they can select without your having to assemble these into author-selected subsets.

For example, a user might want to see cooking topics according to these categories:

- recipes (step-by-step procedures)
- Italian from Compagna, the area around Naples
- featuring tomatoes, basil, or mozzarella
- baked or sauteed
- entree or appetizer

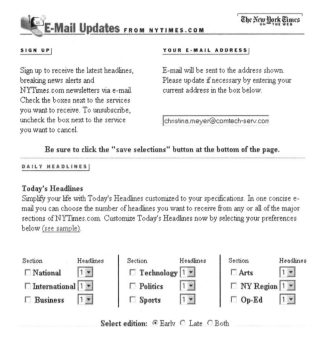

Figure 8-7 *The New York Times* provides users with a page to customize its content.

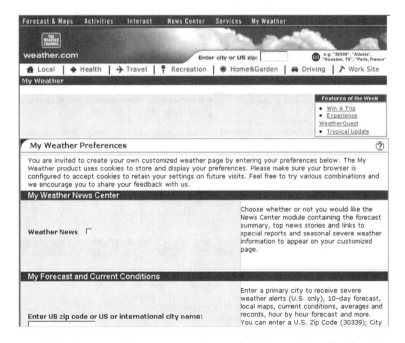

Figure 8-8 Weather.com allows users to choose their home city and select the weather reports and maps they want to receive.

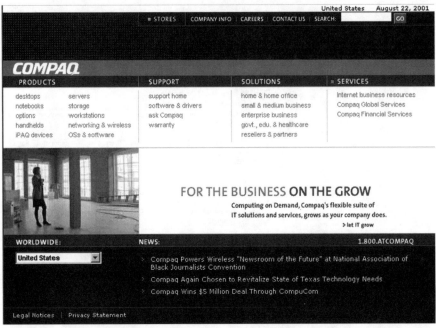

Figure 8-9 Compaq Computer provides versions of its Web site in multiple languages.

By selecting from among these categories, either through a personalization-specific selection screen or through navigation and metadata-governed bookmarking, the user creates a personal view of the topics available on the site.

On subsequent visits to the site, the personalized view is offered to the users as a regular starting place. They are able to add or delete categories at any time.

The personalized view can be drawn from static information resources on the Web site, or the view can be constructed by drawing upon topics in the repository. Then, the user is provided with updates to the information as soon as they become available.

Intranets and extranets already offer considerable opportunities for the information architect to customize resources going to individual users or external customers. Security provisions enable the architect to restrict what may be seen by a vendor, a customer, or an employee.

Personalization of the content by the users themselves has become associated with portals.

Delivering with portals

The concept of the e-workplace portal includes both customization and personalization, as well as dynamic and static delivery of content. Portals enable users to view the information they need to perform their jobs (role specific) by signing on only once to a browser-based environment. Content presented in the users' window is likely to come from diverse sources, including databases that might have required separate login commands in the past. All the separate signing-in procedures are consolidated into one portal sign-in, simplifying the user's access.

Once the user is signed in, all sorts of information becomes available in several ways:

- selected according to a business function (financial information for the finance function)
- selected according to an individual's role and responsibilities in the organization (sales revenue reports for the sales manager)
- selected for personal reasons by the individual (frequently updated stock prices for specific stocks)

Some information might be available because it is related to a specific business function. For example, everyone in the finance department gets daily updated information about revenue and expenses.

Some of the information might be selected by the information architect according to an individual's job title and set of responsibilities. For example, the sales manager needs a daily report of the sales made by the staff, while members of the sales force need to see a graph of their sales for the past month or year. The portal designer assigns information according to the business roles played by different individuals in the organization. Information coming from various databases such as the sales volume report will be updated dynamically on a regular basis.

Other information might be available to all employees but personalized to each individual. For example, individual employees can see their accrued vacation and personal leave or their insurance information.

Information resources can also be personally selected, usually from a list of available ones. Some employees might decide to get up-to-the-minute stock market information delivered to their portals, flight schedules for their business trips, or weather reports for their destinations. The system needs to be hooked into external information feeds to make this sort of information immediately available.

Personalization options in a customized portal environment provide opportunities for individuals to create electronic My Books that are updated regularly from repositories of data objects and information topics. As soon as information is updated, changed, or even deleted from the repository, the individual with a portal knows about the change.

Not only can the users decide to include or exclude certain information from the portal, they can often rearrange the layout of the screens to suit personal preferences, at least within the confines of the design options provided. Figure 8-10 shows a portal page for a budget manager who has selected options that are interesting and necessary. Figure 8-11 shows a similar page personalized by a brand manager. And Figure 8-12 shows the choices of a line manager. One user wants

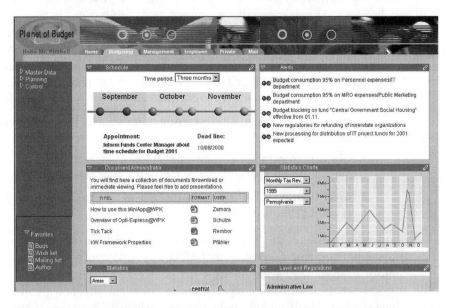

Figure 8-10 The Budget Manager prototype portal uses statistical data, scheduling information, and information about laws and regulations to manage the budget. (A prototype portal design published courtesy of the SAP Design Guild. See www.sapdesignguild.org. Copyright by SAP AG.)

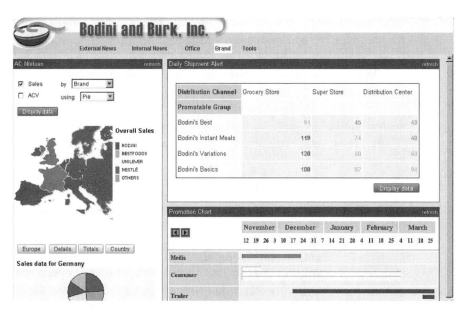

Figure 8-11 The Brand Manager prototype portal uses information about customers, competitors, and the market to manage the growth and positioning of the product. He needs to keep up-to-date about the supply, distribution, advertising, cost, and profit of the product. (A prototype portal design published courtesy of the SAP Design Guild. See www.sapdesignguild.org. Copyright by SAP AG.)

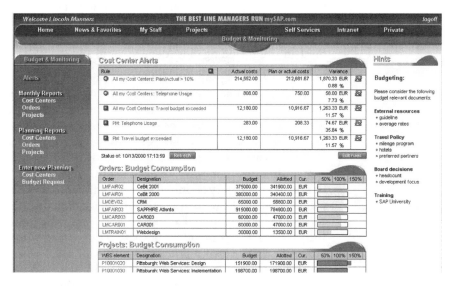

Figure 8-12 The Line Manager prototype portal uses information from the Web to manage personnel and costs. Reports and alerts help him manage costs and budget consumption for orders and projects. (A prototype portal design published courtesy of the SAP Design Guild. See www.sapdesignguild.org. Copyright by SAP AG.)

information selections to appear in a menu on the right side of the screen. Another wants to open a secondary window to view certain information. Sometimes even colors and backgrounds can be changed according to personal taste.

When you develop a workplace portal, you are likely to want to provide access to content residing in a variety of proprietary systems and databases. The grove standard for managing diverse, proprietary content sources provides a method to enable such links.

Eric Freese, senior consultant at Isogen, describes the grove concept in the following vignette.

Groves provide a way to process data from various formats using a single application programming interface (API). What this means to an information architect developing a Web site or intranet portal is that documents can be accessed and links built between them, no matter what the source format, at a level that may not be feasible in their current form. In other words, groves could enable non-proprietary links between Microsoft Word documents, Lotus 1-2-3 spreadsheets, or any other format of document that may be used within the enterprise.

The grove paradigm is defined in an international standard, known as HyTime, which defines, among other things, a methodology for linking between data objects in an open, standardized way. Groves are used to break a document object down into structural pieces that may then be referenced using HyTime links. However, the grove model is also useful when using other linking mechanisms including those defined for use on the Web.

To build a grove, a property set for the document object type (Word, for example) must be developed. The property set is essentially an SGML document that defines the hierarchical structure into which the source document is to be broken. The structure can be as simple or complex as necessary. In the case of Word files, the structure is usually very wide and flat because there is typically not a lot of structure in most Word documents. A database table might be narrower and deeper since they are highly structured. The property set can be written to take advantage of any special features of the information that may be useful in further processing, such as links that point internally within a document. Once the property set is defined, a processing program, called a parser, is developed to organize the document into the pieces defined by the property set. The parser may work directly on the file being processed, or it may use the API for the tool used to develop the file. If the parser is developed effectively, it can be used to handle any number of documents developed in a given format.

Parsers convert the documents within an information collection to a specified format to generate a bounded object set (BOS). The BOS is the complete set of documents within the collection. All linking has to occur within the confines of the BOS. Typically the BOS is represented within a computer's memory and not on some storage device, although it may be possible to do so. Once all the documents have been built into the BOS, they all look the same to a program capable of processing groves.

The conversion to non-proprietary formats is where the real win occurs when using the grove paradigm.

Once the BOS has been constructed, any piece of data looks like any other piece, making it very simple to write code to process the data, no matter its source format. For example, you can process the data using the single API mentioned earlier. Programs developed to work on grove-enabled data will continue to work, even if new types of data are added to the BOS using new parsers. This uniformity of structure also allows a single addressing model to be used where data can now be linked at levels lower than just the document level, as is the case when it is tied up in some proprietary format. Possible applications might include: creation of a set of web pages, insertion of links between all the different pieces of information, conversion into a single unified format, insertion into a repository, etc.

The grove paradigm is a very revolutionary concept because it, in effect, removes one of the biggest forms of leverage that software vendors hold over their customers: namely the proprietary format of the data. If a tool stores your data in a way that only it can read it, then the vendor has a firm grip on your data. The grove paradigm allows information owners to release that grip and reclaim full rights and ownership over their information. It also allows information owners to reuse and re-purpose the information in ways not originally intended but that currently meet the requirements of the enterprise.

Adding user-generated information

Personalized content, dynamically delivered to customers or individual users becomes more relevant to those users when they can add their own content. In a portal environment, provisions should be made for users to create new content and check that content into the repository. Allowing users to annotate topics provides them with an additional tool to personalize the information to their needs.

J D Edwards, a company in the Enterprise Resource Planning environment, goes even further. They deliver their database of software documentation to their customers and give the customers the keys to the database itself. Using the content-management solution, customers are able to add their own content to the repository. Typically, they will add business procedures and policy information that guides their employees in the proper use of the financial and human resources systems. They might also customize portions of the information repository in the same way that they customize the software.

Many companies change details of a software interface to accommodate their business practices. If they cannot change the documentation to match the interface changes, their employees are often left with useless help systems and online manuals. The information in these systems no longer matches what they see on their screens. J D Edwards and other enterprise software developers are using content management to enable customers to change, delete, and add business-critical information.

Creating a content plan for dynamic content

A content plan for a dynamic content-rich Web site contains much the same information as the content plan for a static site with the addition of descriptions of how content will change to accommodate customer needs. The descriptions of each section in Table 8-2 direct you to explain why and how you have decided to take advantage of dynamic delivery.

Creating dynamic Web sites provides both an opportunity and a challenge for information architects who specialize in content-rich business-to-business site development. It is easy to envisage presenting traditional business data on an intranet or extranet. Much of this data is already available in the enterprise through different databases and analysis systems. A good example is Enterprise Resource Planning software that provides myriad opportunities to present corporate financial data for planning and analysis purposes.

It is less obvious how to handle other types of information dynamically. You have to look closely at the need for information that changes regularly. Some of that information will be collected from support services. They seem to have a constant stream of newly identified bugs and fixes or simply known problems with no resolution yet. Users don't want to wait until the next release to find out how to solve problems.

Information that originally is presented in a support-services context can be transformed to standard technical manuals or documentation resources either automatically through the direct reuse of modules or through the intervention of technical authors.

Developers of technical information need to think creatively about the opportunities for dynamic assembly of topics and the development by the user of My Book. If the best resource a customer has is the set of information he or she has developed personally, then you need to find ways to enable personalization and ensure that the selected information resources are updated in a timely manner. Not only will the user create My Book, but the personalized content will remain up-to-date without the user's intervention.

Table 8-2 A content plan outline for a dynamic Web site

Section	Description
Purpose statement	Explain the business requirements that you are meeting in the design and development of the content portion of your Web site.
	Emphasize the business decisions that led to your decision to make some aspect of the site dynamic.
	Discuss the reasons for providing customization and personalization as site functions and how these capabilities will advance business goals. Be sure to carefully articulate what business purpose you are optimizing for.
Audiences	Describe the audiences for whom the content is being assembled. Include references to the user profiles that you have already established for your audiences.
	Divide the descriptions into audience groups. Ensure that you anticipate the roles, responsibilities, workflow, and other dimensions that might interest your audiences.
Tasks	Describe the goals and tasks that you expect for each audience group outlined previously. Explain how the design of the site's content will meet the needs of each audience group and support its goals.
	Explain how the users' goals and tasks will be better supported through dynamic updating, customization, and personalization of the content.
Usability goals	List the usability goals that you have established for the Web site. A typical usability goal might include the time it takes a typical user to find the information he or she needs.
	Usability goals might also describe the performance goals for the users. In stating a user performance goal, describe how the user will be more able to reach a goal and perform a task if the Web site is well designed.

Table 8-2 A content plan outline for a dynamic Web site (continued)

Section	Description
Performance goals	Describe how the Web site must function if it is to meet the user requirements for speed and functionality.
	Dynamic updates—describe how well the dynamically updated information being fed to the users will perform. Designate the time frame for the updates.
Architectural rationale	Explain why you have designed the arrangement of the content as you have. Describe the organizational plan you have for the content including how it will appear to the user, what types of links will be available from each topic of content, how the navigation is intended to work, how searches will function.
	Discuss the impact on the site architecture made by your choices of dynamic delivery of information.
Sources of dynamic information	Describe the sources of the information you will deliver dynamically to the Web site or portal. List the databases from which information will be drawn, including both data and information resources.
	If some information will come from outside your organization, explain what data you want to include. Discuss the syndication options if needed. Explain how syndicated information will be obtained and delivered to the users.
	Decide just how dynamic the information will be. Information that changes either too frequently or too slowly might be frustrating to the users.
Paper prototype	Include a paper prototype (can be a rough sketch) of how the pages of the site will be structured. The paper prototype should support and illustrate your architectural rationale for the site.
	If you are providing users with the capability to personalize the look of their portal or window, show examples of the range of personalization options you will provide.

Table 8-2 A content plan outline for a dynamic Web site (continued)

Section	Description
Use scenarios	Provide the use scenarios that describe exactly how a user with a particular goal will find the required information resources.
	Begin with the primary use scenario for each user group. Then include the secondary scenarios and explain exactly how they are intended to function.
	Include all use scenarios related to the dynamic delivery of information to the site.
Customer tracking	If you intend to track how customers navigate through the information, ask questions, or create searches, explain how your tracking will work. Discuss the data you want to collect and how that data will be used to further customize the information provided to the customers on their subsequent visits to the site.
	Describe your security procedures for ensuring that data about the actions of individual customers or employees will be kept secure.
	Explain how you will inform users of the tracking activities on the site.
Security	If you intend to provide a portal with a single sign-on, explain how the sign-on will work and how you intend to handle securing access to the various databases that will provide information to the portal.
Taxonomy	Describe the categories you intend to use to label information on the site. Describe how the word choice matches the user's words for describing functions and tasks.
	Describe how the labels on the site will map to the dimensions you are using in your metadata to provide access to topics in the database.
	Explain how the users will access their choices for customization and personalization. If you intend to use selection screens or lists, provide examples of how they will appear to the users.
Site Map	Provide a rough sketch (at least) of the organization of topics on the site. A graphic representation of the navigation should assist you in clarifying the organizational and navigational plan for the information topics.

9

Developing a Single-Source Strategy

"Finally, just the information I need…and no more!"

Because information in your repository is stored as unique elements, you can use the same documents, chapters, sections, or content units in different deliverables. You can assemble compound documents built from smaller modules stored in the repository. You can update the modules and have the updates immediately reflected in all the compound documents that contain those modules. You can even modify a module in one set of compound documents without changing it in another set, at the same time maintaining a relationship by linking the two similar but not identical modules together. These strategies for reusing information are referred to as single sourcing.

In Chapters 4 through 6, you learned about a three-tiered structure for categorizing and organizing your information. The top level is represented by the Information Model which provides a framework for how the information is going to be delivered to customers. The middle level is represented by the information type which provides you with a structure for writing independent modules of information consistently. Within the information type, content units hold the specific text, graphics, data, and rich media delivered to the customer.

This three-tiered structure (Figure 9-1) allows you to manage content at many levels of granularity. You can then deliver the content to static media such as print,

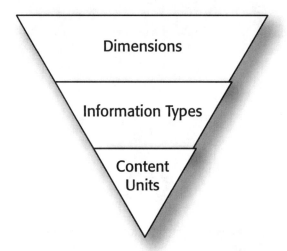

Figure 9-1 As you learned in Chapter 4, *Creating an Information Model*, the Information Model consists of dimensions that are further refined into information types and content units.

PDF, and static Web, and deliver content dynamically by enabling customers to select the content most relevant to their needs. The three-tiered structure allows you to categorize and label content at many levels. You can add labels in the form of metadata to individual files that represent whole documents or sections and chapters of larger documents. You can add labels within structured documents to further categorize content units.

Depending upon the design of your database, you can deconstruct structured modules and store your information as individual content units. You can also find and retrieve individual content units within structured documents if your content-management solution enables you to address the content units separately.

In this chapter, you learn how to

- plan a single-source strategy to reuse information
- decide on the appropriate level of granularity at which to manage and reuse content
- ensure that your Information Model provides you with the appropriate metadata for each level of granularity
- build static output directly by using metadata to find modules of information and create compound documents to embody your content plans

- build dynamic output by using metadata to retrieve updated modules from the repository and allow customers to determine their own structure for compound documents
- use a top-down strategy by starting with an existing document, removing content that is not needed in the new output, and modifying other elements for the specific context being built

The capacity for multiple reuse of identical content, plus the capability to create and maintain relationships between similar but not identical content, provides you with the capability to single source your information delivery in ways that not only greatly increase your efficiency but also enable you to deliver more custom, targeted information to your customers.

Not all organizations need to use a single-source strategy for all or some of the information. Many organizations simply want to publish entire discrete modules to their Web sites. However, in some organizations, depending largely upon the types of content they need to deliver or the variety of output media they want to support, single sourcing will provide a significant opportunity for cost savings and increased quality.

Planning a single-source strategy

Your organization needs a single-source strategy as part of your content-management solution if you

- produce multiple versions of the same product
- publish information in multiple languages for many countries
- deliver similar information among multiple output media
- have frequent multiple releases of products on short time schedules

The purpose of the single-source strategy is to write once and use the modules of information many times, revise once to update everywhere, and translate once.

Your strategy derives directly from your Information Model. The model establishes the framework through which you need to categorize your information. From this framework comes the metadata that you use to label information in the repository so that you can retrieve it and reuse it.

Multiple versions of the same product

Medtronic, manufacturer of implantable medical devices such as pacemakers, has instituted a single-source strategy to increase its efficiency, reduce development costs of its information deliverables, and reduce translation costs. In their initial project following their pilot project, they published ten versions of their user documentation from a single-source repository. Of the ten versions, five were for the US and five were for countries outside the US. The five outside-the-US manuals were then translated into nine languages.

Among the ten versions of the product, about 80 percent of the information is the same and can be completely reused. If any of this reused information changes during the development life cycle, it can be updated once and changed everywhere almost instantaneously.

Approximately 20 percent of the information is unique among the product versions. That information is maintained separately or is reused among a subset of the product versions.

The information is developed in separate modules that are assembled to form the final print deliverables (they are currently required by the FDA to deliver paper documents with each device). The print-composition process, which used to be done by individual authors, is now automated. The modules are assembled from the repository following the sequence established in the content plans for each product version. Formatting is added automatically at the end of the process, helping the team reduce its production time for multi-lingual manuals from three to five days to minutes.

Figure 9-2 provides an example of the completed pages of a Medtronic pacemaker manual.

To facilitate the publication of information in ten languages, the translation and localization team translates the modules in the repository, rather than the English print deliverables. They use the same print-composition process to assemble the ten different documents in each language. As a result of this single-source process, they have been able to substantially reduce translation costs and cycle time while also increasing translation consistency.

Planning started early with the development of an Information Model that provided the categories of information. Metadata is used to label individual content units, e.g., according to product line, model, geography, and topic area. A document-build list, based on the metadata, is used to automatically create appropriate covers, front matter, and back matter for each published version of the manuals.

The publications team achieved a number of impressive gains: faster time to market because of reduced production and translation schedules, increased efficiency from reusing information modules in multiple deliverables, increased efficiency by updating once and changing everywhere appropriate, and reduced translation costs and fewer errors by translating once and using the translated text in multiple deliverables.

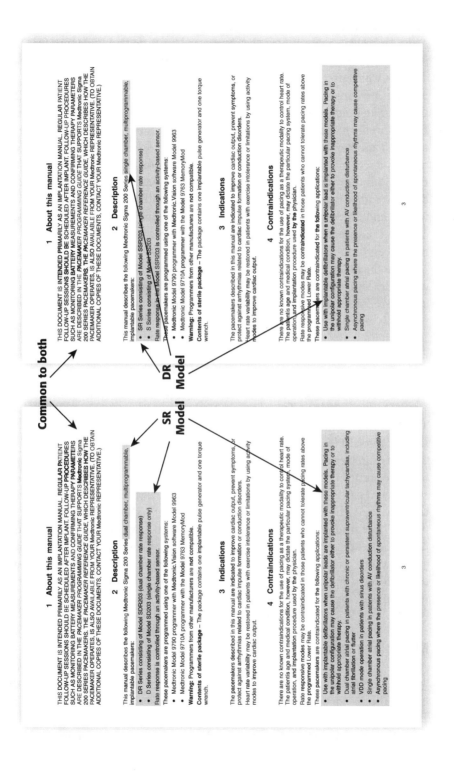

Figure 9-2 Through a single-source strategy, Medtronic reuses on average 80 percent of the information among the manuals for different versions of its pacemaker products. Some information, averaging approximately 20 percent, is unique to each pacemaker manual. (©Medtronic, Inc. 2001. All rights reserved.)

Multiple versions in multiple languages

A similar single-source strategy has been used by Tweddle Lithography for the past six years. Tweddle uses a content-management repository and a single-source strategy, which uses source modules in SGML, a superset and parent of XML, to manage very large volumes of information in multiple versions. The information is written in functional modules, focused on subsystems within a vehicle. One subsystem might explain how to use the radio, another the air-conditioning system, and another how to properly maintain the vehicle. Each subsystem is developed by a writer who is responsible for all the versions of the information throughout the product line. For example, one manufacturer might have many different radios that it uses in its vehicles. The "radio" writer is responsible for writing and properly adding metadata to each module depending upon which model of radio is being discussed. Much of the process is automated, including the process of moving documents through the review workflow.

Once the modules are complete, they are assembled automatically into individual guides with unique content modules for each vehicle type, as well as a significant percentage of information that is common across all vehicles. The assembly process is guided by the metadata that originates in the Information Model.

In addition, the database itself is translated into multiple languages. The localized versions include information that is unique to each country in which the vehicle is sold. That unique information is appropriately tagged. The final production is automated.

As a result of their single-source strategy, which uses source modules in SGML, Tweddle has been able to realize significant cost and time efficiencies. They are looking forward to publishing in multiple media in the future.

Both examples are typical of single-source strategies in companies that support multiple versions of products. Instead of writing each manual separately or even cutting and pasting text and graphics from one version to another, the information developers have relied upon single sourcing to reduce costs and increase efficiency. They are able to focus their efforts on the quality of the content rather than on trying to keep everything in sync manually. They should be able to design new presentation formats for the information in electronic media without having to touch the existing modules. New styles for electronic delivery are simply applied upon output from the repository.

Multiple methods of delivery

A single-source strategy is also extremely valuable in organizations that deliver information for multiple purposes. For example, an organization might produce both end-user documentation and training materials to support its products or services. Some of the information used in each situation will be unique; other information can be used in common, reducing the cost of developing and maintaining it. In this case, an Information Model includes the metadata for delivering information for multiple purposes.

A developer of accounting software decided to combine the efforts of its information and training developers by single sourcing information in multiple deliverables. They developed an Information Model that labeled some information for training materials, some for user manuals, some for the context-sensitive help system, and some for all three, as illustrated in Figure 9-3. Members of the team produced information appropriate for all outputs; specialists in each area produced the information unique to particular outputs. The trainers, for example, added unique laboratory exercises to the training modules. They were able to create specific exercises for the different industries of their customers and identify these with metadata. In this way, rather than use generic exercises, they were able to develop unique training for each type of customer.

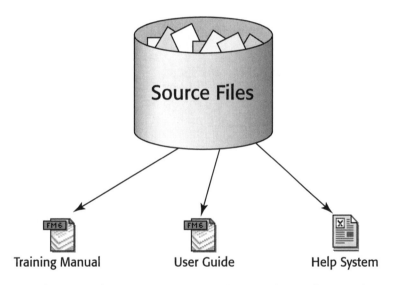

Figure 9-3 The same information or variations of information can be reused to create training manuals, user guides, help systems, and many other deliverables.

By single sourcing, the duplication of effort was significantly reduced and the savings were considerable. Previously, information and training had been separate organizations, each developing much of the same information resources and not sharing anything between them. Development efforts were duplicated not only by the information developers but by the subject-matter experts and reviewers as well. Each of these groups had to provide information and feedback on virtually the same subject matter more than once.

With the reorganization of the department, combining information development and training, staff members are able to reuse information and avoid duplication. Because team members can focus more on customizing the content to particular customers, they are able to increase the quality of the information deliverables at the same time that they reduce costs and time to market.

Multiple output media

Many organizations have already implemented a single-source strategy to provide for multiple output media. The same document is prepared for print, transformed to PDF and HTML, delivered on the Web or on CD-ROM, reformatted for a context-sensitive help system, or even sent to a handheld device, as illustrated in Figure 9-4. The content is identical in each case, with format changes made to accommodate media differences. At this basic level, single sourcing is primarily a technical and format-design problem.

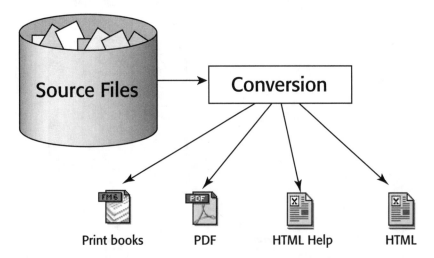

Figure 9-4 Many organizations already single source their information deliverables by converting the same files into multiple output formats, such as print, HTML, HTML help, and PDF.

Frequent multiple releases

One of the large telecommunications companies, faced with multiple releases of information to support their software, developed a single-source strategy based on producing structured documents in SGML and storing modules for reuse in a content-management system. Because additional functionality would often be added to the product during the software-development life cycle, the information developers not only had to maintain multiple versions of the information, but versions that changed frequently, as illustrated in Figure 9-5. At one time, they were simultaneously maintaining as many as nine released versions of information.

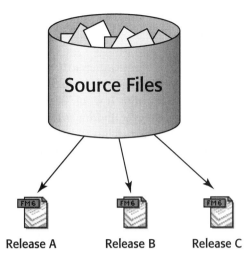

Figure 9-5 Multiple versions of a release can be maintained and tracked within a content-management system to produce a single final release.

Each of these released versions continued to change as bugs were fixed and functionality adjusted based on feedback from customers. Changes might affect one, two, or more different versions of the information. The information developers not only had to keep track of changing information that was common to all the interim releases, but they also had to track some modules that had variations in the content. Eventually, all versions had to be reconciled to match the final, official new version of the software—which meant that each module or set of related modules had to be reconciled and made the same.

Technical publications, legal documents, new business proposals, policy statements, internal procedures—each of these kinds of information is likely to benefit from a single-source strategy. The key is to plan carefully at the outset through the development of a comprehensive Information Model.

To ensure that your Information Model supports a single-source strategy, consider the categories you need to establish for your metadata. You can label information in many ways:

- by product model
- by delivery medium (training, documentation, paper, electronic)
- by language and country
- by interim release
- by final versions
- by customer requirements

Each category provides the opportunity to identify information modules for multiple outputs.

Training is inherently difficult to create and deliver because of the wide range of knowledge and experience that students bring to the classroom. It would seem impossible to speak directly to the needs of every individual's level of experience and knowledge, but this need is precisely what drives the new content management strategy of Prosoft Training. Using a Web-based assessment, students select certain courses based on their current knowledge. Only the courses students don't pass are developed into Web-based training or a printed manual. As Vice President of Research and Development, Judson Slusser's goal is to "find [a user's knowledge] gap and then fill it. Employers only need to make an investment in what their employees don't know."

Driven by their customers' need to have customized technical skills training programs in addition to training programs targeted to a student's existing knowledge, Prosoft Training began investigating what it would take to deliver customized content in print and on the Web to its academic and corporate customers. After discovering the Shareable Courseware Object Reference Model (SCORM), Prosoft felt they had found an effective way to create "learning objects" that could be mixed and matched into multiple deliverables and were ultimately customizable, but it required that their courseware be structured in XML. It was quite a radical transition from the somewhat structured content they wrote in Microsoft Word using standard templates to a full-scale structure using XML written with Epic Editor and a highly structured DTD. Their new structured content is stored and managed using Oracle iFS and produced into print and to the Web with the Arbortext E3 Engine.

By creating learning objects rather than full-scale courses, Prosoft Training combines bits and pieces from multiple courses to create unique courses on-the-fly and according to customer specifications. Additionally, the actual content is targeted to the user community, instructor or student, from the same source material. Because the instructor manuals contain the core basic content with more in-depth information for the instructors, Prosoft Training derives the student manuals from the instructor manuals.

Not by accident but through careful thought and planning, a structured environment has given Prosoft Training the flexibility to turn on a dime and deliver exactly what their customers need whether they can anticipate those needs or not. Prosoft Training is also researching how to respond to recent customer requirements to translate all of their courseware for international customers who currently only have access to translated versions of the exams. A modular content-management system will make that possible.

Contributed by Tina Hedlund, Comtech Services, Inc. and Judson Slusser, Prosoft Training.

Deciding on the appropriate level of granularity

One of the most critical decisions to make in developing your single-source strategy concerns the granularity of the components you want to manage in the database. For many organizations, the appropriate and easily defined level of granularity is at the level of the document. Each document is stored as a whole and labeled with a metadata wrapper that describes the content for retrieval and reuse. Such documents can be unstructured, that is, they need not have any labels or tags associated with their internal workings. They can easily be produced using standard desktop applications and won't need to be based on style sheets or require tags to be used again. However, the lack of styles means that they will probably have to be output using the same application they were developed with. For example, you can store a memo about a decision made at a meeting. The memo might be available to be reused in another context, a report on the decision made that month. However, the memo is likely to be published using the same office application with which it was created.

To gain the most from single sourcing, you are more likely to want to store information at a finer level of granularity than whole documents. Probably the most familiar example of single sourcing is the often-used device of storing graphics as separate entities that are linked by reference in a document rather than being cut and pasted into the document in each location where they are needed. If the graphic is updated, the document that references the graphic will always contain the most recent version.

In other situations, you will need individual modules or even content units to be easily available for reuse.

Book-level granularity

Organizations that produce lengthy books containing multiple chapters and sections can easily single source those large subsections of information for reassembling. Let's say you have many models of a computer product, some that use battery power (the laptops and handhelds) and some that do not (the desktops and servers), as illustrated in Figure 9-6. You want to include a chapter on power conservation for those with batteries but have no need for this chapter in the devices without batteries. If you store each chapter as a separate entity in the repository, you have developed a single-source strategy at the chapter level.

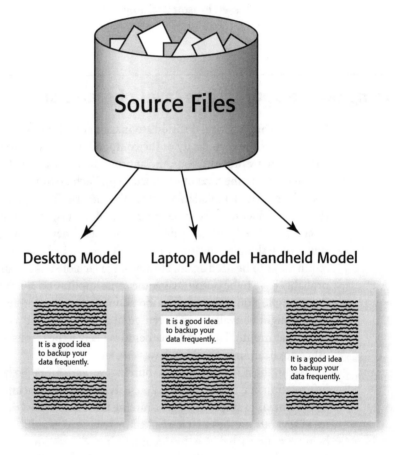

Figure 9-6 The same module of single-source information can be published in a manual for desktop, laptop, and handheld models. Reuse, in this case, is at the chapter level.

Module-level granularity

In other cases, chapter-level granularity will not be fine enough to support an organization's single-source requirements. Take, for example, an insurance company that develops custom insurance policies for each client. Some of the information in the policies is the same across multiple clients, but many modules are included in some policies and excluded from others. By creating a single-source strategy at the module level, the organization can construct new policies from the component modules in the database. When a module is changed, the new version is immediately available for use in any new policies being constructed.

Many organizations have found that certain critical information needs to be stored separately because it is so frequently reused. A company that manufactures chainsaws was able to reuse its safety warnings among many of the company's products. Individual warning paragraphs were stored in the repository to be reused in multiple documents and to be reused in several places in a single document. If the warning stored in the repository was changed, the revised warning appeared everywhere in all their publications, electronic and paper. This company was able to concentrate on developing warning statements that were easy to understand by their users and met regulatory requirements. See Figure 9-7.

The extent of the cost savings with reuse of information at the granular level of a section or even a paragraph is hard to predict. But one manufacturing company was able to avoid a cost of nearly half a million dollars simply by single sourcing its warnings and cautions. In addition, the single-source strategy provided them with a safety net. Because the information in the warnings and cautions was always the same everywhere, they avoided potential litigation that might have resulted from a warning that was not properly written.

Content-unit-level granularity

Sometimes the level of granularity needs to be even finer than individual modules. Some projects require single-sourced information at the paragraph, sentence, and even word level.

Multiple versions of a new business proposal might need to be altered at the paragraph level by including information specific to a particular client's request for proposal or request for information, as illustrated in Figure 9-8. Technical information might need to change at the level of the cells in a table to accommodate differences among customer's configurations of equipment. One equipment company, for example, produced different parameter tables for each customer using its products. Much of the data in the tables was generated automatically from configuration databases and included automatically in the deliverable documents.

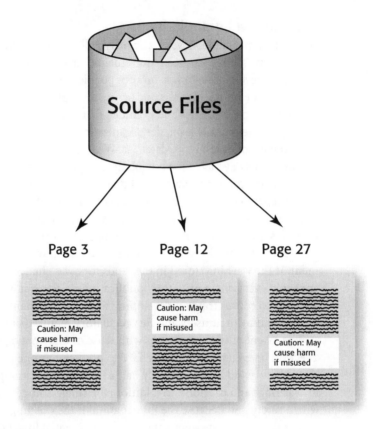

Figure 9-7 Warning statements are used often and in many places. Using a single-source strategy, they can be written once, stored in the content-management repository, updated once, and reused many times.

Word-level granularity

In a large number of cases, individual words need to be changed to accommodate changes in the targeted audience and the business requirements.

An organization might want to control individual words in a document so that they can be altered. Word-level granularity might be appropriate for country-specific measurement units, product names, variant spellings of words, and so on.

In some cases, all the information in two documents can be the same except for the name of the product. In this case, a general entity reference was created in the DTD to define the product name so that it can be updated. The value of the entity is changed for each output. For example, you might not currently know what your final product name will be. In your DTD, define the general entity reference to read <!ENTITY product "Product Name Not Yet Determined">. In your XML documents, your authors type the tag &product;. During production, the general

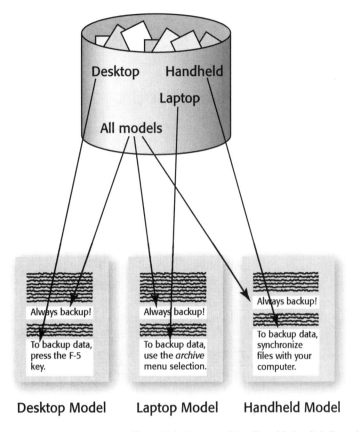

Figure 9-8 Content common to all models is reused in all published deliverables, while the information specific to each model is also published.

entity reference is changed to the new value you define in your DTD. Unless you change the value, the words "Product Name Not Yet Determined" will appear in place of &product;. The value is easily changed to reflect the appropriate product name.

Word or phrase changes can also be handled by metadata attributes in XML. For example, in the US a bank note is spelled "check", while in Canada it is spelled "cheque." By defining the variant values as metadata, you can insert the appropriate value during production. (<variant us="check" canada="cheque"/>) See Figure 9-9, which illustrates this concept.

The opportunities to define information modules at many levels of granularity are endless. However, each grain of detail added to the mix increases the complexity of the content-management process.

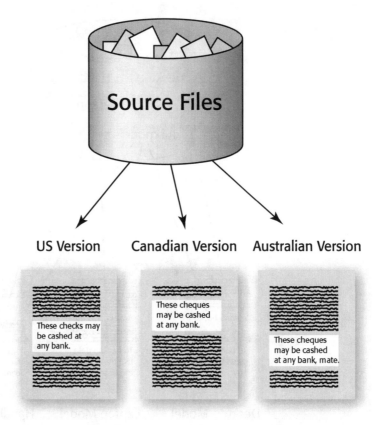

Figure 9-9 Single sourcing is used at the word level to identify regional differences. In the US a bank note is spelled "check," and in Canada, Australia, and the United Kingdom, it is spelled "cheque."

Ensuring that your metadata supports your single-source strategy

Your information architects are responsible for coming up with a categorizing framework that will support all the different information configurations that you need to reach your single-source goal. At each level of granularity that you manage, you will need a set of metadata tags.

Consider the examples in the previous section. Large book-like collections can be labeled at the section level with metadata that identifies characteristics to differentiate them for possible reuse. If, for example, you have entire chapters or sections that are specifically targeted for particular models of a product or particular user profiles, then the metadata must support these variations in the content.

You might need to identify individual modules by any number of characteristics. A module might be used only in training materials, not in reference information. A module might appear only in one type of contract and not in others. A module might be appropriate for a print version of a document but not for an electronic version. In each situation, you use metadata tags to identify the individual modules for reuse in a variety of contexts. In the XML sample in Figure 9-10, the first line indicates that this procedure module will be used in four different deliverables—print, eBook, PDF, and Flash.

At the content unit level or the level of individual words and phrases, metadata tags provide you with access to a categorizing framework. A word might be spelled differently in the US and Canada. If you want to generate versions of the information with the correct spellings, the spelling variations will need to be labeled appropriately. If you have warnings or cautions required in some countries and not others, the metadata tags correctly label which module or content unit goes where. In Figure 9-10, the substep is only used if the user has the ActivSync version of the program. In the second substep, a variant name = ActivSync permits authors to change the name of the variant as necessary.

Building compound documents out of reusable content units

After content has been well labeled with appropriate metadata at all the levels of granularity required by your Information Model, you are ready to use the metadata to create compound documents that are specifically targeted to the user and business requirements you have identified.

The most direct method is for individual authors or production specialists to create a new compound document based upon a new DTD and to pull in the modules and content units needed for a particular targeted audience. If the modules and content are well labeled, you can use search routines based on metadata attributes, tag names (XML elements), and even full-text search to find the appropriate pieces. Then, you insert them into the compound documents as file entities according to your content plan, referencing the file that exists in the repository with a link rather than by cutting and pasting it into a new document.

If you make changes to your compound document and it has already been moved to a Web server, you will have to update the content on the Web server from the compound document in your working repository. In most cases, you will be able to create a workflow that automates the updating process once the changes have been approved.

```
<procedure output="Print, eBook, PDF, Flash">
<title output="Print, eBook, PDF">Send a meeting request</title>
<title output="Flash">Meeting request</title>
<introduction>
<p>Schedule a meeting and send a meeting request through a
synchronization program or an email service. You must enter contacts
with email addresses in the Name and Address application and set up
the Send/Receive application to send and receive email before you can
send a meeting request.</p>
<p>For more information about entering contacts, see Work with
Names and Addresses. For more information about setting up the email
application, see Use the Send/Receive.</p>
</introduction>
<step>From the Start menu, tap DayTimer</step>
<step>Tap Start</step>
<step>Tap First</step>
<step>Tap the down arrow</step>
<step>Tap the email service you want to use to send a meeting
request and tap OK </step>
<substep name="Synchro">Otherwise, tap Synchro to send a
meeting request through the synchronization program. Tap New to
create a new appointment</substep>
<step>Enter the information</step>
<step>Tap the Participants field</step>
<step>Tap the contacts you want to invite to the meeting</step>
<step>Tap OK to add the participants</step>
<step>Tap OK to schedule the meeting</step>
<substep>Send/Receive automatically creates a meeting request
and sends it to the attendees the next time you connect to the Internet
<variant name="Synchro">or your network or the next time you
synchronize</variant></substep>
<hint>Hint: If you make a change to the meeting information, the
application asks if you want to inform the participants about the
changes.</hint>
</procedure>
```

Figure 9-10 This XML-tagged document has a variety of metadata. The first line defines the document as a procedure that can be output in several forms. One substep is optional when Synchro is employed. The variant name in the second substep enables authors to change the name, Synchro, if the product name changes before publication.

Building customized documents out of reusable content units

Customized documents are easy to build out of reusable content units if you have prepared your Information Model to account for variations. At a leading telecommunications manufacturing company, the content-management team designed a process that allowed them automatically to generate custom technical content for their customers. They categorized their technical information according to the hardware and software functions available to customers. Then, when they were ready to publish a new release of the product, they released the database of technical information with a customer database that recorded which functionality was owned by each customer. They produced custom content for CD-ROM delivery to each customer. The satisfied customer received a unique CD-ROM referenced only to the functions in their portfolio rather than a collection of all possible functions.

As this example demonstrates, you can build custom compound documents by using programmed instructions that automatically gather the appropriate sections, modules, or content units and render them in your final form, which can include print, CD-ROM, and other online and Web deliverables. In effect, you use your content plan to generate a compound document automatically.

If you are directing content to the Web, your programmed instructions can also create Web pages that are based upon a set of hypertext links. The dynamic compound document that is your Web page design draws in the modules from the repository and assembles them on the Web page according to the rules you have established in your content plan and style sheet. The original modules are individually stored and can be modified at any time. Then, the hyperlinked Web page can be immediately updated with the new content at the modular level.

Typically, you have to revise an entire Web page if you update the modules in your working repository and then send the new content to the Web server. However, technology now makes it possible to update only portions of a Web page with new content rather than revising the entire page. That means a more responsive system for the users and less time spent downloading whole pages to the browser.

Building documents from the top down using existing compound structures

The examples I have used so far have shown how compound documents can be built from the bottom up by assembling modules and content units and larger entities. Use technology that lets authors build documents from the top down. A good example of a top-down technology is The Environment from Ecosystems.

The top-down approach means beginning with an existing compound document. The author begins by saving a new compound document. Then, he or she reviews the modules and content units in the compound document, deciding to delete some, add others by reference from the repository, and modify some of the content units based on the requirements for the new audience. The author saves the document (Save As) to create a new instance in the repository.

During the process, a top-down look like The Environment builds a decision list, based on the actions of the user. The decision list relates each content unit to a specific version of a compound document (a copy type). The decision list and the copy type are used to construct the new instance in the repository and create the appropriate bi-directional metadata links. The author can use the links to navigate through the repository and merge branched modules and content units.

For example, a sales manager needs to create a new business proposal for a new customer. She finds an existing proposal that was created for a similar customer last month and uses this as the starting point. The existing proposal is a compound document made up of modules and content units that have been stored in the repository. The sales manager creates a new document that is linked to the modules in the repository.

The new compound document is now completely up-to-date because any changes to the modules in the repository have been reflected in the compound document. The sales manager begins by removing modules from the compound document that don't apply to the new customer. The new customer, for example, does not want the standard workflow component. The sales manager brings in the information from the repository on the custom workflow component to replace the standard description. Then, the sales manager modifies the introductory module by describing the new customer's business problem and summarizing how the proposed solution will provide benefits and a rapid return on investment. She also modifies the schedule to reflect the current times and dates and makes some changes to the cost modules to reflect the new pricing strategy.

Each of the modified modules becomes a new entity in the repository, linked to the original source modules and also available for reuse in the future. If someone else uses one of the new modules that the sales manager has created, she can track that reuse through a reporting function. In addition, a workflow system might automate a notification to each owner of a compound document when one of the modules has been changed. That way the owner could elect to accept the change or to delete the link between the two modules, thus creating two entities in the repository.

In creating a compound document in this manner, you must be careful to create a new version of the whole document for the new situation, or you run the risk of making a change to a pre-existing version of the proposal. You will want to archive the pre-existing version so that you know exactly what you delivered to your client before starting to make changes in a new version.

You should also avoid proliferating too many "child" versions of the modules, each tagged for a particular situation. Too many different versions without adequate archives of the published versions will quickly become too confusing to track.

10

Authoring for Reuse

"Now, this module is for the novice. It has more detail than the expert version."

M ost authors, especially those who don't write regularly, create copy so individualistic that it cannot be mixed easily with material written by others. Many prefer to stamp their own style on everything they write so they can call it their own. Unfortunately, when the customer tries to use information from one module with information from another, confusion often results.

If you want to mix and match information to meet the needs of an individual customer, that information must have a uniform structure and style. If you want to reuse information in multiple outputs, you must ensure that it is designed for reuse in the first place.

That means retraining authors to work within content and structure guidelines. It also means that content units containing variable elements (product A works this way, product B works another way) are written so that those elements can be interchanged.

For many organizations today, authoring for reuse is a new kind of writing. For organizations that want to repurpose information dynamically in a Web environment, it is a key differentiator.

In this chapter, I give examples of authoring for reuse, including normalizing existing content that has significant as well as insignificant differences. I also introduce the concept of variable content that depends upon the dimensions selected in the Information Model. I give examples of how content managers can focus on the development of variable content that can be dynamically interchanged to meet the needs of individual customers.

In this chapter, you will learn

- how to begin a single-source, content-management project
- how to make authoring assignments
- when and how to add editing for consistency and continuity
- how to manage the review and approval process
- how to plan for localization and translation
- when to incorporate a minimalist strategy

Starting with a content plan

Is it possible to start writing individual topics without reference to a larger structure like a book, a chapter, or a section? Can you write one topic of a help system without knowing what the other topics will be? Do you need a content plan before you start? But what if the structure will be flexible? What if the topics you write will be used in more than one context? What if they're in no context at all and the user can access them as individual topics without reference to anything else?

There are lots of things an author needs to know before beginning to compose topics. Who is the audience? What audience needs will this information support? What is the scope of the information? Which topics should be included? Which excluded? How detailed do the topics need to be? Which details should be omitted? Which included? These decisions cannot be made in isolation.

To begin writing modular content, you must start with a content plan. A content plan, as I discussed in Chapter 7, *Developing Content Plans for Static Web Sites*, provides the rationale for the document or documents being created. It includes an analysis of the users, their business requirements, the tasks they want to perform, their environment, usability goals, and other issues critical to the decisions about how to structure and style the information.

Based on your knowledge of the users and their information needs, you plan the topics and address their relationship to one another. The content plan lists the topics to be developed in terms of their consequence for the users.

Figure 10-1 illustrates a portion of the content plan for an administrator's manual for a small-business telephone system. In the proposed table of contents, the authors have listed the tasks that they need to address for each segment of the user community. Some tasks are for everyone; some are only for users who want to do tasks that affect individual telephone sets; other tasks are for those who want to customize the way the telephone system as a whole behaves. Finally, they included a group of tasks performed only by those who had purchased an additional product. In each case, they determined what users wanted to do and balanced those needs against the functionality available in the product. Many times,

Content Plan—Small Business Phone System

Client company/project: Small Business Phone System
Writing project manager: Jim Brown
Tentative start date: January 19

Please review this content plan and return your comments to the project manager by 2:00 p.m., February 2.

Please contact Jim Brown at 555-7586 if you have any questions about the content plan.

Publication Content

The *System Manager's Guide* is designed specifically for the audience described previously. It is a task-oriented guide to modifying telephone and system features. It includes the following:

- Preface
- Chapter 1, "Getting Started"
- Chapter 2, "Modifying Telephone Features"
- Chapter 3, "Modifying System Features"
- Chapter 4, "Modifying Restrictions for Telephones and Lines"
- Chapter 5, "Station Message Detail Recording (SMDR)"
- Appendix A, "Reading BCD Values"
- Appendix B, "Forms"
- Glossary
- Index

Overview by Chapter

Preface

The Preface introduces system managers to the *System Manager's Guide*. It briefly explains the document's purpose and design, and it describes the document's organization, including brief descriptions of the five chapters and two appendices.

Chapter 1. Getting Started

Chapter 1 introduces system managers to the SBPS telephone system and to the *System Manager's Guide*.

Chapter Objectives

After reading Chapter 1, users will

- recognize the installation form
- know which features the system manager can change and which features the SBPS technician must change
- recognize special terms used in the *Guide*
- understand the kinds of telephone equipment available with the system
- understand what they need to know before they can begin modifying the system
- understand the basic steps for modifying both telephone and system features.

Chapter Organization

Chapter 1 includes the following sections:
What features can I change?

- This section explains in general terms the system-wide features and the individual features affecting only one telephone that the system manager can change.

Understanding this guide's conventions

- This section explains the terms used to identify the people who are involved in setting up and using the telephone system.

Equipment

- This section lists the five kinds of telephone equipment available in the SBPS system and explains how to use the telephone to modify features.

Figure 10-1 This example shows a portion of the content plan for the administrators' manual of a small-business phone system.

they found functionality in the product that led us to ask, "Why would anyone want to use this." They either left the functionality out or put it at the end of the list.

In this content plan, the authors decided to write for administrators who already knew how to use telephones but didn't know how to program a telephone system. They paid considerable attention to the names of the topics, because they knew that titles were critical in making information easy to access. They also decided to organize the topics in the print manual in alphabetical order within each sub-category. All tasks in this case being equal, it was hard to tell which tasks were likely to be done and in which order. Aside from the basic tasks of logging onto the telephone system and adding name and password, most of the other tasks were interchangeable.

Once the authors had the content laid out in the plan, they could address exactly how to structure each information type. The principal information type was, of course, the procedure. They decided in the interest of simplicity and space to eliminate the logon steps from each procedure. The logon steps were made more-or-less accessible by printing them on the inside back cover of the book—sort of a quick reference device for print. Once they had learned the logon routine, the users could log on the same way each time.

Each procedure followed exactly the same strict structure. The style was worked out in a model procedure that embodied the set of rules for the authors and editors to follow. With the structure fully developed, the writing could be parsed out to members of the team with the assurance that everything would come together successfully in the end.

Was every topic to be included at the beginning of the content planning process known? Certainly not. Topics were both added and deleted along the way. But with a strong modular design in place, they could easily accommodate new information.

Although the information in this content plan was developed for print, it could easily serve for online delivery. In fact, online delivery would eliminate the complication of not beginning with the logon procedure. The logon procedure could be linked to every procedure and be available to any user beginning at any point in the tasks.

With dynamic delivery capabilities, the modular structure of the information would have served users even more effectively. They would have been able to list the tasks they needed in any order that made sense to them.

One section of the administrators' manual constituted a larger chunk of information, the introductory tutorial. The authors decided to include a tutorial because they had learned that the basic task of programming a telephone system using only the keys on the phone and no display was difficult. The tutorial gave users an opportunity to practice the task so that they would not need all the complicating details repeated in every procedure. If the information had been delivered online, the practice tutorial could have been referenced from any point at which the users might have entered. The tutorial module, longer than a typical procedure, represents a single module of information.

Content planning of this type can be done by an individual author. However, in a content-management environment, you might want the content planning to be done by the information architect or by a collaborative team of authors rather than by an individual. If you plan to share topics among various deliverables, they all need to be planned with that intent in mind. The individual authors, then, have to consider that the topics will be placed in more than one context for the users. The structure set for each information type must take into account the multiple reuse.

Focusing on the topic at hand

Once the content plan is in place and the structure determined, the authors can turn their full attention to the subject matter. They can concentrate on determining how to best communicate the information to the users without worrying about the sequence. In fact, when you write to a fully developed content plan, you can write topics in any order. You don't have to follow a sequence determined by the table of contents of a book. You also don't have to worry about transitions, phrases such as "as you read in chapter 1" or "based on the description in the previous section." Those relationships will be determined in the final assembly of multiple compound documents that result.

Although topics can be written in any order, when writing each topic, you should consider what the users must already know for the topic to be of interest to them when they access it. Otherwise, you might find yourself repeating explanations of introductory material or adding an overwhelming number of cross-references.

You might also need to avoid the common practice in book-like documents of creating narrative filler to move the reader through a text. Prefiguring discussions that are limited to "what will be covered in this chapter" or filler that tells the reader "that next will appear information on this topic" have no value in modular text. Readers, as you know from frequent observation and usability assessments, do not read continuously unless there is value to be found in following a sustained narrative. Much technical and procedural information is best presented in modular chunks. The narrative linking is unnecessary because the readers do not process the text linearly. Rather they skim and skip until they find just the information they want to read.

Since the advent of desktop publishing in the early 1980s, many authors have moved away from a focus on content and communication to a focus on page design. WYSIWYG text editors encouraged this concentration, frequently to the detriment of the subject matter and the communication. Structured authoring, on the other hand, shifts the focus back to the user and the information because the format is determined upon output rather than during the authoring process.

A focus on content rather than format is likely to have a positive effect on efficiency and productivity. Less time is spent "tweaking" the format of a topic, chapter, or book than occurs with WYSIWYG publishing. According to PG Bartlett, Vice President of Marketing at Arbortext, their studies have shown that authors spend up to 50 percent of their time formatting instead of developing content. Authors can be 50 to 100 percent more productive when they are relieved from the responsibility of page formatting.

Following a predetermined structure

Structured writing, based upon well-defined information types and content units, is especially useful in assisting less practiced authors to write topics that come up to the quality of more experienced authors. If the authors are using an XML or SGML editor, they have the additional advantage of relying on validity checking to ensure they haven't omitted a required content unit or put content units in the wrong order. Many text editing tools check validity at the same time the writer is entering text, providing messages indicating the nature of the problem.

For the structure to be checked in this way, you must use a DTD. If the writer simply enters XML or SGML codes without a DTD, there is no way to check for structural validity. The DTD provides a collection of rules that indicate how the topic is to be structured. A topic is valid if it follows all the rules in the DTD. Figure 10-2 shows an example of a message that indicates a mistake in following the rules in the DTD.

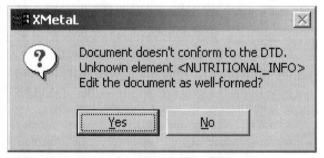

Figure 10-2 This example of a message in XMetaL indicates that the element <NUTRITIONAL_INFO> in an XML document isn't defined in the DTD, and the XML document is invalid.

For less practiced authors, especially those who do only minimal writing in their jobs, you might want to provide text-entry forms or wizards to aid in producing valid structures. At AAA of California, the architecture team provided business specialists with easy-to-complete forms as they developed business policies and procedures. As a result, the policies and procedures were reasonably well written, complete, and well structured. They were also completed in record time because no one had to invent a writing style.

Forms-based writing works best when the information is highly structured and little variation is allowed or desired. Information to be published to the Web often meets these preconditions and can therefore use a very restricted set of page designs or information structures to accommodate novice authors.

Forms and wizards can be designed to produce XML-tagged documents without the authors knowing that the tags are being added. In that way, you can avoid the process of training authors throughout the enterprise in using XML tags. Figure 10-3 provides an example of form-based information authoring.

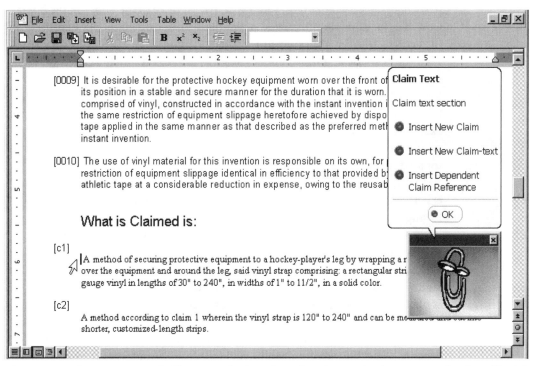

Figure 10-3 This screen sample illustrates the form-based, tagless authoring process developed by i4i for the US Patent Office.

Of course, as I have mentioned earlier, the chief beneficiary of structured for forms-based writing is the intended user of the information, in this case the patent reviewers. When writing is structured and conforms to well-defined information types, the user finds topics that are organized in the same way, contain the same kinds of content, and are easy to identify at a glance.

Making writing assignments

In information development, it is traditional to assign one author to one book, a complete document that usually contains information about many aspects of a project or product. For example, the library for the small-business phone system consisted of four documents: an administrators' guide, a manual for telephone users, a quick reference card, and a technical service manual. A typical staffing of such a project would assign individual authors to the three large manuals. One of the authors would also likely design the quick reference card, possibly with the help of a graphic artist.

Each volume in the library covers many of the same subjects, written for each user group. Using a collaborative writing team, you could assign each writer to a particular subject matter that would span two or three of the books in the library. Consider, for example, the process of handling "music on hold." The end-user can turn this feature on or off for an individual phone. The administrator decides what music to use and which phones in the system to turn on for this feature. The installer connects the music source to the system and provides the functionality for the administrator to handle. One author working on this functionality could handle all the related topics for each user group. The author becomes an in-depth expert on the particular aspect of functionality, focuses on what the various user groups need to know about the function, and is best able to decide when to write topics or content units that can be used in common among the deliverables.

In this collaborative model, authors become the subject-matter and customer experts for a particular type of information, developing all the topics used throughout the library collection. The information in the library on each topic is likely to be much more consistent in this scenario than if different authors are assigned to write for different user groups.

The same is true in a scenario involving delivering in multiple media. The same author who writes information for a user manual might be responsible for the context-sensitive help topics, the training materials, and the wireless version of the subject matter.

At Tweddle Lithography, authors are assigned to content areas and write all versions of the information for all vehicle models. The authors are able to make better decisions on the information that is common to all and the differences that must be accommodated. As a result, the authors write different versions that become interchangeable parts when the final owners' manuals are assembled.

Assigning metadata

A critical element of developing content to be handled by a content-management system is the metadata attached to every topic. The metadata is defined by your Information Model and can be inserted at a number of levels in a topic.

The simplest level is at the beginning of the topic in what is called the "root element." At this level, the metadata labels the topic according to the dimensions of the Information Model. For example, you might have a topic for a technical manual that is labeled as a procedure, software version 2.0, English original, authored by Sam, edited by Jean, first drafted on 8/1, revised on 8/7, and approved by Daphne on 8/15.

The root element in XML would look like the following:

```
<procedure version="2.0" language="English" author="Sam"
editor="Jean" approver="Daphne" first_draft="8.1" revision="8.7"
approval="8.15">
```

If all this information had to be directly entered by the author at the beginning of the topic, it would take time and be inaccurate. However, much of the topic-level metadata can be automated. For example, the workflow provides the information about the author, editor, and approver and automatically enters the dates on which activities occurred. Other metadata can be added to the topic by setting defaults. If you know that Sam always writes in English, is working on version 2.0 and has selected a procedure template, you can automatically add metadata to that effect.

In addition, most XML and SGML authoring systems provide easy-to-use dialogue boxes to use for selecting metadata. The author opens the dialogue and selects the appropriate attributes and values from a predetermined list based on the Information Model.

Metadata added within a topic might require more understanding on the author's part. For example, authors using an XML editor such as Arbortext's Epic Editor are able to add metadata to content units that indicate that a particular content unit has more than one version. Metadata might also indicate that two paragraphs are interchangeable depending on the product model. The author adds an entity name with the appropriate metadata values to each version of the paragraph. FrameMaker provides a similar facility with values called conditional text. Other systems use other terms for the same practice of adding tags to identify variations on a content unit, a sentence, or even a word. See Chapter 9, *Developing a Single-Source Strategy* for a discussion of text variations for single sourcing). Figure 10-4 provides an example of using metadata within a text to label variations.

Authors can also use entities to avoid having manually to change text that is likely to change during the course of the topic's development. For example, prod-

```
<task product="Model Cr Press" id="Troubleshooting">
<title>Drive motor does not start</title>
<taskbody>
<steps>
<step audience="Maintenance"><cmd>Ensure that the
Emergency Stop button is not engaged.<cmd></step>
<step audience="Operator"><cmd>Check the operator console
for any safety controls, such as guards or limit and pressure
switches, that may still be engaged.<cmd></step>
<step audience="Maintenance"><cmd>Ensure that the driver
selector switch is in the proper position.<cmd></step>
<step audience="Operator"><cmd>Ensure that the key selectors
switch on the Bar station is in the Run position.<cmd></step>
<step audience="Maintenance"><cmd>Check the tool pack
cover sensors to ensure that they are registering
properly.<cmd></step></steps>
</taskbody></task>
```

Figure 10-4 An example of metadata used to identify variations in the text to be independently assembled and rendered for maintenance engineers and operators.

uct names often change several times before a product is released. An author can use an entity such as &product; in the text (as long as this entity is defined in the DTD or XML document). Figure 10-5 shows an example of entities used in a text. Then, when the document is published, &product; is replaced by the final name of the product.

```
<?xml version="1.0"?>
<!DOCTYPE shortdesc SYSTEM "\concept.dtd" [
<!ENTITY product "Model CR Press">
]>
<shortdesc>This section presents a brief overview of the operating
instructions for the &product; consolet. Because the consolet is designed
and built to each customer's particular needs, it is impossible to provide
exact operating procedures in this guide. Instead, this section provides
information about the function controls and monitor display messages
that are applicable to most &product;es.</shortdesc>
```

Figure 10-5 The product entity (&product;) will be replaced with the words "Model CR Press" during production. Entities can be defined in the XML document or in the DTD.

Authors might also be asked to use tags to identify particular terms in a text. Consider, for example, a legal brief that contains references to statutes. If the author identifies with a metadata tag each critical reference, the tag can be used to facilitate searches of briefs in the future. To determine which terms or phrases require metadata tags, the information architect must establish a taxonomy of key terms and synonyms in the Information Model that will become the metadata tags and attributes.

A system of tags should be used, rather than having individual authors create their own. Ad-hoc tagging makes the information more confusing because it does not correspond to the tags used in other similar documents. Along the same lines, it is best to predetermine a set of indexing terms to be used across a library rather than permit each author to determine index terms independently.

Creating links

When topics are being written for online delivery, a critical element will be the links between related topics. For example, in the small-business phone system described earlier, the authors wanted to link each procedure to the basic logon procedure rather than repeating the logon steps every time. To do so, the authors had to create a link between the procedure at hand and the referenced procedure, much as they would have created a cross-reference in a printed book.

To incorporate a link in an XML or SGML topic, the author uses a metadata tag that identifies the target of the link. The simplest example is a link that goes to just one place, like the one to the logon procedure. However, authors can also use links that go to more than one place. Such extended links allow authors to create links that might go to different versions of the logon procedure, one for novices and another for experienced users. Figure 10-6 shows a link added to an XML document.

```
<task>
<title>Preloading and centering the redraw carriage</title>
<taskbody>
<prereq>Before you begin this procedure, the redraw carriage must be installed
in the press and the upper cam followers rotated to their highest position. Make
sure that the way strips and way followers are clean and smooth. If they are not
remove, rework, and install the way strips and way followers as explained in
<cite xlink:form="simple" href="installwfollow.xml">Removing, installing, and
setting up the way followers</cite>.
<note>In this procedure, you might have to move the drive system by
hand&#x2014;&#x2014;or <cite xlink:form="simple" href="bar.xml">"bar"
it.</cite></note>
</prereq> </task>
```

Figure 10-6 This example shows an XLink added to an XML document.

Links can also be defined systematically to relate one category of information to another. You might, for example, want to link a procedure to a policy in every case, or to link all policies to their corresponding procedures. By designing a link strategy, you can ensure that certain links are always available without having to rely on individual authors to insert links into their documents.

The topics that you link to from a topic you have developed might, of course, be revised by another author an even deleted. Authors need to be notified if a topic is changed or before it is deleted. In many content-management systems, it is possible for all authors to learn if a topic they are working on is linked from another topic. It is a good practice to check the link management system before revising or deleting a topic to ensure that the relationships between topics are maintained. Many workflow systems provide automatic methods for managing links, including email alerts to the owners of linked topics in the repository.

Adding index terms

In addition to adding links to a topic, authors can add index items if they have been defined as elements in the DTD. Indexing in XML and SGML works like indexing in any document. Authors add index terms to the text to produce a list of index items. Those index items might be rendered as "back of the book" index pages in standard print documents, index links in PDF from the index pages to the content unit in the text, indexes in online help systems, and indexes in HTML documents.

Index items inserted by authors into the text should follow an index standard for terminology, especially if indexes are to refer to multiple volumes in a library or multiple topics authored by different people. The information architect and the editors should work together to develop a master list of index terms to be used by all authors. Authors should also be able to add index terms to the master list to handle specific content in the topics they write. Figure 10-7 shows an index term inserted in an XML document.

```
<concept product="Model CR">
<title>Overview of the redraw motion assembly</title>
<prolog> <shortdesc>The redraw carriage assembly is located in front of the
ram assembly next to the die housing assembly.</shortdesc></prolog>
<conbody><p>The <i1>redraw operation</i1> is the most important function
in the can making process. The <i1>redraw carriage</i1> presses the
<i1>redraw sleeve</i1>into the cup and then pushes the cup through the
<i1>redraw die</i1> to change the cup diameter.</p></conbody>
</concept>
```

Figure 10-7 Index terms are identified by the element <i1>.

Developing style guidelines

Structured authoring of modules for reuse in different contexts requires that all authors adhere to style guidelines. Compound documents, containing topics written by several authors, should read as if one person wrote them.

I recommend that style guides be developed or revised to specify the style requirements for structured topics. Style guides have always included terminology, syntax (for example, requiring that action steps begin with a verb), and content guidelines. A style guide that encompasses a content-management system should also include

- descriptions of each information type including its purpose and when to use it, with examples of well-written types
- descriptions of each content unit in every information type, with examples of well-written content units
- a catalog of metadata dimensions in the Information Model and how to apply them
- a catalog of entities used to label content units and phrases, and words within content units and how they are to be applied
- instructions for inserting links and under what circumstances to add links
- instructions for inserting index terms and how to use common terminology for indexing

Style guidelines should be developed during the planning stages of your content-management project and refined as you move through your pilot project and into your initial rollouts of larger projects. The guidelines become the training manual for authors using the new content-management system for the first time.

In addition, style guidelines might include instructions for using a simplified vocabulary for authoring to ease understanding and translation. Organizations such as Caterpillar and Boeing have long used standardized vocabularies and simplified English to control the language in their documents.

Editing to the guidelines

Developing a repository of modules that can be interchanged to create multiple deliverables requires a collaborative environment. Authors need to work together to ensure that the topics they write follow the standards of their information types and adhere to the style guidelines. But having authors take on all the responsibility for adhering to standards and guidelines will not ensure consistency.

To develop a repository that will provide maximum opportunities for reuse and avoid duplication of effort, I recommend that every organization develop an editorial review function. The purpose of editorial review is to ensure that guidelines are followed and that modules can be effectively strung together in compound documents.

As in an object-oriented development environment, the goal of structured, modular writing suffers from the tendency of authors to want to craft topics in their own styles. Authors are perennial nitpickers, deciding that something written by another person is just not good enough. Instead of reusing an existing module, they decide to write one that reads better.

Content-management systems also require that authors find the appropriate modules to reference in the repository, either by using search routines or by understanding what topics are being written by other members of the collaborative workgroup. Unless it is easy for authors to find the topics they need, they will tend to write their own, adding to the duplication or near duplication of topics.

Normalizing text

An important task of an editorial review team is to find duplicates and eliminate them as well as to find near duplicates and decide if they really should be different. In database language, this process is called normalizing. If you begin your content-management project by importing modules from legacy sources, you are likely to have a huge normalizing task ahead of you. When I reviewed 39 separate manuals for very similar models of one product line, I found hundreds of near duplicates that needed to be resolved and normalized. The near duplicates, sometimes called fuzzy matches, resulted from authors dispersed through the organization and in different countries, the lack of editorial review, and a process of drift, often caused by differences of opinion among reviewers.

To normalize the text, the editor must compare the near duplicates and decide if stylistic variants can be resolved immediately or consult with the original authors or subject-matters experts to decide which of the multiple versions is correct. In many cases, you will find that elements of each version are correct and need to be combined into a new, more complete version. In other cases, you will find, as I have, that much of the detail separating the multiple versions is unnecessary for the users. Among the 39 separate manuals, I found many instances in which technical details irrelevant to the users had been added, resulting in differences from what had been a common initial text. By removing the extraneous details, I was able to resolve the differences and end up with a simpler, more reusable version.

Establishing a review and approval process

The editorial review that I described previously is not the only component of the review process. A document that will be made available to a large number of people, either inside or outside the organization, should be reviewed and approved before it can be published to the Web. The editorial review focuses on the guidelines for writing based on the information types and content unit definitions. The editorial review also checks for the correct application of metadata and other XML or SGML tags if they are being inserted into the topic. Editorial review does not test for correctness or compliance with company policy. These issues must be handled by other people within the information-development workflow.

If you have a workflow system as part of your content-management solution, you can automate the review and approval workflow. Figure 10-8 provides an example of a workflow process. As soon as the author completes a topic, the editor is notified. The editor opens and edits the topic and notifies the author that it is ready for revision. Next comes the expert or peer reviewer. This reviewer might be someone inside the group or individuals who need to review the topic for correctness and completeness. Once again, the workflow system notifies the subject-matter reviewer that the topic is ready for review. The same process holds for other individuals or groups who have to review and approve the topic before it can be published.

Figure 10-8 shows the user's view of a workflow assigned to a project in XyEnterprise's Content@ desktop interface. The example illustrates a simple editing pass on an existing document. The split-screen view provides both the graphical display and a display that shows exactly when the project moved from one task to the next.

The detailed view in Figure 10-9 shows each step in the workflow by activity and highlights the current task. Each activity displays the assigned role and due date.

A review-process problem occurs when authors are preparing individual topics or groups of topics but not entire documents. Many reviewers assume that they have to review large documents and are not used to seeing smaller chunks. Because the compound documents will be assembled during the production and delivery stage, they are not necessarily available for review.

You need to develop a new review process to accommodate a new way of authoring in a content-management environment. In some cases, you will ask people to review and approve individual topics. In other cases, you might need to assemble several topics into a group (a section or a chapter of a book, for example), so that the reviewers can see at least one context. You might want to prepare content that focuses on a particular subject area and send the entire assembly out for review.

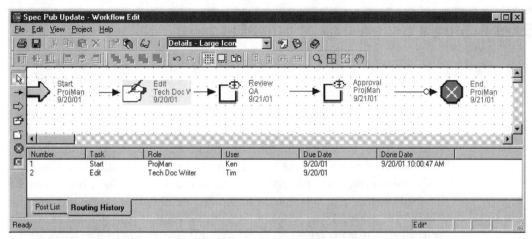

Figure 10-8 The split-screen view of the XyEnterprise Content@ workflow interface provides both a graphical display and a display that shows exactly when the project moved from one task to the next. (©2001, Xyvision Enterprise Solutions, Inc. All rights reserved. XyEnterprise and Content@ are trademarks of Xyvision Enterprise Solutions, Inc. in the United States and other countries.)

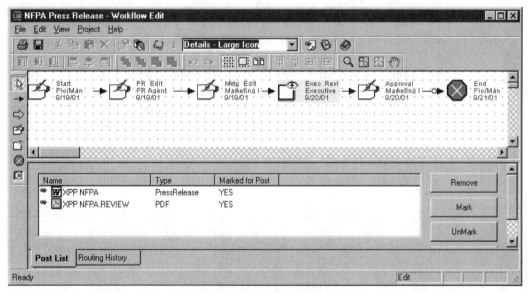

Figure 10-9 The Post list in the bottom panel shows the documents or objects that will be posted as new versions to the database at the end of the project, in this case a Word document and a corresponding PDF. Both outputs are created through an automated process that is executed between the edit and review steps of the workflow. (©2001, Xyvision Enterprise Solutions, Inc. All rights reserved. XyEnterprise and Content@ are trademarks of Xyvision Enterprise Solutions, Inc. in the United States and other countries.)

Tweddle Lithography developed a system by which they send a compound document consisting of the topics for one subject area to the reviewers. Because the automotive engineers themselves specialize in certain functions, they review only what is applicable to their specialty. To facilitate the review process, the workflow system automatically converts an assembly of topics into a PDF. The PDF is emailed to the reviewer, who is asked to mark changes online using Adobe Acrobat. The changes and comments are then sent back to the authors. It took some time for the engineers to get used to this process until they realized how much time it was saving them.

Another problem is that of an individual reviewer who wants to change something in a topic that will limit its reusability. Because topics are used in many contexts, the authors learn to keep the multiple contexts in mind during the writing process. The reviewers also must learn to be aware of multiple contexts during the review process. A procedure changed by one reviewer can appear in tens of different compound documents or might be available dynamically in contexts selected by users.

Information developers must resist idiosyncratic revisions, the addition of interesting but irrelevant details for the users, and changes that do not follow the style guidelines. A training program or briefing that introduces reviewers to the new policies is in order. Ground rules need to be established and respected if the integrity of the modules in the repository is to be maintained.

The rules I describe here are not at all unique to content management; they have been long applied to other corporate databases. People working with a customer relationship management (CRM) database, for example, must follow the rules on how customer information is entered, changed, or deleted. In my organization, for example, there is a rule that a new customer contact cannot be added to the CRM without adding a note explaining the circumstances surrounding the addition.

Financial databases, especially, have rules surrounding how information must be entered, validated, changed, or deleted. The same type of rules need to be instituted for your content-management system.

Planning for translation

One of the most significant returns on investment for many organizations pursuing a content-management solution comes through reduced translation and localization costs. Modules that are written once can be translated once and reused many times. Instead of translating multiple copies of the same information in multiple outputs, the outputs are produced once from the modules stored in the repository.

Many content-management systems support translation by storing translated versions of each module in the repository with links back to the original language version. For example, Chrystal Software's Lingua allows you to maintain parallel versions in multiple languages in the repository. When someone changes a module in English (if that is the source language), the identical modules in every other language are changed back into English. As a result, the translation coordinator knows precisely which modules need to be retranslated.

Using translation memory tools

In addition, many content-management systems support the integration of translation memory tools. A translation-memory system stores the words, phrases, and paragraphs that have already been translated and assists the translators as they proceed through the modules. For example, if authors frequently use the sentence, "Click OK," as part of a software procedure, the translators translate the sentence one time. The sentence becomes part of the translation memory. Every time the translation-memory system encounters that sentence, the translated version is automatically substituted for the original English. As modules are translated, the memory grows, enabling the translator to work faster and more efficiently.

Some content-management systems store the translation memory in the repository. Then, when a module is revised and the new English text reintroduced into the various language versions, the translation memory is automatically applied. If the new text uses the same terminology and style as the previous text, much of it will be translated automatically.

Including translation and localization in the project

Translation organizations often do not have experience translating in a content-management environment. You should involve them early in the planning for content management if their role is a substantial one. At the very least, you must involve them in the early stages of the pilot project.

Translation organizations work as cottage industries, in which the actual translators work at home, their work coordinated by the translation vendor and your own translation coordinators. You must ensure that the vendor you have selected understands your requirements for translating at a modular level.

Although almost every translation vendor uses translation memory tools, few have had experience working with content-management systems. Consequently, you will need to educate your vendors about your system and your expectations. Many of the content-management vendors now provide clients that allow for remote access to the repository, usually through a Web browser. They also provide for a centralized translation memory so that individual translators do not have to have their own tools. You might be able to connect your translators in this way. In other cases, you might have to package your modules before sending them to the translators, effectively removing them from the repository and from version control.

Many translators are also unfamiliar with XML or SGML and do not know how to accommodate the tags. Systems have been developed to hide the tags so that the translators don't see them and don't have an opportunity to corrupt the tags by inadvertently changing or deleting them. Translators also have to learn about the automated publishing system you have implemented for delivery of various output. They should review the style sheets being applied to ensure that they work well for the expansion effect. Remember that most languages have longer words than English and expand the space they need in the final deliverables. Asian and Middle Eastern languages have different reading orders, right to left or top to bottom. Your styles need to accommodate these differences so that no tweaking of the final output is required.

Work closely with your translation coordinators, the translation vendors, and your content-management vendor to ensure that you have the appropriate process in place and the technology to support them. The goal, of course, is to reduce translation costs overall. One organization I work with was able to reduce the translation costs for its pilot project by 60 percent. Another rarely has to translate more than 15 percent of the text from one product release to the next.

You can realize a significant ROI by including your translation process within your content-management solution. However, the savings will be greatest if you maintain consistency in the development of modules, rely on editorial review to ensure that style guidelines are followed, and establish policies that encourage reuse rather than rewriting.

Remember that if you write once, store, and reuse many times, you also need only edit once, test once, review once, approve once, and translate once. A sound reuse strategy provides one of the best methods of realizing your ROI goals.

Pursuing minimalist strategies

Moving to a single-source strategy within a content-management system is an ideal time to consider minimalism. Minimalism researchers have shown time and again that users learn more effectively when they are given just enough information to perform a task. The longer the information resource, the less likely that someone will read it and understand it enough to perform tasks successfully. By decreasing the verbiage and focusing only on what is needed by the user, authors are more likely to help users perform tasks.

Long chunks of text delivered on the Web are not used as frequently as shorter chunks. Reading online is ordinarily more difficult than reading on paper, especially when the text on the Web was originally developed for print. Proponents of effective Web writing styles recommend that information chunks be shorter and smaller than in other media.

To pursue a minimalist strategy, consider the following:

- Know what your users really need to know by studying them directly.

- Concentrate in your writing on supporting task performance, not overwhelming users with concepts, theories, or background.

- Eliminate unnecessary verbiage in the form of long introductory material, overviews, advance organizers, book-like transitional phrases.

- Make the content visually readable by separating steps with white space, differentiating between purpose statements ("To do X, you must complete the following steps"), action steps ("1. Click OK"), and feedback statements ("the dialog box appears"). Use as few words as possible to communicate purpose, steps, and feedback in instructional text.

Less is often more

A division of one of the international telecommunications companies pursued a minimalist strategy by eliminating 75 percent of the information from their manuals. Instead of conceptual overviews, background discussions, and theory, they concentrated on straightforward, step-by-step instructions. They eliminated most of the purpose and feedback statements that had dominated the old versions. As a result of these drastic changes, their customer service calls increased. Users were actively reporting mistakes in the text. Their investigation of the complaints showed that the errors had been in the old, voluminous documentation for years. Now, for the first time, customers were actually reading the documentation and finding the errors. Customer satisfaction with the new minimalist strategy was significantly higher than satisfaction had been with the older versions of the information.

Minimalist information that excludes unnecessary details is more reusable than detailed and verbose versions of the same information. The simpler the writing style that you advocate in your organization and the more attention that is paid to reducing the number of words in light of the users' needs, the more likely that the same text will be reusable in any number of contexts.

The more idiosyncratic the text, the more it reflects personal styles and the favorite subjects of the authors and reviewers, the fewer opportunities you will find for reuse. Idiosyncratic, verbose text is not only more expensive to maintain, it increases your translation and localization costs because it is less responsive to translation memory tools.

A minimalist strategy is not simple—it takes courage to eliminate text. The foundation is, once again, the users' experience. If users are able to use simpler, shorter, more targeted information, you have saved them time and yourself money. You have reduced development costs, increased reuse, and reduced translation costs as well.

Fostering a reuse strategy

You will find that fostering a reuse strategy and maintaining a repository of information resources from which you can continually draw will be difficult. One part of your strategy should include making everyone aware of what is available in the repository. In Chapter 11, *Staffing for Content Management,* I discuss some of the roles and responsibilities that are emerging with content management. Note the description of the role of repository administrator. Members of your team need to be well informed about the content in the repository, how it is organized, how it can be effectively searched, how to reuse components, and how to rewrite the subject at hand for reuse.

The responsibility of the authors is not just to write what they choose, but to take part in the process of content management. It means respect for the processes and guidelines instituted to keep the repository clean. It means following the processes in place whenever possible rather than trying to work around them.

You might also want to address reuse organizationally. Less experienced authors can be assigned to write carefully-defined topics. More experienced authors and information architects can bring existing information and newly written topics together. By separating duties, the incentive to reuse instead of re-create is increased.

Authoring for reuse requires change in the current practices in most organizations. As with any significant process change, you will be best served by instituting a change-management program. Change management focuses on communication and training. Communication helps to dispel concerns and doubts about the new processes. Training makes everyone comfortable with how the new technology works and how it will work to their benefit.

Be careful not to dismiss concerns about the quality of work and creativity. People might feel threatened by a process that promises reductions in cost through greater efficiencies in their jobs. I try to assure people that everyone has more than enough work already, especially if they want to deliver information to users with any degree of quality and responsiveness. Saving time on repetitive and redundant tasks makes time for quality.

11

Staffing for Content Management

O rganizations that specialize in developing content will need to transform the workplace to succeed at content management for dynamic delivery. Organizations that have never focused on content development and management before will find that they need to develop or hire people with a new and different set of skills. A successful content-management environment means having content specialists who know what customers need, information architects who can develop comprehensive Information Models, editors who can ensure that individual authors create reusable content units, authors who can work in a structured writing environment, and publishing specialists who define what the output is going to look like in multiple media.

In this chapter, I suggest ways to restructure an organization by creating new specialties. I also discuss ways to counter the opposition you are likely to meet when you try to create a professional content-development workplace.

In this chapter, you review the process of developing and implementing a content-management solution and learn how to

- staff your content-management project at the pilot stage
- add job skills and responsibilities for the long term

Content-management development process

In Chapter 1, *Is Content Management in Your Future?* I outlined the five phases of a content-management project, beginning with Phase 1 in which you assess your needs and develop a plan. Once your plan has been accepted, a schedule created for your pilot implementation, and funds available for technology, you need to follow a well-defined development process as outlined in Figure 11-1.

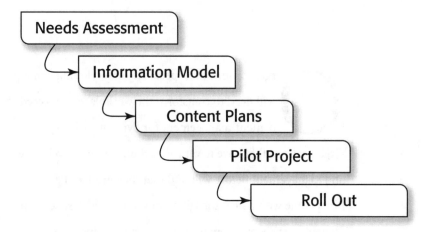

Figure 11-1 The recommended workflow for the content-management project.

Develop an Information Model

In keeping with Phase 2 of your project, you develop your Information Model, which includes

- establishing the metadata dimensions for your information resources
- defining structured information types
- adding content units to each information type
- writing a DTD or schema to support your authors and enforce the rules established in the information types.

You are now ready to acquire new authoring tools and train the authors in the new processes. At this point, you will need guidelines for authors to use for training and reference during the changeover.

You can begin authoring using a DTD without having your content-management system in place. However, you will find that you have a lot of manual tracking to do, especially if you are instituting a single-source reuse strategy.

Develop a presentation design

At the same time that you are developing your Information Model, you can begin work on how you will present information to the users. Content plans are the primary tool to define exactly what static deliverables your authors will create from the topics they are writing. Content plans provide a means to design how users will navigate through information on your Web site and how you will assist them in generating customized and personalized versions of the information.

No matter what your output, unless you are using desktop publishing or other presentation software to author and publish directly (Word in/Word out or FrameMaker in/FrameMaker out), you will need to create a variety of style sheets for every output media. The most complicated to produce are the style sheets that govern print output because they require you to define a very large set of variables.

If you are delivering to the Web through HTML, you will need cascading style sheets as well as a full-scale Web interface design if your information resources are to be accessible by everyone in your user community.

Implement the content-management system

Depending on schedule and finances, you should have completed your acquisition of a content-management system by the time your Information Model is done and you are working on your presentation design. If your authors are already writing in an XML or SGML editor, you need to ensure that there is a smooth transition to the content-management system. It must be easy to check in and check out modules, search for information using metadata as well as full-text search, reuse information by creating compound documents, and communicate with other authors through the workflow system. You should also ensure that a good bridge is established from your authoring tools to your repository. The best solution allows authors to perform repository tasks from inside the authoring tool.

As you implement your content-management system, you are likely to be involved in integrating repositories throughout your organization, linking to repositories that hold traditional quantitative and business data, and acquiring information resources externally, possibly through syndication.

Deliver information to users

In my experience, the most complex part of the process will be the delivery to users. The final production process requires that all the pieces be well integrated and that the work proceed smoothly from authors to repository to delivery. Defining exactly how the delivery process will function can be relatively simple if you are delivering only static (author-defined) information. Enabling dynamic delivery, with customization and personalization, requires significantly more work in designing the Web interface, defining Web interactions, monitoring performance, and ensuring that all the pieces function as designed.

To accomplish your content-management project successfully requires the skills and talents of a number of individuals. Some of these individuals will come from inside your organization. In most cases, they'll need training to come up to speed on the new requirements of their jobs. In addition, you might want to bring in new people who have skills you are lacking internally or work with consultants until the pilot project is either up and running or complete.

Staffing your content-management project

Depending upon the size and responsibilities of your initial content-management project, you will need to designate a group of people who will work collaboratively to deliver a successful implementation. Some of the team members might need to be dedicated full time to the project; others must be available part time during the entire project, with full-time work coming at intervals. A basic content-management team consists of people with these skills:

- project manager
- information architect
- information designer
- interface designer
- authors
- editors
- translators
- repository manager
- application programmer
- database administrator

In most cases, each person on the team will take on multiple responsibilities during the project. After the pilot project is completed, team members continue to work on further rollouts of the process and ongoing analysis and redesign activities.

A content-management project is never done. The activities involved in understanding the users' changing information needs, responding to the needs of the authoring community, improving processes, and keeping abreast of technology improvements don't end with a successful initial implementation.

In small organizations, the ongoing responsibilities should be assumed by people who are interested in developing their skills and who are adept at multi-tasking. In large organizations, individuals will find new careers in several of the job areas outlined here.

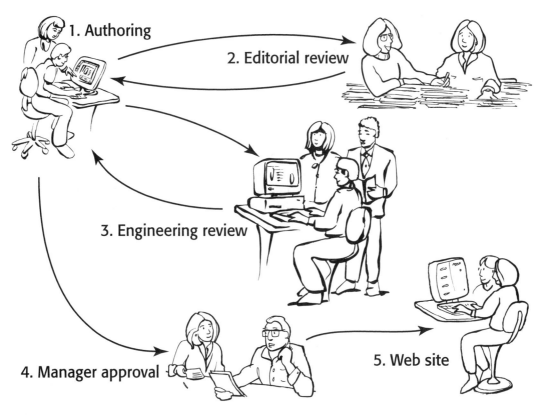

Figure 11-2 This scene illustrates the flow of modules among team members in a typical content-development workflow.

Project manager

The project manager is responsible for ensuring that a sound plan has been established for the content-management implementation and that the plan is adhered to during the course of the project. To be effective, the project manager must have a strong vision of the project's goals, so that he or she ensures that the goals are achieved even when compromises are necessary.

Given the goals of the project and a plan in place for achieving them, the project manager recruits the rest of the team members, assigns their roles and responsibilities, and works with them to develop the schedule, design the budget, and plan the work activities. A typical workflow among team members is illustrated in Figure 11-2. As resource manager for the project, the manager negotiates with other managers to ensure that people are available when needed for the project, especially if they have other job responsibilities.

As the project proceeds, the project manager tracks the schedule and budget, recording the time spent on each activity, focusing the relationship of time spent to time planned. He or she uses this information to make schedule adjustments, request additional team members be added to the project, and prepare requests for additional funding, if necessary. In tracking the schedule, the project manager needs to know what constitutes a completed deliverable and make frequent assessments in consultation with team members about progress toward the deliverables. See Chapter 1, *Is Content Management in Your Future?* for details on the deliverables for each stage of the project.

Most content-management implementations require the assistance of outside consultants. The project manager takes responsibility for negotiating contracts with vendors and consultants and ensuring that the schedules and deliverables are met. The implementation team from the system vendor is likely to be different than the team that sold you the system. The project manager must work closely with both teams to ensure that everyone from the vendor's organization understands the project goals and usability requirements, especially the newcomers to the project. The project manager should not assume that the vendor representatives have adequately communicated among themselves.

The project manager takes responsibility for selecting system integrators and consultants, in consultation with the internal information technology organization. Qualifications should be carefully reviewed for internal and external team members. An internal technology enthusiast might not have the skills to implement effectively and maintain the schedule.

Finally, the project manager has a critical role in communicating with the rest of the organization. Lots of people will be watching closely, some of them hoping that the implementation will fail so that they'll be able to go back to their standard work routine. The project manager should create a communication plan and schedule to dispel doubts, answer questions, and let everyone interested in the project know what is going on. Several well-orchestrated presentations of the solutions will serve to meet communication goals.

Information architect

The information architect is most likely to be the "new kid on the block." Information architecture is an emerging discipline. Only in the last few years have I begun to see job descriptions that outline the responsibilities and qualifications of this role. Many of the advertisements for information architects have emphasized a Web-focus, most likely because so many organizations have decided to move information delivery to the Web. The following job description appeared recently on a the job line of the San Francisco Bay Area Computer-Human Interaction society:

> We are looking for talented Information Architects with demonstrated ability to help deliver highly compelling and usable business solutions. These architects will design the organization, labeling, navigation, and indexing systems to support navigation, searching, and browsing through very large, highly complex and comprehensive Web sites. We need experts in the fields of information visualization and user-interface design who are driven by a passion for making the user experience as easy and productive as possible and ensuring that users can easily find the information they need. This job combines concepts from usability research, user interface design, library science, and traditional architecture.
>
> Job Description:
>
> Identify the mission and focus of a Web site; determine who will be using the site, who is building it, strategic and business goals, key usability principles, technical constraints, and future needs.
>
> Develop high-level conceptual models of business processes.
>
> Perform functional and task analysis to determine transaction flow.
>
> Determine anticipated user paths, logical process flows, and how to balance efficiency with ease of use.
>
> Construct a structure and method of organization of information; organize site content into categories and assist in creating an interface to support those categories.
>
> Map the entire structure of a site and organize the positioning of pages within sections, developing a functional and intuitive plan to get the user from point A to point B on the path of least resistance.
>
> Design the organization, labeling, navigation, and indexing systems to support both browsing and searching to ensure that users can easily find the information they need.

The clear emphasis in this description is on Web interface and interaction design. Although this emphasis is appropriate, the responsibilities of the information architect's job should be broader. In fact, I recommend that the architect and design jobs be separate, especially in organizations large enough to afford specialization.

The information architect is chiefly responsible for the Information Model. To develop the Information Model, the architect must know how to analyze business, authoring, and delivery requirements and mold these into a vision of the user's experience of the future and an outline of the workflow scenarios that will have to be supported by process and technology. The project manager and the information architect work together closely to define the project plan and write the requirements for the content-management solution.

In creating the Information Model, the architect develops the metadata dimensions from the business requirements and works together with the information designer and the authors to identify information types and content units. The architect specifies the design of the DTDs and provides review and quality assurance for the work of programmers, vendors, or consultants who construct the DTD. As the DTDs are being developed, the information architect writes the guidelines for authors that explain how the DTDs are to be used.

With an Information Model in place, the information architect turns his or her attention to the interaction design of Web delivery and delivery in other media. The information architect is responsible for creating the content plans for delivery in both static and dynamic environments. Through the process of defining how the output will function, the information architect interacts with specialists in interface design, programming, traditional book production, and so on.

Some job descriptions indicate that an information architect be a technology specialist as well as a designer. One job description for a Senior Information Architect states

> Senior Information Architects should be schooled in the techniques of information representation, hypertext design, and the technologies of meta-data (data modeling, XML). Also necessary is a background in HCI, UI design, DHTML, CGI, TCP/IP, relational databases, general client/server architecture, and a strong understanding of Internet technologies (DBs, ecommerce, and front-end technologies such as HTML, JavaScript, DHTML, CSS and ActiveX).

It's certainly important for an information architect to be knowledgeable about technology, but I believe that the responsibilities for Information Modeling and interaction design are already broad enough. Most organizations would be better served to include application-programming specialists on the team to ensure that the technology delivers the intended functionality. In a field that is changing so rapidly, I find that system integrators and vendor application consultants are often most qualified to know what is new, what is stable, and what will actually work.

Information architecture encompasses analysis of user and business requirements, development of an Information Model, creation of content plans for static and dynamic delivery in multiple media, tracking and analysis of user response, ongoing adjustments and changes to the Model, and continuing education of authors, editors, designers, and others involved in the implementation of content management.

Information designer

The role of the information designer complements that of the information architect. Of course, one individual might wear both hats but you are more likely to find that the skills are sufficiently different that you need two people. Information design is rooted in traditional typesetting and document layout. Information designers are responsible for ensuring that text, graphics, and rich media are easily scannable and readable and users can differentiate among levels of hierarchy (heading levels, for example) and among content units (different semantic content).

If you are delivering information in print or PDF, you need someone who knows about good page design and typography in this medium. If you are delivering to a browser or other electronic output, you need an information designer who is actively studying visual presentations in these quite different media.

In many cases, information designers will have backgrounds in graphic design. It's important, however, that the information designer you bring onto the content-management team is interested and experienced in working with technical content and long and complicated text and graphics. I have seen many corporate Web sites designed as if they were video games. Information-rich Web sites are complex collections of large volumes of information. However, turning them into overly graphic, video-game-like sites is not the answer. Good page and screen layout is necessary.

In fact, it is very difficult to find exemplars of excellent practice in this area. Too often, you find a book-oriented library dominated by PDFs. Search mechanisms are often badly defined, challenging users from both a search and a navigation perspective.

Structure, navigation, and search all need to work effectively together if a design is to be successful. Beware if someone claims that users prefer searches to navigation. That most likely indicates that navigation is impossible from the user's perspective.

The information designer and the interface designer described in the following sections might be the same individual. However, you need to ensure that the individual has sufficient experience and expertise in both specializations to be effective.

Interface designer

If your information designer is not an expert in user-centered interface design (UCD) or your information architect is not skilled in UCD, you need an experienced interface designer on the team. The design of an information-rich Web environment must be handled very carefully. You visit many sites where information resources are very difficult to find. Typically, users encounter long lists of books and collections. The collections sometimes lead to more collections, which lead to more books. The books become interminable tables of contents that are navigated by drilling down through section after section.

The user interface of an information-rich Web site must be designed with the end users foremost. To be successful with such a design requires experience with the UCD process:

- Begin by gathering information about the user communities, preferably through direct contact.
- Define a set of user personas and user scenarios or use cases that establish how interaction of user and information resources is likely to occur.
- Prototype a design that supports both primary and secondary use cases.
- Conduct usability tests of the prototype and refine.
- Develop the site and test again for usability with representatives from each user community.
- Once again, refine and refine again before going live.

I would expect your interface design expert to be familiar with UCD processes like this and quickly establish an iterative design agenda. I would hope as well that your interface design specialist be expert in document design principles, especially in research that demonstrates how different individuals interact with content and context.*

Your interface design expert should be more than a graphic designer or an expert in coding Web pages. The real need in this instance is for someone who intimately understands how people access and understand information.

Authors and information developers

In Chapter 10, *Authoring for Reuse* I described some of the changes likely to occur for the authors in your organization if you adopt a single-source strategy. Even with more broadly defined content management, you will find that authors need training and assistance in understanding and working productively in the new environment.

I separate the authoring community in most organizations into two groups: enterprise authors who create documents as an adjunct to their other business or technical activities, and professional authors or information developers who are primarily involved in creating technical and business documents. The information developers will be chiefly responsible for a reuse strategy.

Most enterprise authors are used to working independently on documents, usually without regard to their role in the diffusion of information and knowl-

---

* Karen A. Schriver, 1996. *The Dynamics of Document Design: Creating Text for Readers.* New York: John Wiley & Sons.

edge. They usually don't think about how others will find their documents, especially others who are outside their immediate workgroups.

Enterprise authors will need to be trained in using a content-management system to check in their documents, even if they experience no change in the tools they use to create documents. They will need guidance to include the appropriate metadata unless you intend to automate all metadata. You should, of course, create default values for much, if not all, metadata from enterprise authors to avoid asking them to select too complicated a set of values. If you ask enterprise authors to select metadata values, you need to provide training, a help system, and an easy-to-use interface. Preferably, your solution will include a simple dialogue box with default values and selections made from drop-box lists. The easier the system is to use, the more likely it is to be used successfully and regularly.

Enterprise authors might also be more comfortable using wizards or forms to add structured information to the content-management system. Unstructured information usually can be included using their familiar tools such as the Microsoft Office products, WordPerfect, standard email, and others. The only requirements you need to make include adding metadata and being careful to check documents into the content-management system so that they come under version control and workflow.

If enterprise authors are to be included in standard workflows, they will also need to learn to check out documents from the content-management system, even if they don't regularly author documents. If checking out is likely to be awkward, you might want to automate the check-out and check-in processes through your workflow system.

Professional authors, including those who produce technical information, training materials, development documents, technical support information, and formal business documents are most likely to move to a structured writing environment. That environment might include authoring in XML or SGML to produce standard documents according to predefined information types.

To support your professional authors or information developers, you should provide formal guidelines and training for writing in the new environment. If your information developers are moving to an XML authoring environment, they will need training on the new tools as well as training to use the new content-management system. In addition, they will need guidance in using the new DTDs effectively. If you are using information type-specific DTDs, your information developers will need to know how to select among them as they write topics, how to use the internal structure (the content units) properly, and how to add metadata at several levels. For more detail on handling metadata to accommodate a reuse strategy, see Chapter 10, *Authoring for Reuse.*

Information developers are often most experienced at working alone rather than on a collaborative team. Teamwork might be the most challenging change for them. You must decide how much teamwork you want to include in your new processes.

Information developers might continue to work independently to produce entire books on their own and still have the documents they create handled through the content-management system. On the other hand, if information developers create modules that become interchangeable parts among many output deliverables, they will need to know what all the other team members are doing. Less experienced information developers will produce highly structured modules; more experienced information developers will construct compound documents and develop reuse strategies.

If your process includes an information architect who creates a comprehensive information plan for a project and communicates the plan for the final deliverables to the team, the information developers will find themselves authoring modules according to functionality, user profile, type of deliverable, and so on. All the modules created by every team member will then come together in compound documents or be integrated into static or dynamic Web sites. A project of this sort will succeed only if people learn to work together.

Editors

When you integrate your information developers into a collaborative team, editors become a required part of the development process. If you want to ensure that your enterprise authors develop information that meets standards, follows guidelines, and is available for reuse in a variety of compound documents, editors will also play a significant role.

The editors are responsible for ensuring that modules developed independently by a host of different authors end up being compatible in compound documents or in a Web presentation. Editors ensure that structure and stylistic rules are followed so that modules can be combined without unduly jarring the users and affecting readability and continuity.

When Suncorp, a major Australian insurance and banking concern, completely rewrote its internal policies and procedures, a structured writing program was developed by an information architecture and instructional development team. They designed new policy and procedures templates intended solely for online delivery through a corporate intranet. They instituted a strict template and writing rules to ensure that the procedures, in particular, would be uniformly written and promote ease of use. The information architecture team taught the business specialists to use the templates and follow the rules to draft new procedures. Once the drafts were ready, they were first edited by the architecture team. Team members ensured that the templates and rules had been followed. They edited for terminology, consistency of expression, and minimalism. No core procedure could be longer than one screen in the display.

After editing, the procedures were reviewed and approved by business managers and others in the organization. When the new procedures were deployed, they were very well received by the user community and resulted in significant cost savings. Savings came because the procedures were easy to find and read. As a result, users consulted and followed the procedures rather than making up their own and doing something that was against policy.

The editing task is handled most efficiently if it is built into the workflow. As soon as an author has completed a document and checked it in as complete, the workflow system directs it to the editor. The editor has a process in place and a checklist of standards, including terminology. These are applied to the document quickly. If need be, the document is returned to the author to make the changes. Some minor changes might not require author review. Once the author has made the changes, the workflow system directs the document through the approval process. Again, the document might be returned to the author and editor until it is deemed ready and the approvals are complete.

Translators

In many organizations, translation is an integral part of the document-publishing process, especially if documents are released to a multi-lingual user community. Translation must be built into the content-management system and be supported by the workflow system. Once a document has been approved, it proceeds to translation. The workflow system routes the document to the translator's workbench, where systems like translation memory are applied.

In some organizations using content management, translators work on modules in the repository, often before compound documents are created. The translators are responsible for developing modules in multiple languages and storing them in the repository as they are completed. In one such process, the translator received notification of completed modules as part of a daily work schedule and completed modular translation as soon as the modules were ready.

In other organizations, traditionally, translation occurs only after all the compound documents are complete. Some of the multi-language content-management systems accommodate this process. A typical multi-language system stores the entire translated documents in parallel with the original language document.

Content management, if it includes a comprehensive reuse strategy, can significantly reduce the amount of translation work. If modules are well structured, writing consistently with the help of editing, and modules and content units reused wherever possible, translation is significantly more efficient. Translation memory systems become more efficient when writing is consistent, even more so when modules and content units are identical.

Content management also aids translators as they work on revisions. In most cases, the content management system enables the translation coordinators to analyze exactly where changes have occurred to the original text. Analysis tools enable the coordinators to direct the changed text to the translators easily and quickly, as well as maintain a detailed word count for cost analysis.

Translators who have never been involved in a content-management, single-source system must be trained in the new processes. They should be well informed at the early stages of the information-development process, even during information architecture, so that they understand how modules will be developed and how they will eventually fit together in multiple contexts.

To facilitate the translation process in a content-management environment, project managers, editors, and information developers must respect the information architecture. By collaborating closely on content, terminology, and structure, the team members will make work easier for the translators who might be required to translate modules without larger contexts.

Repository manager

Teams working in a collaborative authoring environment that includes a single-source strategy have noted the emergence of a repository manager's role. The repository manager ensures that the authors understand what is available in the repository, how the modules are moving through the workflow, and where information modules are stored in a workgroup folder view. The repository manager should be responsible for assisting in the development of searches to ensure that all relevant modules become available to authors.

Because content management requires that the repository be free of duplicates, near duplicates, and corrupted files, the repository manager keeps an eye on everything that is being checked in and out. The manager should establish policies about check in and check out, requirements for metadata application, and other guidelines that ensure that the integrity of the repository be maintained.

Application programmer

You might find it possible to dispense with an application programmer on your content-management staff if you work consistently with a vendor or system integrator. In either case, however, you need access to individuals who are skilled in new technology that supports content management. Much of the system integration work requires programming skills that go far beyond basic tagging in XML or HTML.

On your team should be those responsible for building and maintaining DTDs or schemas and supporting authors who have issues about the structures and systems in place. The application programmer provides the support to customize the authoring and repository environment, handle interactions and exchanges of information resources, and develop scripts to handle output. A knowledge of XML and related technologies, such as

XML Schema, XSLT, CSS, DSSSL, XSL-FO, XHTML, RDF, XTM topic maps, XLink, XBase, XInclude, DOM, SAX, XPath, XPointer, XQuery,

is important to have inhouse or through a regularly available consultant. For definitions of these technologies, see xml.com. Remember that the programmer or technology expert implements the Information Model and output designs developed by the information architect and information designer. In fact, it is particularly important that the development of templates not be viewed as a technical activity but as a design activity implemented through technology. When DTDs or schemas are designed at the same time they are being writing, you often find yourself with designs that look exactly like existing, unstructured documents.

In addition to all of the technologies associated with an XML environment, the application programmer should have experience with Java and Perl.

Database administrator

Content management means that you will have a database in which your information resources are stored. That database must be administered. Someone with database experience needs to configure the database management system, work with the hardware, be responsible for user administration including permissions and security, handle backups and regular maintenance, and communicate with vendors to troubleshoot problems.

Skills involving Web, network, and system administration might also be necessary. These special skills should be available through your information technologies organization or from outside consultants.

If you intend to support documents that are coming into your organization from third parties, you will need a person responsible for translating them into forms that can be stored and used in your repository. Someone experienced in database programming would be useful as a resource to the team.

Updating job skills for content management

Content management is such a new endeavor for information developers that few people are available in the market with the skills described previously. Many organizations find themselves appointing interested individuals to the new and emerging jobs and helping them find training and other experiences to develop their skills and knowledge.

Training

Besides being trained in the particulars of your installation, including attending vendor training, your team members need training in many areas. If your information developers are also responsible for collaborating with the information architect, the information designers, their peer authors, and the editors, translators, and repository manager, additional training will be necessary. Topics such as

- structured writing for reuse
- collaborative writing, i.e., working with a team
- information architecture
- repository management responsibilities
- writing for translation

should become an integral part of your content-management training program.

Particular individuals on your team might need training in XML and the related technologies I mentioned earlier. Not everyone need learn the intricacies of these technologies, but having one or two on call with a more in-depth knowledge will be helpful to the whole team.

Conferences and exhibits

A growing number of organizations are developing special-purpose conferences to explore the opportunities and challenges of content management. Some conferences are specialized, like the conference devoted to XML programmers called Extreme Markup Languages. XML-focused conferences will be useful for the specialists on your staff. Others might want to attend conferences devoted to single sourcing, enterprise content management, and content management for intranets and extranets. Others might want to pursue knowledge about Web development, including user-centered interface design for the Web, portal development, and usability design. All of these topics are related to the success of your content-management implementation.

Most large conferences include vendor participation in the exhibits. You will find it valuable to use such exhibits to keep up with new solutions based on newly emerging technology. Knowing what the vendors are up to will help you keep abreast of industry changes. For a list of potential vendors, see Appendix B.

Remember, however, that content management is an emerging and highly volatile industry. Vendors are coming into the field in great numbers at the same time others are disappearing because of market changes. In any vendor search, you should be careful to inquire about the financial stability of the companies whose products interest you.

User groups

Many of the vendor organizations have user groups where you can find assistance from others who are experiencing the same challenges. User group conferences are held by most vendors yearly and are helpful to attend. User groups often host their own listservs, Web sites, and chatrooms. They enable newcomers to find out what others have already learned about implementations. They provide an additional resource, beyond the vendor's customer service, for troubleshooting problems.

Organizations such as The Center for Information-Development Management (CIDM) (www.infomanagementcenter.com) provide listservs for those interested in content management and single-source strategies. The CIDM provides a variety of resources for members who are interested in content management.

Those interested in e-learning options as they relate to content management might want to become members of the The Computer Education Management Association (CEdMA) (www.cedma.org).

More resources become available almost daily. My advice is to join one or more organizations, get on the mailing and emailing lists, and pursue links to other organizations and Web sites suggested by participants.

12

Making a Business Case for Content Management

"Now, that's what I call a good investment."

S elling the business benefits of content management in your organization requires that you look carefully at both immediate and long-term gains and at enterprise and departmental solutions. The initial costs to implement a complete content-management solution might be higher than your management is prepared to meet if your focus is departmental or if your predicted gains are too long term. Your job starts with understanding and then revealing the costs inherent in the way content is created, updated, and delivered today. An understanding of the present situation will lead you to a clear vision of why and how the situation must be changed. An understanding of some of the present and hidden costs of content development and delivery will lead you to opportunities for cost reductions. An understanding of how much more effectively you might provide for the information needs of staff and customers will lead you to connect content management with customer loyalty and retention.

You will also find that selling the benefits of content management might be almost as difficult among your colleagues as it is for your decision makers. You must be prepared to face the challenges of change management within your organization.

In this chapter, you learn to

- analyze the current state to reveal hidden (and not so hidden) costs associated with the creation, maintenance, and delivery of content

- identify the benefits that increased control over content will provide to customers, partners, and staff members

- identify the potential cost reductions of implementing a content-management solution

- sell the value of content management to your colleagues within the organization

- manage the change process so that your planning and implementation process is as smooth and successful as you can make it

In the process of building your business case, you are likely to discover that your decision makers don't recognize the costs of poor content management, that they are suspicious of long payback periods and high startup costs, that the information assets are not recognized as having the same or greater value to the business enterprise as other assets, and that the political divisions in your organization, especially in terms of reporting structures, will make it more difficult to achieve the collaboration needed to realize the most important cost savings.

You will also discover that many of your colleagues fail to see beyond their cubicles. They believe that their responsibilities end at their desks or in their departments. They might believe that processes and tools need only to serve their immediate requirements without taking into account the needs of related parts of the organization.

You are also likely to find individuals who are reluctant to change, who fear new directions, or who even fear new technology. They too often fail to recognize that their efforts are part of a larger scheme of making information resources into real corporate assets.

Despite the potential problems you will face, I believe you will find that the effort has far-reaching benefits in efficiencies and quality improvements. All the information you've garnered from this book will help you be successful. It will help you articulate your goals and how you expect to reach them.

Analyzing the current state

Start your process by looking around, first within your own organization and then out to other organizations that produce and use information. Don't forget to include external as well as internal customers in your analysis. Discover just what they like and don't like about the way they get the information they need to do their jobs.

What you are trying to learn is how much it might be costing your enterprise as a whole to ignore the chaos that typically exists around the development and dissemination of content. At the same time, find out just how important information is to the smooth and profitable running of your enterprise.

As you investigate, ask people about the time it takes them to rework content or handle the other problems suggested by the questions presented here. Keep track of the small incremental costs and count how many people in the organization might be similarly affected. The math is easy, and the numbers add up very significantly. Just how much time does it take people in the training department to cut and paste information from the documentation into the training materials, plus reformat the information for a different tool and a different look? A few hours per week, multiplied by everyone in the department, multiplied by the full hourly cost of the individuals' time, can easily add up to several hundred thousand dollars.

Map out the content-development life cycle in your enterprise or even just in your organization. Find out where inefficiencies occur and calculate their costs. The numbers you produce, especially if you are very conservative in your estimates, provide the basis for your cost/benefit analysis.

Estimating checklist

Answers to the following questions may provide you with all the justification you need to improve the process of managing content in your organization.

How many organizations within your enterprise develop content? How much of the content they produce is the same?
As soon as you start looking, you'll be amazed at how many pockets of content development lurk in even small and mid-size enterprises. The larger the enterprise, the more possibilities exist. Even if you start within your own division or line of business, you find a great deal of evidence that content is out of control. I typically find that documents are produced not only by formal "documentation" organizations, but also by training, customer service, product development, logistics, testing, quality control, and so on. The list goes on and on, even if you are focusing only on information that is exposed to external customers. Content is everywhere.

Not only is content being produced everywhere by nearly every one of your professional staff, but much of the content is the same. In one investigation for a major computer manufacturer, I found similar information about spare parts and accessories available in five different customer publications and three additional internal publications.

How many different tools are used to produce and store information in your enterprise?

It's very common for different groups to use different tools to produce information. I have found information resources to be written in Word, Excel, PowerPoint, FrameMaker, PageMaker, Broadvision's QuickSilver, WordPerfect, plus a myriad of other tools. Informal content is often produced using an email program and stored in the email folders on individual hard drives. Some parts of the enterprise store information only in paper form; others store everything on individual hard drives. Some have departmental servers, and others use servers that span departments. All this diverse content infrastructure causes problems in content conversion from one tool to another, as well as additional costs for maintenance and support.

How smooth or difficult is the handoff of information from one organization to another?

I hear over and over again about incompatibilities. One department creates information that meets its own needs but is completely inadequate for the needs of the next department in the information flow. The second department spends minutes or hours filling in the gaps and discarding what is unnecessary to their operations. The lack of an end-to-end information life cycle means that inefficiencies exist everywhere.

How often do people in internal organizations cut and paste, revise and reformat information that is produced by other parts of the organization? How often is the information retyped because the systems used to create it are incompatible?

Many people regard cutting and pasting and even retyping as an ordinary activity. They never stop to count the minutes or hours that it takes them to reuse content produced by other parts of the enterprise. They generally forget about the impact of information that changes but has been reproduced or slightly modified in many different contexts.

How much time is spent reconciling content that is reused in myriad contexts? How much content is never reconciled?

My organization used to spend many hours each month tracking down all the places in which changes had to be integrated into existing information. My staff kept a spreadsheet recording all the instances of reuse so that they didn't miss any. Despite all the hard work that went into trying to keep things synchronized, they know that they didn't always succeed. Over the years, what should have been identical information became more and more different.

In companies with legal requirements around policies and procedures, such differences can become exceedingly costly. One very large company lost a major lawsuit because the content in its corporate policies documents was inconsistent.

How much time is spent recreating information provided by third-party suppliers and other outside groups?

Information coming into your organization is almost never in the form it is needed. Even if it was created using the same technology, the structure and writing styles are often so completely different as to make reuse impossible.

How much is spent on warehousing back versions of information to meet legal or regulatory requirements?

I've been told stories about square miles of warehouse space containing nothing but old documents gathering dust. If someone requires that an earlier version be located, the search times are often monumental. One insurance company keeps every previous version of its policy statements in paper form just in case of future legal actions. It takes them weeks to hunt down the information once it's requested.

If your organization produces information for many delivery media, how much time is spent reformatting and tweaking output?

Many organizations today deliver information in more than one medium. They produce paper, CD-ROMs, Web sites, help systems, and more. In most cases, the content must be converted from one output format to another manually. Because the technology to handle conversions is unable to handle all the idiosyncrasies in the source, people need to tweak the end products to make them acceptable to users.

Given slow and awkward hand-managed processes, the availability of content in multiple sources is often significantly delayed. The delays not only affect product releases, but make it impossible for staff members to be well informed.

If you are translating content in multiple languages, how often is the same content retranslated?

Increased costs of translation have been a significant driver to move enterprises toward content-management solutions and reuse strategies. Not only is it expensive continually to retranslate the same text, it is equally expensive to reformat all the information into multiple deliverables in multiple languages.

Does your company avoid localizing information because the cost is too high?

I find that many companies do little beyond translation because it is too expensive to create more than one version of their information for different local conditions. Unless absolutely necessary, companies often decide that one size fits everyone in the world.

Even when information is localized, the localization is often handled by field organizations in different countries. The changes made are then lost, the translations themselves are often lost, and the whole process and the cost must be repeated over and over again.

How much time is spent by staff members trying to find buried information?
When you begin to multiply hours per month by the number of people in the enterprise, not only can the time spent by each individual be substantial, the costs can skyrocket. When the sought after information cannot be easily found, people consult one another (taking up the time of multiple people), invent their own procedures and policies, rewrite information that already exists and put it through another review and approval cycle, or simply do without.

How often do customers call seeking information that they cannot find? How much does it cost your enterprise to respond to customer calls?
The cost of customer service is exacerbated by a lack of content management. Information is buried in long documents, often poorly linked and difficult to search. Even if the information is available electronically, searching is still slow and frustratingly difficult. Customer service personnel are replete with tales of customers who have already spent hours looking for the information they need. Once they finally call, they are irate.

When customers find information, how often is it so poorly structured as to be unusable?
Customers complain that much of the content they are provided is so poorly written as to be unreadable and so inadequately structured as to be inadequate to help them solve problems and complete tasks. Because departments do not collaborate on content development and often do not agree about style and format, the content they create is so inconsistent that it appears to come from entirely different companies. Customers find that they cannot rely on information that is so inconsistent in structure, style, and depth.

Summary
The questions I've suggested here are by no means the only questions and issues that you will need to address in your organization. More issues will emerge as you conduct your analysis. Consider the cumulative costs of the inefficiencies you expose. A problem that you find with the activities of an individual or a small department is likely to expand if it affects others in the enterprise. In one investigation, I found a content-management problem that cost an individual on average about two hours per month, representing about $150 per month and $1800 per year. However, the same problem likely affected 80,000 staff members doing similar jobs. The cost of this content-management problem cost the enterprise at least $144 million per year, estimated conservatively (the average time spent on the task was conservatively stated at two hours per month; it was likely more).

In many cases, you will find individuals who do not recognize the cumulative cost of their inefficient actions. The ten individuals in a department I analyzed spent on average 40 minutes a day reconciling information among a variety of different product deliverables. Added up, the cost of the reconciliation averaged $250,000 per year, more than enough to cover the cost of a departmental content-management solution.

Remember that you need to address both internal inefficiencies and customer usability and satisfaction issues with the development and delivery of content. You might have the most inefficient process for developing information but very happy customers. Or, vice versa, you might have very efficient internal processes but very unhappy customers. Both cost reductions and customer satisfaction must be part of your analysis and your proposed benefits. I'll address the customer benefits first.

Identifying benefits for customers, partners, and staff

If customers, business partners, suppliers, and staff members cannot find the information they need quickly and easily, a number of problems result. Users of information are frustrated searching through paper documents, Web sites, CD-ROMs, and other sources and being unable to pinpoint the information they need. For external customers, the outcomes are diverse and expensive:

- time-consuming calls to colleagues and support lines
- decreased productivity
- increased downtime
- frustration and annoyance
- ineffective use of products and services

These problems are only the tip of the iceberg. Customers who are frustrated are not loyal. As soon as another product or service becomes available that is easier to learn and use, they jump.

By managing content more effectively, you have the potential of increasing customer satisfaction. Satisfied customers are more loyal and easier to retain. They continue to buy upgrades and add-ons. They renew contracts and recommend your products and services to others.

For partners and suppliers, finding information about doing business with your organization and educating their own customers is essential. The better they are informed about how your products and services work, the more effective they can be in their businesses.

The staff members inside your enterprise are often the most important customers for your information. Not only is content exchanged, it is also reused and repurposed by many departments and individuals. Content is accessed to aid in performing tasks and making decisions. If the information is difficult to find and difficult to use, productivity declines and frustration increases.

Creating customer value propositions

As you work through your analysis of potential benefits, consider making propositions like these:

- It is less expensive to retain existing customers than to find new ones.

- Happy customers are loyal customers who buy more and recommend our products and services to others.

- If you make information easier to find, customers and staff members will be happier and more productive. Information is easier to find if it is categorized and labeled using customer-focused metadata.

- Customers and staff members who can find the information they need quickly and easily are less costly to support and are more productive to their own enterprises.

- If you make information easier to use, customers and staff members will be happier and more productive. Information written with well-labeled internal structure following standard information types is more likely to be complete and understandable.

- Customers and staff members are happier when the information they access is consistent. When they don't get conflicting information from diverse forces, they are assured that the information is correct.

- Customers and staff members are happier when information has been tailored to their requirements. Information that is single-sourced and labeled according to targeted customer requirements is likely to be shorter and easier to use.

- Customers are happier when information has been properly translated and localized to accommodate their different requirements.

- Customers are happier when the information they find is up-to-date and accurate. The faster you can provide them with new information resources and update existing resources, the more pleased they will be and the more likely they will be to turn to electronic sources of information than to make calls to customer support.

- Customers and staff members are happier when they can tailor information to their own needs. Information that can be personalized by the customers themselves increases productivity and job satisfaction.

- Business partners and suppliers who find the information they need to work effectively with your enterprise are likely to sell more product and reduce the costs of doing business. In one case, suppliers were able to reduce the costs of their contract bids because the information they received from the client was consistently structured, complete, uniform, and accurate following the implementation of a content-management solution.

Quantifying the customer benefits

How does customer satisfaction relate to content management? How do you quantify the benefits of having happier customers?

Customer satisfaction is a difficult metric to work with. In crafting your business case for content management, you must predict not only the degree to which improving content quality and delivery will affect customer satisfaction, you must also predict the impact of customer satisfaction on revenue growth. Unfortunately, both customer satisfaction and revenue growth are lagging indicators. You cannot tell if you have affected them until after your content-management solution has been implemented. In advance, you are pretty much limited to predicting some degree of percentage improvement in both metrics.

An added complication is the complexity of attributing any revenue growth at all to a single contributor such as customer satisfaction with information quality and delivery. Many other factors influence revenues, including the global economy, the quality of the product itself, product pricing, and so on.

The contribution of information to revenue growth will also be dependent upon the goals of the company you work for and the positioning of the product that your information supports. Geoffrey Moore, in his seminal marketing work, *Crossing the Chasm*, suggests that companies (or parts of companies) position themselves in one of three ways:

- those that produce leading-edge technologies
- those that provide exemplary customer service
- those that provide reasonable quality at lowest prices

Leading-edge technologies

Companies dedicated to providing leading-edge technologies want to provide information to support innovator and early-adopter customers. Information for these customers must be technically comprehensive and very timely. Leading-edge customers want new products, new features, and the information to understand them as quickly as possible. Content-management solutions that close the loop between product experts and expert customers are most likely to influence product acceptance.

Exemplary customer service

Companies dedicated to providing exemplary customer service need information to support customers effectively. The primary information users are likely to be telephone support personnel, training staff, consulting staff, consulting partners, resellers, and technical support experts. Content-management solutions that provide frequent and rapid updates in multiple media and on multiple platforms is likely to succeed in more effectively supporting customers.

Reasonable quality at low prices

Companies dedicated to providing reasonable quality at low prices also need exemplary information to reduce or eliminate support costs. Low prices provide no margin for expensive customer service. Customers are often on their own to install, learn, and use low-cost products. Information must support them, which suggests that the information must be targeted very precisely to customer needs. Information must be properly localized, translated, customized, and potentially personalized so that customers are successful.

Tracking customer satisfaction

Depending upon the goals of your company, the case you build to demonstrate the influence of information quality on customer satisfaction and revenue will be different. In each case, however, you want to establish methods of measuring customer satisfaction with information, comparing the results after content management to the results before. Cadence Design Systems used customer-satisfaction measures to show that customers were pleased with the increased quality of information available through the Web site. They also tracked calls to customer support attributable to information defects, realizing a 50 percent decrease in calls with improvements to information quality. Given the average cost of a customer call, the information developers at Cadence Design were able to demonstrate a significant cost savings. Does this savings and the increase in customer satisfaction translate into increased revenues? Difficult to know absolutely, but customers who can use information and solve their own problems, independent of calls to customer support, are generally more likely to remain loyal.

Building a competitive advantage

If you can demonstrate that customized information will result in a competitive advantage, you will have a strong business case aligned with many corporate vision statements. If you can demonstrate the adaptive nature of content management, you will be in a much stronger position to argue the advantages of customizing information to a specific customers needs.

Content-management technology provides a way to adapt quickly to a highly personalized marketplace. Instead of producing content multiple times for delivery to multiple media, with XML/SGML technology, you are able to select the content you want to deliver during production.

Information-centric organizations like weather.com and amazon.com use customer information to customize Web output. After finding that many of their users access weather information to determine whether they should golf or garden that day, weather.com customized its information to reflect users' interests. Amazon.com's Web site reflects intelligence they have gathered about user buying preferences.

At the Swedish telecommunications firm, Ericsson, authors use "push the button" technology to create special customized information for each client. They relate ownership information from a client database with information identified by functions clients have purchased. Then, they assemble and deliver customized technical information to each client by CD-ROM. The process literally works at the push of a button, producing highly customized information in a fraction of the time that authors would need to customize the information manually.

Content management offers you the ability to meet customer needs on many levels. It also allows for future growth and adaptability. To deliver information in a highly flexible and targeted way, you must know your customers and their needs. You must focus on your intended market in making your business case and demonstrate how content management will serve your customers and contribute to increased customer satisfaction and market share.

Identifying cost reductions opportunities

Content management provides many opportunities to reduce costs significantly:

- information produced once and used everywhere
- information changed once and updated everywhere
- information delivered in multiple media and on multiple platforms without additional work
- information shared among organizations throughout the content life cycle
- information localized and translated once to produce multiple deliverables
- production activities reduced from weeks to minutes or seconds
- information updated on the Web without further effort to recode or redesign
- new content available on the Web as soon as it is written and approved
- information customized and localized without additional time and added effort

Cost reductions like these are the results of process efficiencies. By reducing the number of steps required to create and deliver information, individuals and even entire organizations save time. Time savings translate, of course, into cost savings.

When content is published to multiple media through automated multi-channel publishing, the savings are impressive. Time to publish can decrease from weeks and days to minutes, eliminating a host of people previously responsible for moving files from working repositories to Web servers and tweaking file formats to make information look good on the Web and in other media.

BMC Corporation used their content-management system to automate the production of several final deliverables. The automation reduced the time to final production from three weeks to minutes, a "push the button" process. The time savings in production enabled the information developers to reduce the time to market of the documentation and increase its completeness and accuracy by better matching the product-release cycle.

JD Edwards significantly reduced the time to market of its internationalized information by fully integrating the translation process with the information-development process. Because modules of content can be automatically moved to the translators' workbench as soon as the authors have completed final drafts in the source language, translated versions are produced virtually simultaneously with the source. VP Ben Martin explains that they have reduced translation and production costs by $3.5 million per year by automatically publishing their content into three deliverables and seven languages.

Medtronic's pacemaker division has been able to reduce writing time by more than 40 percent by creating a repository of modules that are automatically assembled into manuals customized for multiple related products.

Ameritech (now Network Services Staff for SBC), after introducing content management and structured writing, has seen significant cost reductions in authoring and production, as described in the vignette described next.

In their first project, they spun off ten versions of the manual from the original source, five for the US and five for outside the US (OUS). Their first analysis of the results shows that 80 percent of the text is reused in 28 similar manuals. Because modules are translated before they are assembled in the manuals, translation time has been reduced from three days to one day per language. Production in multiple languages has been reduced from three weeks to virtually nothing.

In a recent survey, The Center for Information-Development Management found that the organizations realized cost savings due to their implementation of a content-management solution in the following areas:

- lower costs to translate

- lower costs for final production of information deliverables

- less time spent coordinating by hand modules among different deliverables and different media

- less time spent editing the same text to eliminate differences

- less time spent creating multiple outputs from the same modules
- more significant reuse of modules among departments

Many of the savings listed were realized within the first year of implementation.

Benchmarking against best practices

The experiences of the companies mentioned here demonstrate the importance of benchmarking against those engaged in best practices in content management. In the benchmark studies I have conducted, participants have learned in detail about how companies have managed their content-management initiatives. Benchmarking with companies in the same industry may help you to demonstrate to your management that all your competitors are investigating content management, single sourcing, and structured writing. During our extensive benchmark study of the telecommunications manufacturing industry, we communicated to all the participants that each of the companies in the study had begun to investigate content management, had already implemented an SGML-based solution, had begun to introduce XML authoring, or were actively planning a single-source strategy. The results of the benchmark study enabled managers to make a business case for their investment in planning, design, and implementation based primarily on competitive activities rather than on return on investment alone. I strongly recommend that you use benchmarking to strengthen your business case, either by benchmarking with competitors or benchmarking with industry leaders in related fields.

> The network staff information management team at Ameritech (now Network Services Staff for SBC) had strong reasons for moving to content management and structured writing nearly five years ago. Paper copies of technical information used to implement and maintain SBC networks had become more and more difficult to use. From a business perspective, the company needed to ensure that maintenance and troubleshooting work was being done correctly and consistently across the company. That meant they needed consistent documentation throughout the organization. But, with paper alone, no one could ensure consistency. People hung on to out-of-date copies of information. Versions multiplied as individual departments made their own changes. No one could be sure they had the best, most up-to-date versions of the information.

When the information-development team analyzed the costs, they found that inconsistent information in the workplace contributed to

- Delays in deploying new products and services
- Delays in restoring service when problems occurred in the network
- Time consumed in producing and delivering paper copies
- High people costs of trying to find the right information in nearly 3,000 volumes of highly technical information

The company not only experienced information access and reliability problems with their own information resources; they had the same problems with mountains of technical documentation coming from their suppliers.

The move to an SGML-based co-authoring environment has resulted in significant improvements in productivity and accuracy, as well as dramatic savings in costs. Penny Fairbanks, Area Manager-Information Management, notes that simply making supplier documentation available electronically led to immediate cost reductions because they no longer had to buy multiple paper copies. For example, expenses for one supplier were reduced by 50 percent in the first year after the network project started, and by 96 percent in the second year. Plus, users could search and find information more easily in electronic documents than in paper.

Using uniform information types and content units backed by their SGML DTD has led not only to more savings, but to important gains in productivity and consistency among the authors. Today, information is authored in modules. The network staff team and the authors determine where information must be updated or written anew. Individual subject-matter experts are assigned to write particular modules using a reduced set of SGML standard tags in Arbortext's Epic Editor. All the required authoring structures are in place and, with all formatting information removed, authors are free to focus on content. They find the structured approach makes writing and updating the information uniform and consistent across all authors. Information modules that are common to multiple publications are reused, further cutting authoring and updating time.

In training and convincing authors of the importance of standard structures, the network staff information management team has emphasized the benefit to the users. When the structure is consistent for each information type in all the manuals, users find information faster and read it more quickly and easily.

With the co-authoring environment, SBC is able to update its technical information 7 days a week, 24 hours a day. Subject-matter experts are responsible for ensuring that their information modules are up-to-date and accurate. Once approved, the new modules are published to the SBC intranet. Once a day, an automatically produced email is sent to network employees, notifying them of updates to the repository with hypertext links between the email and the HTML and PDF modules on the Intranet.

Employees are provided a comprehensive search mechanism to find exactly the information they need in the thousands of modules. SBC urges the users to search for the modules they need, print if they need to, and properly dispose of the print version when they've completed a task. They urge everyone to consider the online version as the official version and to always check that they are using the latest version of an information module.

As a result of the content-management initiative, SBC has cut the costs of authoring and using information. Since the mergers of SBC, Ameritech, Southern New England Telecommunications, and Pacific Bell, they are delivering more information without adding people to the co-authoring team. Information is now consistent and accurate throughout the network division, enabling significant gains in productivity and performance. The official version of each information module exists in only one place—the intranet repository. They expect the gains to continue with their planned quality improvements to the information environment.

Promoting internal efficiencies

Internal efficiencies are the result of the process changes that contribute to cost savings. If you are moving to a content-management solution, consider the opportunities to streamline your processes and reduce the time required in the information-development life cycle.

Domain-specific teams

Changing the way authors develop content is the first step in efficient content development. Many organizations with a viable single-sourcing strategy in place have found that the only way they can ensure content reuse is to assign authors to knowledge domains rather than to books or whole products. In these restructured organizations, authors create content in a single content domain or subject matter. For example, authors at Tweddle Lithography might specialize in automotive heating and cooling systems rather than writing individual manuals for each vehicle model. Authors can easily identify which information is common to all and which must be specialized for particular models.

The information developed by each domain team in a highly structured XML/SGML authoring environment is assembled into final manuals for individual product models, users, countries, and many other dimensions of use.

Robust search mechanisms

If you are maintaining multiple information products that are similar but not the same and tracking the common information manually, you can expect to reduce time and costs by implementing a content-management solution. Content-management systems automatically track related information and, typically, use robust search engines that allow authors to search for the modules they need.

Workflow automation and the review cycle

Process improvements can result by automating the flow of work from creation, through editing and reviews, to approvals. With any content-management solution, you can create easily reviewable versions of XML/SGML content as part of an automated workflow and send them to subject-matter experts to be reviewed. Within the assembled documents are modules that are common to all and modules that are unique to targeted audiences. At Tweddle Lithography, the targeted modules are identified by automatically generated marginal notes so that the editors and reviewers understand the distinctions. If, for example, you produce three models of a product that vary somewhat, instead of editing three different manuals, your editors and subject-matter experts review the common information once.

Multi-channel reuse

Opportunities to share and reuse information from other departments makes internal processes more efficient. The most natural information exchange and greatest opportunity for collaboration is between documentation and training. Although the delivery differs, the content is very similar. Within your organization, there are many opportunities to collaborate and facilitate information reuse. You must talk to other departments to determine what information they use and how they use it so that processes can be streamlined and reuse facilitated.

Investigating cost reduction opportunities

Because individual departments are judged by the costs of their internal processes, they often avoid trying to improve the efficiencies of processes that cross departmental lines. Standard cost accounting looks at local operational costs, not at the costs of processes between operations.

In building your business case for content management and single sourcing, you must measure the costs of inefficient inter-departmental processes. Begin to estimate what it costs your company to create and manage information in departmental silos.

Look for opportunities for interdepartmental and intradepartmental collaboration:

- where is the same information developed in more than one department
- what information is produced by one organization and then reused by cut and paste or modifying and retyping
- where is the same or nearly the same information published in different forms
- where is information translated and localized into multiple languages and modified according to the requirements of different countries
- where is information being modified according to the requirements of different product models, clients, platforms, industries, and so on

In each of these situations, you should be able to quantify the costs of the redundant or inefficient activities and calculate how much lower costs might be with better management of content.

Carla is an instructional designer and trainer at ABC equipment manufacturing. She produces training programs for client equipment operators and maintenance technicians. To develop the training, Carla works on new versions of the product as soon as they are available, learning exactly how they work. She interviews the engineers and quality-assurance personnel to understand the new and improved functionality and uncover any of the possible glitches that might affect her customers.

As she gathers the information, Carla produces training manuals that include product descriptions, conceptual and process overviews, and step-by-step procedures for operating and repairing the equipment. She produces slides based on the training materials and sets up laboratory exercises on the equipment.

Chris works for the same company in the information-development department. He works on the same hardware and software equipment that Carla does. He also interviews the engineers and quality-assurance personnel. He reads specifications, attends the product-development meetings, gets copies of the software to run as it is being developed, and is in the loop for all the frequent changes being made to the product. He even works with the assembly team in manufacturing to anticipate troubleshooting and diagnostic issues so he can include them in the documentation for field technicians.

As he gathers information, Chris prepares operator's manuals and repair manuals for the same technicians and operators who attend Carla's training classes.

Both Carla and Chris send their documents to the same engineers and testers for review. The information is presented somewhat differently, but it is essentially the same. Carla adds tutorial exercises linked to typical customer scenarios that she is familiar with. Chris doesn't have the same scenarios available to him, although he knows that typical situations are valued by customers.

James is responsible for localization and translation at ABC. He contracts with a vendor to have the training materials and technical manuals translated in eight languages. In each case, the translators independently translate the training materials and the manuals. They use a corporate glossary that has been developed for technical terminology and translated in advance. Because Carla and Chris both use the glossary in their documents, the translation glossary works well. The translation vendor also uses translation memory tools. Unfortunately, only about ten percent of the text in either source responds to translation memory. The training materials and manuals are written quite differently.

As it turns out, you also discover that three other authors in Chris's department are producing manuals for three other models of the equipment. You estimate that 45 percent of the content among the four manuals for the four product versions is the same (or almost the same). These manuals are also translated using translation memory technology, but because they are written somewhat different, the translation memory is not as effective as it could be.

Calculating potential cost savings

In looking at a scenario like the one illustrated for ABC, first learn how much time Carla and Chris take to produce their materials for a new product. In particular, find out how much time they spend with the engineers and testers. Then, compare the training materials and the manuals. Estimate how much of the content is substantially the same. Finally, calculate how much time would be saved if the redundant text could be produced once and used in both contexts. Add the savings in interview time if the engineers and testers were interviewed only once. Then calculate the costs saved by translating the redundant text once instead of twice. Add up all the cost reductions you find in your investigation. They represent the opportunities you have to reduce the costs attributable to your organization and contribute directly to the increased profitability of your company.

Continue your investigation by calculating the cost of moving both training materials and manuals through a production cycle. How many different outputs are produced? Training materials are printed and delivered on CD-ROM in HTML. The manuals are printed, converted into context-sensitive help for the product software, produced as HTML for the Web, and converted to PDF for another CD-ROM. Discover how much time is spent producing all these deliverables manually. Find out how many different tools are used in the conversion processes. Calculate how much these production processes cost and multiply by all the languages you are producing, because production must be repeated in each language. Consider how much would be saved if all the production processes could be automated if the source information is produced in a format-neutral environment such as XML or SGML.

Cost reductions are possible on many fronts:

- By reusing information between departments, you reduce the cost of producing multiple sources of the same information.

- By working with the writer and instructional designer to structure their information, write in modules rather than books, and reduce the verbiage using minimalism, you improve the opportunities for reuse.

- By reducing the verbiage and creating structured source information, you reduce translation and localization costs.

- By translating before assembly, you ensure that you are translating once rather than many times.

- By automating production activities, you virtually eliminate final production costs in multiple languages and for multiple media.

- By automating production and delivery activities, you virtually eliminate the time it takes to prepare materials for the various delivery options, significantly decreasing time to market for all models of the products.

- By getting all the authors to use the same modules in common among the four models of the equipment, you reduce the costs of information-development time throughout the content life cycle.

- By creating a repository of information modules and making them available to the customer-support knowledge base, you reduce customer-service costs.

- By writing modules once and assembling them into multiple deliverables, you eliminate redundant development activities throughout the content life cycle, including editing, subject-matter reviews, testing, and approvals.

Use the information you gather to calculate current costs and estimate future costs. Be conservative in your estimates. Promise less than you might want to predict to ensure that the decision-markers have numbers they are comfortable with. Don't overhype the cost-reduction results. Add in the costs of designing, developing, and implementing a possible content-management solution. Don't skimp on these costs—be as honest as possible. Talk with vendors; find the names of organizations that have implemented similar solutions. Ask them about their cost reductions. Benchmark with others in your industry and with organizations that are leading the implementation of content management.

Carla, Chris, and the three other authors each work about six months to produce the training and documentation for a new product line. Based on fully burdened costs for 80 percent of the time of five people for six months, you estimate the cost of their projects to be approximately $300,000.

Seven engineers and three product testers spend about 80 hours each reviewing and editing the various documents for all the product models. That's not counting the time they spend providing almost the same information to five different people. The review time alone represents 800 hours or $75,000.

Production activities to produce all the different outputs cost another $60,000 for each set of deliverables and take about three weeks to complete.

Translation and localization, including all the extra desktop publishing activities, cost the company approximately $425,000 for eight languages, one set of training materials, and four sets of manuals. Localization and translation take six weeks on average to complete.

> James spends about three months on this set of documents, which represents one fourth of his fully burdened cost of about $30,000.
>
> The full cost of training and documentation for four product models in eight languages is about $910,000.
>
> What if you could reduce these costs by 40 percent? That would represent a cost savings of $364,000 for each six-month project. Is a 40 percent cost reduction reasonable? How would it be achieved?

Leveraging infrastructure costs

To implement the solution described for Chris, Carla, and James requires an investment in a content-management infrastructure. The investment includes

- an XML editing environment for the professional authors in the organization
- conversion tools to handle legacy information resources
- a content-management system that is supported by a database repository capable of handling multiple languages
- publishing tools that accommodate output in multiple media

In addition, the investment includes the cost of implementation. In most cases, implementation costs will include consulting in

- the feasibility of implementing content management and the outline of a proposed solution
- information architecture to develop a sound Information Model for the organization
- the evaluation of the opportunities for reuse among departments within the organization
- the development of the technology requirements and assistance in evaluating and selecting a vendor
- the development of DTDs, an assembly and linking structure, and style sheets for input and output
- the services of a system integrator to ensure that all the pieces work together

For a small group such as Carla's, the total cost of a content-management solution is likely to be $100,000 to $250,000. Those costs expand for larger implementations, although not necessarily proportionately.

In addition, Carla's organization will engage in their own analysis and possible redesign and restructuring of their information resources into modules that follow the standards of their Information Model. For a small group, I estimate that the internal time to analyze, structure, design, and revise requires between 2500 and 4000 hours of staff time, in addition to consulting time. More time is required if more of the design work is done inhouse. The staff time is likely to represent an investment of between $200,000 and $350,000.

The total investment for a content-management solution will be somewhere between $300,000 and $600,000. For this reason, Carla needs to look beyond documentation, training, and translation to find ways of amortizing the investment across more development centers. If customer support, marketing, and sales see the value of managing their content and reusing content among more departments, the total cost of the development can be shared.

Based on the experience I have had assisting organizations to implement content-management solutions, a 40 percent savings within one product life cycle is not unusual. In Carla's case, that 40 percent represents $364,000 twice a year. If her team can implement their content-management solution in one year, they will easily return their total cost by savings in time spent writing the same content multiple times, reconciling the content to ensure consistency, and producing multiple versions of the content in multiple languages. The cost savings realized in the first year will continue to accrue in subsequent years with minimal investment in infrastructure upgrades. As long as Carla's team stays with standards and avoids proprietary systems, they should be able to migrate their information sources from a current solution to future solutions as they emerge.

According to Forrester Research, companies moving into content management should expect costs of approximately $4 per page for implementation. That translates to $400,000 for a company managing 100,000 pages of content.*

Calculating your Return on Investment (ROI)

The ROI of your content-management solution must be calculated well in advance of your implementation. If you are fortunate enough to have well structured information resources and a degree of cooperation and collaboration among parts of your organization, you should be able to implement an initial solution in a year. A complete solution, integrating more of the organization and developing a complete end-to-end solution in a large organization might take two to three years to implement. Nevertheless, cost reductions and quality improvements should come quickly enough to satisfy those who must approve the initial infrastructure and consulting investment. In fact, using experienced consultants and system integrators will ensure that you realize a significant ROI more quickly than if you try to do it alone.

---

* John P. Dalton, January 2001. "Managing Content Hypergrowth," Forrester Research, Inc.

At a major telecommunications carrier in the US, the training development team developed a integrated XML-based solution, using Enigma's DynaWeb, to provide a workplace information tool to maintenance technicians. The system is centered on troubleshooting workflows that link directly to relevant technical content that the technicians need to solve service problems. As a result of markedly improved access to information, the carrier has cut training time almost in half, from eight weeks to 4 1/2 weeks.

New technicians are taught to use the workflow system to find the maintenance procedures they need. In a survey conducted to evaluate the training program, the new technicians were pleased with the resource:

- 79 percent believed that the new workflow system enabled them to work more independently without having to rely on more experienced technicians for help

- 25 percent indicated that having access to the workflows increased their confidence in doing their jobs

- 89 percent said they regularly use the workflow/reference application

Cadence Design Systems

In 2000, Cadence Design Systems, a developer of electronic design software, implemented their Electronic Document Management System (EDMS) using Documentum. The EDMS enabled them to

- Handle an increasing number of product releases per year

- Manage a growing number of books in their library

- Reduce the number of processes used to create documents across the company

- Eliminate the time required to find the appropriate versions of documents for a release

Since implementing their EDMS, Cadence has experienced significant cost reductions to deliver their documents in HTML and PDF.

- In 2000 alone, they calculated savings of $570,000 by eliminating the manual creation and testing of online menus for each product release. The menus permit users to find relevant documents in the electronic library. By navigating from menus with generic tasks or menus with product names, users can find documents associated with the subject matter in which they are interested.

> ■ The EDMS automates the creation of self-extracting executables (UNIX tar files or PC ZIP files). The savings for this task was nearly $150,000 in 2000.
>
> ■ Cadence also saved more than $10,000 in 2000 by automatically tracking documents through version control.
>
> One manager reported "The EDMS saves me an average of an hour a week on tracking and maintaining information on the books I'm responsible for. But, better than that, I know the information I'm getting from the system is up-to-date. And, I can ensure closure on the handoff for books I've given to another group."
>
> The EDMS has given Cadence the ability to map documents to a changing set of product, group, and family categories and ensure that one document uses a constant set throughout its life cycle. This ability lets them process updated documents for old releases and use new product names and groups for new products, something that would have been impossible before.
>
> In all, the EDMS has permitted Cadence's Knowledge Transfer Organization to standardize and streamline the process they use to produce documentation, saving them time and money. At the same time, the system is flexible enough to grow into future needs. ■

The carrier has experienced a 184 percent return on investment for each group of new employees going through the training. The per group cost of training has been reduced from $81,000 to $28,000. Given that they train between 600 and 700 new employees per year, the total cost savings have been incredible.*

To calculate your potential ROI, you must know what your costs are today. Given your current costs of managing content, calculate the cost reductions you could expect from improving and automating processes. Then consider the costs of implementing a solution, including both development and technology costs. If you can pay back the cost of the investment with the cost savings within one to two years, you are likely to have a viable project.

Selling content-management to your colleagues

Convincing your colleagues in your department and other parts of your organization might be considerably more challenging than convincing management to

---

* I want to thank David Davidoff of Enigma for his help in researching this return on investment.

invest in content management. Your colleagues and staff members will have the task of moving to a structured writing environment, creating modules instead of whole documents, working on collaborative teams, learning new tools, and focusing on content rather than format. They are likely to be asked to write modular information that will appear in multiple contexts, some of them under the control of end users.

Despite the challenges, I have been surprised and pleased by the enthusiasm of most information developers I have worked with. They appear to like the challenge of working in a new way and appreciate the opportunity to learn about new technologies. Those who are more interested in developing excellent content view the elimination of tedious desktop publishing and media conversion tasks positively. They want to get back to the real business of authoring.

The greatest challenges come from those who have not developed domain knowledge, having based their careers on document formatting. For these individuals, you might offer the challenge of taking over the design and maintenance of a wide variety of style specifications. They will need to design, develop, refine, and maintain style conversion capabilities for all the various media you need to produce.

You might encounter a concern about a loss of creativity. People who are most concerned about a loss of creativity are often attached to their books. They think of their information in terms of a book paradigm. Structured writing moves content away from books and into modules. In might be important to point out to those concerned about creativity that they can become the information architects of the team, using their creative bent to develop the Information Model itself.

Involving colleagues in the design of your solution

The greater the involvement of colleagues in the design of your content-management solution, the greater their feeling of ownership of the results. In some of the most successful implementations I have tracked, team members were consulted and involved from the beginning. They participated in the development of a vision statement, in the initial feasibility studies, in the development of the Information Model and structured authoring, and in the selection of a supporting technology. Rather than feel that the new environment was being forced upon them, they became dedicated to ensuring the success of the solution.

Having everyone involved is not always the easiest way to conduct a project. One manager called to tell me about the problems she was having getting the instructional designers and information developers to agree upon common content. They couldn't even agree upon the definition of a step in a procedure. Eventually, however, they worked out their differences and developed an excellent solution that gave everyone more time for creativity in content development and training delivery.

On their first pilot project using the new content-management system, Carla and Chris work together to plan the modules they will product for the training materials and the reference manuals. Chris, with his closer contacts in the development organization, is ready to produce the task-oriented procedures and the troubleshooting solutions. Other writers on the team will develop the detailed reference information through their work with the testers and the product developers.

Carla is very comfortable developing concept modules and process overviews. She also will produce the lab exercises to accompany Chris's tasks. She will fill out the task-oriented information with scenarios of use that she gets from working closely with the customers.

Carla, Chris, and the other writers are all using the new XML editing system. They have four DTDs for each of the information types: reference, task, concept, and troubleshooting. They attended a training session on the editing tool and worked on the DTD development with the consultants. They are very comfortable with the new structures because they helped develop them.

The engineers and testers have agreed to review individual modules rather than entire books. In fact, they are looking forward to reviewing content once instead of several times.

Once the content modules are reviewed and approved, Carla and Chris will work with Sam, the new information architect in the group, to ensure that the modules flow smoothly into the content plans. Sam has developed topic maps with their implementation consultants to aid the output into compound documents for print and PDF and for a heavily linked Web site. He is also working with a designer to produce the style templates for print, HTML, the help system, and their new delivery to a PDA.

James, the localization and translation manager, has also been in the loop from the beginning of the design. He has prepared a process in which his translators will work on a specially packaged module version in which all the XML tags are locked. They can translate between the tags but not disturb the tags.

He has told the translators that they will be translating independent modules rather than books, with no desktop publishing. The new assembly and publishing process automates the production process completely.

James is hoping that the new structured modules will increase the effectiveness of the translation memory tool. Terminology is fine because everyone adheres to the company glossary, but he needs more similarity in the writing styles.

The team expects to be able to produce the multiple versions of their information by building output that uses a combination of modules that are common to all, common to most, and unique. Because each of the modules will be translated only once, instead of many times, James is predicting a 60 percent cost reduction in translation. The elimination of the production cycle with its desktop publishing in multiple languages already means a 40 percent reduction.

Selecting an initial project

One of the most effective ways of involving colleagues in the development of your content-management solution is to stage initial projects carefully. I recommend a series of small implementations. First, they allow you to show a return on the infrastructure investment quickly. Second, they allow you to develop a team of potential leaders who have worked their way through the difficult problems and are prepared to lend their expertise to the next round of projects.

In selecting your initial project, consider the project duration, the scale of the information resources, and the importance of the project to the organization. I recommend selecting a project that can be completed in three to six months after the Information Model has been designed and implemented in an XML or SGML-based system. Select a project that has a moderate number of resources, either new ones to be developed or resources that are reasonably well structured already. Avoid projects that require substantial rewriting of poorly structured legacy information. Select a project that has a strong leader and knowledgeable and enthusiastic staff members. Recognize that these staff members will become the leaders for subsequent projects in a phased rollout. Finally, consider a project that is important to the organization's success. A new product release, the development of a new way of delivering information to users, opportunities for revenue growth—all these possibilities will help you maintain the visibility of the work and demonstrate the opportunities for quality improvements as well as cost reductions.

Projects in growth mode are expanding so fast that they often don't have problems obtaining funds. The initial investment in a content-management solution is most likely to be returned over a short period of time. Additionally, a project that promises a rapid increase in revenues or an increase in a user base contains opportunities to leverage content from early adopters to majority users if the project goes into a high-growth mode. Growth projects do not have to produce an immediate high ROI because they are expected to increase in value for several years.

Sustaining projects are expected to maintain their existing market share, although they might show moderate growth. The choice of a sustaining project for your initial implementation must be able to show a strong ROI, as well as a strong return on capital employed.

Harvesting projects involve mature products that are not being expanded but are expected to earn a steady income. In these situations, long-term goals and savings are not valued. Short-term projects and savings will be valued more; therefore, projects in harvesting mode might not be successful candidates for content management unless you can show opportunities for significant cost reductions and potential reduction in the number of staff required to maintain the products through the support chain. However, if you can show decreased costs of support, harvesting projects might be attractive.

You must, therefore, select single-sourcing projects carefully. If you begin with projects in growth or sustaining modes, you are much more likely to get the initial start-up funds you need. Once start-up costs are invested and processes are defined, you can make a business case for the inclusion of projects that are in harvesting mode. Once you have a content-management system and single-source processes in place, goals and savings will shift to short-term and fit with the financial goals of harvest projects.

Involving the staff

Staff members are often most eager to become involved in high-growth projects that offer considerable visibility in the organization. If you have a capable and enthusiastic team that wants to invest time and energy in a new implementation of content management, involve them in a high-growth project. However, ensure that they are likely to be successful by providing them with significant opportunities for learning. Involve them in the design of the Information Model, provide tools training, and give them chances to attend and present at industry conferences. Recognition, despite the hard work involved, is the best reward.

Take a learning and growth perspective

To deliver innovative information solutions, realize how content management will impact future learning and growth opportunities within your organization. You must emphasize in your business case current opportunities lost when employees are not challenged to work outside their comfort zone. In a content-management, single-sourcing environment, staff members will be challenged to

- learn new technologies, such as XML
- become subject-matter experts in a knowledge domain
- learn to create more structured and usable information
- become specialized in new career areas such as information architecture and Web-based production

New knowledge and experience will open doors to other opportunities to innovate as staff members become more expert. These staff members become more valuable to your organization as they develop significant expertise in new technologies and best practices. Innovation does not occur in a stagnant environment. Providing innovative work opportunities motivates your best employees, the ones you want to retain.

Critical success factors

The business case you build must be specific to your department, your organization, and the market and customers your products serve. Many of the ideas presented in this chapter might be used to make your case, but they must be tailored to your environment to be effective. The true benefits of content management will be identified by your customers and your staff and will be the driving force for the arguments you present in your business case.

Look around your organization and ask yourself if

- long, complex documents are moved from department to department, with each individual group applying the content differently
- information crosses departmental walls to be created, revised, approved, and used
- information changes frequently in response to product changes, changes in services, regulatory requirements, market forces, and more
- significant numbers of people are dedicated to creating and maintaining information throughout the organization
- these same people rewrite content rather than reusing existing content, leading to inaccuracies, inconsistencies, and long delays in deployment
- much of the information produced has a long information life
- the information resources exist in a web of interrelationships and cross references

- barriers in your information-development process keep you from getting products to market quickly, innovating new services, informing employees of policy and procedure changes, and satisfying the information needs of your customers
- the demand for information resources is great inside and outside your organization
- large numbers of people in diverse user communities need information to be productive and effective in their jobs
- your information is governed by legal or regulatory rules

You don't need to experience all these issues to find an opportunity in the development of a content-management solution. You just need to start somewhere in planting the seeds of recognition.

Content becomes information, and information becomes knowledge. Knowledge leads to better decisions and more effective implementation of processes. As such, content is a corporate asset that has been seriously overlooked in the past. Technologies have become available in the last several years to make managing content viable. But, as I have argued throughout this book, technology is not sufficient to provide a solution. You and your colleagues are responsible for the design, development, and deployment of effective content inside your organization and to your customers. Begin to manage that content today.

Appendix A: Content Management Requirements Checklist

I n Chapter 2, *Implementing a Content-Management Solution,* I discussed many different ways of thinking about and planning for a content-management solution. I cannot emphasize enough the importance of creating a detailed requirements document before you approach vendors to learn about their products' capabilities. If you begin to look at products without an explicit definition of your needs, you are likely to become confused about the similarities and differences, strengths and weaknesses, of all the product combinations you will see.

With requirements in hand, you provide vendors with a well-defined way to respond to you. They are able to tell you which of your requirements are easily met with standard functionality, which must be customized, and which are not easily implemented with their solutions. You can use your requirements as a checklist, particularly if you have prioritized them (critical, necessary, nice to have).

Define your requirements according to the four components of a content-management solution outlined in this chapter: output requirements, storage and retrieval requirements (repository), assembly and linking requirements, and authoring requirements. Remember that authoring, storing, assembling, linking, and retrieving are all specific in light of your vision of the user experience in finding and using information resources.

The checklist below offers some but certainly not all of the questions you should address and answer as you define your requirements. Expand or contract the list as necessary. The questions are designed to help your planning process. Some will not apply to your organization. Others might not reflect current practices but might suggest ideas for how you want to deliver information in the future. The chapters in the book expand upon these questions and suggest ways in which you might want to organize your information.

Output requirements (assembly, linking, publishing)

Describe how you want your information to be available to your users. State your vision of the user experience and specify how the information needs to be available in different forms.

- Do you want to target different versions of your information to different internal business and user groups, customer groups, or individual users (external: buyers, installers, planners, system administrators, end users, and so on; internal: business departments, employee services, engineering, product development, marketing, sales, and so on)?

- Do you want to prepare different information according to market segments? For example, you might create different examples and case studies in information targeted for manufacturing companies versus service organizations.

- Do you want to differentiate information based on product type or model? For example, you might have information that is specific to subsets of a product.

- Do you have versions of your products that deliver some percentage of identical or similar functionality? What is the percentage of shared functionality?

- Do you now deliver or do you intend to deliver information in multiple languages, localized to the particular needs of a regional or local user community?

Current delivery methods

- What output types do you produce today (print, online context-sensitive help, Internet, intranet, extranet, CD-ROM, PDA, WAP, etc.)?
- What different types of information, potentially using the same data, are now being produced in your larger organization (product catalogs, support information, new business proposals, policies and procedures, product-development documents, training materials, reference documents, user manuals, frequently asked questions, marketing communications, data sheets, etc.)?

Future delivery methods

- What output types would you like to be able to produce in the future?
- Do you expect to deliver information through the Web? Do you hope to broadcast to handheld devices? Do you want information to be integrated with a software product interface in the form of context-sensitive help?
- Do you want your customers to be able to configure their own information from a Web site, a CD-ROM, or other electronic device?
- Do you want to be able to update information at any time?
- Do you intend to give customers access to customer support information (for example, a customer support database) as well as more formally produced information?
- Do you want to be able to connect customer information to other information about your product and its buyers? Would it be useful to anticipate the specific configurations of the customers' use of the products as soon as they enter a Web site? Do you want to identify customers according to logons and passwords?
- Do you want to be able to track users or customers in their progress through your Web-delivered information? Do you want to know what information they have visited?
- Would you like to obtain immediate feedback from customers when they arrive at a particular information resource? Do you want to know if the customers find the information to be useful or to respond to their questions?

Web Delivery

Describe how you will deliver information to your Web sites. Discuss both static and dynamic delivery methods as they might apply to the vision of the user experience that you are constructing. Explain how the users will be able to access information easily.

Static delivery

- Do you currently deliver only static content to your Web sites (Internet, intranet, or extranet)? Static content is designed and developed by authors or Web designers and remains the same on the Web site until updated.

- How often do you update static content?

- Are you concerned with the amount of time now required to update static content? Is updating delayed because of manual processes?

- Do you have static content on your Web sites that is now out-of-date?

- What plans now exist for updating static information in a more timely manner?

- Does your static information include resources that are syndicated from other organizations?

- Does your static information primarily consist of entire large documents available in PDF?

- Do users typically download and print information from your Web sites?

Search mechanisms

- What search mechanisms do you have in place to access static information?

- Are you using full-text search exclusively? Have you tested your full-text search system to determine if it returns information accurately?

- Does your search system include Boolean search mechanisms? Are you confident that your users know how to use Boolean relationships adequately to refine their searches? Do your users typically avoid advanced Boolean search tools as confusing and unsuccessful?

- Have you studied the success of your search mechanisms with your users? Are they satisfied that they can easily find the information they need?

Navigation

- Are you satisfied with the navigation throughout your Web sites? Do you know that users can find information through navigation? Have you learned that users avoid navigating in favor of search because they are confused by the navigation or believe that it takes them too long to find relevant information?

- How many levels (clicks) must users typically navigate before finding relevant information?

■ Are users easily able to make choices from the home page and at every level of your Web sites? Do they believe they are getting closer to or farther away from the information they need?

■ If you have an Information Model in place, do your Web sites reflect the Information Model? Is the navigation governed by the Information Model? Is this Information Model affecting Web navigation organized in terms of users or in terms of the internal structures of your organization?

Dynamic delivery

■ Are you aware of Web sites that offer dynamic delivery of information to users based on user profiles or other considerations?

■ Do your Web sites now offer dynamic delivery of information?

■ Are users able to reach information quickly that pertains to their product configuration, job responsibilities, level of experience, or others?

■ Do you customize your information, delivering unique home pages and other content dependent on users' previous actions on your Web sites?

■ Do you customize information based on user profiles stored within your system?

■ Do you enable users to reconfigure information based on their own needs?

■ Can users develop their own "books" consisting of the modules they want to use?

■ If you are not delivering dynamic information at this time, do you hope to deliver dynamically in the future? If so, what is your vision of the future user experience with your information?

Authoring and acquisition requirements

Describe how your authors will need to work with your content-management system. Describe the technologies and processes that you want to use in the new environment. Explain what types of information you create and whether you want to handle information that you acquire from outside your organization.

Technology

■ What development platforms are now used in your organization (UNIX, mainframe, Windows PC, Macintosh, etc.)?

■ What authoring tools are used (FrameMaker, Word, PowerPoint, Illustrator, etc.)?

■ What files types are created and stored (doc, eps, bmp, jpeg, wav, etc.)?

- Which departments, groups, or users will input information to the repository?
- Which departments, groups, or users will reuse information from the repository to develop their own outputs?
- Is there any information that must be secured from people besides the authors or information owners?

Process

- How often are documents revised? Quarterly? Monthly? Yearly? At any time?
- How often should documents be revised? If information were updated daily, would support costs be significantly reduced? What other costs might be affected?
- How much does information change during the information-development life cycle? Are features and functions added at the last minute? Removed at the last minute?
- Do several information developers ever work on updating the same modules at the same time?
- Do information developers reference graphics stored separately or do they ordinarily embed graphics in the text files?
- Who creates the graphics? How are they stored? How are they updated?
- Do you have a standard scheme for naming files of text? Of graphics?
- Does each department or information-development organization have its own naming conventions? Are documents uniquely named or do their names depend upon their position in a folder/file hierarchy?
- How are documents reviewed (technical review, editorial, peer review, management sign-off, etc.)? Is there a regular review process in place?
- Where are files stored? How are they backed up?
- What is the size of the current information repository? In your department? In other departments?
- How many people have to access the information to create and revise it? How many of these people work on the same information sources?
- How are documents archived?
- Do authors ever work on the same files during a single development process?
- Do you currently have any method of searching your document files for specific pieces of information?

- Does any reuse of information occur today between information developers within the same organization or in different organizations?
- Does any reuse of information occur today between instructional designers or trainers and information developers?
- Does any reuse of information occur between product developers, testers, customer service, and any other information developers in your organization?

Information acquisition

- For what sources will you acquire information?
- Do you use third-party providers for information? How will you receive this information?
- Do you have information coming from inside and outside your organization that is unstructured? Structured?
- How do you want to include both structured and unstructured information in the repository?
- Do you syndicate information from outside sources? How is that information generated and fed to your organization? Do you want to be able to restructure the information before you publish it?
- Do you use information that is stored in other databases? How is the information structured? How will it be combined with other content? How will it be displayed and accessed?

Information Model requirements

Describe the requirements of your Information Model. Refer to Chapters 4 through 6 on creating the three-tiered structure of your Information Model.

High-level model

- How is your entire library of information organized today? Primarily by department? By product line? By development organization?
- Does each sub-library adhere to the same information titles (procedures manual, policies guide, installation guide, system administrator guide, reference manual, or others)?
- Are all of the information titles directed toward specific user groups or are user groups mixed in the documents?
- Is each document that contains a particular type of information organized in the same way (all installation guides, all system administrator guides, etc.)?

- Do you use the same titles for subsections of information in a particular type of document?

- Have you determined which subsections are intended for which user groups?

- Is there any information that is reused throughout the library today (copyright notices, warnings, etc.)?

- Are you in the process of reorganizing any of the information libraries that you now produce?

Detailed model

- How many information types are used in your information libraries? Typical information types are conceptual overviews, summaries, policy statements, procedures, reference modules, training modules, examples, and so on.

- Are the information types organized consistently across your libraries of information? Do you write in a modular way already?

- Do you have conceptual as well as style templates for your information types? Style templates describe the content in terms of its appearance, i.e., paragraphs, numbered lists, bulleted lists, headings. Conceptual templates describe the content in terms of its meaning for the users.

- Is the information reviewed to ensure consistency of content and presentation? How reliable is the review process in identifying inconsistencies and correcting them?

- Do you use a structured writing style to produce consistent content units within your information types? For example, are all procedure titles written in the same grammatical style with the same content? Do your procedures begin with purpose statements when necessary? Do the purpose statements contain the same level of explanation and detail?

- Do you use individual content units of information in more than one place through cutting and pasting?

- Do you have individual content units of information that were once identical but have changed over time? Should they be identical again?

- Do you have a style guide that is consistently used and enforced throughout your organization?

- Does your style guide include content as well as format and process guidelines and rules?

Media

- Is your information library always printed? Do you print documents for some customers on order?

- Do you produce CD-ROMs? Do they contain the same information as your print library?

- Do you deliver information through a Web site today? Is it the same or different from other forms of delivery such as CD-ROM or print?

- Do you deliver online help associated with software? Does the help contain the same or different information as other forms of delivery?

- Do you deliver training materials for Instructor-Led Training? Computer-Based Training? Web-Based Training? Is any of the information produced for training reused elsewhere? Is any documentation produced elsewhere also used in the training materials?

- If you deliver information electronically today, do you provide your users with links to other relevant information? Links to definitions of terms? Other types of links?

- Do you deliver information in any other ways than mentioned here?

User community

- What job tasks or activities do your users perform?

- How do your users organize their work activities? Who does what?

- What are the workflows or process flows typical of your users' organizations?

- How do your users locate and use information throughout their workflow today?

- Which user groups use which information you produce?

- Is your Information Model organized around user tasks and user goals?

- What prior knowledge and experience do your users bring to their activities and tasks?

- Do your authors and editors take that prior knowledge and experience into account as they write and edit? Do they include too much detail? Not enough detail? Do they have enough experience with the users to know how much detail is needed?

- What opportunities exist for delivering information to your users in ways that better meet their needs?

Content management requirements

Describe the requirements your solution needs to support in the design of the repository.

Reuse (see Chapter 10, *Authoring for Reuse,* for more on reuse strategies)

- Do authors need to know when a module they have written is being reused in multiple contexts by other authors? Should this information be available in the authors' editing environment or from a source that must be separately accessed through the content-management system?

- Should authors be able to review visually the relationships (links and reuse) among modules?

- Should authors be able to create children (requiring a small change in content) from a parent object and maintain a link between parent and children to handle future changes?

- Do you require reporting on all instances of reuse across modules and content plans?

Version control

- Do your authors need to access earlier versions of their modules? How quick and easy should access be?

- Do your authors require the ability to promote older versions of a module to the status of current version?

- Do you want your authors to annotate the reasons for changes when they check in a new version of the module to the repository? Do you want to require a notation?

- Do you want to link the notations to engineering change orders or other change tracking methods?

- Do you want the system to save the entire content for each version of a module? Or, do you want the system to store only the differences between the current version and previous versions?

- Do you require a process to archive working versions when you are ready to move a module to final release?

- Must authors be able to access earlier versions of modules from inside their editing environment without having to run a report or access the repositories in other ways?

Localization and translation

- Do you need to maintain parallel translated versions of your modules in the content-management system?

- Do you need to maintain related translated versions with differently localized information?
- Do you want to be able to apply translation memories from within the content-management system to newly written or revised information modules in the source language before submitting the modules to the translators?
- Do you want the content-management system to track all changes in the source modules in the translated versions of the modules?
- Do you need to be able to generate precise word counts of new words to be translated when modules are changed in the source language?

Search and retrieval

- What search and retrieval resources are required by your authors and others working in the content-management system?
- Do authors need to be able to search multiple databases to find information resources?
- Should the search and retrieval process work from inside the author's editing environment? Or, should the authors have to move to the repository in order to search and retrieve?
- Is full-text search required?
- Is Boolean search required?
- Must authors be able to search on metadata values?
- Must authors be able to search using a combination of strategies, including full-text and metadata?
- Must authors be able to limit the extent of a search of any type to a particular database, folder, area, file name, or other file attributes?

Security

- What levels of security are required in your organization?
- Does the security system need to be administered by your information technologists or from within your department- or division-level organization?
- Do you need to limit the visibility of certain parts of the database from authors so that they cannot see that certain objects exist?
- Must authors be able to log on to the content-management system and all repositories from a single point of access?

Check in/check out

- Should authors be able to check out and check in modules from inside their editing environment?
- Do you need to limit access to check out modules for Read Only?
- At what level of granularity do authors need to be able to check out modules or content units within modules?
- Do several authors need to work on the same module concurrently? If so, how should edits be reconciled?
- Are annotations to be required every time a module is checked in?
- Must authors be able to save their work without checking modules back into the content-management system?
- Should there be any ways for authors to access modules without going through the content-management system?
- Should there be an easy way of allowing authors to see that a module is checked out and who has checked it out?

Workflow

- Do you need a workflow system that allows you to automatically route modules from person to person to smooth editing, reviewing, translating, and approving processes?
- Do you need to add scripted actions or programmable actions to aspects of the workflow?
- At what level should individuals or departments be able to create and modify the workflow system?

Database structure

For many of these issues, you will need to consult with your information technologists.

- What file types must the content-management system support?
- What storage capacity do you require for your information databases?
- What performance levels are required (24 x 7, for example), and how many concurrent authors must be supported?
- Do you need the ability to replicate databases at different locations?
- What type of archiving capabilities do you need? Do you need to archive entire back versions of your Web site?
- What about backup capabilities?
- What about other aspects of database administration?

Appendix B: Vendors

Authoring

Product	Description	Contact Information
Adobe FrameMaker+SGML	Using FrameMaker+SGML, authors create and edit SGML and publish into multiple formats with Quadralay WebWorks® Publisher Standard Edition, which ships with it.	Adobe Systems, Inc. 345 Park Avenue San Jose, CA 95110-2704 888-724-4508 www.adobe.com
Altova XML Spy	Altova's XML Spy is not only an editor that validates against DTDs and schemas, it also allows you to write XSLT stylesheets using a drag-and-drop interface.	Altova, Inc. 900 Cummings Center Suite 306-T Beverly, MA 01915-6181 978-927-9400 www.xmlspy.com
Arbortext Epic Editor	Epic Editor is a robust XML editor, allowing development of content for delivery to Web, print, CD-ROM, and wireless devices from the editor. Epic Editor also ships with adapters to facilitate access to Oracle iFS and Documentum.	Arbortext, Inc. 1000 Victors Way Ann Arbor, MI 48108 734-997-0200 www.arbortext.com
Ecosystems The Environment	Exosystems' The Environment is an XML content-management application that integrates into content-management systems like Documentum. It supports a graphical interface into the repository and stores and tracks changes to content, metadata, and structure.	Ecosystems 222 West 23rd Street Suite 1022 New York, NY 10011 212-929-4402 www.eco-online.com
Enigma DynaTag	DynaTag facilitates converting legacy documents such as Word or Adobe FrameMaker with limited structure into XML, either individually or in a batch process.	Enigma, Inc. 200 Wheeler Road Burlington, MA 01803 781-273-3600 www.enigma.com

Product	Description	Contact Information
HyperVision WorX	WorX is a plug-in for Microsoft Word turning Word into an XML editor. Authors assign structure by applying styles.	HyperVision, Ltd. 230 East Ohio St. Suite 210 Chicago, IL 60611 312-274-1206 www.hvltd.com
i4i S/4TEXT	S/4 TEXT integrates into Microsoft Word. A wizard-like interface guides users though the creation of valid XML.	i4i 116 Spadina Avenue Fifth Floor Toronto, Ontario Canada M5V 2K6 416-504-0141 www.i4i.com
SoftQuad XMetaL	Softquad's XMetaL is an easy-to-use XML editor. It lacks built-in conversion capabilities or adapters to content-management systems. XMetal uses cascading style sheets to style output for the screen.	SoftQuad Software Ltd. 161 Eglinton Ave. East Suite 400 Toronto, Ontario Canada M4P 1J5 1-800-387-2777 www.softquad.com

Content Categorization

Product	Description	Contact Information
Autonomy	Autonomy offers a suite of products for storing, indexing, and searching structured and unstructured content. Autonomy uses a combination of models and theories to recalculate and re-index information based on previous searches.	Autonomy Inc 301 Howard Street 22nd Floor San Francisco, CA 94105 415-243-9955 www.autonomy.com
Semio's Semio Tagger	Semio provides a categorization engine that extracts concepts from unstructured data, from which it builds taxonomies and custom content categories.	Semio 1730 S Amphlett Blvd Suite 101 San Mateo CA 94402 650-638-3330 www.semio.com

Content Management Systems

Product	Description	Contact Information
AuthorIT	An end-to-end solution, AuthorIT offers an interface for authoring, a content-management system, and production utilities for conversion into Word documents for print or PDF, WinHelp, HTML, XHTML, HTML Help, JavaHelp, and Oracle Help for Java.	AuthorIT Software Corporation PO Box 300-273 Albany, Auckland New Zealand +64 (9) 915 5070 www.author-it.com

Product	Description	Contact Information
Lightspeed Astoria	An SGML and XML component-management system, Astoria ships with ObjectStore, an object-oriented database management system.	Lightspeed Software 5200 Franklin Drive, Suite 100 Pleasanton, CA 94588 925-224-8730 www.lightspeed.com
Documentum 4i	Documentum, long recognized as a document management system, entered the content management market with 4i. 4i ships with integrated workflow, check in/check out, versioning, and search capabilities.	Documentum 6801 Koll Center Parkway Pleasanton, CA. 94566 925-600-6800 www.documentum.com
J D Edwards Enterprise Content Manager	With J D Edwards Enterprise Content Manager, authors write in Microsoft Word templates and assemble dynamic tables of content.	J D Edwards & Company One Technology Way Denver, CO 80237 877-613-9412 www.jdedwards.com
Live Linx	Live Linx software automates e-Publishing, delivering fully hyperlinked and personalized documents in multiple channels.	Live Linx Extensible Solutions, Ltd. RMPE House, Har Hotzvim PO Box 45168 Jerusalem 91450 Israel 972-2-532-8580 www.livelinx.com
Noonetime Constellation	Noonetime's solutions bridge the gap between structured and unstructured environments by allowing automatic, loss-less content interchange between XML and Microsoft Word, Quark XPress, and FrameMaker.	Noonetime 1900 Wazee Street Suite 1543 Denver, CO 80202 303-296-0567 www.noonetime.com
Oracle iFS	A free download with the purchase of Oracle's database management system, Oracle iFS is a complete CMS. iFS provides the standard library services: check in/check out, versioning, and search capabilities.	Oracle Corporation 500 Oracle Parkway Redwood Shores, CA 94402 1-800-ORACLE-1 www.oracle.com

Product	Description	Contact Information
Trisoft InfoShare	An XML content-management system developed to support a multilingual environment, InfoShare ships with check in/check out, versioning, and search capabilities.	Trisoft NV Jan Van Gentstraat 17 B-2000 Antwerp, Belgium +32 (0)3 238.76.50 www.trisoft.be
XyEnterprise Content@ XML	An XML-based content management system, Content@ integrates with XPP to support high quality print output and ships with integrated workflow, check in/check out, versioning, and search capabilities.	Xyvision Enterprise Solutions, Inc. 30 New Crossing Road Reading, MA 01867 781-756-4400 www.xyenterprise.com

Production

Product	Description	Contact Information
Arbortext E3	Arbortext's publishing tool, E3, allows automatic conversion of XML content for delivery to Web, print, CD-ROM, and wireless devices.	Arbortext, Inc. 1000 Victors Way Ann Arbor, MI 48108 734-997-0200 www.arbortext.com
Curl Corporation's Curl	A content description language, Curl allows incremental updates to Web sites and client-side applications through a browser plug-in. Although the plug-in is large, it allows for fast downloads and client-side processing.	Curl Corporation 400 Technology Square, 8th floor Cambridge, MA 02139-3539 617-761-1200 www.curl.com

Product	Description	Contact Information
Enigma 3C	Enigma 3C provides content, commerce, and collaboration applications to enable content production and content delivery in the support chain. The content delivery process enables the production of content for the Web, on CD-ROM, and for Mobile delivery.	Enigma, Inc. 200 Wheeler Road Burlington, MA 01803 781-273-3600 www.enigma.com
Turn-Key Systems TopLeaf	Turn-Key Systems' TopLeaf renders XML or SGML data as high quality print, PDF, or PostScript, using a commercial typesetting language.	Turn-Key Systems PO Box 1216 Crows Nest NSW 1585 Suite 101, 38 Oxley Street St Leonards NSW2065 Austrailia 612 9906 1577 www.turnkey.com.au
Quadralay WebWorks	WebWorks is an easy-to-use publishing tool that integrates into FrameMaker to produce HTML, XML, XHTML, and all industry standard online help systems using cascading style sheets to format the output.	Quadralay Corporation 9101 Burnet Road Suite 105 Austin, Texas 78758 512-719-3399 www.quadralay.com
WexTech Systems' AnswerWorks	AnswerWorks includes a cross-lingual question-answering engine that allows companies to add a natural-language interface to Help systems and Web-based knowledge repositories. AnswerWorks Answers allows users to phrase questions in everyday language. Users type in questions, and AnswerWorks retrieves the most pertinent topics.	WexTech Systems, Inc. 400 Columbus Avenue Valhalla, New York 10595 914-741-9700 www.wextech.com

Product	Description	Contact Information
XyEnterprise XPP	XPP is a publishing tool for processing XML, SGML, and ACII text into high quality postscript and PDF.	Xyvision Enterprise Solutions, Inc. 30 New Crossing Road Reading, MA 01867 781-756-4400 www.xyenterprise.com

Bibliography

Books

Applehans, Wayne, Alden Globe, and Greg Lagero. *Managing Knowledge: A Practical Web-Based Approach*. Reading, MA: Addison-Wesley, 1999.

Boiko, Bob. *Content Management Bible*. New York, NY: Hungry Minds, 2001.

Brinck, Tom, Darren Gergle, and Scott D. Wood. *Usability for the Web: Designing Web Sites that Work*. San Diego, CA: Morgan Kaufman Publishers, 2001.

Dick, Kevin. *XML: A Manager's Guide*. Boston, MA: Addison-Wesley, 2000.

Dillon, Andrew. *Designing Usable Electronic Text: Ergonomic Aspects of Human Information Usage*. Bristol, PA: Taylor & Francis, 1994.

Donnelly, Vanessa. *Designing Easy-to-use Websites: A Hands-on Approach to Structuring Successful Websites*. Harlow, UK: Addison-Wesley, 2001.

Dumas, Joseph S. and Janice C. Redish. *A Practical Guide to Usability Testing*. Norwood, NJ: Ablex Publishing Corporation, 1993.

Ensign, Chet. *SGML: The Billion Dollar Secret*. Upper Saddle River, NJ: Prentice-Hall, 1997.

Fleming, Jennifer. *Web Navigation: Designing the User Experience*. Sebastopol, CA: O'Reilly & Associates, Inc., 1998.

Hackos, JoAnn T. *Managing Your Documentation Projects*. New York, NY: John Wiley & Sons, 1994.

Hackos, JoAnn T. and Dawn M. Stevens. *Standards for Online Communication*. New York, NY: John Wiley & Sons, 1997.

Hackos, JoAnn T. and Janice C. Redish. *User and Task Analysis for Interface Design*. New York, NY: John Wiley & Sons, 1998.

Jackson, Ken and Sonya Keene. *FrameMaker to HTML: Single Source Solution for Paper and Web*. Reading, MA: The Harlequin Group Limited, 1997.

Kaplan, Robert S. and David P. Norton. *The Balanced Scorecard: Translating Strategy into Action*. Boston, MA: The Harvard Business School Press, 1996.

Maler, Eve and Jeanne El Andaloussi. *Developing SGML DTDs: From Text to Model to Markup*. Upper Saddle River, NJ: Prentice Hall PTR, 1996.

Moore, Geoffrey A. *Crossing the Chasm: Marketing and Selling High-Tech Products to Mainstream Customers*. New York, NY: Harper Business, 1995.

Moreville, Peter and Louis Rosenfeld. *Information Architecture for the World Wide Web*. Sebastopol, CA: O'Reilly & Associates, 1998.

Musicano, Chuck and Bill Kennedy. *HTML and XHTML: The Definitive Guide, 4th edition*. Sebastopol, CA: O'Reilly & Associates, 2000.

Nakano, Russell. *Web Content Management: A Collaborative Approach*. Boston, MA: Addison-Wesley, 2001.

Nielsen, Jakob. *Designing Web Usability: The Practice of Simplicity*. Indianapolis, IN: New Riders, 1999.

Price, Jonathan and Henry Korman. *How to Communicate Technical Information: A Handbook of Software and Hardware Documentation*. Menlo Park, CA: Benjamin/Cummings Publishing Company, 1993.

Price, Lisa and Jonathan Price. *Hot Text: Web Writing that Works*. Indianapolis, IN: New Riders, 2002.

St. Laurent, Simon. *XML: A Primer, 2nd edition*. Foster City, CA: M&T Books, 1999.

Sano, Darrell. *Designing Large-Scale Web Sites: A Visual Design Methodology*. New York, NY: John Wiley & Sons, 1996.

Schriver, Karen A. *The Dynamics of Document Design: Creating Text for Readers*. New York, NY: John Wiley & Sons, 1996.

Svenonius, Elaine. *The Intellectual Foundation of Information Organization*. Cambridge, MA: Massachusetts Institute of Technology, 2000.

Tomsen, Mai-lan. *Killer Content: Strategies for Web Content and E-Commerce*. Reading, MA: Addison-Wesley, 2000.

Turner, Ronald C., Timothy A. Douglass, and Audrey J. Turner. *README.1ST: SGML for Writers and Editors*. Upper Saddle River, NJ: Prentice Hall PTR, 1995.

Veen, Jeffrey. *The Art & Science of Web Design*. Indianapolis, IN: New Riders, 2001.

Vering, Matthias, et al. *The E-Business Workplace: Discovering the Power of Enterprise Portals.* New York, NY: John Wiley & Sons, 2001.

Periodicals

CM Focus, The Magazine for the Content Management Professional
A features and case study-based journal published by the Ark Group that features articles from global companies and contributions from leading academics. For more information or to subscribe, visit www.cmfocus.com.

The Gilbane Report, Content, Computing, and Commerce—Technology & Trends
An educational journal published by Bluebill Advisors that covers information technology and standards. For more information or to subscribe, visit www.gilbane.com.

KM World Magazine
A magazine from Knowledge Management World that provides information about improving your business performance. For more information or to subscribe, visit www.kmworld.com.

<TAG>: The SGML Newsletter, The Technical Journal of the SGML Community.
Newsletter published by Architag International that covers industry-wide applications of SGML. For more information, visit www.architag.com.

Web Sites

SAP Design Guild
A place where you can exchange information and opinions on visual and user interface design issues and take advantage of SAP design resources. Visit www.sapdesignguild.org.

Single Source Listserv
A mailing list hosted by Comtech Services, Inc. for people in the technical communication industry interested in creating reusable information across multiple dimensions. Participants can post questions and participate in discussions via email related to content management and reuse. Visit http://www.comtech-serv.com/sslistserv.com.

Content Management
Comtech Services, Inc.
The Web site of Comtech Services. Comtech focuses on helping you provide effective products and information to your customers and employees. Visit www.comtech-serv.com.

Transformmag.com Content Management Channel
A focused channel dedicated to Content Management on the Web site of *Transform* magazine, Reinventing Business with Content and Collaboration Technologies. Visit www.transformmag.com/contentmgmt.

SGML

The SGML newsgroup

The place where you can discuss everything about SGML. Subscribe to comp.text.sgml.

XML

DITA

Provides an introduction to the Darwin Information Typing Architecture developed by IBM. Visit www-106.ibm.com/developerworks/library/x-dita1/index.html.

XML.com

A Web site that provides XML development information, XML resources, and XML specifications. Visit www.xml.com.

W3C

The W3C's Architecture Domain on XML. Visit www.w3.org/xml.

WebReference.com

The Webmaster's Reference on XML that includes tutorials, tools, standards information, and product reviews. Visit www.webreference.com/xml.

XML School

This Web site provides information to help you learn what XML is, the difference between XML and HTML, and how to use XML in your applications. Visit www.w3schools.com/xml.

The Directory of XML Resources

This Web site provides a directory of XML applications, tutorials, and other information about XSL, XML, XSLT, and DTD. Visit www.xmldir.com.

Personalization

Personalization Consortium

This Web site provides links to resources pertaining to customer relations, knowledge management, marketing and advertising, personalization, and privacy. Visit www.personalization.org/resourcelinks.html.

Index